Handbook of Management Accounting

Handbook of Management Accounting

Edited by David Fanning

Gower

Published by
Gower Publishing Company Limited
Aldershot, Hants, England

British Library Cataloguing in Publication Data

Handbook of management accounting
  1. Managerial accounting
  I. Fanning, David Christopher
  658.1'511   HF5635

ISBN 0-566-02236-2

Typeset by Guildford Graphics Limited, Guildford, Surrey
Printed in Great Britain by
Redwood Burn Limited, Trowbridge, Wiltshire

Contents

PART TWO: ACCOUNTING FOR MANAGEMENT CONTROL

PART THREE: SELECTED MANAGEMENT TECHNIQUES

PART FOUR: SPECIAL ASPECTS OF MANAGEMENT ACCOUNTING

Preface

This handbook has been planned to give an authoritative and rounded overview of the current state of management accountancy and the contributions range from the essentially practical application of management accounting techniques to the more sophisticated discussion of advanced ideas and developments. The contributors have been chosen with a view to presenting a coherent appraisal of management accounting in the 1980s, with some emphasis on the adventurous and the forward looking. The contributors are acknowledged and articulate experts in their respective fields; many are of international standing and they are drawn from the business, professional and academic worlds.

The handbook is directed towards the needs of financial executives, managers, cost and management accountants, and teachers, both within the United Kingdom and in English-speaking countries abroad. Managers and accountants will find in the contributions clear explanations and assessments of the theories and practices of management accounting. The contributions also provide readers with the information and criteria for evaluating and improving their own systems and performance. Teachers will find in the handbook a comprehensive and up-to-the-minute summary and exposition of management accounting techniques from both a theoretical and a practical viewpoint.

While each contribution is complete in itself, necessarily representing the views and experiences of its author, an overview section introduces each of the four parts into which the book is divided. Those overviews place the succeeding chapters in context and highlight the degrees of cohesiveness between otherwise apparently disparate treatments. Each chapter is introduced by an editorial synopsis of its main contents and contribution to the processes and practices of managerial accounting.

An underlying theme of many of the contributions to this collection is the recognition of the changed nature of present day management accounting. As several contributors argue, management accounting is now characterised by a readier acceptance of the lessons and implications of many sciences and disciplines outside the traditional influences of financial and cost accounting. While the background and training of most management accountants has not changed significantly during the past quarter of a century, and such perennial topics as budgets, variances, standard costs, and divisional performance have remained priorities in teaching and training programmes, there are welcome signs that the 'newer' sciences of organisational behaviour, information economics, control theory and the like are coming to play an important role in modern management accounting education and experience. Accordingly, one of the principal purposes of this book is to describe and evaluate those influences and to demonstrate ways in which they can provide powerful aids to present-day planning and decision making. Equally, however, the book has a role to play in the discussion and exemplification of the more traditional techniques used by management accountants. So, while the range of contributions and their individual coverage may seem to offer an uneasy combination of the practical and the academic, the cohesiveness of the handbook stems from its recognition of the present state of the art of management accounting and its advocacy of desirable and essential future developments.

These aims are central to the Editor's opening introduction, which describes the conceptual foundations on which management accounting rests and the development of a wider theory of management accounting in recent years. In Fanning's view, there has been an increasing acceptance of considerations deriving from economic, informational, behavioural and conceptual analyses of the nature and role of management accounting. He claims that the past three decades have been characterised by a relative lack of impact by management accounting research on management accounting in practice, and the introductory chapter offers a number of suggestions for improving the direction of research and development.

The first part of the handbook deals with the strategic plans and decisions of an organisation and the best ways in which management accounting can assist these processes. The contribution by Simmonds offers a comprehensive analysis of the strategic role that management accounting should play in planning and decision making. In that author's view, the pre-eminent function of the management accountant is to provide essential information for strategy formation and adjustment. There is a strong need, he argues, to move away from the all-too-common predilection for standard costing and data derived from existing, conventional accounting systems. According to Simmonds, it is this traditional data-recording orientation that has out-dated the development of management accounting as an effective strategic function.

The other contributions in the first part of the book cover those strategic processes of direct relevance to the planning and control of the business organisation. Sizer's chapter concerns itself with one of the most important considerations: the selling price decision and the impact of cost-volume-profit analyses. Pricing decisions are of particular importance in periods of inflation and the author offers valuable guidelines and techniques for managers faced with such difficult decisions. The chapter by Dobbins and Pike describes some of the more commonly used techniques for assessing capital projects, and the contribution by Groves analyses and appraises the use of mathematical models in planning and control. The models described and evaluated by Groves reflect three approaches to modelling: the inventory models, the mathematical programming models, and the forecasting models. The emphasis in Groves' chapter is on the description and explanation of ways in which quantitative modelling techniques can help provide management with better information and the contribution represents a valuable illustration of those basic techniques. In his chapter, Bromwich reinforces the book's concern with planning and decision making by arguing for a better use of traditional standard costing and variance analysis techniques. Bromwich calls for a switch in the emphasis of such systems – from their traditional concern with controlling operations to one of informing and planning future operations.

Part Two of the handbook deals with specific uses of accounting methodologies in the control of business operations and investigates a number of routine techniques. Brown reviews and evaluates the frequently misunderstood approaches of absorption costing and marginal costing, while MacArthur presents a wider ranging analysis of different, and often non-traditional, forms of budgeting.

The question of standard costing is addressed again in this part, by Jones; the emphasis here, however, is on the nature and significance of the variances themselves. In the concluding chapter in this section, Fanning examines the delegation by top management of the freedom to make decisions and the subsequent accountability of the decision-taker. In practice, responsibility accounting gives a manager considerable discretion and a concomitant degree of accountability for the results of his actions. Fanning returns to that theme – the performance of divisional and line managers – in a wider based chapter in the fourth part of the book.

Specific management techniques are discussed in the third part of the handbook, which contains four chapters describing examples of specific techniques for the control of organisations rather than giving a complete picture of the whole range of available techniques. Hollis analyses the range of mechanisms available to achieve cost reduction, Fanning discusses methods of loss prevention, and Pike and Dobbins deal with the questions of planning and controlling business projects. Santocki argues for a wider acceptance of the auditing of management's performance and activities. The management accountant has a vital role to play in that process and the evaluation of the strengths and weaknesses of a management team is obviously crucial to the strategic well-being of an organisation.

The final section of the book contains a number of chapters dealing with special aspects of the management accounting function. In the opening contribution, Groves moves away from the technical emphasis of most of the earlier writers in the book. In dealing with the organisational and behavioural processes underlying the techniques and mechanisms of management accounting, Groves introduces the practising management accountant to the complex and parlous nature of organisations and the impacts and effects of even routine control and reporting measures. The next two chapters examine the special problems and practices of the divisionalised organisation. Fanning's chapter details the many difficulties and obstacles associated with the measurement and control of divisional performance and introduces the important characteristic of controlability as a yardstick in the measurement process. Davies describes and discusses the theories and mechanisms of transfer pricing, arguing for the provision of adequate and relevant management accounting information.

In an analysis of the application of management accounting skills and techniques to one area of business activity, Hill describes and evaluates the role of management accounting in the physical distribution of goods, a cost item which is often neglected to an alarming extent. The concept of added value and its pertinence to management decisions are discussed by Cox, and the applications of management accounting to the affairs and activities of not-for-profit organisations are described and analysed by Bennett. Each of those chapters extends the normal boundaries of management accounting in an innovative way and the contributions add valuable new dimensions to the customary model of a management accountant. The concluding chapter by Fanning draws together some of the pervasive arguments from earlier contributions, particularly those that point towards the need for a revised or extended theory of management accounting. The chapter sets out a framework for such a theory, taking a systems view of the modern organisation and its informational and strategic needs.

The handbook is not intended in any way as a management accounting 'textbook' or 'encyclopaedia'; rather, it plans to offer the manager and the management accountant a blend of the practical, the traditional, the theoretical and the innovative. It is presented in the belief that its coverage will be of value and interest to its target readership and in the hope that its clear exposition and able advocacy of fresh and demanding ideas will encourage practitioners and teachers to widen the boundaries of conventional management accounting.

The task of gathering and editing a collection such as this draws heavily on the patience and forbearance of all concerned, not least the contributors who willingly accepted an invitation to squeeze yet another task into their already crowded days and nights. Above all, a particular debt is owed to Malcolm Stern, editorial director at Gower, for his enthusiastic and long-suffering espousal of the cause of this handbook and his tolerance of the vicissitudes of the editorial process.

Sincere acknowledgements are due also to many people whose courteous and selfless advice and guidance helped make this a better and more rounded collection. Any recognition of helpful participation must include a goodly number of undergraduate and postgraduate students who have afforded the Editor and the contributors valuable opportunities to try out new material and polish arguments and presentations. Hinc lucem et pocula sacra!

David Fanning

Notes on contributors

Duncan Bennett, FCMA, FCCA, RAPC, is a Colonel in the Army and Head of the Management Accounting and Costing Services unit. He has been a regular army officer since 1948 and has had considerable experience in the 'not-for-profit' field, dealing with state finance, charitable trusts and cash administration. A founder member of the ICMA's Defence sub-branch, he is a member of the Institute's Public Sector and Education & Training Committees.

Michael Bromwich, BSc (Econ), FCMA, IPFA, is Professor of Finance and Accounting at the University of Reading. Author of *The Economics of Capital Budgeting* (Penguin, 1976; Pitman, 1980), and co-editor of *Essays in British Accounting Research* (Pitman, 1981) and *Auditing Research: Issues and Opportunities* (Pitman, 1982), he is a member of the Accounting Standards Committee and of the ICMA's Council. An experienced writer and researcher, he is a member of the Industry & Employment committee of the Social Science Research Council.

J. Lewis Brown, MSc, FCMA, FCCA, FBIM, is Lecturer in Management Accounting at the City University Business School, having spent earlier parts of his career in industry and in further and higher education institutions in Britain and Iran. He has special interests in corporate planning and inventory control and has jointly written *Cost Accounting and Costing Methods* (Macdonald and Evans, 1978) and *Managerial Accounting and Finance* (Macdonald and Evans, 1982).

Bernard Cox, FCMA, FCCA, is Technical Director, Research, of the

Institute of Cost and Management Accountants, having previously held accountancy appointments with Marconi, EMI and Westland Helicopters. He is the author of *Value Added* (Heinemann, 1979) and joint author of *Management Accounting in Inflationary Conditions* (ICMA, 1976). He has a special interest in value added incentive schemes and is pursuing doctoral research in that topic at the City University Business School.

Jeffrey Davies, BA, MA, ACMA, is a principal lecturer and Head of the Division of Accounting and Finance at the Polytechnic of Wales, Pontypridd. Joint author of *Pricing in Practice* (Heinemann, 1975), *Managerial Economics* (Macdonald and Evans, 1977), and *Investment in the British Economy* (Heinemann, 1980), his earlier career included periods with Rolls-Royce and at the North Staffordshire Polytechnic. Among his research and teaching interests are the initiation and development of small firms.

Richard Dobbins, MSc, PhD, FCCA, is Senior Lecturer in Financial Management at the Management Centre of the University of Bradford. He is editor of *Managerial Finance* and the author and co-author of a considerable number of books and articles, including the *Handbook of Managerial Finance* (MCB Publications, 1977) and *The Growth and Impact of Institutional Investors* (ICAEW, 1978). An experienced lecturer and consultant, his earlier career included periods in public and private accountancy practice and in cost accountancy.

David Fanning, BSc, PhD, is Lecturer in Business Administration and Accountancy at the University of Wales Institute of Science and Technology, and he has written a considerable number of newspaper and journal articles on business and finance. The author of *Marketing Company Shares* (Gower, 1982), *Public Companies* (ICAEW, 1983), and other books, and editor of *Pension Funds: Issues in Accounting and Finance* (MCB Publications, 1981), his main teaching and research interests are in the areas of managerial accounting and business finance.

Roger Groves, BCom, MSc, PhD, FCA, is Sir Julian Hodge Professor of Accountancy at the University of Wales Institute of Science and Technology, having spent earlier parts of his career in a professional accountancy practice and in university teaching positions in Britain and America. Joint author of *Company Finance in Europe* (ICAEW, 1975), he has written numerous articles in professional and academic journals on various aspects of accountancy and finance. He is a consultant to a number of manufacturing and service companies.

Gordon Hill, BSc, ACMA, CEng, MIChemE, MInstE, MIMC, is a director of A.T. Kearney Ltd, management consultants, and the author of a number of publications on management subjects. Formerly a research scientist with the National Coal Board and an experimental engineer with Johnson Wax, he has specialized as a management consultant in materials management and physical distribution. He is a member of the board of the Centre for Physical Distribution Management and of the Council of the Institute for Physical Distribution Management.

Anthony Hollis, MBE, ACMA, RAPC, is a Major in the Army and Chief Technical Officer in the Management Accounting and Costing Services unit. He was awarded the MBE in the 1982 New Year Honours List on the basis of his work on cost reduction schemes while Transport Management Accountant in London. An army officer for 27 years, Major Hollis has a strong interest in government and public sector accounting, and he has served with all three logistics corps in the Army.

C. Stuart Jones, MSc, FCMA, ACIS, JDipMA, is a lecturer in accounting at the University of Hull, following appointments in financial management and planning with Massey Ferguson and Chloride. He is the author of *Successful Management of Acquisitions* (Beattie, 1982), and of several articles in the professional press. His special interest is in the post-acquisition control of merged firms and the role of management accounting in that control task.

John MacArthur, MA, FCCA, is Assistant Professor in Accounting in the School of Business of the University of Northern Iowa. Previously a lecturer at the University of Wales Institute of Science and Technology, his research interests include management accounting practices and the particular problems of nationalised industries.

Richard Pike, MA, PhD, FCA, is Lecturer in Finance and Accounting at the Management Centre of the University of Bradford. His earlier career included teaching appointments and he was group planning controller with the Burton group, responsible for the capital planning process. His main teaching and research interests are in the field of capital investment, but he has published extensively on a variety of accounting and finance topics.

Janusz Santocki, BCom, MPhil, FCA, is Senior Lecturer in Auditing at the City of Birmingham Polytechnic, following earlier appointments in further education and ten years in professional chartered accountancy. He is the author of *Case Studies in Auditing* (Macdonald and Evans, 1978) and *Auditing: A Conceptual and Systems Approach* (Polytech, 1982). With special research and teaching interests in auditing, he has written a number of articles in professional and academic journals.

Kenneth Simmonds, BCom, MCom, DBA, PhD, FCMA, FCIS, FInstM, is Professor of Marketing and International Business at the London Graduate School of Business Studies, having spent earlier parts of his career in industry and in teaching positions in the United States and in Britain. The author of *Strategy and Marketing* (Allan, 1982) and joint author of *International Business and Multi-national Enterprises* (Irwin, 1982), he has written a considerable number of articles in professional and academic journals on topics in management and strategy. He is a director of a number of public companies and a member of the ICMA's Education & Training committee.

John Sizer, BA, FCMA, FBIM, is Professor of Financial Management and Head of the Department of Management Studies at the University of Technology, Loughborough. Previously holding academic appointments at the University of Edinburgh and the London Graduate School of Business Studies, he is an experienced and active consultant and adviser to a number of international companies, including Bowater, Philips and British Steel. He has contributed a large number of papers and chapters to a wide range of publications and is the author of *An Insight into Management Accounting* (Penguin, 1979), *Case Studies in Management Accounting* (Penguin, 1979), and *Perspectives in Management Accounting* (Heinemann, 1981). He has edited and contributed to *Readings in Management Accounting* (Penguin, 1980).

List of illustrations

Tables

List of illustrations

1

The Nature of Management Accounting

David Fanning

This introductory chapter seeks to explain the foundations of management accounting and to describe some of the more important elements in a rounded management accounting information system. To many observers, management accounting seems technique-bound, an emphasis more in keeping with the old style label of cost accounting than with the present-day purpose of assisting management to plan and control the activities of the modern organisation. The modern management accountant is more than a cost accountant or a financial accountant in the sense that all cost and financial information prepared or appraised by accountants is of central interest to management. In recent years, there has been an increasing awareness of the information needs of management and of the various influences and constraints on planning, control and decision making. The boundaries of management accounting are no longer defined by narrow, process or procedure-based techniques; there is a ready recognition of the importance of conceptual, behavioural, informational and economic considerations. While appreciating the extent to which practical and academic research have helped the development of management accounting, the chapter is critical of recent and current initiatives and offers suggestions as to the better direction of research in this important area.

For too long management accounting has been regarded as a variant of cost accounting and considered as dealing almost exclusively with costs and prices. As the contributions to this book demonstrate, that view of management accounting is incomplete and inappropriate. Definitions of management or managerial accounting can be found in most textbooks and guidebooks, and the British professional body, the Institute of Cost and Management Accountants, has issued its own definition on which most writers base their interpretations. The professional definition of management accounting is:

> the application of professional knowledge and skill in the preparation and presentation of accounting information in such a way as to assist management in the formulation of policies and in the planning and control of the operations of the undertaking.

As Sizer (1979) has recounted succinctly, the use of the term 'management accounting' derives from the identification of a third accounting function in addition to those already existing – the determination of the effects of a firm's activities and the evaluation of its assets and liabilities, and the preparation and verification of information for control purposes. To those two functions was added that of assisting management to plan and control the policy-making and decision-taking activities of the modern complex organisation. Sizer links this development to the 1950 visit to the United States of a management accounting team and the subsequent publication of its report. The professional body accepted the conclusions and implications of the report and changed certain of its examination and accreditation procedures. Not until March 1972, however, was the title of the institute changed from that of 'Cost and Works Accountants' to its present name. Not surprisingly, many cost accountants resisted the change and looked askance at the 'intrusion' into their closely defined and unexceptional discipline of concepts and techniques deriving from more sophisticated management and behavioural sciences.

The evolutionary nature of contemporary management accounting has been stressed by many writers. For example, Anton, Firmin and Grove (1978) argue that:

> Cost and managerial accounting, like accounting in general, are dynamic, evolving disciplines.... [There has been a] conceptual expansion in order to provide relevant accounting data to decision makers. These conceptual developments include the consideration of management information systems, decision models, behavioral science, budgeting, cost estimation

and control, not-for-profit performance evaluation, internal pricing, and various decision oriented problem areas.

This view of the redefined nature of management accounting has been reinforced by the adoption of a conceptual 'systems' approach to the modern enterprise – an approach exemplified by the seminal work of such writers as Amey and Egginton (1973).

The foundations on which management accounting rests have been described ably by Belkaoui (1980) and the following discussion derives from that writer's presentation.

THE CONCEPTUAL FOUNDATIONS

There are four principal conceptual foundations of management accounting: accounting foundations; behavioural foundations; organisational foundations; and decisional foundations. As argued by Belkaoui:

> Management accounting is designed, first, to supply information to internal decision makers of a given organization, second, to facilitate their decision making, third, to motivate their actions and behavior in a given direction, and, finally, to promote the efficiency of the organization. It is accounting-based and individual-, organization-, and decision-centered. Thus, management accounting requires an accounting, behavioral, organizational, and decisional grounding.

A proper appreciation of each of these foundations will help in the design of a management accounting system which will respond adequately to the needs and demands from within and without the organisation. On the other hand, a failure to understand any of the conceptual foundations will probably lead to deficiencies in the system and failures in the provision of adequate responses.

Belkaoui identifies four basic characteristics, or problems, one of which relates to the conceptual strands. The accounting characteristic is

> one of determining the ways in which accounting information may be accumulated, classified, analyzed, and adapted to specific problems, decisions, and day-to-day conduct of an organization.

The required elements have been identified in the literature – the objectives, qualities, concepts and techniques of management accounting. The organisational characteristic is

> one of tailoring the internal reporting system to the organizational structure and to the significant elements which approximate the patterning and order inherent in organizations.

The third characteristic, the behavioural problem, is defined as

> one of adapting the internal reporting system to the different factors that shape the 'cognitive make-up' of individuals within the organization and affect their performance.

These factors include the way in which the individual sees the objective function or goals of the organisation, which may be to maximise wealth or welfare, the various components of any motivational structure, and the decision processes acceptable to or desired by the individual. The decisional problem or characteristic is

> one of determining the types of decision and decision systems, the type of information and information system needed.

and many such frameworks have been proposed in the literature.

The accounting foundations

Accounting provides information, through the presentation, verification and interpretation of financial data, for two distinct yet closely related purposes: reporting the activities and condition of an organisation to outside parties with a legitimate interest; and decision making within the organisation. The practice of external or financial accounting addresses itself to the first purpose, while the practice of internal or management accounting deals with the second. Both practices or schemes involve the production and distribution of accounting data, albeit different data for different uses.

In that management accounting is concerned with internal problem solving, it requires much more than the application of generally accepted accounting principles to the process of recording economic activities. As Belkaoui recognises, management accounting techniques do not

> conform to any set of prescribed rules, and much may be left to the decision-maker's philosophies.

The frame of reference used in management accounting is, therefore, much broader than that used in external or financial accounting. That significant difference has been recognised by many professional and academic commentators. Since the objectives of external and internal reporting differ markedly, the concepts underlying the two practices differ in several important respects and a separate conceptual framework must be developed in management accounting. Such a framework will include the objectives of management accounting, the qualities to be sought as essential attributes of management accounting information, the concepts to be established as the foundation for the body of knowledge represented in the framework and the techniques and procedures of the internal accounting systems. Belkaoui argues that these elements have not yet been integrated into a formalised management accounting framework, but that they exist separately in the literature.

He advances several citations of the objectives of management accounting, presenting a list of four goals or priorities:

1 the planning functions of managers;
2 organisational problem areas;
3 management control functions;
4 operating systems management.

For any management accounting information to help to attain such objectives, the qualitative characteristics or properties of that information must be such that the value of the information is enhanced or at least maintained. Belkaoui cites the following list of standards or qualities to be applied to internal or managerial accounting:

1 relevance/mutuality of objectives;
2 accuracy/precision/reliability;
3 consistency/comparability/uniformity;
4 verifiability/objectivity/neutrality/traceability;
5 aggregation;
6 flexibility/adaptability;
7 timeliness;
8 understandability/acceptability/motivation/fairness.

While most of these characteristics are good and readily acceptable as desirable standards for financial reporting, each is worth examining a little more closely in the particular context of management accounting.

Relevance is in the mind of the user; in other words, relevant information is the information provided on any variables in the objective function of the user and

> must be very close to the definition implicit in the objective function.

Relevant information is that which bears directly or closely on the action planned or the result desired.

> Relevance depends on the particular user receiving the information and on his or her particular decision. Some variables may be relevant to one user and not to others, and to one type of decision and not to others.

The characteristic of mutuality of objectives refers to the degree of consistency or congruency between the objectives of information users and those of the organisation as a whole. Equally, the goals of the information preparers or processors must be congruent with those of the organisation.

The characteristics of accuracy, precision and reliability call for little explanation, although there is a need for any management information system to set thresholds or upper and lower limits of reliability and precision. Similarly, the quality of consistency and the related characteristics of comparability and uniformity are unexceptionable, although their desirability may vary between long-term and short-term decision processes. Undue insistence on consistency, comparability and uniformity may hamper the better analysis of long range planning decisions based on unstructured information and about non-repetitive situations. On the other hand, short-run performance control and planning rely heavily on structured information and repetitive situations.

In management accounting terms, it is not so crucial that information should be as neutral as the data processed in financial or external reporting. It is a sine qua non of both practices, however, that information should be verifiable and traceable and that, as far as possible, measurements are made objectively. The neutrality of the information will obviously be impaired by a measurer's personal interest in the data. Nevertheless, where information is used for allocating resources or settling claims, neutrality is a most desirable characteristic.

Aggregation has serious disadvantages in management accounting, not least being the loss of identifiability and pertinence. In order to cope with voluminous detail and to reduce the cost of data handling, some aggregation is obviously necessary. The particular needs of the organisation concerned and the associated costs and benefits will dictate the degree of aggregation which is acceptable.

In like manner, higher levels of flexibility and adaptability are far more valuable in management accounting disclosure than in financial accounting information. The degree to which basic data may be used to generate several different types of information and report is arguably much more important in internal disclosure than external. Adaptability of information to the special needs or characteristics of the organisation concerned is equally important, and may involve some tailoring or harmonising to relate the information generated to the planning and control processes of the organisation.

Timeliness is a quintessential feature of management accounting information and may best be seen from two viewpoints: the intervals between which such information is prepared, and the delay in preparing and distributing the information. Timeliness may, of course, be affected by other considerations such as cost or accuracy.

The final set of qualities relates to the extent to which the user is able to use the information. The ability

> of the user to ascertain the message submitted . . . the recognition by the user that the problem specification and measurement criteria have been met . . .

are the characteristics of understandability and acceptability. Fairness refers to the characteristic of neutrality mentioned earlier, while motivation relates to the attempt to secure goal congruence. In brief,

> management accounting information should be understandable, acceptable, fair to the user, and a motivation to the user to perform in a desired manner.

Moving next to a consideration of the concepts to be encapsulated in a management accounting conceptual framework, Belkaoui developed a list of concepts identified in 1972 by a committee of the American Accounting Association as follows:

1 measurement;
2 communication;
3 information;
4 system;

5   planning;
6   feedback;
7   control;
8   cost behaviour.

Belkaoui argued that these concepts represent those foundation components essential to a proper 'grasp of the management accounting process'.

Measurement is the quantification of past, present or future economic phenomena, on the basis of past or present observations and according to defined and acceptable rules. Communication refers to the process of moving from measurement to information, while information in this definition encompasses financial information, production information, personnel information, and marketing information.

The concept of system refers to the existence of two or more interacting networks or components within an organisation. The total management information system, will include an accounting information system as a subsystem, and the management accounting system will represent a subsystem of that subsystem. Planning requires setting objectives, formulation of policies and choosing appropriate mechanisms for their accomplishment. Feedback prompts the revision of plans to accommodate new events or situations; thereby the output of a process becomes, in its turn, an input to that same process in order to initiate control. Control involves the continuous monitoring of performance and its evaluation to determine the degree of coherence between actions and plans. Any evaluation of actions is based on the identification, classification and estimation of costs. Cost behaviour is, therefore, essential to any control process.

There is almost infinite scope for disagreement as to what constitutes a full range of management accounting techniques. While most textbooks contain certain fundamental – even traditional – methods such as standard costing, very few attempts have been made to establish a wide ranging checklist of management accounting techniques. The 1972 report of the AAA committee mentioned above proposed an accounting structure, which is reproduced as Table 1.1. While that structure omits the behavioural, organisational and decisional foundation models to be discussed later, it does represent most of the techniques discussed in the literature.

Table 1.1
Management accounting techniques

INTRODUCTORY MATERIAL
> Systems theory and accounting; communications, measurement and information concepts; criteria development; feedback and control mechanisms; information systems; accounting for management planning and control; cost concepts and techniques.

COST DETERMINATION FOR ASSETS
> Job order and process costing; standard costing systems; direct versus absorption costing; by-product and joint product costing; cost allocation practices; accounting for human resources.

PLANNING
> Strategic planning; continuous planning; investment decisions; comprehensive budgets; cost-volume-profit analysis; problems of alternative choice.

MANAGEMENT CONTROL
> Responsibility accounting; cost centres; financial performance centres; investment centres; centralised versus decentralised structures; goal congruence concern; transfer pricing; evaluation methods; performance reporting.

OPERATIONAL CONTROL
> Internal control; project control; inventory control.

From the above, it may be seen that, as Belkaoui argued,

> Management accounting has its foundations in the discipline of accounting, although it recognizes the potential benefits of borrowing relevant techniques from other disciplines.... Although generally perceived as a set of techniques, management accounting includes most of the components of a conceptual framework.

The behavioural foundations

The aim of management accounting is to influence the behaviour of individuals within an organisation and to direct their efforts to the best advantage of that concern. Thus, management accounting demands a good grasp of the fundamentals of behavioural theories, in particular, the corporate and/or individual goal shaping and seeking processes – the objective function, in other words, the motives and needs of the individual, and the decision making processes in organisations.

Business entities are complex organisations and most writers on the subject have discussed the identification and attainment of specific goals and of such typologies as goals *for* an organisation and goals *of* an organisation – see, for example, Etzioni (1964) and Thompson (1967). Others, such as Perrow (1961), have argued the distinction between official goals, as clearly stated but commanding few resources, and operational goals, as the future states towards which most of an organisation's means and resources are committed.

Each discipline examines profit oriented organisations in a different way, establishing different objectives in line with its particular orientation. Economics, for example, sets a single determinant for organisational behaviour: profit maximisation. On the other hand, organisational and management theorists have advanced several behavioural theories of the firm. The economic or behavioural model is not entirely suitable, however, in a management accounting context, although both approaches have influenced the three models of business behaviour most amenable to management accounting:

(a) shareholder wealth maximisation;
(b) managerial welfare maximisation;
(c) social welfare maximisation.

Since each of these three aims possesses attractive attributes for management accounting purposes, a brief discussion of their respective characteristics and merits is apposite.

The objective of shareholder wealth maximisation is a pervasive thread in most textbooks on corporate strategy and finance. The rationale behind the model rests on achieving peak returns on capital and is generally interpreted as maximisation of the price of the firm's equity shares. Management is assumed to wish to act in the best interests of the shareholders and, therefore, to wish to plan and control actions and their outcomes to achieve that end. The model is naive, however, in that it ignores other operational goals which, legitimately and usefully, may be pursued by management in its progress to shareholder wealth maximisation. Sales maximisation, growth maximisation, market share maximisation, and so on – each of these is a realistic fellow traveller. The problems arise when there is a conflict between apparently harmonious goals. Such conflicts may lead to the rejection of decisions that would be accepted under the wealth maximising criterion.

Managerial welfare maximisation has been seen by several writers as a realistic model of experience in most organisations with widely held equity; managers act in their own best interests. The maximisation of managerial welfare may be achieved in several ways – maximising size or turnover, rate of growth, or managerial usefulness. Again, the possibility arises that managements will adopt suboptimising behaviours designed to serve their own ends rather than those of the organisation. Management accounting techniques will be adopted which are in the best interests of the managers rather than the owners.

Given that societal and environmental pressures on organisations are increasing apace, the objective of social welfare maximisation has achieved greater prominence in recent years. The advocacy of social responsibility for modern corporations has brought with it the notion that businesses should maximise social benefits and minimise social costs. As a consequence, different corporate purposes or goals may be adopted, resulting in other reporting techniques (for instance, social accounting or human resource accounting) and different underlying management accounting techniques.

The theories of motivation are central also to an understanding of the behavioural foundations of management accounting. Some five or six theories of motivation are identified in the relevant literature. Each theory has implications for management accounting; as Belkaoui summarises:

> Each of these theories either identifies what factors within the individual and his or her environment activate high performance, or attempts to explain and describe the process of how behavior is activated, what directs it, and how it is controlled and stopped.

Briefly, the predominant theories may be listed and categorised as follows:

1   Need theory – individuals are motivated to satisfy a hierarchy of needs in a sequential way, from physiological needs through to self-actualisation needs (Maslow, 1943).
2   Two-factor theory – job situations are affected by two factors; satisfying factors and dissatisfying factors, ranging from achievement and recognition to status and job security, with satisfiers being labelled 'motivator' factors and dissatisfiers 'hygiene' factors (Herzberg, Mausner and Snyderman, 1959).

3 Achievement theory – individuals like being challenged and wish to be innovative, powerful and respected (McClelland, 1961).
4 Value/expectancy theory – individuals act in ways dictated by the expected outcomes or rewards for such behaviour, with effort and performance being linked to reward (Vroom, 1964).

The motivation theories identify the environmental and situational factors and designate the management accounting techniques which will be most likely to activate high performance.

The question of which techniques to use in a given situation is influenced also by the decision making models employed by management accounting information users in that context. Again, some four or five major models of decision making have been developed in the literature. Broadly, those models have conformed to four main perspectives:

1 The rational view – individuals choose the most attractive or beneficial outcome from a series of outcomes resulting from a series of alternative acts or courses of action.
2 The satisfying view – individuals satisfy rather than optimise when making operational decisions, introducing a subjective rationality into the decision making process and basing decisions firmly on individuals' actual knowledge.
3 The organisational procedures view – individuals follow closely and act according to a fixed set of standard procedures, acting in terms of goals and on the basis of expectations.
4 The individual differences view – individuals follow particular decision making styles, which will be more appropriate for some situations than for others, being, for example, dogmatic or authoritarian, heuristic or analytical, perceptive or organisationally bemused. (For a useful treatment, see Keen and Scott Morton, 1978.)

The implications for management accounting are clear. Informational reports should be compatible with the cognitive and decision making styles of their users. The rule-of-thumb manager may be less appreciative of quantitative management accounting techniques and reports than the analytical manager. By definition, analytical

management accountants should not assume that all users are and should be like themselves.

The organisational foundations

The role of management accounting in the organisation is defined by the elements of organisational structure and by the theories of organisation advanced in the literature. Equally, such determinants define the best techniques and approaches to be adopted by management accountants.

Taking the elements of organisation structure, it can be seen, in summary, that organisations portray a number of structural characteristics pertinent to the management accounting function:

1 Organisations are fairly permanent and complex interactive systems – they are going concerns, they are exclusive in terms of membership, they include interdependent members.
2 Organisations have clearly defined organisational structures – whether vertically, horizontally, or uniquely differentiated – with implications for such topics as authority and responsibility.
3 Organisations give rise to different and complex relationships between individuals – functional controllers, line managers, shopfloor workers, and so on.
4 Organisations have different views of the function and role of the management accountant, and part of that role may be to convince organisational members of the value of management accounting information.

Organisational behaviour is complex and confusing, and a number of theories of organisation have developed in an attempt to explain that behaviour. In brief, the four persistent theories may be described as follows:

1 The rational perspective – members of an organisation work together in a methodical manner to achieve organisational goals, with organisations embracing one of three types of legitimate authority following profiles: traditional, charismatic, or bureaucratic (Weber, 1947).
2 The classical or scientific management perspective – organisations seek to use resources to give optimal efficiency, by setting standards and imposing planning and control at all levels (Taylor, 1947).
3 The human relations perspective – organisations depend on human elements and need participation from individuals and groups of individuals, to whom social conditions and situations are important (McGregor, 1960).

4   The natural system perspective – organisations behave in unplanned, spontaneous or natural ways, with a life of their own,
adapting continually to altered environments, developing a
corporate personality, depending on subsystems and their autonomy, their members and their interdependence (Katz and Kahn,
1966).

The decisional foundations

Belkaoui argues that:

> A fundamental objective of management accounting is to
> facilitate and support all aspects of an organization's decision-
> making. To accomplish this objective, management accountants
> should be aware of the kinds and levels of decisions involved in
> order to identify those particular areas where management
> accounting techniques and information would be most relevant
> and useful.

A number of different conceptual bases for viewing decisions and
decision systems have been advanced in the literature.

Anthony (1965) proposed a hierarchy of decision systems: strategic
planning decisions, management control decisions, operational
control decisions. Each area of decision making calls for different
approaches to planning and control and each requires different
information. If the information requirements are seen along a
continuum, and the attributes of the information described in
various ways, the information required by strategic planners can be
seen to be markedly different from that required by operational
controllers. For example, strategic planners will require summary
data, whereas operational controllers will require detailed data;
similarly, strategic planners may work best with qualitative information, whereas operational controllers will require quantitative
information.

While Anthony concentrated on the purpose of the decision
making activity, Simon (1960) presented a decisional framework
concerned with the processes of decision making or problem
solving by individuals. He identified three stages or phases: intelligence (in which the problem is identified, the information collected,
and the criteria or goals established); design (in which various
courses of action are considered and analysed); choice (in which the
best alternative is selected).

Other writers have suggested combinations or extensions of those views. Forrester (1961) saw decision making as a response to the gap between the objectives of the organisation and its accomplishment of those objectives. Dearden (1965) argued for both a horizontal and a vertical categorisation of decisions; horizontally by the type of decision, vertically by the kind of information handled.

Belkaoui summarises the position thus:

> ... these frameworks constitute the decisional foundations of management accounting by providing the basis for making resource allocation decisions about information systems, in general, and management accounting, in particular. They suggest the types of information needed for different categories of decisions and decision centers.

He presents a strong case for a combined theory of management accounting, as shown in Figure 1.1.

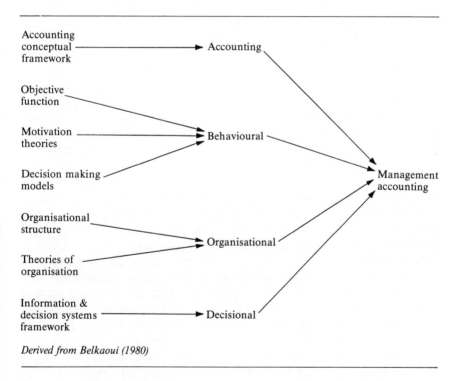

Derived from Belkaoui (1980)

Fig. 1.1   Conceptual foundations of management accounting

To gather together the strands of the above arguments, each of the four foundations for management accounting can be characterised by appropriate decisive factors. The accounting foundations are determined by the extent of the derivation of management accounting techniques from basic accounting concepts. The behavioural foundations are determined by the objective function, by motivation theories and by models of decision making. The organisational foundations are determined by the elements of organisational structure and by the theories of organisation. Finally, the decisional foundations are determined by the framework of information and decision systems.

RECENT DEVELOPMENTS

In broad terms, developments in or of relevance to management accounting in recent years may be grouped in three ways: those which represent extensions or developments of conventional techniques; those which represent techniques with implications for management accounting; those which derive from other quantitatively based disciplines.

The first category includes such techniques as standard costing, marginal costing, zero base reviews, management by objectives, cost-volume-profit analysis, life cycle costing, and the like. In the second category – those with implications for management accounting but of far wider application – are included corporate planning, strategic modelling, network analysis, value analysis, organisation and methods techniques, and so on. The third category includes such quantitative techniques as operational research, linear programming, linear regression analysis, discriminant analysis, and the like. A thorough and wide ranging review of these developments has been provided by Hart (1981).

Notwithstanding the body of published research over the past decade, it has to be said that most of the analysis undertaken in this area in recent years has had little or no impact on management accounting in practice. In part this is because practitioners do not want a unified theory of management accounting; they are happy to have a conceptual framework for each segment of their practice. Management accounting practice is diversified by nature and a general theory of management accounting would appear to offer little to practitioners.

If that is the case, and the evidence points clearly in that direction, future research in management accounting must be practically oriented. Research in management accounting must arise from and be directed to meeting the present and future needs of internal users of management accounting information. It follows that management accounting research must be user-oriented. Two essential elements of such research must be model building and empirical testing. Models directed at practitioners are too often excessively mathematical and notation-bound; to be useful, models must have verbal equivalents and, above all, be practicable in the run-of-the-mill situation faced by most management accountants. A practical test of one model would be worth many dozen exemplifications of theoretical models with unquantifiable variables and arcane relationships. Empirical testing is an essential element of scholarly research, particularly in financial and management accounting, and should be conducted on a longitudinal basis. The case study approach has been derided by a number of scholars, but they have failed consistently to suggest anything better. Observations carried out over time in a few organisations, where managers are watched at work, where decisions are analysed, where inputs and outputs are described and recorded – these are the fundamental techniques of research in management accounting. Theoretical and desk research are revealed regularly to have little weight in practice and their products have found little support amongst practitioners.

There appear to be four significant strands to any possible future research. First, it is essential to discover the nature and characteristics of the problems faced by management accountants. What do they want to solve or understand? Second, the current narrow horizons of management accounting need to be extended. Third, there must be a move away from the predilection for results which are susceptible to quantitative and statistical analysis. Qualitative information can be just as valuable, and frequently more so than quantitative data. Fourth, the vehicle for future management accounting research must be more broadly based and less hidebound. Rather than a qualified management accountant researching a likely problem within the confines of his own academic discipline, there needs to be a multidisciplinary team, encompassing behavioural scientists, information scientists, accounting specialists, political scientists, organisational scientists, and so on. Above all, research must be realistic to be relevant.

REFERENCES AND FURTHER READING

American Accounting Association, *Report of the Committee on Courses in Managerial Accounting.* New York: AAA, 1972.

Amey, L. R., and Eggington, D. A., *Management Accounting: a Conceptual Approach.* London: Longman, 1973.

Anton, H. R., Firmin, P. A., and Grove, H. D., *Contemporary Issues in Cost and Managerial Accounting.* 3rd edn. Illinois: Houghton Mifflin, 1978.

Anthony, R. N., *Planning and Control Systems.* Cambridge, Mass.: Harvard University Graduate School of Business Administration, 1965.

Belkaoui, A., *Conceptual Foundations of Management Accounting.* Reading, Mass.: Addison-Wesley, 1980.

Dearden, J., 'How to organize information systems', *Harvard Business Review,* March–April 1965.

Etzioni, A., *Modern Organizations.* Englewood Cliffs, N.J.: Prentice-Hall, 1964.

Forrester, J. W., *Industrial Dynamics.* Cambridge, Mass.: MIT Press, 1961.

Hart, H., 'A review of some recent major developments in the management accounting field', *Accounting and Business Research,* Spring 1981.

Herzberg, F., Mausner, B., and Snyderman, B., *The Motivation to Work.* New York: Wiley, 1959.

Katz, D., and Kahn, R. C., *The Social Psychology of Organizations.* New York: Wiley, 1966.

Keen, P. G., and Scott Morton, M. S., *Decision Support Systems: an Organizational Perspective.* Reading, Mass.: Addison-Wesley, 1978.

Livingstone, J. L. (ed), *Managerial Accounting: the Bevhavioural Foundations.* Columbus, Ohio: Grid, 1975.

Maslow, A., 'A dynamic theory of human motivation', *Psychological Review,* 1943.

McClelland, D. C., *The Achieving Society.* New York: Van Nostrand, 1961.

McGregor, D., *The Human Side of Enterprise.* New York: McGraw-Hill, 1960.

Perrow, C., 'The analysis of goals in complex organizations', *American Sociological Review,* 1961.

Simon, H. A., *The New Science of Management Decision.* New York: Harper & Row, 1960.

Sizer, J., *An Insight into Management Accounting.* Harmondsworth: Pelican, 1979.

Taylor, F. W., *Scientific Management.* New York: Harper & Row, 1947.

Thompson, J. D., *Organizations in Action.* New York: McGraw-Hill, 1967.

Vroom, V. H., *Work and Motivation.* New York: Wiley, 1964.

Weber, M., *The Theory of Social and Economic Organization.* New York: Free Press, 1947.

PART ONE
PLANS AND
DECISIONS

OVERVIEW

The first section of this handbook focuses on the strategic nature of management accounting and on the improvement of management information to facilitate better and more relevant decision making. The generation of management accounting information is not, of itself, either particularly difficult or, more sadly, especially helpful. To serve its proper function, management accounting needs to widen its horizons and deepen its analyses. The chapters in this first part concentrate on those objectives and propose a variety of mechanisms and concepts designed to enhance the current practices of management accounting.

In the opening chapter, Professor Kenneth Simmonds of the London Graduate School of Business Studies argues persuasively for the speedy recognition of the strategic role of management accounting. He criticises the present practitioners of management accounting for continuing to emphasise the analysis of recorded costs and for neglecting to strive to improve the decision guiding potential of management accounting information. Information clearly affects strategy, and management accountants play an important role in shaping and preparing that information. This aspect of the management accountant's contribution to managerial decision making is considered further by Professor John Sizer of the Department of Management Studies at the University of Technology at Loughborough. Selling price decisions and the underlying analysis of costs and volumes are among the most complex and difficult decisions faced by management. In the absence of relevant information, of practical value to the decision-taking manager, such decisions are taken inappropriately and often shortsightedly.

Dr Richard Dobbins and Dr Richard Pike of the Management

Centre of the University of Bradford examine another critical field of management decision making – the assessment of capital investment opportunities. The intrinsically practical orientation of that discussion is continued by Professor Roger Groves, of the Department of Business Administration and Accountancy at the University of Wales Institute of Science and Technology in Cardiff, in the overview of three quantitative models applicable to management accounting problem solving. From simple techniques to relatively sophisticated procedures, the two chapters offer both an appreciation and a starting point for more complex, higher order methodologies. Such techniques form the foundations on which the preparation and interpretation of management accounting information must rest if the conceptual edifice is to have any stability. Such a conceptual framework will only survive if its products are seen to optimise managerial decision making.

In the final chapter in this section, Professor Michael Bromwich of the Department of Economics at the University of Reading returns to his long running criticism of one of management accounting's fundamental techniques – that of variance analysis. In his view, the emphasis of such systems must be switched from control to planning and effective decision making, and he advances several suggestions for such a reorientation of traditional management accounting thinking.

2

Strategic Management Accounting

Kenneth Simmonds

Because strategic decisions determine the competitive market position of a business, they are the managerial decisions in which the greatest sums are at risk. As the author of this chapter argues, since the value of information lies in avoiding the cost of mistakes that would have been made otherwise, it is in the formation of strategy that the greatest value of management information will arise – where the mistakes can be most costly. It follows that management accounting should see it as a primary task to provide for management the essential information for strategy formation and adjustment. Yet, despite management accounting's name, proclaiming its metamorphosis from cost accounting, the tendency to place analysis of recorded costs to the fore still outweighs the embryonic and generally abstruse efforts to analyse managerial decision making and design accounting information to improve the process. In Professor Simmonds' view, a consideration of strategic questions is most noticeable by its absence. Information clearly affects strategy. Whether or not the management accounting profession seizes the opportunity to lead aggressively in providing this information, the design of management accounting systems will eventually come to be dominated by its provision, simply because of its value in use. If management accounting lags behind, others will take pride of place. The author demonstrates that management accounting has a strategic purpose. In his assessment, strategic management accounting is poised on the threshold; the stimulus of the recognition of the legitimacy of a strategic focus is bringing a belated response. 'Strategic management accounting is ready to flower as a prime function of the management accountant.'

Were information for strategy to be made the first and primary focus of management accounting, the profession would take its greatest change of direction since Garcke and Fells produced *Factory Accounts* in 1887. The change from cost analysis to value of information analysis is radical. This does not mean, however, that strategy has only recently been perceived as one of the purposes of management accounting. A clear case for the strategic role of cost accounting, as it was then, was put forward as long ago as 1932 at an international cost conference of the National Association of Cost Accountants. Since then, however, for every treatise that has proclaimed the accountant's role in strategy, a thousand papers have outlined some picayune aspect of a standard cost system. Even where there has been an attempt to look at strategic uses, the bias has been strongly towards the provision of data from the existing accounting system.

In recent years, American academic accountants, in particular, have given a lot of attention to the relationship between accounting and management information systems. The Committee on Foundations of Accounting Measurement of the American Accounting Association held the view in 1971 that, despite the two extreme schools of thought that put either accounting or management information systems as a subset of the other, the answer lay somewhere in between. In its report (American Accounting Association, 1971), the committee saw two distinct fields with some degree of overlap:

> Should accountants extend their effort to cover the entire area of management information systems? Essentially, this questions whether the intellectual skills required to be an 'expert' in accounting are easily transferred to the whole area of management information systems. At present, it must be concluded that they are not. This opinion is based on the fact that there is a certain advantage, at least initially, in limiting our efforts only to financial data, because processing and analysis of non-financial data require technical knowledge unfamiliar to accountants. Besides, the processing and analysis of financial data alone offer challenges and opportunities that will not be exhausted in any forseeable future.

One can question whether the committee's diagnosis was correct. A strong case could be made that the lack of attention to management decision requirements lies at the core of the problem – not the lack of technical skills in recording non-financial data.

The same report went on to evaluate decision-making and information needs, but instead of looking at real needs, hypothetical situations were tabulated. The conclusion was reached that the more users there were and the more decisions to be made from a data source, the greater the need for an accounting system consisting largely of primary measures with most aggregation occurring at the time of decision making. The orientation was back to the details of the accounting system not forward to the details of the decisions. It is this traditional data-recording orientation that has held back accounting (Simmonds, 1972).

Curiously, another American Accounting Association committee which reported at exactly the same time seemed to sense that the role of accounting was threatened by providing and analysing information. It seemed also, however, to see most hope for management accounting in the area of strategic planning.

Somewhere, over the years, the accounting profession appears to have lost its belief in its natural leadership in providing strategic management information. Gone is the clarion call of the 1930s. Perhaps the cause of the doubts is the concentration on the technicalities of information supply, rather than a deep concern for the purpose of the information supplied. A closer look at strategy formation, however, gives a picture of tremendous needs for appropriate accounting information.

THE ESSENCE OF BUSINESS STRATEGY

The word 'strategy' is derived from the Greek word *strategos,* meaning a general, and the Greek verb *stratego,* describing generalship. The concepts of military strategy were discussed by early writers like Homer and Euripides, and at one point Socrates likens the duties of a general and a businessman, both planning the use of resources to meet objectives in the face of competition.

Despite the long history of writing on strategy, however, the field of business strategy is predominantly a creation of the past two decades with its own set of subtle business terms and meanings that have become firmly embedded in the business policy and marketing literature. One attempt in the mid-1960s to relate the emerging field of business planning to modern principles of military strategy showed a very considerable distance between what the military saw as strategy and the business concept of strategic planning (Caplan, 1965).

There are generally agreed to be three distinct levels of business strategy: corporate strategy, business strategy, and functional area strategy (Hofer and Schendel, 1978). At the corporate level, the allocation of resources among different businesses is the prime concern. At the level of the individual business, strategy is concerned with the thrust of competitive actions in that business alone. Functional level strategy is further limited to the configuration of business variables falling within the purview of the particular function. This hierarchy of strategy levels parallels organisational levels. At each subsequent lower level, the scope of the strategist is further constrained and subject to the strategy of the higher levels.

This chapter focuses predominantly on the second level of business strategy. In many ways, this level of strategy dominates the other two. Without well considered business strategies as a basis, it would be foolish to develop an elegant corporate strategy and even more foolish to build a detailed functional strategy.

The precise definition of strategy in business situations is less clear. Published definitions vary, with each text adding its own ideas and emphasis. To many, strategy refers to the plan, the end product of strategy formation, with no emphasis placed on the strategic nature of the configuration of actions included in the plan. Some include the objectives as part of the strategy, others see the objectives as what the strategy is to achieve, and some argue that the strategy defines the goals. Others distinguish between goals and objectives. In some cases, the strategy is depicted as a planned series of actions; in other cases, it is a series of decisions about actions; occasionally, it is a set of rules for making decisions. Many mention allocation of resources as the essence of strategy, and some refer to the time scale of achievement, seeing strategy as long term relative to tactics as short term. Emphasis is occasionally placed on determining strategy according to a particular situation and in other cases the environment is picked out for analysis to arrive at the strategy. Some specify a review of market scope and a few mention competitive position.

To some extent these differences in definition stem from identification with different levels in the business organisation, but in most cases the divergencies lie less in underlying concepts of strategy than in the attributes the writers chose to emphasise. Largely unmentioned in definitions, yet implicitly accepted by the way strategy is described, are a range of generally agreed elements of the business situation against which business strategy is designed. It is these elements which shape strategy to the contemporary business situation, and give business strategy quite a different meaning from the strategy of war. It is these elements, too, which condition the information needed. Both the strategy and the information are determined by the nature of the game or the conflict.

Of course, business does not conform to one standard pattern. But by reducing the confusion of reality to some basic elements, patterns of strategy have become examinable. Eleven such elements that apply to the majority of business strategy writing are proposed as follows:

1   Strategy is applicable to business within defined boundaries. While the boundaries may change, the strategy applies at any specified time to actions affecting a delimited area of demand and competition.
2   There are direct competitors. These competitors sell essentially the same products or services within the defined demand area. Indirect competitors operate outside the defined business and their products are not direct substitutes. Indirect competition is usually ignored or covered by the concept of price elasticity of demand.
3   There is zero-sum competition between the direct competitors for the market demand, subject to competitive action affecting the quantity demanded.
4   Demand within the defined market varies over time. This variation in demand is largely independent of supplier strategies and is often referred to as the product life cycle. At its simplest, it is depicted as a normal curve over time with regularly growing then declining demand.
5   Strategy unfolds over a sequence of time periods. Competition evolves through a series of skirmishes and battles during the product life cycle.
6   Single period profit is a function of (a) the price level ruling for the period, (b) the accumulated volume experience of the firm, and (c) the firm's achieved volume as a proportion of capacity.
7   Market share has intrinsic value. Past sales levels influence subsequent customer buying, and costs reduce with greater single period volume and accumulated experience.
8   Competitors differ in market share, accumulated experience,

production capacity, and resources. Competitors are unequal, identified and positioned.

9   Objectives differ. Firms composed of ownership, management and employee factions and operating a range of different businesses have different objectives. Strategic business thinking, however, will usually express these as different time and risk preferences for performance within an individual business, measured in monetary terms.

10   Within a given situation, a core of strategic actions will determine changes in competitive position. Non-strategic, or contingent, actions will support strategic actions and should be consistent with them, but will not change competitive position significantly.

11   Identification of an optimal core of strategic actions requires reasoning and diagnosis, is not attained through the application of a fixed set of procedures, and is situational. In short, thinking is required.

Together, these eleven elements build a picture of business strategy as the choice of a core of actions through which position in a market relative to competition is manipulated over time to maximise the firm's objectives. In a sense, business strategy presents a framework for modelling certain strategic elements of real situations so as to produce the most favourable result, much as a complex game – not at all unlike the game of Monopoly. A circuit of the board in Monopoly is like the single period of the business strategy. Just as period financial performance is not, on its own, a measure of a firm's strategic performance, so, too, in Monopoly. Performance over a circuit is not judged solely by the increase in cash and historic cost of property assets. An assessment of any change in the strategic position of one player relative to other players is also required. To the extent that a property enables a player to build up a limited monopoly position on a segment of the board and charge monopoly rents or to prevent a competitor doing so, then it has a strategic value.

Monopoly has other similarities to contemporary business strategy – for example, the concept of a changing core of strategic actions. At some stages in the game, strategic gain is seen as buying the maximum number of properties, at others it is forcing up the prices others pay, draining competitors' cash resources, forming coalitions or reinforcing a limited monopoly by building houses.

This last is very similar to the proliferation in model development adopted by some market leaders.

THE DEFINITION OF A BUSINESS

What is a unit of business? The question was first raised in exactly this form by Clark (1923) in his classic *The Economics of Overhead Costs*. Nevertheless, the problem has recurred over the years in economics, accounting, marketing, and now strategy literature. Possibly marketing literature is now the most sophisticated in its measurements.

The difficulty is not so much with the concept of a unit of business in static terms, but rather with the concept applied to dynamic competition when every attribute on which a definition rests can change or disappear. It would be generally agreed that in its static definition a business provides products or services in the face of competition to meet market needs. Furthermore, it may be defined either by product, competition, or market attributes. The preference, however, is to lean towards definition based on market attributes which indicate a gap in the chain of product substitutes. It is when competition cuts across an accepted definition that the difficulties arise. Mathematical economists have tended to step around the problem by defining the product, and hence the business, in ever more precise terms until it becomes unique. Economists with an industrial bias, however, have inclined towards a variable unit economics in which the business is re-defined on a changing attribute base according to the strategic needs.

It is this latter approach that seems to match best the concepts of business strategy. Strategic definition of a business is prompted by the need to adjust actions to build or defend the unit of business. Just as a campaign for a military commander may cover a large or a small area, so may a strategic move for a businessman. For the true strategist there can be no fixed definition of a business. Units will need to be changed and reformed in step with perceptions of the need for defence or the opportunity for advance.

Strategy texts, not surprisingly, lay great emphasis on the definitions of strategic businesses and segments. For example, Abell and Hammond (1979) argued that:

Knowing how to segment a market and knowing when and to

> what extent to differentiate the offering to each segment is often
> the most creative part of strategy formulation,

while Porter (1980) held that:

> Usually there are a small number of strategic groups which
> capture the essential differences among firms in the industry.

Management accounting clearly has a major role to play in enabling the identification and definition of the appropriate business units at any time. To do so, the management accounting system must be designed so that management can be both stimulated to consider what might be appropriate units for strategic action and also able to search further in a process of confirming or rejecting possible units of action. Classification and indexing thus become crucial issues. The problems of classification, coding and flexibility are not new to management accounting. These are the bases on which cost accounting was founded (Risk, 1956).

Thus, the requirement to design the management accounting system to enable diagnosis of the units of business requiring strategic attention, does not require a major reorientation of the technical aspects of classification. The missing ingredient is the acceptance of strategic competitive position as the determinant for identifying units. To achieve such acceptance, the findings of contemporary research into the patterns of competitive strategy will need to take their place at the beginning of management accounting. 'What should we cost?' should be confronted before 'How do we design a cost system?'.

COMPETITION AND RELATIVE COSTS

The need to defend a business unit against aggressive competition and the opportunity for initiating offence to build its performance can both exist at the same time, because each business stands in a different strategic position against different competitors. Other things being equal, competitors with a cost advantage are threatening and those without such an advantage are weaker.

The recent concern for strategy gained its initial impetus from an article by Hirschman (1964) showing how the learning curve phenomenon could affect relative costs and hence strategic positions. Measuring cost in constant money terms, he showed how a straight line relationship could be obtained between cost and cumulative units produced when plotted on a double logarithmic scale. On an arithmetic scale with linear coordinates, however, the relationship plots as a curve with a rapid initial decline that later tails off. Hirschman showed the slope of the logarithmic curve was such that for each doubling of the accumulated production experience, the unit cost would fall to around 80 per cent of the previous level, depending on the mixture of man and machine work involved:

> The phenomenon has many names: 'manufacturing progress function', 'cost-quantity relationship', 'cost curve', 'experience curve', 'efficiency curve', 'production acceleration curve', 'improvement curve', and 'performance curve'.

Hirschman's formula for the curve was straightforward and he argued that the curve should be used as a basis for management planning and action to secure such cost reduction. He also argued that the concept applied to industries and to nations could be defensibly projected ahead because of the inevitable nature of the human drive for survival against competition – the cause of the dynamic nature of the environment.

Hirschman's ideas were picked up by The Boston Consulting Group, related to price experience, and, as the 'experience curve' approach, widely popularised as a basis for business strategy. A whole range of elegant strategy concepts was built upon this experience effect (Boston Consulting Group, 1968). If costs can be made to decline predictably with total accumulated production, then the competitor who has produced the most units should have the lowest cost per unit and the highest profits. Figure 2.1 shows a cross-section of an industry's performance at one point in time with Competitor A leading in production experience and profits and Competitor C only breaking even. Faster growth in sales than the competition would reflect in increased market share and either reduce cost disadvantage or increse advantage. Market share thus has an intrinsic value through its effect on relative costs. Early experience with a new product could confer an unbeatable lead over the competition and the leading manufacturer should be able either to reduce price or increase customer value, further increasing volume and eventually forcing some lagging competitor out of the industry.

Long before the experience curve was propagated, economists had argued from empirical evidence that long term instability in competition and decreasing costs were widespread (Wiles, 1956). So these ideas are not new, yet despite many careful attempts to

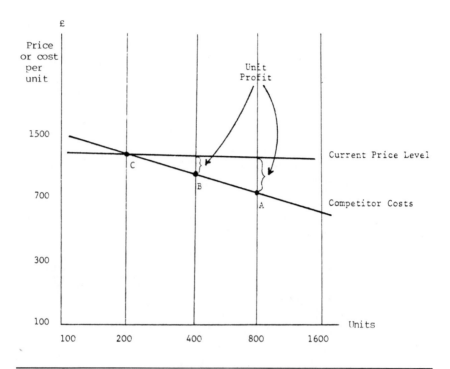

Fig. 2.1   Accumulated production experience, relative cost and profitability for three competitors (log/log scale)

measure long term cost functions, economists did not succeed in establishing a standard shape for the curve – and certainly not that of the experience curve. Against those efforts the evidence produced by experience curve proponents looks rather sparse. It is possible that the experience effect is merely a reflection of well spread gains in national productivity and would not hold its linear relationship in periods in which productivity decreased.

While management accounting should incorporate the experience curve into its body of knowledge, it should not do so at the expense of the tried and true concepts of short run cost curves. Short run cost variation is still here, and may be the clue to much strategic action. It is noticeable that in many mature industries such as steel, motor vehicles, consumer electrical goods, competition has come from behind to overtake firms with huge accumulated experience. Competitive breakthrough in some segment areas has forced the established leader back up a short term cost curve at a much steeper slope than the longer term experience curve. Defence becomes retrenchment and retrenchment rout as financial resources are drained. Figure 2.2 indicates what may have been happening. For a short time, the expanding competitor B may record rising marginal costs causing average costs to fall more slowly than when plant is optimally adjusted to the increased volume. Nevertheless, such an expanding competitor can very quickly reduce costs to the level of a much larger retrenching competitor. In this figure, the section of the short term cost curves for production below 'normal' capacity assumes the experience effect completely overridden by the under recovery of fixed overheads.

However questionable the factual basis for the experience curve, what is clear for management accounting is that relative costs are

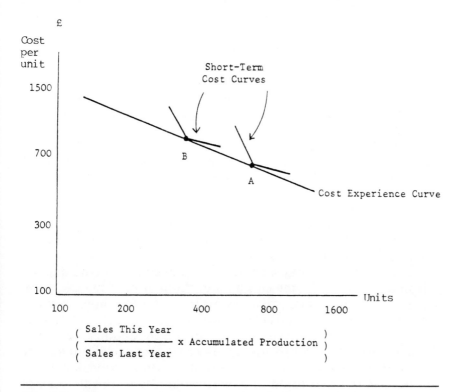

Fig. 2.2   Short term reversal and the vanishing experience effect (log/log scale)

crucial to strategic action. An actual level of cost is of limited value for helping management's strategic thinking – even if honed to five decimal points. Without knowledge of relative competitor costs, the firm does not know whom to attack, nor how strong a defence should be. In those circumstances, management must take strategic decisions in the dark.

Despite the importance of relative cost, it is rare to find management accounting systems designed to collect comparative competitor costs, price and volume data. Accountants have even been known to argue that it cannot be done. It can. It is surprising how much production people know about competitors' plants. Management accounting skill that can construct internal budgets from minimal data can be just as readily turned towards external costing despite minimal competitor data. If little is known internally, it may be possible to question equipment suppliers about other installations they have made, or spend money on travel and observation. A new camera could be more valuable than another office calculator! Detailed value assessment of competitor products can also go a long way to showing cost differences.

Competitor cost assessment will probably involve more than national competitors. Today's competition is largely multinational. Even if international competition is not yet felt directly, a competitor may be building up accumulated experience and a cost advantage in a market with a higher price level unimpeded by leading competition. Again, where the international competition is more developed, competitive cost assessment may require quite complex investigation. For example, it might require reconstruction of a competitor's international production system. Economies stemming from component production on a scale far beyond that required for any individual market are not necessarily revealed by studies of performance in the end product markets.

Accounting skills may also be utilised to comparative financial advantage. It has become common to think of covering exchange risk to the revenue or capital accounts in terms of the home country currency; that is, the currency in which the accounts are kept. A foreign competitor, however, may cover in another currency, bringing a potential for relative gain or loss. Strategically, it may be appropriate to cover in the same currency as the competitor. There are occasions when to do otherwise would be to run the risk of relative loss in some market just when the competitor was most likely to attack.

Price experience

Variations in costs from those of competitors are not the only indicators of strategic advantage or vulnerability. A competitor may use price policy to gain market share or, potentially as dangerous, holding prices up to gain higher profits. Precision is needed to highlight the effects of price variations over time because significant changes in competitor fortune so often result from a chain of small variations mounting up over the years.

Under inflation, most real price reduction takes place through firms holding prices while costs escalate, or raising prices less than the cost inflation. Moreover, the timing of price setting and hence strategy review is forced upon management by the rate of inflation rather than chosen as part of the strategy. Frequent price changes caused by rapid inflation make it even more important for precision in measuring progress.

While external reconstruction of competitor costs requires skill and imagination, collection of competitor prices is much more straightforward. Of course, few competitors sell just one product at one price, but it should not be difficult for management accountants to build a weighted price index for a competitor. Where competitor revenues are also available, these may be used to check the accuracy of such an index, or as an alternative in the calculation.

There is a legal requirement in the United Kingdom for companies to disclose the turnover and profit of substantially different classes of business. Emmanuel and Gray (1977, 1978) have shown that, from published reports, it should not be difficult to segment data down to a three-digit Standard Industrial Classification code by industry, but segmentation by customer industry is rarely possible. While disclosure to competitors has not been foremost in financial accountants' minds, the failure to define what constitutes a separate segment highlights the scanty attention paid to strategy within accountancy. The general impression is that most accountants, and auditors, overlook segments identified and used by management for strategy formulation if they are not classified as products within the chart of accounts.

Volume and demand

Given price and cost data, the missing ingredient for strategic management accounting is volume. But current volume is not enough; the size and pattern of future demand is all important to strategy formulation. After all, strategy concerns performance over the entire conflict, not a summation of separate performance in a succession of periods.

Market share is one indicator of the link between cost and profit performance for a single period and long term, or product life cycle, profit. It is a proxy for the future earnings flows, enabling rudimentary assessment of the economists' concept of profit in place of the one-period accountants' profit. Movement in market share further indicates the extent to which a firm is gaining or losing position, while relative market share indicates the strength of the firm compared with important rivals.

The incorporation of market share assessment into management accounts seems one of the most obvious steps in moving towards strategic management accounting. The simple addition of market share change enables any set of accounts to be viewed much more intelligently. A high profit obtained through holding prices above competition may indicate a real loss of present value from reduced market share and relative cost position. Conversely, low profits may be more than justified by rising market share and relative cost advantage.

Probably it will not be many years before financial accounting also moves to publication of market share data. Definition of markets will require more attention, but is far less fraught with theoretical difficulty than, say, asset valuation. Weighted and consolidated market share data would be significant in interpreting consolidated accounts, even for a multinational conglomerate.

Though a valuable indicator of strategic position, market share discloses nothing about the size, pattern and duration of expected demand. Yet present value of a market share can be severely curtailed if, for example, demand fluctuates dramatically or is expected to drop rapidly. The management accountant assessing various strategic alternatives will want to employ the best forecast available rather than rely on market share as a proxy. To date, the strategy literature has not advanced far in its use of market forecasts or in the sensitivity testing of strategies to variations in demand. General statements like high and low growth, maturity, decline and decay are sprinkled throughout the strategy literature as bases for prescribing broad lines of strategy.

A great deal of effort has also been expended in trying to identify a standard product life cycle and relate strategy to it. Demand that followed a regular bell shaped pattern over time with predictable growth and decay would make strategy calculation so much simpler, and there is substantial evidence that product adoption does follow such a shape. Beyond the introductory adoption period, however, no such standard pattern has been found. Moreover, merchandising effort by competitors may condition the product life cycle, even though it is conventional to regard demand for generic products, as opposed to brands, as being little influenced by supplier activity.

While management accountants are unlikely to take over the task of forecasting from marketers and econometricians, its need for the best possible forecasts as input for strategic calculations gives management accounting a vested interest in monitoring the quality of the forecasts. There is certainly a role for monitoring this vital input into strategy and planning, and probably a case for the management accounting audit taking over from the marketing audit. Precision is needed when formulating a business strategy, particularly in interpreting the cost effects over time.

RETURN ON COMPETITIVE POSITION

The emphasis that accountancy and finance have placed on return on investment over the years has subtly transmuted into a widely and deeply held belief that return comes from the investments themselves. In a typical comment, Van Horne (1971) held that:

> The capital expenditure decisions of a firm are, perhaps, its most important decisions. The scarce resource of capital is allocated to investments from which benefits or returns are expected over varying future periods of time. Consequently, the future success and profitability of the firm are dependent upon investment decisions made previously.

Furthermore, investments are nearly always regarded as either physical assets that are valued and described in the accounting records or accumulated costs of creation – as for research and development of a new product. This whole belief pattern is further supported in many firms by the way in which investment forms are drawn up and administered. Sales and profitability are shown as coming from the physical asset with, frequently, no mention of competitive market position.

The truth is very different. Sustained profit comes from the competitive market position. New production investment to expand sales must imply a change in competitive position and this change should be the focus of the investment review forms. Without it, the calculations must be a nonsense.

Return from investment in competitive position will differ according to the future demand pattern. In a high growth market, for example, the doubling of accumulated experience is rapid and the opportunity for correspondingly high cost reduction is equally great. A firm that can increase its market share in a high growth market stands to gain considerably. It is also possible that the cost of doing so will be low because the gain is achieved from the market growth without taking business away from competitors. In many situations, competitors are only aware of competitive attack when their sales fall.

The competitor or competitors from whom the market share is taken can also affect the return on investment in competitive position. A fast growing competitor, aggressive in pricing and likely to continue until stopped, is a threat to an existing position. Sales taken away from such a competitor can have much greater value than the intrinsic worth in the sales themselves. Added to the cost reduction value and profitability of the sales gained would be the profit saved by retaining business the competitor would otherwise have taken.

If strategic thinking is allowed to filter through the entire breadth of conventional management accounting, it will inevitably change the way investment is regarded. Calculations of returns from changes in competitive position will replace the return on investment forms and be used for expenditures frequently classified now as revenue expenditures. Generally, there will be a comparison of returns between the existing position of 'no action' and a strategic proposal. It will also become common to calculate competitors' positions under the alternatives in order to provide a picture of the relative gain or loss and assess the stability of the competitive situation.

A simple worked example, will serve to illustrate the type of calculation that will be needed. Firm X is considering a proposal to invest an amount of £100 000 in product improvement and promotion to bring these up to the levels of its major competitor, Y, and expand its market share from 25 per cent to 35 per cent. Competitor Y, with 20 per cent of market share, has been gaining gradually on X and, if X takes no action, Y is expected to erode X's market share to the extent of 1 per cent of market each year. X calculates that the product improvement and promotion will switch 4 per cent of the market from Y and 6 per cent from smaller competitors. Currently, the price stands at £10.00 per unit, with X making profits of 5 per cent on sales and Y making 3 per cent. Costs decrease on an 80 per cent experience curve and X and Y have accumulated experience of 200 000 and 150 000 units, respectively. Cost of capital, used for discounting, has been set at 15 per cent a year. Prices have tended to decline at about 3 per cent a year in real terms, held up by the smaller competitors and by the fact that both major competitors would expect the other to follow. Based on calculations of likely relative costs, X's management accountants can see no reason for this pattern not to continue, as it would be more or less in line with the cost experience of the second firm under either alternative.

Forecasts of the market for six years and calculations of volumes, costs and profits for both X and Y are presented in Tables 2.1 and 2.2, and it can be seen that the investment is more than justified. Note how much clearer the evaluation can be when the competitor data is included as a test of the validity of the calculations. Were data on the smallest firms included, confidence would be even stronger, eliminating the feeling that Y might gain by attacking them, with repercussions for X. On the other hand, the small firms could be protected in special market segments able to survive with lower spending on quality and promotion. Also omitted is any allowance for short term cost increase as a result of the actual volume decrease for Y and the smaller competitors in the first year. In this case, such an allowance would strengthen the decision to spend, but it might lead to a higher price level.

Resources, cash flow and portfolios

The ebb and flow of competition against any one firm is normally of much longer duration than a few accounting periods. It can be very difficult to defeat even a small competitor outright. Threatened competitors will draw on reserves and reorganise to defend their position. Since 1959, successive generations of business school students have studied and discussed the appropriate reaction for Scripto Pens when attacked head on by Bic in the ball point pen market. Despite the resounding defeat suffered by Scripto, the firm limped on over the years and suddenly launched an aggressive and

Table 2.1
Base case: take no action

Year		1	2	3	4	5	6
Market size	(000 units)	100	100	120	150	180	180
Market price	(£)	9.70	9.41	9.13	8.86	8.59	8.33
FIRM X							
Market share	(%)	25	24	23	22	21	20
Sales	(000 units)	25.0	24.0	27.6	33.0	37.8	36.0
Accumulated sales	(000 units)	225.0	249.0	276.6	309.6	347.4	383.4
Increase in acc. sales	(%)	12.5	10.7	11.1	11.9	11.2	10.4
Experience effect – reduction in cost per unit	(£)	.34	.28	.30	.33	.30	.28
Cost per unit (current = £9.50)	(£)	9.16	8.88	8.58	8.25	7.95	7.67
Profit per unit	(£)	.54	.53	.55	.61	.64	.56
Total profit	*(£000's)*	*13.5*	*12.7*	*15.2*	*20.1*	*24.2*	*20.2*
Present value deflator @ 15%		1.0	.870	.756	.658	.572	.497
Present value of profit	(£000's)	13.5	11.0	11.5	13.2	13.8	10.0
COMPETITOR Y							
Market share	(%)	20	21	22	23	24	25
Sales	(000 units)	20.0	21.0	26.4	34.5	43.2	45.0
Accumulated sales	(000 units)	170.0	191.0	217.4	251.9	295.1	350.1
Increase in acc. sales	(%)	13.3	12.4	13.8	15.9	17.1	18.6
Experience effect – reduction in cost per unit	(£)	.36	.34	.37	.42	.45	.47
Cost per unit (current = £9.70)	(£)	9.34	9.00	8.63	8.21	7.76	7.29
Profit per unit	(£)	.36	.41	.50	.65	.83	1.04
Total profit	*(£000's)*	*7.2*	*8.6*	*13.2*	*22.4*	*35.9*	*46.8*

Table 2.2
Investment alternative: £100 000 in product improvement and promotion

Year		1	2	3	4	5	6
Market size	(000 units)	100	100	120	150	180	180
Market price	(£)	9.70	9.41	9.13	8.86	8.59	8.33
FIRM X							
Market share	(%)	35	35	35	35	35	35
Sales	(000 units)	35.0	35.0	42.0	52.5	63.0	63.0
Accumulated sales	(000 units)	235.0	270.0	312.0	364.5	427.5	490.5
Increase in acc. sales	(%)	17.5	14.9	15.6	16.8	17.3	14.8
Experience effect – reduction in cost per unit	(£)	.46	.40	.42	.44	.46	.40
Cost per unit (current = £9.50)	(£)	9.04	8.64	8.22	7.78	7.32	6.92
Profit per unit	(£)	.66	.77	.91	1.08	1.27	1.41
Total profit	*(£000's)*	*23.1*	*27.0*	*38.2*	*56.7*	*80.0*	*88.8*
Present value deflator @ 15%		1.0	.870	.756	.658	.572	.497
Present value of profit	(£000's)	23.1	23.5	28.9	37.3	45.8	44.1
COMPETITOR Y							
Market share	(%)	16	16	16	16	16	16
Sales	(000 units)	16.0	16.0	19.2	23.0	28.8	28.8
Accumulated sales	(000 units)	166.0	182.0	201.2	224.2	253.0	281.8
Increase in acc. sales	(%)	10.6	9.6	10.5	11.4	12.8	11.4
Experience effect – reduction in cost per unit	(£)	.28	.26	.28	.31	.34	.31
Cost per unit (current = £9.70)	(£)	9.42	9.16	8.88	8.57	8.23	7.92
Profit per unit	(£)	.28	.25	.25	.29	.34	.41
Total profit	*(£000's)*	*4.5*	*4.0*	*4.8*	*6.7*	*9.8*	*11.8*

so far successful attack in late 1980. This time the attack appeared as an erasable ball pen directed at the 21 per cent of the American ball point market which had been captured by Gillette's Paper Mate division with its 'Eraser Mate'.

Given the ever present possibility of competitor reaction, it is not sufficient to base strategic actions on an assessment of their direct contribution to the firm's profits and market share. Ideally, any decision should reflect an assessment of the effect on competitors' profits and market shares extended to forecast the pattern of conflict over the longer term. This pattern of conflict will, in turn, depend on competitors' resources and liquidity as well as their profits. Sometimes, competitors will lack the resources to retaliate; at other times, some competitors will be protected within a profitable market segment and will remain unaffected by competitive attack.

More than any other business function, management accounting has the skill for such competitor assessments. The skill needed amounts to accounting for competitors, from outside, and projected ahead to a suitable strategic horizon. Such 'competitor accounting' is usually complicated by the fact that most firms operate more than one business. Thus, each competitor is sitting at several Monopoly boards, not just one. Resources may be switched from board to board as appropriate. The objectives and time preferences for profits from any one business will probably vary between competitors, owing to their differing requirements for other businesses. To handle this portfolio complication, the starting point would be an analysis of the competitor's actions and statements in order to identify his objectives for each business. An initial classification into three objectives of 'build', 'maintain', or 'harvest' can then lead to a projection of the cash flows from each and from the entire competitor portfolio. Underlying the assessment will be the concepts of balanced cash flow and balanced risk, for the competitor organisation. Again, these assessments fall within the skill of the management accountant more than other functional specialist. Some form similar to that reproduced in Table 2.3 would be helpful in assessing competitor cash flow portfolios. At a more advanced level, some firms have set up an entire competitive intelligence system (Porter, 1980), and some have developed interactive computer models.

Table 2.3
Competitor business portfolio – five year cash flow projections

Business title	A	B	C	D	TOTAL
Competitor classification	Grow	Maintain	Grow	Harvest	
Profits					
Depreciation					
Working capital reduction					
* * * *					
* * * *					
* * * *					
Total cash in					XXX
New investment					
Working capital expansion					
* * * *					
* * * *					
* * * *					
Total cash out					XXX
Net cash by business					XX
Research and development				XX	
Finance charges				XX	
Taxation				XX	
Dividends				X	XX
Surplus or deficit					X

STRATEGIC MANAGEMENT ACCOUNTING AS AN OPERATING SYSTEM

A fashionable claim in the strategy literature has been that strategy is a function of structure (Chandler, 1962, for example). It might be more accurate, however, to move the emphasis away from organisa-tion structure and place it on accounting measurement. Managers have a tendency to do what is measured and not to do what is not measured. Few management accounting systems are adequately structured to measure strategy.

Budgeting is one area where management accounting has traditionally laid a claim to expertise and every business budget implies a strategy of some sort. Yet the format traditionally adopted for budget preparation negates strategic reasoning! There is a noticeable absence of any attempt to incorporate data which depict the situation with regard to customers or competitors or even to highlight strategic variables. Tabulations of spending under different accounts provide no indication of which is carrying the core of any strategic thrust or defence. Worse than this, it has become a tradition to measure spending against past levels for the same account heading. So ingrained has historical internal comparison become that the same six-column pattern appears in firm after firm:

	Month			Year to Date	
Last year	Budget	Actual	Last year	Budget	Actual

Admittedly, broader planning data are available for some firms, although it is usually outside the management accounting system. In a few, zero base reviews (Pyhrr, 1970) have removed the 'historisis' effect. These developments do not change the underlying truth, however. Budgeting as widely used is anything but strategic.

If strategic management accounting is to become a reality, some fundamental changes must be made to the format of management accounting records, plans and reports. Amey (1979) has argued that planning budgets should be separated from control budgets because they serve different purposes and a good plan might not yield a good control. Such a move, however, runs the risk of failing to control strategy as the moves unfold. Why should not management accounting reports be routinely presented in a strategic format with, say, columns for 'Ourselves', 'Competitor A', 'Competitor B', and so on? It would make a welcome change from the usual six columns!

The more data that are formally incorporated into management accounting reports to indicate buyer response to spending on different variables, the easier it will be to identify actions which build competitive advantage. The more that can be incorporated about competitor spending and the cost-volume-profit conditions which they face, the more informed can be the estimate of their reactions.

Incorporation of strategic reasoning is even more important than data. Competition with numerous opponents and multiple reactions is complex; it is not solved by a simple set of decision rules. What will identify a good budget is sound reasoning that holds up well when tested against the market, competitor and cost facts. It may not be possible to prove that a strategy is optimal, but it is certainly possible to establish degrees of quality for strategies advanced to match a given situation. If forms are altered to include terse statements of strategic reasoning, the reasoning may be measured against the outcome. If it is so measured, it will become more dominant and perhaps less prone to unsubstantiated rules of thumb.

Changes in competitive position generally build gradually through the ebb and flow of many moves and counter-moves. Thus strategy is a field in which an ongoing precision can pay off handsomely. Management accounting has the concepts and the skills to provide that precision; it does have a strategic purpose. With formal acknowledgement of the legitimacy of a strategic focus and a firm step away from the search for information from internal cost analysis, strategic management accounting is ready to flower as a prime function of the management accountant.

(Editorial note: This chapter is an edited version of a paper presented to a technical symposium of the Institute of Cost and Management Accountants at Pembroke College, Oxford, in January 1981.)

REFERENCES AND FURTHER READING

Abell, D. F., and Hammond, J. S., *Strategic Market Planning: Problems and Analytical Approaches,* Englewood Cliffs, N.J.: Prentice-Hall, 1979.

American Accounting Association, *Report of the Committee on Foundations of Accounting Measurements,* New York: AAA, 1971.

Amey, L. R., 'Budget planning: a dynamic reformulation', *Accounting and Business Research,* Winter 1979.

Ansoff, H. I., *Corporate Strategy,* New York: McGraw-Hill, 1965.

Boston Consulting Group, *Perspectives on Experience,* Boston, Mass.: Boston Consulting Group, 1968.

Caplan, R. H., 'Relationships between principles of military strategy and principles of business planning', *in* Anthony, R. N., *Planning and Control Systems,* Cambridge, Mass.: Harvard University Graduate School of Business Administration, 1965.

Chandler, A., *Strategy and Structure,* Cambridge, Mass.: MIT Press, 1962.

Clark, J. M., *Studies in the Economics of Overhead Costs,* Chicago: University of Chicago Press, 1923.

Emmanuel, C. R., and Gray, S. J., 'Segmental disclosures and the segment identification problem', *Accounting and Business Research,* Winter 1977.

Emmanuel, C. R., and Gray, S. J., 'Segmental disclosures by multi-business multinational companies: a proposal', *Accounting and Business Research,* Summer 1978.

Hirschman, W. B., 'Profit from the learning curve', *Harvard Business Review,* January–February 1964.

Hofer, C. W., and Schendel, D., *Strategy Formulation,* St Paul, Minn.: West Publishing, 1978.

Porter, M. E., *Competitive Strategy,* New York: Free Press, 1980.

Pyhrr, P. A., 'Zero-base budgeting', *Harvard Business Review,* November–December 1970.

Risk, J. M. S., *The Classification and Coding of Accounts,* London: Institute of Cost & Works Accountants, 1956.

Simmonds, K., 'From data-oriented to information-oriented accounting', *Journal of Business Finance,* 1972.

Van Horne, J. C., *Fundamentals of Financial Management,* Englewood Cliffs, N.J.: Prentice-Hall, 1971.

Wiles, P. J. D., *Price, Cost and Output,* Oxford: Basil Blackwell & Mott, 1956.

3

Pricing and Cost-Volume-Profit Analysis

John Sizer

Selling price decisions are difficult and complex, and the management accountant should provide financial information relevant to the decision in hand. In particular, he should present information on the impact of such decisions on cost-volume-profit relationships. High rates of inflation, price controls and recessions have increased the importance of such information. Managements have the difficult task of deciding to what extent higher costs could be passed on to customers in higher prices. A knowledge of cost-volume-profit relationships is essential in differential cost analysis of problems of choice, because the alternatives frequently differ in total volume and in the composition of volume. As Professor Sizer has argued elsewhere (Sizer, 1976), the management accountant's role is crucial in that respect:

> *In considering pricing policy in inflation, an attempt must be made to make a contribution which is of real practical value to the manager faced with the problems of formulating a pricing policy against the background of an increasingly dynamic and uncertain external environment, and which recognizes that pricing is one element in a multi-dimensional marketing programme.*

Cost-volume-profit analysis, or breakdown analysis, stresses the relationship of the factors affecting profit. Used properly and appropriately, cost-volume-profit analysis offers valuable information for managerial decision making on a wide range of business actions. Additionally, it forms an essential component of management's strategic processes.

It will be recognised that in many multi-product, multi-market companies, pricing is not simply a process of setting figures at which a company's products are offered to customers, but rather it is part of a broad and complex field which also embraces problems of determining characteristics of products to be sold, segmenting markets, choosing sales promotion methods, determining channels of distribution and obtaining a satisfactory volume of business. This chapter concentrates on cost-volume-profit analysis aspects of selling price decisions. It starts with a simplified example and moves towards the complexities of the real world. Inevitably, in a single chapter all these complexities cannot be considered fully. The author has examined elsewhere (Sizer, 1972 and 1979) the relationship between price and non-price variables in the marketing mix, and (Sizer, 1981) the wider subject of pricing policy in inflationary conditions.

A SIMPLIFIED EXAMPLE

When considering a selling price decision or a decision concerning the non-price variables in the marketing mix, the product and marketing managers should have sufficient understanding of the relevant cost and revenue concepts to be able to ask the management accountant the right questions and evaluate the significance of his answers. Provided assumptions are clearly stated, product profit volume charts can be employed effectively to explore both the relevant cost and revenue concepts and the cost-volume-profit relationships.

Let us consider a simple example. It is assumed that the company seeks to fix its prices so as to maximise the total contribution to fixed costs and profit. Unless the manufacturer's products compete directly with each other, this objective is achieved by the price maker considering each product in isolation and fixing its price in each market in which the product is offered at a level which is calculated to maximise the total contribution in that market.

The Bang Bang Manufacturing Company is reviewing the selling price of Product X, a consumer durable, and, after carrying out extensive market research, has estimated the probable annual demands for the product at varying prices shown in Table 3.1. It is estimated that each of these demands can be manufactured and marketed with existing capacity. The forecast average variable cost

Table 3.1
Product X: price/demand schedule

Price per unit	Estimated annual demand
£17.00	8 000
£17.50	7 800
£18.00	7 600
£18.50	7 200
£19.00	6 600
£19.50	5 700
£20.00	4 200

per unit over the relevant output range is constant at £12 per unit, in other words marginal cost equals average variable cost. The separable fixed costs are £25 000, that is the fixed costs associated with the product (such as the product manager's salary) as opposed to the common fixed costs (such as the managing director's salary). The calculation of the price which will make the greatest contribution towards fixed costs and profit is shown in Table 3.2, and it will be noted that the greatest profit improvement would result from raising the selling price of Product X from its existing level of £18 to £18.50, giving a direct product profit of £21 800 as against £20 600 at present.

The information in Table 3.2 is presented in Figure 3.1 in the form

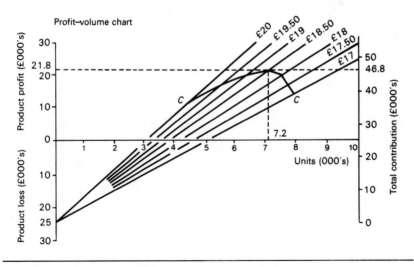

Fig. 3.1   Product X: product profit-volume chart

Table 3.2
Product X: review of alternative selling prices

	£	£	£	£	£	£	£
Selling price	17.00	17.50	18.00	18.50	19.00	19.50	20.00
Marginal cost	12.00	12.00	12.00	12.00	12.00	12.00	12.00
Contribution	5.00	5.50	6.00	6.50	7.00	7.50	8.00
Estimated demand (units)	8 000	7 800	7 600	7 200	6 600	5 700	4 200
	£	£	£	£	£	£	£
Total contribution	40 000	42 900	45 600	46 800	46 200	42 750	33 600
Separable fixed costs	25 000	25 000	25 000	25 000	25 000	25 000	25 000
Direct product profit	15 000	17 900	20 600	21 800	21 200	17 750	8 600
Product break-even Sales (units)	5 000	4 545	4 167	3 846	3 572	3 333	3 125
Percentage of demand	62.5%	58.3%	54.8%	53.4%	54.1%	58.5%	74.4%

of a profit-volume chart. 'CC' is the contribution curve for Product X, and shows the relationship between demand in units, direct product profit, total contribution, and breakeven units for each price. For example, a selling price of £18.50 would result in a demand for Product X of 7 200 units, a total contribution of £46 800, a direct product profit of £21 800, and a breakdown at 3 846 units. In establishing the contribution curve and determining the price which promises the highest contribution, the demand function has been taken into consideration and the cost function is based on a concept of cost (future marginal cost) that is relevant to the pricing decision at hand.

The product profit-volume chart can be related to marketing strategy at different stages of a product's life cycle. The introductory stage can be contrasted with the maturity stage. The product manager may adopt a skimming policy or a penetration policy towards selling price decisions at the introductory stage. Limited production capacity may rule out a penetration policy. A capacity limitation has been imposed in Figure 3.2 which restricts the choice of selling price. P_6 may be chosen with a view to successfully reducing price as (a) the price elasticity of demand increases, (b) additional capacity becomes available, and (c) competitors are attracted into the market.

If the new product introduction is successful, then as demand grows both the position and the shape of the contribution curve change. Alternatively, if there is no production capacity constraint,

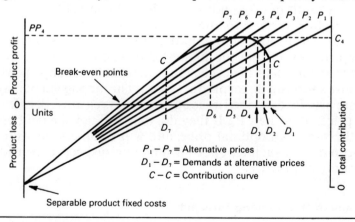

Fig. 3.2 Product X: product profit-volume chart (with capacity constraint)

a penetration price such as P_3 or P_4 may be adopted which yields early high volume accompanied by slow competitive imitation, but lower unit product profit. Again, with the growth in demand the position and shape of the contribution curves will change, but the company relies on the penetration price to maintain its share in a growing market without any need for successive price reductions.

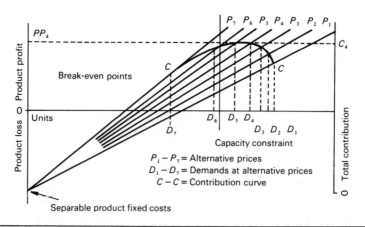

Fig. 3.3   Product X: product profit-volume chart (maturity stage)

At the maturity stage, the firm will have far less discretion over selling prices. Prices will probably have fallen during the growth stage as a result of economies of scale and competitive pressures. Prices decline further in the maturity stage, but may stabilise eventually. The profit-volume chart in Figure 3.3 shows that P_4 is the selling price promising the highest direct product profit. At this stage of the product's life cycle, the firm would probably be wise to maximise short run direct product profit. The management may, for what are usually described as 'long run policy reasons', decide upon some price other than P_4. If they do, they will deviate deliberately from the short run optimal price, and will be able to measure the short run cost of such a policy – which one suspects is considered only rarely in practice.

Accuracy of the demand forecast

It will be appreciated that the determination of the contribution curve 'CC' is dependent upon the accuracy of the demand forecast. When conducting seminars with marketing executives on marginal pricing using profit-volume charts, it is pointed out that the analysis is dependent upon their ability to provide a demand curve. Invariably they agree that they cannot provide estimates. However, after some discussion the following conclusions are reached frequently:

1   It is possible to answer sensitivity analysis type questions from the product profit-volume charts or from the contribution graphs. For example, if the price of Product X is increased to £18.50, how far can demand fall before the total contribution falls below that forecast for the current price of £18.00?
2   The contribution curve 'CC' can be drawn as a band and for each price there will be a range of possible units demanded, product profit and total contribution outcomes. Marketing has long been viewed as requiring mainly judgement, intuition, and experience, but marketing researchers are increasingly combining scientific techniques with judgement and intuition. While market researchers cannot predict accurately the shape of the demand curve, they should be able to attach subjective probabilities to a range of possible outcomes for each possible price. The accuracy of demand curve estimates could be improved, but the cost of refining the estimates generally outweighs the benefit derived from the improved accuracy.
3   Many assumptions underlie the product profit-volume chart and the analysis is only relevant to a limited range of output. It is more realistic to present to management a product profit-volume chart, such as that shown in Figure 3.4, which takes account of the uncertainty surrounding the pricing decision.
4   Normally, at the growth and maturity stages of the product life cycle, the product manager should be concerned with choosing between a limited number of alternative prices on the crown of the contribution curve. The lower and higher prices on the tail of the contribution curve are not normally relevant, except in a severe limited capacity situation or when considering a skimming policy or penetration policy at the introductory stage.
5   The subjective probabilities attached to demand curve estimates by market researchers can be incorporated into probability diagrams to determine alternative outcomes, and graphs or tabulations can be presented which array the probable price/contribution outcomes according to a rational combination of the possibilities involved. Risk profiles can be developed for each

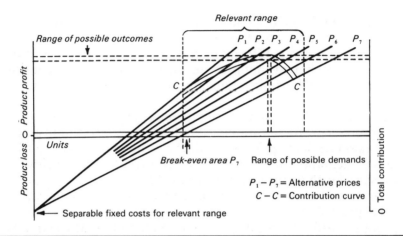

Fig. 3.4   Product X: product profit-volume chart (under uncertainty)

alternative price indicating the likelihood of achieving various total contributions.

The author has proposed a simple risk analysis procedure which uses a discrete probability density function (Sizer, 1970), while a more sophisticated approach has been developed by Flower (1971). Developments in software packages have led to a more widespread use of the approach advocated by Flower.

It may well be argued that, while the results of the types of analyses that employ subjective probabilities look impressively neat and infallible, they are, after all, based on purely subjective judgements. True, no one has yet developed a completely reliable method to measure precisely the price elasticity of demand of any brand or product, particularly where cross-elasticities of demand affect a number of brands. The product manager must estimate intuitively the effects of a proposed price change. He will rarely find precisely comparable circumstances in either his own or his firm's experiences. Subjective judgements of the range of likely outcomes, based on the cumulative experience of executives, are better than subjective most-likely estimates based on the same cumulative experience. As management becomes more accustomed to attaching subjective probabilities to demand forecasts and cost estimates, its ability to make such judgements improves markedly. Analysis formalises something that is always done in management decision processes: weighing the odds.

MOVING TOWARDS THE REAL WORLD

In the above simpified example, it has been assumed that the firm is either a price maker or, if it follows a price leader, has some choice around that leader's price. Situations in which the firm is a price taker or adopts a 'price-minus' approach to pricing can also be explored with profit-volume charts. With the price-minus approach, the company works backwards from a market price to alternative quality-cost-volume-profit relationships. Product managers must not view their responsibility as being merely that of determining the various demand elasticities of brands and products in different markets, but must also consider how they could alter those elasticities so as to improve a brand's or product's competitive position. This means that they must be prepared to shift the relative emphasis given to price, advertising, product improvement, product differentiation, etc, for each stage of the product life cycle in different markets. They may undertake simultaneous changes in price and non-price variables in the marketing mix. Profit-volume charts can be used to explore the financial aspects of such decisions with product and marketing managers.

In a multi-product, multi-market company, products will make different contributions at various stages of their life cycles in diverse markets. In this respect, it is important for the management accountant to recognise that marketing management requires a system for reporting current and forecast segment profitability, since marketing managers need such information when making pricing and other marketing mix decisions. An interesting and useful approach to examining volume-contribution relationships of products and markets, of products within a market, and customers within markets, which can prove effective in communications with marketing managers is the use of contribution graphs or pictures, as represented in Figure 3.5. By assuming constant marginal cost over the relevant output range, equi-contribution curves are derived by multiplying unit contribution on the vertical axis and units. For example, in Figure 3.5 a total contribution of £1 200 can be generated by any of the following combinations: 1 200 units at £1.00 per unit; 2 000 units at £0.60 per unit; 2 400 units at £0.50 per unit; 4 000 units at £0.30 per unit; and so on. The graphs can be segmented to show high and low unit and total contribution areas, and high and low volume areas. Products shown in the bottom lefthand corner (that is, numbers 1, 6, and 10) are candidates for withdrawal

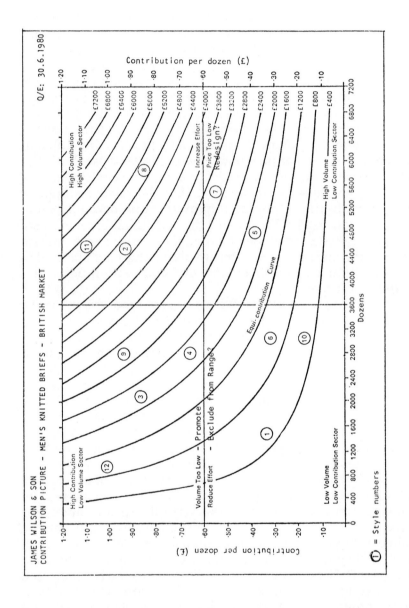

Fig. 3.5 Contribution picture

from the market. The most profitable products are shown in the top righthand segment (numbers 11, 2, and 8); they have high unit contributions and high volume and therefore generate a high total contribution. Against that background, the following case can be studied and analysed.

James Wilson & Son

This case is taken from Sizer (1979) and represents the second part of a longer case study of the same firm. Wilson was an old established company producing a wide range of knitted outerwear, leisurewear and children's outerwear for a variety of outlets. They had premises in Bridge Street and South Street, Milchester, and recently had opened a new factory in North Ashfleet, ten miles south of Milchester. Underwear and leisurewear were produced at Bridge Street and knitwear at South Street and North Ashfleet. The company had an annual turnover of £1.3 million and some 500 employees.

Hawkeye, the management accountant at Wilson, calculated three possible costed selling prices for a garment and these are illustrated for three garments in Table 3.3; overheads were included by multiplying the total labour cost by the overhead recovery rate for the factory in which the garment was to be produced. The sum of the two columns represented total cost and variable cost; for example, the total cost of the boy's jersey was £16.08 and the variable cost £12.66. The three costed selling prices were determined by the following additions to total or variable cost:

1   Total cost plus 8.5 per cent gave a costed selling price of £17.45 for the boy's jersey.
2   Variable cost plus 43 per cent gave a costed selling price of £18.10 for the boy's jersey.
3   Variable cost plus 3-times making-up labour gave a costed selling price of £17.50 for the boy's jersey.

The mark-ups of 8.5 per cent and 43 per cent were calculated by Hawkeye by either relating required profit to total cost (which gave a mark-up of 8.5 per cent) or relating required total contribution to total variable cost (which gave a mark-up of 43 per cent), and the relevant calculations are shown in Table 3.4.

Table 3.3
Wilson – costed selling prices for three garments

	Boy's jersey size 26 in.			Baby's cardigan size 18in.			Maxi-cardigan size 36in.		
	lb.			lb.			lb.		
Yarn usage per dozen: Weight	8.88			2.26			16.44		
Waste	0.56			0.16			1.03		
	9.44			2.38			17.47		
		£	£		£	£		£	£
Cost per dozen									
Yarn cost		7.08			1.93			14.15	
Draw thread and swatches		0.02	7.10		0.02	1.95		0.02	14.17
Needles			0.06			0.06			0.06
Buttons		0.13			0.03			0.50	
Sewing/tabs/tapes		0.26			0.25			0.30	
Plastic		0.90	1.29		–	0.28		–	0.80
Bags/boxes			0.15			0.13			0.30
Knitting labour		0.66			0.46			2.80	
Making-up labour		1.62			0.89			2.29	
		2.28			1.35			5.09	
Holiday pay/increase	(24%)	0.55	2.83	(24%)	0.25	1.60	(11%)	0.56	5.65
Carriage/packing			0.18			0.16			0.18
		11.61			4.18			21.16	
Overheads	(121%)	3.42	11.61	(121%)	2.03	4.18	(135%)	7.63	21.16
		15.03			6.21			28.79	
Commission discount (7%)		1.05	1.05		0.43	0.43		2.02	2.02
Total cost/variable cost		16.08	12.66		6.64	4.61		30.81	23.18
+ 8.5%/43%		1.37	5.44		0.56	1.99		2.64	9.97
Costed selling price per dozen		£17.45	£18.10		£ 7.20	£ 6.60		£33.45	£33.15
Variable cost + 3 making-up labour		£17.50			£ 7.30			£30.05	

Table 3.4
Wilson – knitwear division budget 1970

Budgeted sales	£510 000
Estimated capital employed, with fixed assets valued on an assumed current cost basis	£270 000
Required return on capital employed	15%
Required profit	£40 000
Fixed overheads	£112 000

Mark-up on total cost

$$\frac{\text{Required profit}}{\text{Total cost}} \times 100 = \frac{£40\,000}{(£510\,000 - £40\,000)} \times 100$$
$$= 8.5\%$$

Mark-up on variable cost

$$\frac{\text{Required total contribution}}{\text{Total variable cost}} \times 100 = \frac{£152\,000}{£358\,000} \times 100$$
$$= 43\%$$

The factor that frequently limited the company's capacity to manufacture additional garments was making-up labour. The company had a making-up capacity equivalent to a standard cost for making-up labour of £50 000, and to achieve the budgeted contribution of £152 000 it had to obtain £3 contribution for each £1 standard making-up labour. Therefore, the third pricing rule was variable cost plus three times making-up labour.

Hawkeye used his costed selling prices in the following way. He recommended to Simpson, the sales manager, the highest costed selling price produced by the three methods. Everyone's criterion was then met. Simpson cannot always negotiate the highest selling price and sometimes has to come down below the lowest costed selling price. Hawkeye was very unhappy with any selling price below total cost. For example, maxi-cardigans were very popular at the time and were a recent introduction to the range. For the maxi-cardigan, as shown in Table 3.3, Hawkeye recommended a selling price of £33.45 per dozen; in the event, Simpson sold twelve dozen at

£40 per dozen. Business was hard to come by at the time and the North Ashfleet factory, which produced the maxi-cardigans, was working on short time. Hawkeye could not recommend the price of £30.05 based on making-up labour, because the total cost per dozen was £30.81 and overheads would not have been recovered.

Each quarter, Hawkeye produced an analysis of sales which distinguished between (a) sales below total cost, (b) sales between total cost and lowest desirable selling price, (c) sales between desirable selling price on labour and desirable selling price on variable cost, and (d) sales above highest desirable selling price.

An analysis

The case study is interesting in that Hawkeye appears to use a 'belt-and-braces' approach to pricing. He employs full cost plus, the rate of return on capital employed variant, and marginal cost methods to determine recommended 'costed' selling prices for garments.

It will be noted that Hawkeye calculates separate overhead rates for each of the factories, even though two of them appear to be capable of producing the same knitwear. The result is that, as shown in Table 3.3, an overhead rate of 121 per cent is applied to the boy's jersey and the baby's cardigan, while a rate of 135 per cent is applied to the maxi-cardigan. Furthermore, a single overhead rate is applied for each factory. Hawkeye appears not to recognise that there are two distinct parts to a knitwear factory – the capital intensive knitting operation and the labour intensive making-up operation. In Table 3.3, it will be noted, the ratio of knitting labour to making-up labour varies significantly between the three garments. Should there be separate overhead rates for each operation? A machine-hour rate for the knitting operation and a labour-hour rate for the making-up operation? The point is that a number of equally qualified and competent accountants would produce different costed selling prices depending upon the methods of overhead absorption they favour. Further, the calculation of overhead absorption rates has the appearance to many managers of turning fixed overheads into variable overheads.

Hawkeye sees the costed selling price he recommends as the starting point for Simpson the sales manager, from which Simpson arrives at the final selling price.

The strength of Hawkeye's system is that it is directed towards achieving clearly defined objectives, the £40 000 profit and the 15 per cent return on capital employed, and also takes account of making-up labour – the factor that frequently limits the company's manufacturing capacity. When the company achieves or exceeds budgeted sales, provided Simpson gains the 'costed' selling prices, the profit and return on capital employed objectives should be met. Furthermore, Hawkeye directs management's attention to the relationship between his recommended pricing decisions and actual prices, highlighting those prices which appear to deviate from the profit and return on capital employed objectives. No doubt this leads management to consider price/demand relationships.

What Hawkeye's system fails to do is to take account formally of price-volume contributions for individual garments or the impact of pricing decisions on the company's cost-volume-profit relationships. In those circumstances, a budgeted profit-volume chart would assist. Individual pricing decisions will determine the weighted average profit-volume ratio and also the volume of sales. Variations in the profit-volume will increase or reduce the break-even sales volume and also the profit or loss for a given sales volume. Therefore, should Hawkeye be placing greater emphasis on segmental volume-contribution analysis when presenting his analysis of actual pricing decisions? (In fact, as shown in the first part of the case (Sizer, 1979), he had developed a comprehensive computer-based segmental reporting system.)

The weakness of the system as described in this case is that it does not provide Simpson with guidance on how to take account of and anticipate price-demand-contribution relationships when working out a final selling price, particularly when the company is operating below capacity. Thus, Hawkeye would have been unhappy to recommend the maxi-cardigans at a selling price of less than £33.45 and appears happy that Simpson had sold twelve dozen at £40.00 a dozen. He seems to have taken into consideration that, at a lower price of, say, £30.00 a dozen, Simpson might have sold not twelve but, perhaps, fifty dozen when 'business is hard to come by'. Twelve dozen at £40.00 per dozen gives a total contribution of £201.84 (that is, $12 \times (£40.00 - £23.18)$, whereas fifty dozen at £30.00 per dozen would have given a total contribution of £341.00 (that is, $50 \times (£30.00 - £23.18)$. Simpson should take account of future as well as current market conditions. He could use contribution graphs, such as that shown in Figure 3.5, to provide price-demand-contribution relationships and indicate which garments to promote, which to redesign, which to exclude from the range, and which to give high priority.

Alternatively, Hawkeye might develop a ready reckoner for Simpson so that he could quickly compare alternative selling prices – estimated sales volumes in terms of total contribution. Of course, Hawkeye and Simpson might have to develop a good working relationship which would encourage Simpson to request the information he needs and allow Hawkeye to provide informal advice on price-volume relationships.

THE IMPACT OF INFLATION

A full discussion of individual pricing decisions in inflation is beyond the scope of this chapter. However, the impact of high rates of inflation on cost-volume-profit analysis can be highlighted.

The high rates of inflation experienced in recent years have increased the importance of pricing decisions. The continuous pressure on profit margins has forced companies to review prices frequently, and in many cases continuously. An essential first stage in the pricing decision process is a comprehensive monitoring system that signals the need for a price review (Oxenfeldt, 1973). Such a system should be forward looking and aim to identify some of the shifts in demand that occur in the market place and the future trends in costs and product profitability. Furthermore, segment reporting has become more relevant, not only because the high rate of inflation and successive budget measures affect products and markets in different ways but also because the significant shift of net disposable income that has taken place makes current socio-economic groupings unreliable guides to disposable incomes.

The monitoring system should signal the need to review prices, and product profit-volume charts may be used for this purpose. Two situations may be analysed: a high rate of inflation and rising real disposable incomes; and a high rate of inflation and falling real disposable incomes.

High inflation and rising incomes

With a high rate of inflation and rising real disposable incomes, period costs, variable product costs and breakeven volume for existing prices are increasing continuously, but it is likely that the income elasticity of demand effects will allow the higher costs to be passed on in higher prices. The contribution curve is likely to move upwards and to the left and compensate for the increase in variable

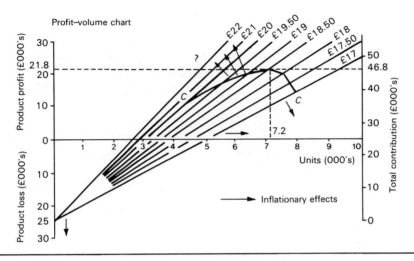

Fig. 3.6   Effect of inflation with rising real disposable incomes

costs and period costs. The company is likely to generate a higher total contribution and direct product profit in money terms at the optimal price, assuming any prices legislation allows the company to charge its target price. These effects of inflation are shown in Figure 3.6. While increases in costs and breakeven volume for a given price can be forecast with reasonable accuracy, the move in the contribution curve cannot; an effective monitoring system should assist in that direction.

High inflation and falling incomes

Consider now the situation in a period of high inflation and falling real disposable incomes. Period and variable costs still rise continuously, but as real disposable incomes fall the income elasticity effects no longer compensate for the increase in costs. The contribution curve may move *downwards* and to the left as consumers move onto lower indifference curves. The shape of the contribution curve may change as demand switches to cheaper products or to substitutes, or as some consumers stop purchasing the product. As shown in Figure 3.7, many companies in 1975–77 found themselves in a position of rising costs, falling demand, and disappearing total contributions. The optimal price was no longer that allowed by prices legislation or some higher price, but a lower price difficult to determine. In that situation, companies were forced to take a long

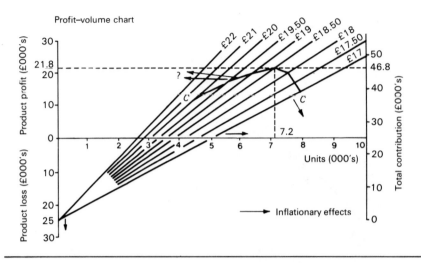

Fig. 3.7 Effect of inflation with falling real disposable incomes

hard look at both variable product costs and period costs.

At the time of writing, companies in the United Kingdom are considering pricing decisions and examining cost-volume-profit relationships against a background of a deep domestic recession and relatively high interest rates, a stagnant world economy, and high rates of cost inflation. All these factors reinforce the inflationary effects in Figure 3.7 and force companies to review the profitability of products and markets, and reduce their capacities and related period costs.

A similar analysis can be hypothesised for producers of industrial goods. An important difference is that the customers in these markets are professional buyers. In a recession, companies marketing industrial products can soon find themselves in a buyers' market. A similar profit-volume chart can be developed, for example, for a firm producing industrial components, by substituting alternative percentage contribution margins or profit-volume ratios for alternative prices. The effect of a high rate of inflation in a period of recession is very similar. Period costs are rising, contribution margins are being eroded by increasing variable costs, and demand is falling at the same time. It is very difficult to raise prices in a buyers' market; if losses are to be avoided, it will be necessary to reduce period costs.

There is a clear need for segmental reporting and contribution picture analysis of the impact of falling demand and rising costs on products and markets, for comprehensive forecasting and monitoring systems, and for effective cost control systems and cost reduction programmes.

It must be recognised that margins are more important than volume when a company has liquidity and profitability problems in a declining market. A company that attempts to maintain or increase volume by reducing prices and cutting margins in a period of rising costs and declining market size may suddenly find it has no margins!

To sum up, a high rate of inflation increases the importance of pricing decisions. An essential first stage in individual pricing decisions is a comprehensive monitoring system which signals the need for a price review. Managements have the difficult task of deciding to what extent higher costs can be passed on in higher prices. They have to examine price-volume-contribution relationships of different products in different markets. They have to estimate the position of contribution curves on product profit-volume charts. As such, cost-volume-profit analysis is an essential technique for the management accountant concerned to produce relevant information for managerial decision-making.

REFERENCES AND FURTHER READING

Flower, J. F., 'A risk analysis approach to marginal cost pricing: a comment', *Accounting and Business Research,* Autumn 1971.

Oxenfeldt, A. R., 'A decision-making structure for price decisions', *Journal of Marketing,* January 1973.

Sizer, J., 'A risk analysis approach to marginal cost pricing', *Accounting and Business Research,* Winter 1970.

Sizer, J., 'Accountants, product managers, and selling price decisions in multi-consumer product firms', *Journal of Business Finance,* Spring 1972.

Sizer, J., 'Pricing policy in inflation: a management accountant's perspective', *Accounting and Business Research,* Spring 1976.

Sizer, J., *Case Studies in Management Accounting,* Harmondsworth: Penguin, 1979.

Sizer, J., *An Insight into Management Accounting,* 2nd edn. Harmondsworth: Penguin, 1979.

Sizer, J., *Perspectives in Management Accounting,* London: Heinemann/ Institute of Cost and Management Accountants, 1981.

4

Capital Budgeting Techniques

Richard Dobbins and Richard Pike

This chapter describes some of the more commonly used managerial techniques for assessing capital projects. The authors give brief explanations of the use of net present value, internal rate of return, profitability index (cost/benefit ratio), payback period, return on capital employed, earnings per share, certainty equivalents, risk-adjusted discount rate, simulation, and the modern approach to investment appraisal based on the capital asset pricing model.

Financial management theorists generally assert that the objective of the firm is to create as much wealth as possible. Wealth is created when the market value of the outputs exceeds the market value of the inputs. In assessing all capital projects, managers should follow the net present value rule, which states that a project is acceptable if the present value of anticipated incremental cash inflows exceeds the present value of anticipated incremental cash outflows. We are aware that studies of managerial behaviour reveal that managers pursue objectives relating to sales, market share, employees, assets, and personal satisfaction. However, the fundamental objective of industrial and commercial enterprises is the creation of consumable goods and services.

Managers create wealth by ensuring that the market value of the firm's outputs is greater than the market value of its inputs. Cash and obligations flow in from customers and cash and obligations flow out to suppliers of goods, labour, services, and capital items. Within that framework, all projects can be assessed by calculating the net cash flows accruing to the firm, using the net present value rule described below, after taking into account the risk and timing of cash flows associated with the project.

NET PRESENT VALUE

As already stated, the objective of the firm is to create wealth by using existing and future resources to produce goods and services now and in the future with greater value than the resources consumed. To create wealth now, the present value of all future cash inflows must exceed the present value of all anticipated cash outflows. The net present value (NPV) rule is illustrated as follows:

$$NPV = \sum_{t=1}^{n} \frac{R_t}{(1+k)^t} - C$$

where R_t = expected net cash inflows; k = the required rate of return on the project; C = the immediate capital outlay. In words, the net present value (NPV) of a project is the sum (Σ) of all anticipated net cash inflows (R_t) from now ($t=1$) to the end of the period in question (n), discounted at the project's required rate of return (k), less the cost of buying into the project (C). A brief example will serve to make the matter clearer.

Table 4.1
Net present value of a project

Risk class	Discount rate	Present value of cash inflows Yr 1	Yr 2	Cost	NPV
A	10%	£54	£50	£100	£4
B	13%	£53	£47	£100	£0
C	16%	£52	£44	£100	−£4

The initial capital outlay to finance an investment is £100. Anticipated net cash inflows are £60 received at the end of Year 1 and £60 received at the end of Year 2. The firm operates in a low risk industry and divides its various projects into three categories: class A where the risk is low and the required rate of return is 10 per cent; class B where the risk is average for the industry and the required rate of return is 13 per cent; class C where the risk is high and the required rate of return is 16 per cent. Evaluating the project from the NPV viewpoint and using the NPV formula given above will provide the estimates illustrated in Table 4.1, which shows the NPV of the project under each of the three risk classifications.

If the project is classified as low risk, the cash flows are discounted at a rate of 10 per cent. The Year 1 cash flow has a present value of £54 and the Year 2 cash flow has a present value of £50. The present value of the inflows is therefore £104 and, after deducting the initial outlay which has a present value of £100, the project has a net present value of £4. The project should be accepted; it has a positive NPV. It creates wealth, albeit small. If the projected cash flows are achieved, the market value of the firm should rise by £4.

On the other hand, if the project is classified as high risk, the cash inflows are discounted at a rate of 16 per cent and the NPV is estimated at −£4. The project is unacceptable; it has a negative NPV. Its acceptance would have the effect of reducing the firm's market value by £4. Clearly, it would not be wise to exchange £100 today for future cash flows having a present value today of only £96.

If the project is classified as average risk, the discount rate used is 13 per cent, yielding a NPV of £0. The project is just acceptable; it yields 13 per cent.

From this simple example, we can draw three important conclusions: (1) project acceptability depends upon cash flows and risk; (2) the present value of a given expected cash flow decreases with time; (3) the higher the risk of a given set of expected cash flows (and the higher the applied discount rate), the lower will be its present value, that is, the present value of a given expected cash flow decreases as its risk increases.

The NPV rule is not difficult to apply in practice. The tedium of using formulae and power functions has been reduced by the creation of discount tables. Extracts from a set of discount tables are presented in Table 4.2, which shows values of £1 received in the future and of £1 received annually for a number of years. The column headings in the table are discount rates which increase from left to right. The rows represent increases in time from Year 1 to Year 10. To find the value today of £1 expected to be received in one year's time assuming a required rate of return of 10 per cent, it is only necessary to find the value in row 1 (that is, Year 1) located in the column under 10 per cent. The value shown is 0.909, giving an answer of £0.909 or 90.9p. How much is the same £1 worth if the required rate of return (discount factor, cost of capital, percentage factor) is increased to 16 per cent? The value indicated is 0.862, giving a value of £0.862 or 86.2p. It will be seen that all the values in

Table 4.2
Discount tables (extracts)

PRESENT VALUE OF £1 RECEIVABLE

Discount rate	10%	13%	14%	16%	22%	25%	34%
Year							
1	0.909	0.885	0.877	0.862	0.820	0.800	0.746
2	0.826	0.783	0.769	0.743	0.672	0.640	0.557
3	0.751	0.693	0.675	0.641	0.551	0.512	0.416
4	0.683	0.613	0.592	0.552	0.451	0.410	0.310
5	0.621	0.543	0.519	0.476	0.370	0.328	0.231
6	0.564	0.480	0.456	0.410	0.303	0.262	0.173
7	0.513	0.425	0.400	0.354	0.249	0.210	0.129
8	0.467	0.376	0.351	0.305	0.204	0.168	0.096
9	0.424	0.333	0.308	0.263	0.167	0.134	0.072
10	0.386	0.295	0.270	0.227	0.137	0.107	0.054

PRESENT VALUE OF AN ANNUITY OF £1 RECEIVABLE

Discount rate	10%	13%	14%	16%	22%	25%	34%
Year							
1	0.909	0.885	0.877	0.862	0.820	0.800	0.746
2	1.736	1.668	1.647	1.605	1.492	1.440	1.303
3	2.487	2.361	2.322	2.246	2.041	1.952	1.719
4	3.170	2.974	2.914	2.798	2.494	2.362	2.029
5	3.791	3.517	3.433	3.274	2.864	2.689	2.260
6	4.355	3.998	3.889	3.685	3.167	2.951	2.433
7	4.868	4.423	4.288	4.039	3.416	3.161	2.562
8	5.335	4.799	4.639	4.344	3.619	3.329	2.658
9	5.759	5.132	4.946	4.607	3.786	3.463	2.730
10	6.145	5.426	5.216	4.833	3.923	3.571	2.784

the table fall from left to right, confirming our earlier conclusion that present values decline as the discount rate increases. Furthermore, all the values get smaller as the table progresses into the future (from top to bottom). As a further simple example, the present value of £1 000 receivable in Year 10 and discounted at 25 per cent is calculated at £107 (that is, £1 000 × 0.107).

The lower section of the table shows the present value of an annuity of £1 receivable annually for a number of years. An annuity is a sum of money paid or received each year. To find the present value of £1 receivable for each of the next ten years assuming an interest rate of 10 per cent, it is necessary to find the value in row 10 located under the 10 per cent heading. The value shown is 6.145 which gives an answer of £6.145 (that is, £1 × 6.145). If the interest rate is increased to 16 per cent, the annuity is worth £4.833. Again, it is possible to demonstrate the power of discounting by way of a further simple example. The present value of an annuity of £1 000 payable for 10 years at a rate of 25 per cent is £3 571 (that is, £1 000 × 3.571).

INTERNAL RATE OF RETURN

The net present value rule offers the best available answer to the accept/reject problem. An alternative approach is to calculate an investment's internal rate of return, sometimes called the yield. The internal rate of return is the rate of return which equates the present value of anticipated net cash flows with the initial outlay. To calculate the internal rate of return (IRR), it is necessary to solve the following formula for r:

$$0 = \sum_{t=1}^{n} \frac{R_t}{(1+r)^t} - C$$

that is, r is the rate of return which gives a zero NPV. A project is acceptable if its yield or internal rate of return is greater than the required rate of return on the project (k). This method of project appraisal gives exactly the same accept/reject decision as NPV. Projects with positive NPVs will have values of r greater than k. In the case of the simple example used above, the project's yield is 13 per cent:

$$\frac{60}{(1 + .13)} + \frac{60}{(1 + .13)^2} - 100 = 0$$

If the project is class A then it is acceptable as the yield of 13 per cent is greater than the required rate of return of 10 per cent. If the project is classified as B, it is just acceptable, but it would be rejected as a class C project. Managers are recommended to use the NPV method, if only because it is easier to handle. Without the use of a computer the IRR calculation can be a laborious business.

PROFITABILITY INDEX (COST-BENEFIT RATIO)

A third reasonable method of assessing capital expenditure decisions is to use a profitability index, sometimes called the cost-benefit ratio. The profitability index (PI) is the present value of anticipated net future cash flows divided by the initial outlay. The only difference between the NPV and PI methods is that when using the NPV technique the initial outlay is deducted from the present value of anticipated cash flows, whereas with the PI approach the initial outlay is used as a divisor. In general terms, a project is acceptable if its PI value is greater than 1. Clearly a project offering a PI greater than 1 must also offer a net present value which is positive.

In the simple example used above, PI values can be calculated easily. As a class A project, it has a PI of 1.04; as a class B project, its PI is 1.00; as a class C project, its PI is 0.96.

PAYBACK, RETURN ON CAPITAL EMPLOYED, AND EARNINGS PER SHARE

The NPV rule helps managers to make wealth-creating decisions. There are, however, several other techniques for assessing capital projects which may give misleading indications as to whether or not an investment should be accepted. Three popular methods examine the project payback period, the return on the capital employed in the project, and the effect on earnings per share.

The payback period is the length of time required to recover the initial investment. This method is unacceptable because it involves the subjective establishment of an acceptable payback period – say 2½ years, for instance. Should managers ignore, therefore, substantial payoffs in years 3 and 4?

Return on capital employed is calculated like 'accounting profit' as a percentage of the capital employed. This must be dismissed as a rule of thumb or heuristic approach. The technique does not use cash flow, ignores the timing of returns and ignores risk.

Earnings per share is calculated by dividing 'accounting profit' by the number of shares in issue. Again, this calculation ignores cash flows, timing, and risk.

The acceptability of a project in rational terms depends on cash flows and their timing and on an appreciation of the risk involved. In consequence, the latter three methods must be rejected as inappropriate. As the following example demonstrates, they can give faulty recommendations as to acceptability.

The results of a project are shown in Table 4.3, with an immediate cash outlay of £20 000 required to finance the project. The firm's policy is to depreciate the initial outlay in equal instalments over the estimated project life, giving depreciation charges of £5 000 a year. For a project of this risk class, the firm's required rate of return is 14 per cent. The firm issues 20 000 ordinary shares of £1 each to finance this, its only project.

Table 4.3
Results of a project (£s)

Year	1	2	3	4
Incremental cash inflows	14 000	22 000	14 000	10 000
Incremental cash outflows	6 000	14 000	6 000	4 000
Net cash flows	8 000	8 000	8 000	6 000
Depreciation	5 000	5 000	5 000	5 000
Accounting profit	3 000	3 000	3 000	1 000

Using the various methods discussed earlier, we can calculate a number of decision directed values. The payback period is 2½ years, with £8 000 being received in each of year 1 and year 2 and £4 000 in the first half of year 3. Return on capital employed can be calculated as follows: accounting profit divided by average capital employed. Average capital employed is the £20 000 initial investment less successive years' depreciation charges, averaged on the basis that depreciation charges properly accrue evenly through the year. So for year 1, average capital employed is beginning capital employed (£20 000) plus ending capital employed (£15 000) divided by 2 – giving an average of £17 500. For year 2, average capital employed is £15 000 plus £10 000 divided by 2 – £12 500. Similar calculations can be carried out for years 3 and 4. Accounting profit for each year is given in Table 4.3, and the resultant rates of return on capital employed are calculated as: year 1 – 17.1 per cent; year 2 – 24.0 per cent; year 3 – 40.0 per cent; year 4 – 40.0 per cent. Are those returns on capital employed acceptable? The general assumption is the greater the return on capital employed, the better. Those rates of return clearly depend on the firm's depreciation policy, among other things. Such arbitrary accounting procedures do not enable managers to make rational wealth-creating decisions.

Turning to the earnings per share approach, it can be seen that earnings per share (EPS) for each of the first three years is 15 pence – £3 000 divided by the 20 000 ordinary shares in issue. For year 4, the EPS figure falls to 5 pence. Again, it is not clear whether these rates are acceptable. Once more the assumption is the greater the EPS, the better.

The NPV approach gives a theoretically better decision, and results in the following calculation of NPV:

$$\text{NPV} = £8\,000 \times 2.322 + £6\,000 \times 0.592 - £20\,000$$

The project is acceptable on the positive NPV criterion.

Moving to the IRR technique reveals that the internal rate of return on the project is between 19 per cent and 20 per cent (actually, 19.3 per cent), rendering it acceptable on the basis that the yield on the project is greater than the 14 per cent required rate of return.

The PI method reveals an index of 1.1 (£22 128 divided by £20 000), giving an acceptable result with a PI greater than 1.

On balance, then, the NPV rule is a practical and rational approach to project evaluation. Notwithstanding its intrinsic faults, however, payback analysis is the most popular technique used by managers. This may stem from the ease of calculation. Perhaps, then, both techniques should be used: NPV because it gives a guide to the amount of wealth being created, and payback because it probably tests a manager's instinctive reaction to cash at risk and because it is very easy to calculate.

RISK ANALYSIS

It was stated earlier that the acceptability of projects depends upon cash flows and risk. Cash flow is operational cash receipts less operational cash expenditure and investment outlay. In the NPV formula, R_t is the difference between operational cash income and operational cash expenditure, and C is the amount of new investment. Where additional cash/investment outflows are anticipated in future periods, they can either be deducted from the cash flows in those future periods or be discounted back to the present and added to C. Both approaches have an equal effect on NPV.

Most managers can readily appreciate cash flows. Risk is a more difficult operational concept to grasp. Intuitively it is not liked. In attempting to maximise the market value of the company, it can be assumed that neither shareholders nor lenders like it. Providers of capital expect to be compensated for risk exposure. Risk cannot be avoided and it must be taken into account when estimating the required rate of return on a project.

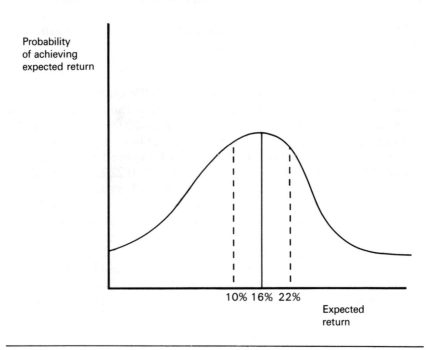

Fig. 4.1 Distribution of returns on a project

Risk relates to the volatility of the expected outcomes; the dispersion or spread of likely returns around the expected return. In Figure 4.1, the expected return on a project is 16 per cent. Statisticians calculate that 67 per cent of the actual returns will lie within one standard deviation of the expected return. (The standard deviation is a measure of dispersion or spread.) On average, four out of six actual outcomes should lie within one standard deviation of the expected outcome. Accordingly, in Figure 4.1, four out of six outcomes should, on average, lie between 10 per cent and 22 per cent, with 6 per cent being the standard deviation in this instance. On the other hand, two out of six outcomes will lie outside one standard deviation. On average, one time in six the outcome will be above 22 per cent (upside potential). Unfortunately, one time in six the actual return will be less than 10 per cent (downside risk). This is known colloquially as the 'one-in-six rule'.

Investors do not like risk and the greater the riskiness of returns on a project, the greater the return they will require. There is a trade-off between risk and return which must be reflected in the discount rates applied to investment opportunities and their outcomes.

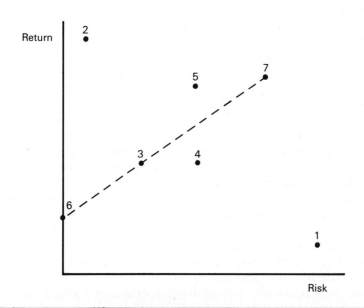

Fig. 4.2 Risk-return relationships for alternative projects

Figure 4.2 shows the risk-return relationships of seven projects. Which is the best available project? Which is the least desirable? Which investment should be chosen between, say, 3 and 4 or 4 and 5? Which is the nearest project to backing a horse? What kind of investment might 6 be? These and other questions can be answered succinctly.

The best available project is number 2. It is a high return and low risk project, and represents the most desirable combination of those characteristics. The least desirable project is number 1, which is a low return and high risk project. Investment number 3 will always be preferred to investment number 4, because it is a lower risk project for the same return; similarly, investment number 5 will always be preferred to investment number 4, because it has a higher return for the same level of risk. The project nearest in character to backing a horse is number 7, because it has high risk and high return. Project 6 is a zero risk investment with a certain outcome. Such an investment might be a short dated government security, where the exact interest rate is known in advance.

If it is assumed that the line joining projects 6, 3, and 7 represents the trade-off between risk and return in the real world, the three projects can be examined further. Since those projects are on that risk-return line, they have zero net present values; their expected returns are just enough to compensate for their riskiness. Investment number 6 might be a short term investment in a government guaranteed security; investment 3 might be a unit trust investment; investment 7 a complete gamble. Different investors can be logical in their choice patterns and yet select either 6 or 3 or 7. Equally, an investor could choose to invest anywhere along the risk-return line 6-3-7 by investing proportions of his total investment in mixes of the three projects or investments – thereby diversifying within his portfolio.

Modern capital markets are very competitive and are therefore efficient in the sense that the prices of securities generally reflect all available information relating to those securities' anticipated cash flows and risk. In those markets, it would be difficult, though not impossible, to earn returns greater than those generally expected for the level of accepted risk. Most securities and portfolios lie fairly close to the hypothetical line 6-3-7.

Managers, however, operate in product markets which are neither perfectly efficient nor perfectly competitive. It is a manager's job to locate projects, such as numbers 2 and 5, which have positive net values and therefore offer wealth-creating opportunities. Not surprisingly, this is a fairly difficult task. It is easy to find projects, such as numbers 4 and 1, which have negative net present values.

Several rules of thumb have been devised for taking risk into account in the investment decision making process.

Subjective discrimination
Managers can assess their intuitive or 'gut' reactions to risky projects

and accept 'less risky' projects with similar net present values. While 'unscientific', this method is fairly easy to adopt in practice.

Certainty equivalents

A more numerate approach is to reduce the estimated future cash flows to their certainty equivalents and then discount at the chosen rate of interest. The NPV formula should be adjusted as follows:

$$NPV = \sum_{t=1}^{n} \frac{aR_t}{(1 + k)^t} - C$$

where aR_t represents the adjusted cash flows. An obvious problem with this method is that it is difficult to devise a rational approach to cash flow adjustment.

Simulation

The computer facilitates a probabilistic approach to forecasting cash flow along the lines pioneered by Hertz (1964, 1968). Probabilities can be assigned not only to the net cash flows but to all those factors affecting the wealth-creating ability of the project – for example, units sold, selling price, investment outlay, residual values of plant, fixed and variable costs, and project life. Once the risk variables are identified, and the probability distributions estimated for each variable, the computer program selects at random a large number of possible outcomes. A sufficient number of outcomes will result in a clear picture of the investment's risk-return profile. This approach provides a great deal of information about the risk-return characteristics of an investment, but it does not provide an accept/reject solution. Furthermore, it is often very difficult to devise probability distributions for factor inputs, and it can be expensive to use the computer to generate a very large number of random selections.

Risk-adjusted discount rate

A method which is fairly easy to handle and which is theoretically appealing is the risk-adjusted discount rate approach. Perhaps the easiest way to take risk into account is by classifying projects into risk categories, as suggested earlier. Having established those risk classes, the NPV formula can be adjusted as follows:

$$NPV = \sum_{t=1}^{n} \frac{R_t}{(1 + k_a)^t} - C$$

where k_a is the risk-adjusted rate of return. A major problem with this approach is the difficulty of establishing the risk classes for different companies in industries of diverse risk. A project of average risk for a company in a high risk industry would demand a higher return than a project with average risk in a low risk industry. Modern portfolio theory has provided many insights into the trade-off between risk and return in efficient capital markets and the 'new' methods for assessing capital projects are rather similar to the risk-adjusted discount rate method.

THE MODERN APPROACH

A refinement of the risk-adjusted discount rate method is derived from modern financial theory. So far, this chapter has discussed the total risk of an investment. That total risk (variability of outcomes) can be broken down into two constituents, namely the specific project risk and the general or market risk.

The specific risk of an equity investment in a quoted company relates to the company itself, regardless of general movements in the economy. This specific risk can be removed by diversifying across a number of companies. Many studies show that investment in 15 to 20 companies can remove between 80 per cent and 95 per cent of this specific risk. Since that risk can be avoided, stock markets offer no rewards for taking on specific risk. Investors are rewarded for taking on part of the economic or general risk – the market risk.

The theory is that the expected return on an equity investment is a function of the investment's market risk. Furthermore, this can be measured for a quoted company by plotting the periodic returns for a given company or group of companies against the periodic returns on the All-Share Index as a reasonable surrogate for the UK economy. This is illustrated in Figure 4.3. If the return on a company rises 10 per cent when the return on the index rises 10 per cent, and if the return falls 10 per cent when the index falls 10 per cent, then those periodic returns could be plotted and the line of 'best fit' through all the points would be a 45° line as shown for Security B.

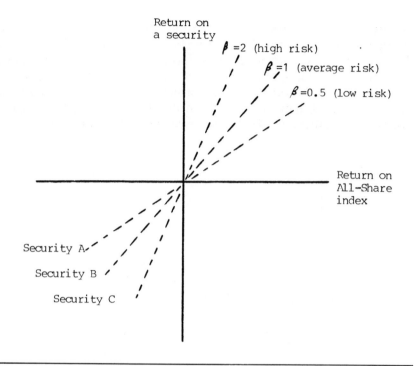

Fig. 4.3   Returns on securities

The slope of the line, its beta, β, would be 1.0; the beta coefficient is therefore the measure of a security's market risk. Most companies have a beta fairly close to 1.0; a high risk investment like Security A might have a beta of 2.0 (with periodic returns rising or falling by 20 per cent when the returns on the index rise or fall by only 10 per cent); a low risk investment like Security C might have a beta of 0.5 (with periodic returns rising or falling by 5 per cent when the index returns rise or fall by 10 per cent). These beta values, measures of market risk, are now available from several sources – for example, in the quarterly Risk Measurement Service of the London Business School.

A company's beta, adjusted for corporate leverage effect (Pike and Roberts, 1980), offers a guide to the weighted average beta of all the company's projects; it does not give betas for individual projects, products or divisions. These would have to be estimated by relating individual project betas to the firm's average project or by relating anticipated cash flows from individual projects to unanticipated changes in the economy. Estimating betas for individual projects is therefore not easy; corporate betas change over time, are subject to a wide range of error, and historic betas are generally used as proxies for future betas. Nevertheless, this approach to adjusting required rates of return for market risk is probably the most theoretically acceptable method available for assessing capital projects.

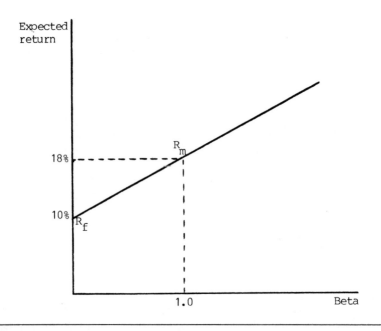

Fig. 4.4   The capital asset pricing model (CAPM)

The capital asset pricing model (CAPM) illustrates the trade-off between risk and return, as shown in Figure 4.4. As stated, the expected return on an investment or portfolio is determined by its market risk as measured by beta, rather than total risk because the specific risk can be removed by diversification. The risk free rate of interest, R_f, may be represented by the certain rate of return on a short dated government security; the return on the market, R_m, is the return on the all-share index, which clearly has a beta of 1.0 because it moves up and down perfectly with itself. A straight line through R_f and R_m is the capital asset pricing model, representing the trade-off between risk and return. The expected return on any project, investment or portfolio is dictated by its beta. An investor can invest all resources in R_f or in R_m. Furthermore, an investor could mix R_f and R_m and lie anywhere along the line R_f-R_m. For risk-lovers, it would be possible to push further up the line by borrowing at R_f and investing at R_m. The line R_f-R_m represents the minimum rate of return acceptable on all investments, because it represents the opportunity cost, that is the forgone opportunity of equal market risk.

It is necessary to adjust the NPV formula for risk in accordance with the capital asset pricing model. The new formula is:

$$NPV = \sum_{t=1}^{n} \frac{R_t}{[1 + R_f + \beta (R_m - R_f)]^t} - C$$

by replacing k, in the required rate of return in the earlier NPV formula, with $R_f + \beta (R_m - R_f)$. To be more theoretically correct, interest rates and risk premia should be forecast for future periods, but this is complex and questionable.

If it is assumed that the after tax risk-free rate of interest is 10 per cent and that the expected after tax return on the all-share index is 18 per cent, the market risk premium is 8 per cent. Using those rates, the average required rates of return for the three companies shown in Figure 4.3 can be calculated as follows: Company A has a beta of 0.5; k = 10% + 0.5(18% - 10%) = 14%. Company B has a beta of 1.0; k = 10% + 1.0(18% - 10%) = 18%. Company C has a beta of 2.0; k = 10%+2.0(18%-10%)=26%. These expected returns are averages, of course, as discussed earlier and for individual projects or products it would be necessary to carry out the kind of relational exercise described earlier (see, for example, Broyles and Franks (1975)).

Perhaps the best that can be done is to establish the required rate of return on a company's average project and then relate other projects to this average. It should be possible, for a company with an average beta of 1.0, to classify all projects into, say, five risk classes – as shown in Figure 4.5.

A worked example

As a practical example of risk analysis, the following case has been used by the authors in many situations and offers several useful guidelines.

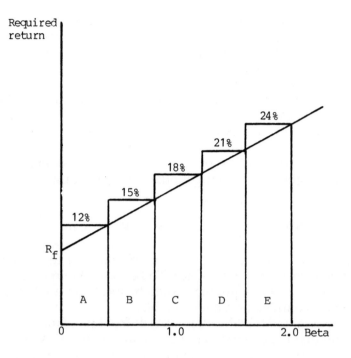

Fig. 4.5 Company's project risk classes

Delta Engineering Limited is an all-equity company, under-taking high risk maintenance contracts in the UK oil industry. Its historic beta coefficient has been estimated at 1.5.

At the beginning of 1983, the directors are considering tendering for a maintenance contract worth about £600 000 gross for each of the next five years. The directors believe that this contract would be about twice as risky as the company's average project. The financial director estimates that the constant after tax risk-free rate of interest will run at 10 per cent and that the overall after tax return on a weighted average portfolio of industrial investments will run at 18 per cent. Having made several serious errors in the past when attempting to forecast future interest rates and risk premia, he is now a firm believer in the efficient market hypothesis that the best estimate of future rates and premia is existing rates and premia.

Equipment costing £400 000 would be required straightaway at the commencement of the contract, although the usual tax benefit (a first year allowance of 100 per cent of the equivalent tax payable on a profit of the same order as the equipment cost) would be received at the end of 1984. The equipment could be sold at the end of the contract for around £100 000 (which income would attract tax and that tax would be payable at the end of 1988). The incremental costs associated with the contract would run at £150 000 each year, including depreciation charges, and the company expects to pay corporation tax throughout the period at the rate of 52 per cent, payable approximately one year after the 31 December financial year end.

Table 4.4
Delta Engineering – contract estimates (£000s)

Year	1983	1984	1985	1986	1987	1988
Incremental income	600	600	600	600	600	—
Incremental expenditure	(150)	(150)	(150)	(150)	(150)	—
Operational cash flow	450	450	450	450	450	—
Taxation @ 52%	—	(234)	(234)	(234)	(234)	(234)
After tax cash flow	450	216	216	216	216	(234)
First year allowance (on £400 000)		208				
Balancing charge (on £100 000)						(52)
Sale of equipment					100	
Net cash flow	450	424	216	216	316	(286)

In assessing the project, the directors are advised to take a CAPM approach to risk analysis. Doing so, the financial director calculates the figures reproduced in Table 4.4. The required rate of return, k, can be calculated as follows: $k = 10\% + 3.0(18\% - 10\%) = 34\%$. The beta used is 3.0 – twice the company's average beta of 1.5. Using the discounted cash flow factors for 34% (see the final column in Table 4.2), the NPV of the contract can be calculated as shown in Table 4.5, and it is calculated that the contract would have a net present value of £352 202. In those circumstances, the contract is clearly acceptable, offering a wealth-creating opportunity even after taking its riskiness into account.

Table 4.5
Delta Engineering – discounted cash flows

Year	Net cash flows	34% Discount factors	Present value
1983	£450 000	0.746	£335 700
1984	£424 000	0.557	£236 168
1985	£216 000	0.416	£ 89 856
1986	£216 000	0.310	£ 66 960
1987	£316 000	0.231	£ 72 996
1988	(£286 000)	0.173	(£ 49 478)
		Total present value	£752 202
		Capital outlay	(£400 000)
		Net present value	£352 202

REFERENCES AND FURTHER READING

Bierman, H., and Smidt, S., *The Capital Budgeting Decision,* 4th edn. New York: Macmillan, 1976.

Broyles, J., and Franks, J., 'Capital project appraisal: a modern approach', *Managerial Finance,* 1975.

Hertz, D. B., 'Risk analysis in capital investment', *Harvard Business Review,* January–February 1964.

Hertz, D. B., 'Investment policies that pay off', *Harvard Business Review,* January– February 1968

Levy, H., and Sarnat, M., *Capital Investment and Financial Decisions,* 2nd edn. Englewood Cliffs, N.J.: Prentice-Hall, 1982.

Pike, R., and Roberts, B., 'How to adjust investment hurdle rates for risk', *Management Accounting,* June 1980.

Sharpe, W. F., *Portfolio Theory and Capital Markets,* New York: McGraw-Hill, 1970.

5

Mathematical Models in Management Planning and Control

Roger Groves

This chapter considers three approaches to modelling – inventory models, production and investment planning models, and forecasting models. As Professor Groves argues, quantitative models can be of considerable assistance to management and help both to control day to day activities and to plan future activities. The three models considered in this chapter are comparatively elementary, and more sophisticated models are in common use. Nevertheless, the author's treatment presents a comprehensive introduction to the use of mathematical models in control and planning. It is essential, of course, that the user of these models should appreciate their limitations and drawbacks. The usefulness of mathematical models depends very much on their key ingredients and the effects of measurement errors can be far-reaching, especially where fundamental decisions are being taken. Notwithstanding those reservations, accountants and managers are coming to rely more and more on mathematical models, particularly those susceptible to representation in a computer program. The increasing use of sophisticated data processing equipment has enabled managers to build, adapt and use mathematical models as effective aids to optimal managerial decision making.

Models are representations of reality – whether physical representations, such as model cars or aeroplanes, or conceptual representations, such as models of the economy. Accounting and financial reports are models also, because a model portrays the multi-faceted inter-relationships between factors in a real life situation.

Many models are expressed in mathematical form to help analyse the quantitative aspects of a problem. Building a model can help in the discovery and description of the patterns of order that underpin business operations. Through their formal structure, models can identify the relevant factors in a decision making process and, by supplementing the intuitive or heuristic judgments of managers, can lead to better decisions.

Frequently, models are criticised on the grounds that they over simplify reality, by being based on restrictive assumptions, or that they ignore important underlying factors, or that they are static representations of a dynamic environment. Without doubt, in their contexts all those criticisms could be maintained, but at the same time there are numerous examples of successful applications. The real test is that of costs versus benefits; comparing the benefits accruing from the alternative techniques for decision making (including modelling) with the costs of providing and processing information under each approach.

This chapter deals with three approaches to modelling, the first being inventory models which are representations of the buying and storing processes of stock and work-in-progress. The second approach is the use of mathematical programming algorithms in the planning and control of production and investment planning. The third section looks at models used for forecasting.

INVENTORY MODELS

Systems for the planning and control of corporate inventories have been in operation successfully for many years. The objective of these systems is to ensure that an organisation holds the smallest amount of inventory or stock, as economically as possible, to suit its internal or external needs. The quantity of inventory for each different item of stock or work-in-progress will be computed by using a model so as to minimise the total of related costs. The model discussed here can be applied to raw material stocks, work-in-progress, and finished good stocks, though the examples will concentrate on bought-in items, for example, raw materials.

Two main inventory policies can be modelled. The first, the re-order level policy, is based upon replenishment at certain inventory levels, while the second, the re-order cycle or periodic review policy, replenishes at regular times. Each policy has distinct and different advantages. The periodic review policy enables the regular raising of a single order for numerous items from a common supplier, thereby saving money, but probably requires higher stock levels to be carried, which costs money. Use of the re-order level policy, reduces the probability of 'stock-out', through the greater awareness of stock levels gained from frequent reviews.

Obviously all these points must be borne in mind in the choice of group policy for items held in stock. So must the investigation of costs associated with ordering and carrying inventory, or with being out of stock.

Using the re-order level policy as the example for modelling, the major objective of managing inventory is to discover and maintain the optimal level of investment in inventory. The optimum level will be that quantity which minimises the total costs associated with inventory. Costs of ordering stocks can include:

1   the preparation of the purchase or production order;
2   the costs of receiving the goods;
3   the documentation processing costs;
4   the intermittent costs of chasing orders, rejecting faulty or un-acceptable goods, etc;
5   the additional costs of frequent or small-quantity orders.

Carrying costs – that is, storing and holding costs – will include the following:

6   storage space costs;
7   required rate of return on investment in current assets;
8   obsolescence and deterioration costs;
9   insurance and security costs.

Stock-out costs are the most difficult to assess and incorporate in a model, especially a simple one, because they are based on qualitative, subjective judgements such as loss of customer goodwill, workforce alienation, loss of market share, and so on. Normally such costs would be incorporated in the more sophisticated models, which are outside the scope of this chapter, but managements must not neglect to consider the quality of service provided and should undertake an implicit valuation of each level of service.

Before discussing the simple model in more detail, it will be of value to direct attention to the question of actually calculating stock-out cost. As Horngren (1977) emphasised:

The most difficult cost to determine is stockout cost, consisting mainly of the forgone present and future contribution to profit from losing an order because of lack of inventory ...

and he went on to argue that managers might choose to maintain a suitable level of safety or buffer stock according to the maximum probability of being out of stock or a minimum probability of not being able to meet all demands from customers. If there are no demands during the time an item is out of stock, there are no stock-out costs and no forgone contribution to profit. If there are demands but customers are prepared to accept substitutes, again there are no stock-out costs and no forgone profit. On the other hand, if there are unsatisfied demands and a consequent loss of present and future business due to dissatisfaction, the stock-out costs will prove substantial. Thus, most inventory control techniques concentrate on maintaining a minimum stock level, however derived, rather than on minimising stock-out costs.

Economic order quantity and order timing

The two main questions to be answered, then, by this model are: What is the optimal order quantity? When should orders be placed? The optimal size of the order for an item is known as the economic order quantity (EOQ) and is calculated so that total inventory costs are at a minimum for that particular stock item. Total inventory costs for an item of stock are computed for a given period – usually a trading year – by combining the costs of ordering and the costs of carrying that item. Using simple notations.

$$C_t = C_o + C_s$$

where C_t is the total inventory cost, C_o is the cost of ordering, and C_s is the cost of carrying. The pattern of supply and demand for the item is assumed to be known with certainty and the various costs are assumed constant over the period under review.

The cost of ordering is the cost of placing a separate order multiplied by the number of separate orders placed in the period. If D is the annual demand for the item, if q is the size of each order, and P is the cost of placing a single order, then

$$C_o = P \times (D/q)$$

Similarly, the storage costs can be calculated easily. Assuming that S

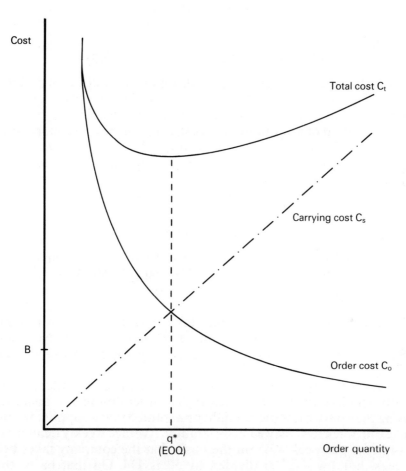

Note: The incorporation of safety or buffer stock would have the effect of moving the
carrying cost line upwards, beginning, say, at point B, and having the same slope. The
effect would be to reduce the quantity q^*.

Fig. 5.1 Evaluation of economic order quantity

is the annual cost of carrying one stock item, and that throughout the year, on average, half the stock is on hand all the time in addition to the safety or buffer stock, B, decided upon, then

$$C_s = S \times (B + q/2).$$

That gives

$$C_t = P \times (D/q) + S \times (B + q/2)$$

and, by using calculus to find the minimum value of C_t, an optimal value of q can be found, q*, the economic order quantity. Figure 5.1 shows that the point of intersection of the two cost lines, C_o and C_s, gives the point of minimum total cost, because the costs of ordering and of carrying tend to offset one another. The fewer the orders, the lower the costs of ordering but the greater the size of each order and the greater the costs of carrying.

As a result of the differentiation of C_t, the value of q* is derived from the following:

$$q* = \sqrt{2DP/S}$$

If the cost of placing an order is £5.00, if the annual demand is 5 700 units, and if the annual unit carrying cost is £1.50, then

$$q* = \sqrt{2 \times 5700 \times 5.00/1.50} = 195 \text{ items.}$$

The company would, therefore, make 29 orders during the year, each for 195 items, so as to minimise total inventory costs. Note that the safety or buffer stock has no bearing on the EOQ, only on the timing of orders.

The usual length of time between the placing of an order and its fulfilment has an important bearing on order timing. For instance, using the above example, it might be assumed that a supplier would take one week to satisfy each order fully. Average weekly demand is 114 items per week, say; on the basis that the company takes two weeks' holiday – 5 700 divided by 50 is 114. On that basis, the company should re-order when stock falls to 114, the minimum re-order quantity or level. However, the supplier may not always meet the order within a week, or there may be a greater than average call-off by production, so a buffer stock of, say, a further week's average demand might be required. That would give a re-order point of 228 items. Figure 5.2 presents a diagrammatic representation of the stock movements of the typical item discussed here.

In Figure 5.2, stock is called off until the level reaches the re-order

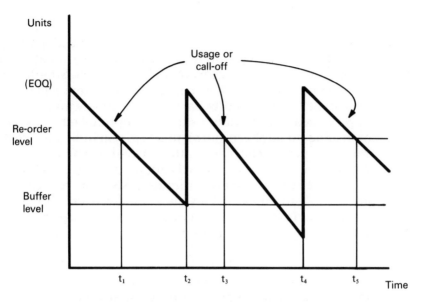

Note: Usage exceeds anticipated rate between time t_2 and t_4, so the re-order level is reached
      earlier, at time t_3. Supplies are received, however, on the regular date, at time t_4,
      occasioning utilization of part of the buffer stock.

Fig. 5.2   Stock movements and the EOQ

level at time t_1 which triggers the order for an amount equal to the
EOQ. Meanwhile, the held stock is still being called-off. The stock is
replenished at time t_2 and call-off continues, with a further order for
the EOQ being triggered at time t_3. Between order time, t_3, and
replenishment time, t_4, the amount called-off exceeds anticipated
demand and part of the buffer stock is used. The cycle continues in
this manner.

   The model just described is the most simple form of the inventory
models and can be made much more sophisticated by introducing
additional variables to incorporate such factors as stock-out costs,
supply and demand irregularities, quality control, and the like.

Accuracy and classification

Considerable amounts of time and effort can be expended in trying to ensure that the most appropriate, accurate and up-to-date cost information is used in the inventory modelling process. Simulation studies have demonstrated, however, that even very large deviations from the so-called 'correct' costs have neither greatly affected the EOQ nor produced large deviations from the optimal total cost per item. For instance, it has been shown that errors in individual costs of the order of 50 per cent have only affected total cost by some 2 per cent – that is to say that the total cost is not particularly sensitive to large inaccuracies in carrying or ordering costs. This reduces the need to use a costly sophisticated inventory model; it also cuts down the time and effort involved in estimating costs for incorporation in any model, thereby reducing the cost of building and using the model.

Before applying the model, it would be helpful to classify the inventory, using characteristics such as value, usage rate, or other important criteria. Often, a small quantity of the inventory accounts for the majority of stock value – designated as, perhaps, Category A stock – and these items need a high degree of control and security. In that case, a re-order cycle model would probably be supplemented by a policy of periodic stock review. Category B items might be less valuable but would still be held in reasonable quantities, so a re-order level model of appropriate sophistication would be used. The low-value, high-quantity group of stock items, those in Category C, would be handled best through a simple reorder model using simple calculations of the EOQ and re-order levels.

In many cases, re-order models and their constituents may not be revised for considerable periods of time – if only because of the costs of alteration, which may well exceed the value of any savings accruing from the revision. Inventory models are used extensively by firms to help plan and control this fundamental part of their working capital, especially as the cost of funds needed to finance inventory is very considerable.

PROGRAMMING MODELS

A second group of models using some form of mathematical programming can assist management in the planning of production, investment, distribution, and so on. The mathematical approach allows the planner to allocate limited or scarce resources in an optimal manner and facilitates the achievement of corporate objectives, such as maximising share prices. The best known and easiest algorithm is the linear programming approach, discussed and explained in this section.

Most enterprises have more than one objective in view, but the financial management literature tends to emphasise the maximisation of shareholder wealth (or, more tangibly, maximisation of share price). The models which employ a mathematical programming approach can accommodate either a single objective or multiple objectives. Linear programming, however, assumes the optimisation of one objective function, subject to any number of limiting constraints. Some of those constraints, of course, could be the minimum hurdles necessary for the achievement of other objectives.

The level, size and sophistication of the model depend on the needs of the user, as well as the costs and benefits attached to building and using the model. They depend also on the faithfulness with which the model represents the situation it purports to portray. For instance, there is no point in building a sophisticated linear programming model, assuming all relationships between variables to be linear, when this is patently not the case.

The first step is to formulate and construct the linear programming model. The exact details of performing linear programming computations are not within the scope of this chapter and explanations and practical examples can be found in any standard treatment of quantitative methods in management or accounting. For the most part, in real life these computations are handled most effectively by preprogrammed software packages or specially written programs for advanced calculators or simple computers. The example used here is concerned with production planning, but could as easily have dealt with investment planning or distribution control.

The fundamental problem or concern of the linear programming model is to establish the specific combination of factors that will satisfy all constraints and, at the same time, maximise the objective sought. It is possible, where there are only two or three variables, to solve this type of problem by heuristic or intuitive methods or by graphical means; when there are more variables, however, such methods become impracticable. In most cases what is needed is an iterative, step-by-step procedure, from the first statement of the available resources and constraints to the final, optimal statement. Such a method is known as the simplex method, which proceeds by the solution of sets of simultaneous equations. The simplex method begins by presenting a feasible solution – typically one in which nothing is done – and proceeds to see if that solution can be improved by substitution. Substitutions continue until no improvement is possible, at which point the optimal solution is deemed to be identified. Descriptions of the simplex method can be found elsewhere, and the following example omits many steps in the procedure.

Production planning

A company makes fishing reels and is considering the quantities to be produced of its three models A, B, and C. By categorising the costs, it is possible to identify the variable and fixed costs involved in the manufacture and selling of the reels. The linear programming approach assumes that sales and production volumes are equal; deviations from that assumption can be investigated by conducting sensitivity analysis after the derivation of the optimal solution. All fixed costs are ignored because they are not affected by changes in volume in the range around the optimal solution. The contribution of each product is calculated and, as in simple cost-volume-profit analysis, the aim is to maximise the short term contribution of the firm's product lines.

The firm will have to contend with numerous restrictions or potential restrictions on production levels or distribution rates. For instance, given the machine population in the factory and a one-shift operation, there is a limit to the number of hours that the machines can be worked; given the van population, there are limits to the quantity that the firm can ship. In both those instances, the restrictions are not completely binding, since they are susceptible to relaxation; the firm could work overtime or a second shift or it could buy or hire additional vans or use alternative distribution methods.

The three types of fishing reel can be re-designated 1, 2, and 3 and the quantities to be produced (and sold) labelled x_1, x_2, and x_3. If the models have respective contributions of £2.00, £3.00, and £4.00, then the total contribution from selling those quantities would be:

$$Z = 2x_1 + 3x_2 + 4x_3$$

where Z is total contribution. The problem then is to maximise Z.

Limits on production possibilities are present in four areas: machine time available; supervisors' time available; assembly time available; and floor space availability for storage of assembled products. Model 1 takes 5 hours of machining time, Model 2 takes 1 hour, and Model 3 takes 1 hour; the maximum availability of machine hours is 8 000 hours (the resource constraint). In equation form, this can be stated as follows:

$$5x_1 + x_2 + x_3 \leqslant 8\,000$$

where a simple solution might be to make 1 600 units of Model 1 and none of either Model 2 or Model 3, or to make 8 000 units of either Model 2 or Model 3, and none of Model 1, or some feasible combination of the three models. Supervisors' time availability is 8 000 hours, with Model 1 requiring 2 hours, Model 2 requiring 4 hours, and Model 3 requiring 2 hours. Equally, assembly time availability is 8 000 hours, with Model 1 needing 1 hour, Model 2 needing 2 hours, and Model 3 needing 4 hours. There are 4 000 square feet of storage space available, and for ease of calculation, it is assumed that each reel will take up 1 sq ft of storage space.

The problem to be solved takes the following form:

$$\text{Maximise } Z = 2x_1 + 3x_2 + 4x_3$$
$$\text{subject to } 5x_1 + x_2 + x_3 \leqslant 8\,000$$
$$2x_1 + 4x_2 + 2x_3 \leqslant 8\,000$$
$$x_1 + 2x_2 + 4x_3 \leqslant 8\,000$$
$$x_1 + x_2 + x_3 \leqslant 4\,000$$

and that x_1, x_2, and x_3 must each be greater than or equal to zero, that is, none can be negative. Here each constraint allows the combined products of x's and their technical coefficients (the individual values ascribed to each x according to the individual time or space requirements for each model) to be less than or equal to the resource capacity.

The fishing reel production problem can be stated as the first solution or tableau in a simplex procedure. The problem is converted from inequalities to equations and set out in tableau form. Conversion takes place by adding 'slack' variables for each inequality associated with the resource constraint equations, so that, for example, the machine hours equation reads as follows:

$$5x_1 + x_2 + x_3 + x_4 = 8\,000.$$

The first tableau for this problem is shown in Table 5.1, wherein the first row, the C_j row, states all the contribution coefficients of the variables in the objective function. None of the variables associated with resource constraints has any contribution, and therefore they have zero coefficients in the objective function. The technical coefficients are given in the third, fourth, fifth and sixth rows under the columns P_1 through to P_7. P_0 is the vertical vector of values for the variables in the solution vector at each stage of computing, listing the quantities to be produced and any unused resources. At the outset, with no production, all resources are unused and available and thus appear under P_0. Z, the value of the objective function, is zero at this point – as indicated by the number in the Z_j row of the P_0 column. When the optimum solution is reached, this element in the tableau provides the calculation of the total contribution from that optimal plan. The elements in the Z_j row are the contributions per unit lost if that variable is to be used in excess of the quantity shown in the P_0 column. The final row, the C_j–Z_j row, lists the values for C_j less the values for Z_j in the row above and represents the net contribution for each variable after each iteration.

The final tableau for this problem is also shown in Table 5.1 and can be interpreted as follows. In order to achieve the optimal contribution of £9 925.19, the firm should produce 1 185.41 Model 1 reels, 740.51 Model 2 reels, and 1 333.21 Model 3 reels. There will be 740.88 sq ft of storage space unused. From that total contribution should be deducted the fixed costs still to be recovered so that net trading profit could be calculated. It should be remembered that this is only the net profit for one trading period.

What this optimal solution provides is an indication of what the future plan should be. If this linear programming solution is used as the basis of the next period's budget, then the approach could be used again at the end of that period to calculate a revised optimal solution. The difference between the original plan and the revised plan is the opportunity loss occasioned by changing circumstances, and the difference between the actual results and the revised optimal plan indicates the operating variances.

Turning to long term planning, by the use of an objective function which maximises the net present value of the possible investments and a set of constraints, some of which are related to cash restrictions over a coming period, the linear programming model can be used just as easily for that type of problem. Such approaches and their associated problems are discussed in Salkin and Kornbluth (1973), Carsberg (1969), and Bhaskar (1978, 1979). The constraint

Table 5.1
Fishing reel problem – simplex tableaux

First tableau

P_1	P_2	P_3	P_4	P_5	P_6	P_7	P_0		
2	3	4	0	0	0	0			C_j
5	1	1	1	0	0	0	8 000	P_4	0
2	4	2	0	1	0	0	8 000	P_5	0
1	2	4	0	0	1	0	8 000	P_6	0
1	1	1	0	0	0	1	4 000	P_7	0
0	0	0	0	0	0	0	0		Z_j
2	3	4	0	0	0	0			$C_j\text{-}Z_j$

Final tableau

P_1	P_2	P_3	P_4	P_5	P_6	P_7	P_0		
2	3	4	0	0	0	0			C_j
1	0	0	.222	−.037	−.037	0	1 185.41	P_1	2
0	1	0	−.111	.352	−.148	0	740.51	P_2	3
0	0	1	0	−.167	.333	0	1 333.21	P_3	4
0	0	0	−.111	−.148	−.148	1	740.88	P_7	0
2	3	4	.111	.314	.814	0	9,925.19		Z_j
0	0	0	−.111	−.314	−.814	0			$C_j\text{-}Z_j$

vector, P_0, in such a formulation would comprise the expected cash amounts available in each of the years in the period under review, as well as other restrictions within which the firm has to work, such as ensuring profit levels are maintained, keeping financial ratios acceptable, maintaining staffing levels, and so on.

Assumptions and limitations

Underlying the linear programming model are a number of assumptions and the practical application of the model may require relaxation of one or more of those assumptions – a practice which has led to the model being criticised. The assumptions implicit in the linear programming model are as follows:

1   Linearity of objectives. It is assumed that the constants of proportionality – for cxample, the rate of contribution per unit of product – do not vary with levels of production, or at least that in practice the linear relationship holds over the relevant range for which the model is designed.
2   Proportionality. It is assumed that the amount of input required by an activity is directly related to the level at which the activity is happening. Doubling the activity level would double the amount of input required.
3   Divisibility. It is assumed that activities and resources are divisible – for example, using 4.15 lbs of raw material to produce 1.75 units of output.
4   Non-negativity. It is assumed that activities can only occur at a positive level – for example, there can be no negative output.
5   Accountability. It is assumed that it is possible to account for the whole physical capacity of each resource, including the unused part – for instance, the 740.88 sq ft storage space in the earlier example.
6   Certainty. It is assumed that the values in the model are known with certainty and will remain unchanged over the range being planned – for example, cost estimates for the production process will be constant, despite any learning effect.
7   Independence. It is assumed that the variables in the objective function are strictly independent of each other.

In practice, the linearity assumptions need not be too constricting, provided that they approximate actual relationships. Divisibility of resources and activities can be accommodated by approximation or by the use of integer programming, which dispenses with this assumption and operates only with integer values. Non-negativity is not an obstacle, because in building the model this possibility can be overcome by introducing a specific variable for the item concerned. Thus, there could be variables for both lending and borrowing in an investment model, so that there were no negative lending outputs but positive borrowing ones.

Both accountability for resources and independence of output variables are easily handled, as mentioned above. However, when making any plans and forecasts it is accepted that the numbers used are only estimates and not known with certainty. Therefore, to answer the 'what if' type of questions that all decision makers pose before making their decisions, it is helpful to provide further information based on sensitivity analysis. Weingartner (1963) explored all the alternative forms of mathematical programming that could be used in the investment decision context and covered those problems associated with certainty.

Sensitivity analysis

The optimal solutions revealed by the final tableau in a linear programming iteration are only valid over a given range. Formally entitled parametric linear programming, sensitivity analysis seeks to determine the range of variations in the coefficients over which the solution will remain optimal. The variations can be classified under five headings:

1 variations in the objective function coefficients;
2 variations in the technical coefficients;
3 variations in the constraint vector coefficients;
4 the addition or deletion of constraints;
5 the addition or deletion of variables.

Jensen (1968) has given a thorough description of the computational and interpretational aspects of sensitivity analysis and standard software packages can provide sensitivity analyses.

Using the fishing reel example and the final tableau shown in Table 5.1, it is possible, for instance, to calculate the relevant range of variations in the constraint vectors. Table 5.2 presents the reduction and increase limits for each resource – on the basis that those are the maximum changes from the original values which can be accommodated before the solution loses its optimality.

Interpreting those limits, it is possible to say, for example, that machine hours could be increased by 6 671 or reduced by 5 340 before the solution decayed; or that storage space could be reduced by 741 sq ft before the solution was impaired – there is no upper limit, since there is a surplus of storage space under the optimal solution.

It is also possible to argue that the values shown in the $C_j - Z_j$ line in the final tableau in Table 5.1 reveal the opportunity costs or shadow prices of one more or less unit of each limited resource. For instance, the loss of one hour of machine time would incur a loss in

Table 5.2
Fishing reel problem – sensitivity analysis

Constraint vectors – relevant ranges

	Reduction limit	Increase limit	Relevant range
Machine hours	5 340	6 671	2 660–14 671
Supervisor hours	2 104	5 006	5 896–13 006
Assembly hours	4 004	5 003	3 996–13 003
Storage space	741	infinity	3 259–infinity

contribution of £0.111; the acquisition of an extra hour of machine time would add £0.111 to the total contribution. If an hour of machine time could be acquired for, say, £3.00 it would not be worthwhile; if it could be acquired for £0.10 it would be worthwhile. A relatively straightforward discussion of these matters can be found in many texts, for example Dev (1980) or Mepham (1980).

Goal programming

Another application of linear programming is in goal programming. This recognises that companies have more than one goal – and that these goals are often of a qualitative nature. It also allows objectives to be ranked. The approach is based on the objective of minimising the variance around each goal, incorporating the goals as constraints. Ranking of goals is identified and effected in the objective function.

Using the fishing reel problem illustrated earlier, it is possible to add two more objectives. For instance, assume that some governmental prices legislation dictates that profit contribution in the coming trading period must not exceed £9 000, and further assume a sales target of £23 000. Take selling prices for the three models as £5.00, £8.00, and £10.00 respectively. Underachievement of the profit target is designated by U_p, while overachievement is designated V_p; similarly, underachievement and overachievement of the sales target are designated U_s and V_s respectively. The profit goal is more important, and is given a weighting of 100 in the objective function. The problem can be stated thus:

$$\text{Minimise } V = 100U_p + 100V_p + U_s + V_s + 0x_1 + 0x_2 + 0x_3$$
$$\text{subject to } 2x_1 + 3x_2 + 4x_3 + U_p - V_p = 9\,000$$
$$\text{and } 5x_1 + 8x_2 + 10x_3 + U_s - V_s = 23\,000$$

and additionally subject to the production constraints present in the problem stated before on page 97. Without going through all the iterations and manipulations, the solution to this problem proposed that no Model 1 reels should be produced, that 1 000 Model 2 reels should be produced, and that 1 500 Model 3 reels should be produced. The optimal solution indicated that there would be no surplus assembly time, but that there would be unused 5 500 hours machine time and 1 000 hours supervisors' time. Additionally, there would be 1 500 sq ft of storage space unused. The mix of products has altered markedly and three of the production facilities are under used. Fortunately, profit restrictions are not one of the problems faced by manufacturing industry – at least at the time of writing!

This section has shown how to choose from a selection of alternatives restricted by resource scarcity and how to satisfy a set of objective criteria.

DEMAND ANALYSIS AND FORECASTING

Prediction features as an important use of quantitative models and all plans are based on someone's estimates of future costs, sales, labour requirements, and so on. Forecasts can be based on intuition or models, of course, but there are obvious attractions in having a set of forecasts based on a quantified and verifiably objective (that is, non-subjective) set of assumptions.

The level and sophistication of the forecasting techniques depend very much on the task to be performed, the speed and accuracy required of the information generated, the costs of preparation and inaccuracy, and so on. This section looks at two relatively straight-forward techniques for forecasting: the moving average model, and the exponential smoothing model.

The procedure for building a forecasting model has five stages:

1 Past data are analysed and the main sources of variation dis-tinguished. There are three principal sources: the trend effect, the seasonal effect, and the random effect. The trend effect over time can be tested by regression analysis, though it shall be assumed here to be linear. Such an analysis may highlight also the cyclical

pattern of any seasonal variation. Any other unexplained variation is assumed to be of random nature.

2   Forecasts are prepared.

3   Possible forecasting errors are calculated, indicating the accuracy of the forecasts and whether there is a trend in the accuracy level which would need attention.

4   Additional factors should be incorporated, such as changes in corporate policy or budgetary guidelines.

5   Forecasts are applied.

Moving average approach

The average of the past period is taken as the forecast for the next period, unless amended for trend and seasonal effects. The length of time over which the moving average is taken depends on the nature of the business, but the longer the period the less sensitive the forecast to more recent happenings. The accuracy of the forecast may be impaired unless it is adjusted for trends or recent developments. Table 5.3 gives details of the sales experiences of a company and forecast sales.

Table 5.3
Sales experiences and forecasts (£000s)

Actual monthly sales	Running 6-month total	Running 6-month average	Original sales forecast	Trend	Running 4-month average trend	Trend adjusted forecast
30.0						
29.0						
31.0						
32.0						
34.0						
36.0	192.0	32.0				
39.0	201.0	33.5	32.0			
37.0	209.0	34.8	33.5	+1.5		
40.0	218.0	36.3	34.8	+1.3		
42.0	228.0	38.0	36.3	+1.5		
42.0	236.0	39.3	38.0	+1.7	+1.5	44.0
44.0	244.0	40.6	39.3	+1.3	+1.45	45.1
47.0			40.6	+1.3	+1.45	46.4

In that example, it is assumed that the company began trading in Month 1 of Year 1; by the end of the sixth month, its total sales have reached £192 000, giving an average for the first six months of £32 000 a month. That average is used as the base for the forecast for Month 7, because the company has decided that it operates on a six-monthly cycle. So, under column 4 for Month 7 this original forecast is shown. The actual sales for the month are £39 000, and the error in forecast is £7 000. The forecast for Month 8 is the average sales for the prior six months – £33 500. Since this forecast assumes that the underlying mean is constant and that fluctuations about the mean are due to random events, then the moving average will lag behind a persistent trend, being an average of past data.

To remedy that defect, the original forecast must be adjusted. Column 5, the trend, is calculated by finding the difference between successive forecasts. The trend for Month 8, therefore, is the difference between the forecasts for Month 7 and Month 8. To smooth the monthly differences, a running average of the trend is taken over a shorter period than the original six months; this is shown in column 6. The average for the previous six months is given in column 3 and reveals the average monthly sales for the middle of that six-month period. Thus, three more months have elapsed between then and the end of the period. To obtain a forecast of sales for the following month, the moving average is augmented by the addition of four times the running average trend for that month – three for the gap from the middle to the end of the period and one for the month to be estimated. For Month 12, for example, the revised trend-adjusted forecast is calculated by combining the original sales forecast (£38 000) and four times the running 4-month average trend ($4 \times$ £1 500), giving a revised forecast for Month 12 of £44 000.

The forecast error between the adjusted forecast and the actual month's sales is much smaller than that between the original sales forecast and the actual sales, because the underlying upward trend has been recognised and incorporated. A multiple regression analysis would give a more accurate and reliable representation of the trend than this simple approach. In that method, an algebraic relationship – a regression equation – is fitted to the past data and projected forward. The data treated could comprise more than one set of dependent variables – not just past sales, but, say, past sales, changes in gross national product, past sales of complementary products, advertising and promotion expenditure, and so on.

Exponential smoothing approach

A weighted form of moving average is used in the exponential smoothing approach and is calculated as follows. A smoothing constant, α, is found by trial and error and assigned a value between 0 and 1. The constant is derived from past data and is incorporated so that the new average equals the latest sales figure and the most recent average both adjusted by the smoothing constant. The equation can be written algebraically as follows:

$$E_t = \alpha\, S_t + (1 - \alpha)E_{t-1}$$

where E_t is the exponentially weighted moving average for period t, where S_t is the actual sales level for period t, where E_{t-1} is the previous period's exponentially weighted moving average, and where α is the smoothing constant. Simplifying that equation gives:

$$E_t = \alpha\,(S_t - E_{t-1}) + E_{t-1}.$$

Like the simple moving average, a trend factor can be built in to improve the the accuracy of the forecast, and this uses also a smoothing factor, β, and a similar estimation equation:

$$M_t = M_{t-1} + \beta(m_t - M_{t-1})$$

where M_t is the weighted trend average for period t to be added to the forecast to get the revised forecast, where M_{t-1} is the previous weighted trend average, where β is the smoothing constant, which has to be calculated from past data, but from experience is best if $0.001 \leqslant \beta \leqslant 0.1$, and where m_t is the weighted forecast error $\alpha\,(S_t - E_{t-1})$.

Table 5.4
Sales experiences and forecasts (£000s) – exponentially smoothed

Actual monthly sales	Original sales forecast	Forecast error	Weighted error	Trend adjustment	Adjusted sales forecast
39.0	35.51	3.49	2.79	2.279	
37.0	38.30	−1.30	−1.04	1.947	41.15
40.0	37.26	2.74	2.19	1.971	39.69
42.0	39.45	2.55	2.04	1.978	41.91
42.0	41.49	0.51	0.41	1.821	43.96
44.0	41.90	2.10	1.68	1.807	44.18
47.0	43.58				45.84

Using part of the data presented in Table 5.3 gives the forecasts recorded in Table 5.4. The forecast sales figures and the trend adjustment for Month 7 (the second and fifth columns of the first line in this new table) made use of data from the earlier periods. Sales, which are growing monthly, are very dependent upon the most recent past period sales, so a high value of α is appropriate, hence $\alpha = 0.8$ in this example. The forecast for Month 8, which we will call F_8, is calculated as follows:

$$
\begin{aligned}
F_8 = E_7 &= \alpha (S_7 - E_6) + E_6 \\
&= \alpha (S_7 - F_7) + F_7 \\
&= 0.8 \ (\pounds 39\,000 - \pounds 35\,510) + \pounds 35\,510 \\
&= 0.8 \ (3\,490) + \pounds 35\,510 \\
&= \pounds 38\,300.
\end{aligned}
$$

The actual sales for Month 8 turned out to be £37 000. Column 1 shows the actual sales that occurred, while the original sales forecast, E_{t-1} or F_t1, is shown in the second column, the error in forecasting being given in the third column. This error term is used to help adjust for trend. For Month 8, the adjustment term is

$$
M_8 = M_7 + \beta(m_8 - M_7)
$$

where $\beta = 0.1$ and where the weighted error term, m_8, is given in the fourth column, calculated as follows:

$$
m_8 = 0.8 \ (\pounds 37\,000 - \pounds 38\,300) = -\pounds 1\,040.
$$

by substitution, the following is derived:

$$
M_8 = \pounds 2\,279 + 0.1 \ (-\pounds 1\,040 - \pounds 2\,279) = \pounds 1\,947.
$$

The current exponentially derived weighted moving average, E_{t-1}, lags behind the current sales level and it can be shown that the size of this lag is $(1 - \alpha)/\alpha$ time periods. The trend line projection must also be lagged, and thus the forecast for i periods from now, t, is F_{t+1} such that

$$
F_{t+1} = E_t + (1 - \alpha)/\alpha \times M_t + iM_t.
$$

The estimated trend is multiplied by $(1 - \alpha)/\alpha$ to bring it up to date and also by i to add the additional trend estimates for the extra i periods. Here i = 1 and hence

$$
\begin{aligned}
F_8 &= E_7 + (1 - \alpha)/\alpha \times M_7 + M_7 \\
&= \pounds 38\,300 + (1 - 0.8)/0.8 \times \pounds 2\,279 + \pounds 2\,279 \\
&= \pounds 41\,150.
\end{aligned}
$$

The adjusted sales forecasts are listed in the sixth column and are more accurate predictors and easier to compute, with less need for data, than the simple moving average technique.

CONCLUSION

The past three sections have endeavoured to introduce three areas in which quantitative models can help management to get better information upon which to base decisions. As mentioned earlier, far more sophisticated models can be built and there are many other areas in which combined mathematical models and accounting can be useful to management – regression analysis in the measurement of costs, decision theory, game theory, service cost allocation by matrix algebra techniques, and so on. The bibliography suggests further reading on the ideas discussed in this chapter and those for which room has not been found.

REFERENCES AND FURTHER READING

Bhaskar, K. N., *Building Financial Models: A Simulation Approach*, London: Associated Business Programmes, 1978.

Bhaskar, K. N., *Manual to Building Financial Models*, London: Associated Business Programmes, 1979.

Box, G. E. P., and Jenkins, R. M., *Times Series Forecasting and Control*, New York: Holden-Day, 1968.

Brown, R. G., *Statistical Forecasting for Inventory Control*, New York: McGraw-Hill, 1959.

Brown, R. G., *Smoothing, Forecasting and Prediction of Discrete Time Series*, Englewood Cliffs, N.J.: Prentice-Hall, 1962.

Carsberg, B., *Introduction to Mathematical Programming for Accountants*, London: Allen & Unwin, 1969.

Demski, J. S., *Information Analysis*, Reading, Mass.: Addison-Wesley, 1972.

Dev, S., 'Linear pogramming and production planning', *in* Arnold J., Carsberg, B., and Scapens, R. (eds), *Topics in Management Accounting*, Oxford: Allan, 1980.

Feltham, G. A., *Information Evaluation*, Sarasota: American Accounting Association, 1972.

Grinyer, P. H., and Wooller, J., *Corporate Models Today*, 2nd edn.

London: Institute of Chartered Accountants in England and Wales, 1978.

Horngren, C. T., *Cost Accounting – A Managerial Emphasis,* 4th edn. Englewood Cliffs, N.J.: Prentice-Hall, 1977.

Jensen, R. E., 'Sensitivity analysis and integer linear programming', *The Accounting Review,* 1968.

Livingstone, J. L. (ed), *Management Planning and Control: Mathematical Models,* New York: McGraw-Hill, 1970.

Mepham, M. J., *Accounting Models,* Stockport: Polytech, 1980.

Miller, D. W., and Starr, M. K., *Executive Decisions and Operations Research,* 2nd edn. Englewood Cliffs, N.J.: Prentice-Hall, 1969.

Salkin, G., and Kornbluth, J., *Linear Programming in Financial Planning,* Englewood Cliffs, N.J.: Prentice-Hall, 1973.

Wagner, H. M., *Principles of Operations Research with Applications to Managerial Decisions,* 2nd edn. Englewood Cliffs, N.J.: Prentice-Hall, 1975.

Weingartner, H. M., *Mathematical Programming and the Analysis of Capital Budgeting Problems,* Englewood Cliffs, N.J.: Prentice-Hall, 1963.

6

Costing for Planning and Decision Making

Michael Bromwich

Above all else, information presented to management for decision making purposes must be useful, and there must be a continual effort to improve the methods of preparing, submitting and interpreting such information. Professor Bromwich argues that the traditional variance calculations of budgetary control and standard cost systems can be made much more useful to decision making. Switching the emphasis of such systems from their traditional preoccupation with control to concentrate upon planning will aid management in a difficult task. The chapter reviews the usefulness of conventional variances for planning and appraisal in relation to both inefficiency in operation and the inaccuracy of original plans and standards. It shows how better information can be derived than that given by the usual variance computations. The author believes that variances of the kind discussed in his chapter can be much more useful to management than the ritual calculation of all-purpose textbook variances. As he argues, it is by no means clear that variances designed for one purpose can be used effectively for another; variances intended to aid planning processes cannot often serve as motivational devices, for example.

Contemporary changes in general purchasing power, major altera-tions in specific prices, and the seemingly extra variability and uncertainty of today's economic environment, among other things, make it imperative to improve the information available to management for decision making. In one particular area, that of variance analysis, traditional emphases can be switched from a predominant concern with control to a more effective concern with planning.

The model used in standard costing approaches compares actual and expected results, significant deviations being identified and isolated for remedial action or reformulation by management. Devices of that type are known as 'feedback' systems, in which the outputs of the system themselves become inputs to the adjustment process designed to ensure that the outputs of the system are those specified originally. Such a typical 'engineering' control system can be depicted as in Figure 6.1. Outputs are given, the process is easily

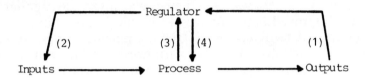

(1) feedback
(2) adjustment of inputs
(3) information flow directly from the process
(4) adjustment to the process

Fig. 6.1 Feedback control system

contained, inputs are specified and are relatively few. The outputs are monitored and can be controlled by the regulator making adjustments to the inputs. Probably the best known feedback model is the conventional central heating system, where differences between actual and desired warmth are used as signals for automatically changing boiler activity.

The model is readily incorporated in the management accountant's control process. If the output of the information system is actual material prices paid, then the error signal becomes a price variance and the regulator becomes the responsible manager. The usual analogue drawn between standard costing and budgetary control systems and feedback control devices illustrates the traditional preoccupation of budgetary and standard costing practitioners with control. Any management accounting textbook will also give clear evidence of this heavy emphasis on control aspects.

The feedback approach to standard costing does, however, bring out very clearly the link between planning and control. In the central heating system, for example, past performance is monitored and, on the assumption that any past error will continue unless corrective action is taken, a planning decision is made about fuel input. Similarly, standard cost variances can only be used to guide future actions, for any mistake is a sunk cost. If a purchasing manager who lost £15 000 last month is sacked, this is due less to his past error than to fears that he may continue to make such mistakes in the future. Unfavourable control variances (better called 'appraisal' variances because of the emotive connotations of the word 'control') are planning variances which serve to highlight the need for improved performance or planning in the future.

One area of feedback theory rich in potential applications to accountancy, involves the use of variances as inputs into planning models and future decisions – that is, feeding forward such variance information.

CAUSES OF VARIANCES

One of the most important differences between simple feedback systems and those of the management accountant is the latter's need to consider the cause of any error signal. In the central heating system, the remedy is clear and the cause is usually of little importance. In the management accountant's system, the cause may be of paramount importance; very different responses may be required to variances resulting from different factors. Indeed, many variances cannot be eliminated, but must be taken into account when re-planning; for example, a price variance following a change in foreign exchange rates.

There are two major causes of variances between standard and actual performances:

1 inefficiency in operation; failure to obtain a reasonable standard in the prevailing circumstances, whether through inability in one form or another or through lack of motivation;
2 incorrectness of original plans and standards; invalidation of original plans and standards through environmental change.

Under the second set of circumstances, reporting variances may result in a revision of plans and the one thing that should not be encouraged is adherence to the original, wrongly-based plans. The process of variance analysis should prove educational in this respect.

Variances calculated from these causes and with the circumstances of the business explicitly in mind will be more useful to management than the ritualistic textbook all-purpose variances. A different kind of variance might then be used for each cause. As Stedry (1967) said, it is not obvious that variances designed to aid planning can also serve as motivational devices.

VARIANCES FOR PLANNING AND APPRAISAL

The present chapter, therefore, reviews the usefulness of the conventional variances for planning and appraisal in relation to the two principal causes mentioned earlier, and shows that information obtained in that way can be more meaningful than that derived from the usual variance computations. The variances highlighting the first cause (inefficiency and poor motivation) may be called 'appraisal' variances. At present, it does not seem possible to suggest an analytical approach to split the appraisal variance between the two underlying causes and a detailed investigation of actual specific variances appears the only solution. However, recent work has contributed substantially towards understanding the motivational effects of accounting methods of planning and control. By isolating off-standard results due to those causes, it is possible to learn something about a manager's past performance. In other words, given the environment faced by the manager and the decisional variables over which he had authority or control, how near did he come to optimum performance?

Both for self-appraisal by the manager and for senior management review of subordinates, only controllable variances are pertinent. Thus, where the environment has changed, performance should be compared with a standard reflecting those changed circumstances, showing how well the manager has grasped new opportunities or coped with an unfavourable environment. The major difficulty lies in the definition of optimum performance; but it can be shown that some useful approximations exist. Any attempt to define optimum performance for changing circumstances introduces a greater element of subjectivity into variance analysis than is usually present, but the associated difficulties are likely to be offset by the provision of more meaningful information to management.

Variances monitoring the second principal cause (poor or inappropriate plans and standards) may be called 'planning' variances – being used to evaluate plans and standards rather than operational performance. When used in conjunction with the variance between original plans and the current appraisal standard (which reflects the prevailing environment), a comparison between unadjusted original plans and actual results can provide a useful check on forecasting skill and ability. Further, and more important, an unfavourable trend in a planning variance could be fed into the decision process for the next period and might suggest revisions of original plans; a persistently favourable variance might hint at new opportunities for the firm.

The subsequent sections deal separately with individual variances on the assumption that many price, wage and overhead variances are not controllable by operating managers. Indeed, many may not be controllable by anyone within the organisation. This is true, for example, of many material prices, where the buying organisation does not have substantial purchasing power, and of many public sector price increases. In such cases, it is not clear that reporting price increases to operating managers serves any useful purpose. Often, even the enterprise's purchasing managers cannot be held responsible for price increases. Price variances, then, can only be used sensibly in re-planning and revising decisions.

It is not clear, either, that information concerning this type of price increase dictates the detailed alterations to standard costing systems that are being attempted by many firms. Indeed, it can be suggested that in situations of rapidly changing prices, such as those caused by major and continual currency fluctuations, many operating managers would be better served if their performance reports emphasised physical quantities. This is one reason why there are doubts about the wisdom of incorporating a current cost 'cost of sales adjustment' (as recommended by SSAP 16) into management accounts in any general way. It might be less confusing to report relevant price changes only to those concerned to decide the enterprise's response to such changes. These doubts are magnified when the 'monetary working capital adjustment' of SSAP 16 is considered, especially since it is difficult to see how the normal methods recommended for its calculation can yield a measure of the real cost of financing the enterprise's operating activities. It might also be better to consider issuing special reports for those concerned with such activities as stockholding, credit management, and short term financing.

As exemplified below, price variances might serve two crucial roles: to monitor forecasting ability, and to aid decision making concerning the enterprise's future responses to the underlying price changes they reflect. The traditional view of variance analysis seems to be that all variances require action within the organisation to regain the original planned state (see Institute of Cost and Management Accountants (1980) and Chapter 10 in this handbook for instance). This concentration on control may lead to neglect of the vital contribution that variance analysis can make towards strategic re-planning. Furthermore, when considering non-controllable variances, an attempt to use them solely for control purposes robs variance analysis of any contribution whatsoever, other than the possible negative impact of distorting decisions. This neglect of variances which reflect non-controllable factors deprives variance analysis of its potentially unique role in providing a formal framework for scanning and understanding the environment. Planning variances, as defined above, can reveal a great deal about changes in the environment.

The remainder of this chapter seeks to justify the above view of standard costing by considering the relevance of several familiar and well used variances to planning and decision making. The suggested procedures should not be applied to all variables in the system; but should be confined to those items considered of special significance to decision making. The variances are considered in three categories: direct cost variances; sales variances; fixed overhead variances.

DIRECT COST VARIANCES

Conventionally, these are categorised as follows:

1 material price variances;
2 material usage variances;
3 mix variances;
4 labour rate variances;
5 labour efficiency variances;

and the following sections examine and discuss each in turn.

Material price variances

The usual price variance – actual material price less standard material price times actual material usage for actual performance – may be of little use for appraising the performance of the purchasing agent or officer, since price changes may be due to market forces outside his control. For instance, oil prices uncontrollable by operational buyers; local authority rate charges and public utility prices offer further examples. In such cases, a more meaningful variance may be derived by comparing the actual price paid with the best available estimate of the market price prevailing at the time of actual purchase. A favourable variance would indicate the buyer's ability to 'beat the market', either by bulk buying or by special arrangements.

A major weapon of the market beating buyer is speculative purchasing, though his ability to engage in this strategy depends on the market in which he buys, the finances of the firm, and his management's attitude. Many salutary experiences in recent years warn against the reckless pursuit of this kind of 'entrepreneurial' behaviour – as witness the costly mistakes made by the cocoa buyers in several large chocolate manufacturing organisations! Various approximate measures of speculative 'success' can be suggested. Where the buyer is ordering quantities larger than seem economically necessary and above those called for in the normal production process, his policy might be justified by a claim that prices were about to increase. By calculating the variance between the prices which actually obtain in the later period (in which those items would otherwise have been purchased) and the buyer's earlier estimates of those prices, his forecasting success can be measured. The profitability of his speculative activities can be gauged by deducting from the actual later prices the lower prices paid plus the holding costs incurred – to which special attention should be paid in times of high interest rates. Given the variability of financing costs, consideration might be given to issuing special reports on the opportunity costs of holding current assets, rather than attempting to incorporate this information in general all-purpose information reports.

The above description illustrates the general point that variances for appraisal purposes should show how well managers did in the prevailing circumstances and should abstract from non-controllable environmental changes.

As a check on forecasts and standards, the usual price variance may be helpful for planning purposes, particularly if used in conjunction with the appraisal variances outlined above. Further, were an appropriate external forecast of prices available, an assessment of relative forecasting skill could be obtained by comparing the mistakes of the general market index with the firm's internal index. Such an external index may be valuable as an approximate measure even if it covers a much wider range of goods or services than the firm uses.

Price variances play a major role as indicators in assessing whether the trend in prices necessitates a change in existing plans – such as to raise final output prices or to change production methods. Here a rate-of-change variance, namely a comparison showing the trend in the price variance over time, may be more helpful than the conventional computation.

It is suggested, therefore, that the usual price variance should be split in two – a planning variance and an appraisal variance. The planning variance shows how the market price differed from that previously assumed, and the appraisal variance measures the buyer's ability in the conditions that actually prevailed.

The planning variance formula is

$$(p_c - p_s) \times mX$$

where p_c is the general market price at the time of purchase (based on external indicators), where p_s is the original standard price, and where mX is the standard material usage for the actual output (where m is the standard usage per unit of output and X is the actual number of units produced).

The appraisal variance formula is

$$(p_a - p_c) \times mX$$

where p_a is the actual price paid. Material usage is evaluated in these cases at standard usage per unit of output in order to avoid complications that arise from the presence of the joint variance.

The usefulness claimed for planning variance is general and is not restricted to those concerned with price changes. The value of these variances for planning may be extended by classifying them in terms of the responses gained. The most extreme type of uncontrollable change is that to which management can respond only by altering future activity in a given way. The only response that a profit

117

maximising management can make to such changes is to alter its future plans to reflect their effects. An extreme example of this type of environmental change would be a new legislative requirement, the provisions of which could be followed only by quitting the enterprise's existing area of activity – if, for example, the manufacture of cigarettes were made illegal.

A further category incorporates those environmental changes that can be modified or exploited by managerial action, even though their occurrence is beyond the influence of management. Many instances of this second type of expectational change could be given. For example, it is unlikely that a firm could influence the world trend in steel prices, but it may escape many of the consequences of such price changes by stockholding in the short run and by using substitute materials in the long run. The higher taxation of 'high tar' cigarettes and the expected decline in the market for such cigarettes might be exploited by a concentration on 'low' or 'medium tar' cigarettes.

The third type of change that might be monitored separately is that generated by alterations to factors within managerial control. This category can be subdivided at least once. One element of the subdivision would then indicate the expected change if no action were planned to correct past inefficiencies; a second, on a similar basis, would indicate the effects of incorrect original forecasts of factors within management's control.

It is recognised that none of the above classifications can be delineated precisely. However, at least some of the advantages claimed for the proposed system should prove relatively robust and insensitive to considerable inaccuracy. These ideas merely extend the concepts underlying existing standard costing and budgetary control techniques and procedures. The variance between the original and revised levels of the variable in question, insofar as those variances could be assigned to uncontrollable factors, woud give a further indication of the uncertainty surrounding the enterprise's activities, particularly when calculated over successive periods to produce a time series of variances.

Further analysis of such variances into those which management could meet only with a change of plan and those which could be offset by appropriate action within the existing plan would point up the nature of the uncertainties facing the firm. Insofar as such variances were controllable and could be analysed into those due to errors in earlier planning and those due to errors in execution of the plan, they would highlight the need for management action to improve efficiency.

Even such modified variances reflect only part of the buyer's responsibility. By bulk purchasing, he may show a favourable price variance – but at the expense of inventory holding cost. Some attempt should be made to lay down inventory standards so that such effects could be detected. Similarly, provided that the information obtained is worth its cost, standards could be set for the buyer's other responsibilities; for example, a transport cost variance would highlight the cost of rush orders and could be charged to the responsible department. One could argue that management accountants have been dilatory in extending their activities in such ways.

Material usage variances

This variance is less likely than the price variance to be affected by uncontrollable changes in the firm's environment; even so, such cases can easily be imagined. For example, poorer quality labour than expected may be used, owing to shortages of skilled workers. Then, for appraisal, actual material usage should be compared with an adjusted standard. However, if the use of inferior labour is due, say, to poor performance in the personnel department, then, in principle, the responsible manager should incur a variance equal to the difference between the revised and the original standard.

In such a situation, where the use of lower grade labour is due to general economic conditions and is therefore non-controllable, the modified variance suggested above should be used for appraisal, but the conventional variance should be used in conjunction with it for re-planning. A conventional usage variance that becomes increasingly unfavourable over time may indicate a need for more capital-intensive methods. This suggests reporting a rate-of-change, as mentioned earlier.

Mix variances

Substitutions between materials (and, indeed, between materials and other factors, and between other factors such as labour and capital) may also be profitable. This may often be the only way of responding to uncontrollable price changes. If such decisions are possible technically, the responsible person should be given an indicator that tells him when they would be profitable. The normal material usage variance gives no such hints to the production manager, since usage is evaluated at standard prices to avoid contaminating the variance with items beyond the manager's control. This may be reasonable – provided signals are given elsewhere in the management accounting system to indicate the profitability of substitution decisions. In general, material usage is priced at standard throughout the system and, consequently, operational management is not informed when it would be profitable to change material proportions.

It might be expected that the mix variance would highlight the possibility of substituting cheaper materials for more expensive ones. However, it cannot do so, since it is priced at standard cost. The variance generally serves the far less important role of an appraisal variance, denoting the cost of changes in mix at given constant relative prices. Furthermore, owing to the implicit assumptions about feasible material substitutions, it does not even do that very well.

Ideally, for planning there should be 'on the shelf' material usage plans for different relative prices – that is, usage recipes giving mixes for different various relative material prices. Depending on prices, some materials will feature in some recipes but not in others, or larger quantities of any specific material will appear in some recipes than in others. These recipes can be used to calculate a planning variance called a 'substitution' variance. For each material actual use is compared with 'off the shelf' optimal usage for the relative prices that actually held in the period, and the difference is valued at the actual price for the period of that material. These components are then summed over all materials to give the total substitution variance. For each material, the following comparison is made:

$$(m - m^*) \times p_a^* X$$

where the new symbols, m^* and p_a^*, are, respectively, the optimal usage for each material and its current price, where m is the actual usage of material per unit of finished output, and where X is the actual number of units produced.

An unfavourable substitution variance would suggest that the use of different material proportions should be considered. This may seem a costly exercise, but it can prove an extremely valuable one. A number of industries such as the oil and chemical industries, follow this procedure. A cake manufacturer, for example, could employ alternative recipes depending on the relative prices of jam, sugar, and other ingredients.

The concept of having different recipes for different relative prices is not restricted to materials and can be applied to any number of factors – capital and labour come to mind, as do alternative energy sources, recipes for both depending on expectations of relative prices in the long run.

Apart from serving as a planning variance, the substitution variance is useful for appraising the executive responsible for decisions of that type. This is an instance of the same variance being used for both planning and appraising. However, if this revised mix variance is to be helpful for appraisal, the reasons for any substitution must be known. For example, there may have been a departure from the optimal mix as a result of a failure in the buying department, rather than any inefficiency in production. For appraisal purposes, the optimal usage, m^*, should represent the best operating management could do in the light of the purchasing department's failure. A separate comparison based on the difference between this optimum (which is available to the production department) and the optimum which should have been attained but for the inefficiency of the purchasing department indicates the cost of the latter. This cost would be useful in appraising the purchasing department's performance and may underline a need for re-planning.

In their usual form, mix and yield calculations give no clear guidance to the correctness of the original technical specifications and, therefore, worthwhile revisions may not be made. The only remedy seems to be routine engineering studies of existing technical specifications.

For these reasons, it seems doubtful whether the calculation of the conventional mix and yield variances would be worthwhile. It can also be shown that many of the above difficulties and reservations could be applied to sales price and mix variances.

Labour rate and efficiency variances

Criticisms of the conventional material price variance also apply forcefully to the labour rate or price variance – actual wage per hour less standard wage per hour times actual hours worked to produce actual output. Indeed, the staffing department may be even more at the mercy of the outside market than the buying department. The conventional labour rate variance may be useful for planning, but it is less likely to make a good appraisal variance.

The conventional formula for labour efficiency variances – actual hours worked less standard hours estimated for actual production times standard wage per hour – is generally regarded as an appraisal variance, any deviations from standard reflecting adversely on the production manager. This is reasonable if the standard reflects the environmental conditions prevailing during the period. If, for example, owing to conditions in the labour market, less than skilled labour had to be used, the standard for appraisal purposes should be adjusted to reflect that fact.

A rate-of-change variance may be useful for appraisal purposes, as the responses of both senior management and the individual responsible manager depend closely on whether any unfavourable variance is expected to persist. Watching the trend in labour, and other appraisal variances, may be helpful in validating standards; a persistent trend should signal a thorough study of existing targets.

In calculating labour efficiency variances (and, indeed, all variances), attention should be paid to all that are mutually dependent. For example, by allowing higher than standard material waste, greater labour efficiency may be obtained; labour efficiency and material usage variances cannot usefully be studied in isolation. The efficiency (appraisal) variance based on current attainable standards and the uncontrollable efficiency variance (planning) due to changes in environmental conditions together explain deviations from forecast capacity due to labour inefficiency. They may suggest that management should employ more capital-intensive methods, consider price increases, or consider switching to a product needing less skilled labour. The two variances together are thus relevant for planning.

Cost of labour inefficiency

The conventional efficiency variance, even when adjusted to take account of attainable standards, may understate the cost of excess labour usage. This cost variance is taken to be the wage payments for which standard performance was not obtained, whereas the true cost is the opportunity cost of production lost due to inefficiency – approximately, the lost total contribution to fixed overheads and profits.

A simple example may help to explain this. Assume that 100 labour hours were taken to produce 90 units of output; the standard output for one hour of labour was one unit. The standard wage rate was £2.50 an hour. The conventional efficiency variance would price the ten extra hours at £2.50, giving an unfavourable variance of £25.00. If the selling price was £25.00 and the standard contribution to fixed costs and profits was £7.50, the real loss associated with those ten hours was the forgone contribution from the ten units that might have been produced – an unfavourable opportunity cost variance of £75.00.

Under the above assumptions, the true cost of labour inefficiency is the conventional variance (provided that the inefficiency was controllable by the manager in question) plus any lost contribution.

On the other hand, the conventional variance reflects accurately the cost of inefficiency if idle capacity is expected in the future and if unsatisfied demand in any period can be carried forward and satisfied in future periods. If overtime has to be worked to make up lost units, however, the cost of such overtime should be included in the variance as a cost of excess wage payment.

The approach suggested above, which entails a forecast of the future effects of past inefficiency, is more subjective than the usual calculations. However, it shows more clearly the effect of substandard performance and illustrates the need to consider its likely impact.

SALES VARIANCES

These may be considered in the following categories:

1   sales volume variance;
2   sales price variances.

Again, these will be considered in terms of their applicability to planning and appraisal and in terms of the real costs of such inefficiences as are identified, bearing in mind lost opportunities and forgone profits.

Sales volume variances

In conventional terms, the sales volume variance is calculated as the difference between actual sales and standard or budgeted sales priced at the standard or budgeted contribution per unit. All such a variance reveals is whether a sales manager has sold more or less than expected. What would be of more interest would be to know how well he has performed. If, for example, the market was such that many more units could have been sold than were actually sold, the sales manager has underperformed (provided production capacity was such that it would have allowed him to market those extra units). In the prevailing circumstances, the sales manager should have sold more.

A simple example will help to emphasise the point. A sales manager for a motor vehicle manufacturer is set a target of 2 000 saloon cars to sell in the coming three months. Each saloon car generates a contribution of £1 750 to fixed overheads and profits. The sales manager actually sells 2 500 saloon cars. However, examination of market trends suggests that, given the increased demand for cars of the type in question, the manager could have sold 3 000 such cars during that quarter. Those details are reproduced in Figure 6.2, which reveals that the budgeted contribution for the period was £3.5 million, whereas the actual contribution was £4.375 million. Conventional sales volume variance analysis would hint at a 'good' variance of £875 000 extra contribution.

Taking an opportunity cost view of the sales manager's performance, however, would reveal a forgone contribution of £875 000. Rather than significantly overperforming, the sales manager had underperformed markedly. The question of whether or not he had beaten an obsolete target is irrelevant. Even though the management accountant's conventional variance has suggested that the sales manager had performed well, the cost to the company of the neglected opportunities – that is, the failure to sell the additional 500 saloon cars – is a true measure of the extent to which he failed.

Equally, if the market for saloon cars of the type in question had declined, the sales manager should be assessed against a more realistic lower standard. To calculate such an appraisal variance precisely would call for better demand information than most firms possess. Here again, however, a close enough approximation may be made to produce useful information. Trend analysis is of considerable assistance in such an approximation, as has been discussed in Chapter 5 of this handbook.

Other, perhaps more qualitative information may also help considerably. Properly weighed, appraisal variances of this type will consistently provide better information than their conventional counterparts. Original plans can be compared with the adopted appraisal standard to give a planning variance. As discussed earlier,

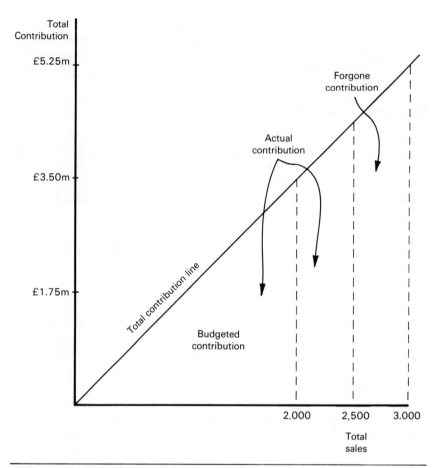

Fig. 6.2 Sales performance

such a variance will reveal useful information about forecasting abilities, shifts in the environment, and the need for revision of plans – particularly if used in conjunction with a rate-of-change variance.

In following the usual rule for pricing lost sales, care needs to be taken to take realistic account of those opportunity costs. It is assumed, in that context, that any such lost sales are lost forever. But to take the saloon car example again, the 500 unsatisfied customers might be prepared to wait for delivery, rather than buying another make or model. In those circumstances, the 'real' opportunity cost to the company would be any loss in the value of money occasioned by the defined actual cash flows generated by the sales. Equally, concomitant opportunity costs may be occasioned by being unable to use that £850 000 now rather than in one or two months' time.

Sales price variances

Typically, the sales price variance is calculated as the difference between the actual sales price and the standard sales price times the actual sales volume. Realistically, however, it is not particularly meaningful to consider a sales price variance on its own. In any relatively stable economic environment, an unfavourable sales price variance will tend to be associated with a favourable sales volume variance; equally, perhaps, the higher the actual sales price, the lower the actual sales volume. Little may be gained, therefore, from splitting the overall sales variance.

It is, after all, unrealistic to expect to sell more than the standard or budgeted quantity without some associated reduction in selling price. The better approach to calculating valuable sales variances is to decide an adjusted selling price upon which to base the variances. Such an adjusted selling price would be derived from an assessment of the price that would have been expected for the actual volume of sales achieved. The adjusted price should be used also for re-calculating the standard or budgeted contribution.

When a marked change has taken place in the external environment, the above procedures are of little use, since both price and volume variances may be favourable for reasons beyond the control of management or even despite management's actions. The variance analysis in those circumstances becomes very much more subjective, depending upon estimates of the best attainable performance in the changed conditions facing the firm during the period in question. Important clues for such a solution would be, for instance, changes in market share and in inventory levels.

FIXED OVERHEAD VARIANCES

Routine treatments of overhead variances encompass the calculation of overhead under- or over-recovery and its division between overhead capacity variance and overhead efficiency variance. In the context of this chapter, it would be better to consider overhead variances from rather more practical viewpoints – those of the opportunities lost through inefficient use of available resources.

In many instances, conventional overhead variance data are redundant, since most will be reported elsewhere as either sales or direct cost variances – being the results of either failing to sell the budgeted quantity or of inefficiencies in production. Perhaps more important, fixed overheads are the current consequences of previous decisions on investment, of labour supply constraints, of public utility policies, and so on, and are by definition fixed for any volume of production within a given range. Overhead recovery rates treat such overheads as variable with production, which is patently unrealistic and at best confusing – particularly as the different, acceptable methods of calculating overhead rates all lead to different answers, all arbitrary and each misleading.

That latter point argues forcefully against incorporating a replacement cost depreciation adjustment (of the type recommended in SSAP 16) into management accounting performance reports. Generally, depreciation expenses are not controlled by operating managers; they become no more controllable when based on the so-called replacement cost of assets.

Unless depreciation is affected by asset usage, those expenses are determined by the investment decision concerning the asset in question. No useful additional information to that obtained by monitoring the investment project as it proceeds is yielded by reporting depreciation expenses.

The need for more useful methods for planning and controlling such overheads represents a major challenge to the management accounting profession. The importance of the task is being increased by several factors which tend to boost the proportion of total costs represented by fixed overheads. Such influences include increasing capital intensity reflecting technological advances, and those changes in employment law and practice which inhibit flexible staffing arrangements.

One approach to this task which seems to show some promise is the establishment of cost centres for major items of fixed overheads. The budgets for such centres recognise that these costs alter with some causal factors, rather than with short run production levels. Assuming that this difficult task can be accomplished, at least in part, the approach advocated so far in this chapter can be used to control and plan those factors normally treated as fixed overheads. The costs of many of those factors are not usually susceptible to bargaining by the firm, however, and this renders the calculation of planning variances for such items of crucial importance, especially if such variances highlight the responses available to the firm to price increases for those factors. Variances for use in appraising the performance of those charged with managing what are normally regarded as fixed overheads require that both the benefits the organisation hopes to obtain from their use can be determined and the factors which cause the amounts of those benefits to vary can be identified. As argued above, appraisal variances should be limited to those causal factors which lie within the firm's influence or control.

When the budget is prepared, the level of expected benefits needs to be determined for each major item of fixed overhead. Setting budgeted amounts of benefit from each overhead item implies a total expenditure on each of those items, assuming certain standards of performance relative to those causal factors which are within the firm's control.

Appraisal variances will measure the degree of achievement of those performance levels. However, it is likely that most variances associated with what are normally regarded as fixed overheads will be of the planning variety – leading to new forecasts of enterprise profitability and to consideration of alternative methods of achieving the desired level of benefits in the changed environment.

Figures for fixed overheads under-recovered owing to production inefficiencies reveal little of real value. For example, if a firm's planned production for a period is 7 000 units, each requiring 30 minutes labour, and if total fixed overheads are budgeted at £28 000 for the period, the conventional overhead recovery rate will be set at £4.00 a unit or £8.00 per labour hour. If actual production is only 6 000 units, the overhead under-recovered is calculated at £4 000 (on the assumption that budgeted and actual labour hours worked are the same). All that reveals, essentially, is that the figure of under-recovery can be explained by inefficiency in the use of labour.

But what is the real loss? It is the cost of the opportunities lost due to the inefficient use of labour – in other words, the labour efficiency variance discussed earlier. If the 1 000 units are 'lost' forever, it is the value of the lost contribution plus the wages paid to inefficient labour (500 hours at the wage rate). If the units could not be sold anyway, the cost is only the labour cost.

Idle capacity cost

In order to check the accuracy of forecasts used in the past to justify investments and to highlight the opportunity cost of unused facilities and help to plan better usage in the future, it is helpful to have a ready measure of the cost of idle capacity.

The best measurement of forecasts and monitoring their validity can be achieved by a simple comparison analysis of planned and actual cash flows and sales volumes. Again, an appraisal standard would be helpful, comparing the levels used to justify an investment and the optimal levels which might have been achieved.

Ascertaining the opportunity cost of idle capacity is more difficult, as choices must be made between a variety of measures of capacity. Due to economies of scale, under which it might be worthwhile to invest in a plant of far greater capacity than is actually required, the notion of technical capacity is inappropriate in many circumstances.

As a first step, management should be provided with an estimate of expected idle capacity for the coming period. That estimate can then be compared with the actual variance caused by idle capacity. Both variances, one for planning and one for appraisal, should be costed at their opportunity cost – the profits forgone due to idle capacity. Spare capacity could, perhaps, be rented out, or it could be used to manufacture another product. If no alternative use is possible, idle capacity has no cost.

The usual overhead efficiency variances can be both misleading and redundant; the traditional overhead capacity variances are not a true measure of idle capacity; only the conventional overhead expenditure variance is useful in the context of this chapter's arguments. Even then, such a variance needs to be pruned of non-controllable items or influences.

(Editorial note: This chapter is an edited version of a paper presented to a technical symposium of the Institute of Cost and Management Accountants at Pembroke College, Oxford, in January 1981, and parts rely on ideas in the author's series of articles on standard costing for planning and control in The Accountant *in April and May 1969. The permission of the publisher to reprint parts of those articles is gratefully acknowledged.)*

REFERENCES AND FURTHER READING

Beyer, R., and Trawicki, D., *Profitability Accounting for Planning and Control*, 2nd edn. New York: Ronald Press, 1972.

Bromwich, M., 'Standard costing for planning and control', *The Accountant*, 19 April 1969, 26 April 1969, 3 May 1969.

Dearden, J., *Cost and Budget Analysis*, Englewood Cliffs, N.J.: Prentice-Hall, 1962.

Horngren, C. T., 'A contribution margin approach to the analysis of capacity utilization', *The Accounting Review*, April 1967.

Institute of Cost and Management Accountants, *Terminology of Management and Financial Accountancy*, London: ICMA, 1980.

Solomons, D., *Divisional Performance: Measurement and Control*, Homewood, Ill.: Irwin, 1965.

Solomons, D. (ed), *Studies in Cost Analysis*, London: Sweet and Maxwell, 1968.

Stedry, A. C., 'Budgetary control: a behavioral approach', *in* Alexis, M., and Wilson, C. Z., (eds), *Organizational Decision-Making*, Englewood Cliffs, N.J.: Prentice-Hall, 1967.

PART TWO
ACCOUNTING
FOR MANAGEMENT
CONTROL

OVERVIEW

The second section of this handbook examines fundamental and routine accounting procedures for aiding management to control the functions and activities of the modern organisation. Essentially, these accounting procedures are concerned with furnishing financial information; combining financial and quantitative data in different ways in the preparation of reports that serve as a guide to management, both in the control of the enterprise and also in planning future activities.

In the first two chapters in this section, Lewis Brown of the City University Business School, London, examines the two predominant costing concepts: absorption or full costing and marginal or variable costing. The essential difference between the two methods is their assignment of specific costs to products. The problem of cost apportionment and the associated impacts on stock valuation and profit determination are crucial factors in the analysis of costs and profitability. The advantages and disadvantages of both systems are described and discussed.

Professor John MacArthur of the School of Business at the University of Northern Iowa develops the traditional or conventional approaches to budgeting and illustrates a number of ways in which budgets can be used more effectively. The chapter concentrates on short run budgeting and introduces the fundamental concept of opportunity costing into the budgetary process, describing and demonstrating the 'economic cost' approach to budgeting. Professor MacArthur also examines aspects of budgeting which are often overlooked in conventional treatments. He extends his refreshing analyses to the budgeting aspects of non-production cost elements, and discusses the incremental and zero-based approaches. One of the persistent difficulties associated with the budgetary process is the adequate recognition and incorporation of uncertainty and probability constraints. The chapter explores those difficulties and suggests a solution.

The determination and interpretation of variations between budgeted outcomes and actual results are the subjects of the final two chapters in this section. In the first of these, Stuart Jones of the Department of Accounting at the University of Hull returns to the topic of variance accounting, providing a comprehensive discussion of variance accounting techniques and their interpretation. The author recognises that variances, in themselves, do not rate managers' abilities; they indicate possible managerial strengths or weaknesses and suggest areas for investigation. After all, variances may reflect a manager's forecasting and estimating shortcomings rather than any operating failure.

The concluding chapter in this section gathers together some of the underlying themes treated earlier; in particular, it discusses a system of responsibility accounting as a management control tool. Describing and analysing the identification and categorisation of controllable and non-controllable costs, the Editor examines the formulation of an organisational responsibility hierarchy and the determination of responsibility costs or revenues. The chapter investigates the different types of responsibility centre and presents examples of responsibility reports for departments and divisions. Responsibility reporting is not without its difficulties, and the chapter lists and discusses a number of problems associated with responsibility accounting systems. The writer sees responsibility accounting as providing a most effective technique to facilitate the harmonious delegation of responsibility and retention of control within an enterprise.

In management terms, control involves implementing planning decisions and monitoring activities to ensure that the goals of the enterprise are attained. Control systems in management accounting should provide the information management needs to implement decisions successfully; they should also indicate when plans for the future require revision, and the direction any changes and their implementations should take. The chapters in this section seek to establish accounting frameworks for providing such information. The role of management control is to ensure that the enterprise carries out its plans and strategies effectively and efficiently; accounting information is vital to the proper fulfilment of that task.

7

Absorption Costing

J. Lewis Brown

Absorption costing, or as it is sometimes termed total costing, is probably the oldest system of cost accounting in operation. Even though it was introduced at a very early stage in the development of cost accounting methods, it is still widely used. Considerable problems are inherent in any application of absorption costing, as the author of this chapter recognises, and yet absorption costing continues to flourish. In fact, a partial adoption of absorption costing is recommended by the Accounting Standards Committee in its standard on stocks and work-in-progress. Since many firms still approach the pricing decision in terms of 'adding something on to total cost', full or total costing provides some information on which to base a selling price decision – but of an imprecise and significantly inaccurate nature, argues the author. The growing use of the contribution margin approach in performance measurement and cost analysis has led to an increasing use of direct or marginal costing for internal purposes, but the advocates of traditional absorption costing methods argue strongly that both variable and fixed costs are necessary to produce goods and, therefore, fixed cost overheads should be inventoried. Distinctions between variable and fixed costs are valuable for a range of managerial decisions, and the traditional absorption cost proponents recognise that value, arguing that such information is readily available from traditional financial statements. The issue to be resolved is one of timing. When should fixed factory overhead be released as expense? At the time it is incurred, as a period cost? Or at the time of sale of stock, as a cost of sale? The issue is narrowed, then, to one of whether or not fixed overhead should properly be part of inventory cost.

Conceptually, absorption costing is a simple and fundamental method of ascertaining the cost of a product or service. The direct cost of manufacturing a product – the cost of direct materials used, direct wages and any other expenses associated directly with the product – is calculated and to that figure is added an estimated amount to cover overheads and profit. Obviously, it is fairly easy to calculate the direct costs but more difficult to decide an equitable charge for overheads and profit. In fact, this problem of calculating overhead cost has proved a controversial topic for many years and has been highlighted by the introduction of an alternative system, known as marginal or direct costing, prior to the second World War. During the first World War, a form of absorption costing called 'cost plus' costing was used extensively, particularly in government contracts for the supply of military equipment. That system was simple: a fixed percentage was added to total cost, to cover profit.

Following its introduction, it is perhaps surprising that marginal costing has not been adopted more extensively than has been the case to date. The problems inherent in absorption costing are so difficult to resolve that many proponents of marginal costing argue that any absorption costing 'solution' is conceptually invalid. Nevertheless, despite the opposition of the marginal costing enthusiasts, absorption costing continues to flourish – so much so, in fact, that the accounting standard on stocks and work-in-progress (SSAP 9) recommends that they be valued at that cost which includes production overhead.

Overheads include any costs not directly attributable to a product or service; in other words, any cost which is not a direct material, direct wage, or direct expense. Usually, such overheads can be divided into three categories: production; administration; selling and distribution. Where appropriate, however, further categories can be created, such as research and development. These categories are established for control purposes, so that costs can be identified for important functions in an undertaking.

The control of overhead expense is an increasingly important function of the management accountant. For many years, there has been a tendency for overhead costs to rise more sharply and more frequently than other cost elements. Reasons for this include:

1 Inflation, under which most expenses, but especially salaries, energy costs, rates and the like, have risen rapidly and considerably.

2   Improvements in control techniques, where the direct costs of materials and material-holding have been reduced.
3   Automation and mechanisation, where labour costs have been reduced but where increased installation, maintenance and operation costs have been incurred.
4   Specialist services, where industrial and commercial enterprises have increasingly resorted to outside specialists – such as market researchers, behavioural scientists, taxation advisers, etc.
5   Advertising and promotional costs and practices, with most enterprises being forced to meet increasing competition by more extensive and more frequent advertising and promotion.
6   Business size, where increases in the size and structural complexity of business enterprises have necessitated the institution and operation of effective and costly control systems.

ELEMENTS OF COST

The main elements of an absorption cost analysis are illustrated in Table 7.1; such a statement shows at a glance the costs of producing each product and the profit for the period.

When that kind of analysis is presented, it is easy to accept the data as a sound criterion for decision making. However, the problem arises: Are the figures reliable, or acceptable? Assuming that accounting records have been maintained accurately, it could be accepted that the sales row is correct and that the totals column is correct, though doubt must be expressed concerning the other figures and estimates in the statement.

It is probably fair to say that the prime cost figures are relatively accurate, allowing for minor errors in charging out hours worked or materials used, but the overhead charges are, at best, arbitrary. This area has caused the greatest part of the controversy between absorption and marginal costing, so it is appropriate to explore the systems of charging overheads to product costs.

The recovery of overhead in production costs is a tedious and far from simple operation. Clearly, much will depend on the nature of the business or industry. If a company produces one type of aircraft at the rate of one a month, this is a different proposition from a company which produces dozens of different types of food products, at least one of which has an output of several hundreds of thousands

Table 7.1
Absorption costing statement (£000s)

	A	B	C	Total
Direct materials	200	500	100	800
Direct wages	100	300	200	600
Direct expenses	20	50	30	100
Prime cost	320	850	330	1 500
Production overhead	180	350	270	800
Production cost	500	1 200	600	2 300
Administration overhead	120	260	170	550
Selling & distribution overhead	80	140	130	350
Total cost	700	1 600	900	3 200
Sales	800	2 000	1 200	4 000
Total cost	700	1 600	900	3 200
Profit	100	400	300	800

of cans a day. Each category of overhead has to be considered separately, so that production cost can be ascertained.

PRODUCTION OVERHEAD

Included in production overhead would be all items of indirect materials, indirect labour and indirect expenses. It is easy to establish the amount of production overhead incurred during an accounting period; the difficult part is to relate those costs to specific production costs. It is proposed that the task should be undertaken in three stages: allocation; apportionment; absorption. The first two stages are concerned with charging overheads to the department or cost centre in which production is being carried out, so that the cost of production is ascertained in respect of each department, while the third stage is concerned with charging the cost incurred by a department to each product being manufactured.

A simple example will serve to illustrate this three-stage procedure. A factory has six manufacturing departments and its total production costs for one month are £1 000 000. The first stage is to allocate or charge direct to the departments wherever possible. For example, salaries of staff engaged exclusively in a department will be charged to that department, and the cost of a service used exclusively by one department will be charged direct to that department. Much of the production overhead cost cannot be allocated in this simple, direct way. The larger part of such cost will have to be apportioned between cost centres.

The apportionment of overheads depends very largely on managerial discretion and corporate policy, but a number of traditional basis are employed. The nature of the overhead will usually determine the choice of apportionment method. The most common methods use floor area, plant value, employee numbers, material values, and technical estimates.

Such overhead costs as rent and rates can be apportioned according to the floor areas of departments. In our example, if the annual rent of the factory amounts to £50 000 for a total floor area of 10 000 sq ft, and if Department 3 occupies 2 000 sq ft, the amount charged to that department in respect of rent will be £10 000 a year.

Overhead costs like insurance or depreciation can be apportioned according to relative plant values. For example, with an annual insurance charge of £10 000 for machinery and plant valued at £400 000 and with Department 2 using plant valued at £100 000, the amount charged to that department in respect of insurance would be £2 500 a year.

Canteen subsidies, health and welfare costs, sports facilities costs and the like can be apportioned according to relative employee numbers. For example, if total annual canteen costs for a factory with 10 000 employees are £100 000 and if Department 4 contains 3 000 employees, the amount charged to that department in respect of canteen facilities will be £30 000 a year.

Material values can be used to apportion the costs of storage and warehousing. If total annual costs for storage amount to £200 000 in respect of £3 000 000 of used materials and if the goods released from storage to Department 6 are valued at £600 000, the amount charged to that department in respect of storage costs will be £40 000 for the year.

Sometimes it may be necessary to consult specialists for guidance on the apportionment of certain overheads. For example, if departments do not receive individually metered supplies of electricity, it may be necessary to ask an electrical engineer to estimate departmental consumptions based on machine power, number of appliances, and so on.

When production overheads have been allocated and apportioned to departments or cost centres, management can be presented with a report of the costs incurred by each cost centre. It must be emphasised, however, that these cost figures will not be wholly accurate. If the apportionment has been carried out realistically, though, they will be at least representative. Accuracy can never be achieved in absorption costing, and even if it were possible the process would be much too costly and time consuming. Nevertheless, the information generated provides management with a useful guide to the cost of operating each department.

Unfortunately, such a report of the costs of overhead ascribed to each department does not mean that the procedure is completed. Our example assumed six manufacturing departments. Additionally, service or functional departments will usually have to be considered. Now, assume that there are two service departments to support the six manufacturing units. So far in the procedure followed, the two service departments would have been allocated or apportioned overhead cost in the same way as the manufacturing departments. However, the costs of service departments cannot be passed on to their end-products because, by their nature, such departments do not manufacture goods. Thus, costs of service departments must be borne by the manufacturing departments, necessitating a laborious process of re-apportioning service costs between production departments.

When a group has numerous service departments, that process may be particularly difficult and complex. For example, if one of the service departments is a canteen, the cost of operating it must be apportioned over all the manufacturing departments and other service departments. Furthermore, service departments may be interdependent; the canteen will feed the boilerhouse staff, while the boilerhouse will supply power to the canteen, and so on. There are a number of acceptable methods which can be used in an attempt to apportion service department costs to production departments, but perhaps the best is that of repeated distribution.

Table 7.2 presents the breakdown of apportioned total production overhead between the eight departments, and shows the estimated service provided by the two service departments to each of the other

Table 7.2
Production overhead apportionment and estimated service provision

Departments	Apportioned production overhead	Estimated service provision	
		Dept X	Dept Y
1	£120 000	10%	20%
2	£200 000	20%	5%
3	£100 000	5%	10%
4	£180 000	10%	20%
5	£140 000	15%	20%
6	£160 000	20%	15%
X	£60 000	—	10%
Y	£40 000	20%	—

departments. Estimation of the proportionate service provision is perhaps the most difficult part of the procedure and might require the cooperation of experts in the field of each service department. The cost of a service department is apportioned to other departments according to the agreed percentage of service rendered. The process is repeated until the cycle is completed, as shown in Table 7.3.

It can be seen from the distribution summary in Table 7.3 that this re-apportionment of overhead is very arbitrary. However, using this approach does mean that all the overhead costs have been charged against production departments so that the final stage of absorbing the overheads into products manufactured in those departments can be completed. This stage is the essence of absorption costing, in that each product absorbs its estimated share of the production overhead.

Overheads must be recovered according to some estimated rate, normally based on a budget. In the majority of industries, it would be quite impossible to use actual recovery rates because the amount of expense incurred would not be known until after the event. It is estimated, therefore, to produce a forecast of the amount of overhead for a future period so that an estimated rate of absorption can be calculated.

Absorption rates

A variety of criteria have been used to decide a rate for the absorption of overheads.

Table 7.3
Production overhead distribution

Departments	Apportioned overhead	Distributions						Total
		X1	Y1	X2	Y2	X3	Y3	
1	120 000	6 000	10 400	520	208	10	5	137 143
2	200 000	12 000	2 600	1 040	52	21	1	215 714
3	100 000	3 000	5 200	260	104	5	2	108 571
4	180 000	6 000	10 400	520	208	10	5	197 143
5	140 000	9 000	10 400	780	208	16	5	160 409
6	160 000	12 000	7 800	1 040	156	21	3	181 200
X	60 000	(60 000)	5 200	(5 200)	104	(104)	(2)	—
Y	40 000	12 000	(52 000)	1 040	1 040	21	(21)	—

The most common are:

1 a percentage of direct material cost;
2 a percentage of direct labour cost;
3 a percentage of prime cost;
4 a rate per unit produced;
5 a rate per labour hour;
6 a rate per machine hour.

Perhaps it is inadvisable to generalise and claim one of those methods to be the best. The circumstances of a particular situation must be considered before a choice is made. In broad terms, however, the fifth and sixth methods seem preferable to the others in most, if not all, cases.

Most overhead costs are incurred as a function of time – for example, rates, rent, salaries and depreciation occur with the passing of time – and so it is reasonable to suggest that, in the interests of consistency, overheads should be absorbed as a function of time. Thus, the hourly-based rates of absorption are to be recommended. Discretion must be exercised, of course, in determining whether labour hours or machine hours are more appropriate.

To illustrate the production overhead absorption rate approach, consider the budget of Department 5 in the earlier examples. The cost estimate for a specific job is being prepared. The production data associated with that job are shown in Table 7.4, and the effects of the adoption of each of the six absorption rate methods listed above are shown in Table 7.5.

Under the first method, a percentage of direct material cost, it can be seen that the production overhead is 50 per cent of direct material cost, so the amount of overhead to be absorbed in Job 99 is £255. This method is normally unsuitable because overhead seldom varies in proportion to direct materials.

The second method, a percentage of direct labour cost, results in Job 99 bearing £220 of overhead cost, on the basis that production overhead is 66.7 per cent of direct labour cost. This method may be reasonable when one factory-wide wage rate applies, but it will not be suitable when wage rates differ from department to department.

Using the third method, a percentage of prime cost, the amount of production overhead to be absorbed by Job 99 is calculated at £240, representing 28.6 per cent of prime cost (on the basis that £160 000 is roughly 28.6 per cent of £560 000 – in the department's 1983 budget).

Table 7.4
Production budget and job estimate

Department 5 – Production Budget 1983

Direct materials	£320 000
Direct wages	£240 000
Prime cost	£560 000
Production overhead	£160 000
Production cost	£720 000
Planned units of output	400
Planned labour hours	80 000
Planned machine hours	16 000

Job 99 – Estimate

Direct material cost	£510
Direct labour cost	£330
Prime cost	£840
Labour hours required	100
Machine hours required	25

Table 7.5
Job overhead absorption rate methods

Absorption method	Prime cost	Production overhead	Production cost
% of direct material cost	£840	£255	£1 095
% of direct labour cost	£840	£220	£1 060
% of prime cost	£840	£240	£1 080
rate per unit	£840	£400	£1 240
rate per labour hour	£840	£200	£1 040
rate per machine hour	£840	£250	£1 090

This method is a combination of the first and second methods, and so shares the weaknesses of both.

The fourth method, using an absorption rate per unit of product, results in a charge of £400 per unit as an average of the estimated production overhead across the planned output of 400 units. This method looks the weakest of the six described, unless all the products being manufactured are of similar or equal value.

The labour hour rate approach, the fifth method, results in the apportionment to Job 99 of production overheads of £200 (on the basis that, in the department's 1983 budget, production overhead represents £2 per labour hour planned). If labour is a predominant factor in the production process, this method is preferable.

Under the sixth method, the machine hour rate approach, the production overhead burden for Job 99 is £250 (on the basis that production overhead in the budget represents £10 an hour). If machinery is a predominant factor in production, this method is preferable.

While the recovery of production overheads by means of a three-stage operation is important, it is essential that overheads should be controlled carefully. Results should be monitored by the use of budgetary control and standard costing systems. A budget for production overhead should be prepared, standard costs and standard recovery rates established, and deviations from the standards set should be analysed as variances.

The absorption of production overhead is central to absorption costing and is the most difficult part of the system. Once the production cost has been established, it forms the basis for calculating total cost. The other principal categories of overhead expense are administration overhead and selling and distribution overhead.

ADMINISTRATION OVERHEAD

All costs incurred in the administration activities of a business will be included in administration overheads, irrespective of whether such costs are materials, wages or expenses. A budget for administration overhead should be prepared so that actual results can be monitored. A monthly budget report should be presented to management giving details of each element of overhead and any significant variance should be analysed and explained.

In terms of expenditure, the control of administration overhead is similar to that of production overhead, that is, control is through budgets and the reporting of variance. Recovery of overhead is a different matter, however. The procedure followed with production overhead is not possible with administration overhead owing to the inherent difficulties of relating any administration expense with a particular product or department. A simple example will underline the difficulties. If the chief executive's secretary receives a salary of £8 000 a year, and the firm produces large numbers of each of dozens of products, how much should be charged to each product?

How, then, can administration overheads be charged to products? No sophisticated or scientific method is available, so a very arbitrary method is usually chosen – namely, charging administration overhead to products on the basis of their proportionate cost of production. The system works as follows.

A company manufactures four products – Alpha, Beta, Gamma, and Delta – and incurs a total administration overhead cost of £500 000. The products incur total production costs as follows: Alpha – £200 000; Beta – £600 000; Gamma – £800 000; Delta – £400 000. On the basis that the four products incur respectively 10 per cent, 30 per cent, 40 per cent and 20 per cent of overall production costs, each product would be charged with those proportions of administration overhead; respectively £50 000, £150 000, £200 000 and £100 000.

SELLING AND DISTRIBUTION OVERHEAD

All costs incurred in marketing and distributing products will be included in selling and distribution overheads. Obvious examples include advertising, salesmen's wages and commissions, warehousing costs, transport costs and product brochures. Control of selling and distribution expense is normally exercised by a cost budget which may be analysed to show targets and results for months, divisions, products, or salesmen. Actual performance is monitored and deviations reported and investigated.

As with administration overhead, it is very difficult to charge selling and distribution overhead to products or departments. A straightforward and frequently used method is to treat selling and distribution overhead in the same way as administration overhead and charge it to products on a production-cost basis. Alternatively, the basis chosen could be production cost plus administration cost.

Using the same results as in the previous illustration, the total cost could be calculated easily by this method. Assuming that selling and distribution overhead is budgeted at £1 000 000, then the four products would be charged with selling and distribution overhead as follows: Alpha – £100 000; Beta – £300 000; Gamma – £400 000; Delta – £200 000. That would give total costs for the whole product range of £3 500 000, attributable as follows: Alpha – £350 000; Beta – £1 050 000; Gamma – £1 400 000; Delta – £700 000.

Alternatively, selling and distribution overhead could be apportioned on a sales-mix basis. Assuming that total sales for all four products were expected to reach £4 600 000, of which Alpha would account for £552 000, Beta for £1 288 000, Gamma for £1 610 000, and Delta for £1 150 000, their selling and distribution overhead could be apportioned as follows: Alpha – £120 000; Beta – £280 000; Gamma – £350 000; Delta – £250 000. The four products would then bear total costs as follows: Alpha – £370 000; Beta – £1 030 000; Gamma – £1 350 000; Delta – £750 000.

It will be appreciated that these methods of charging overheads are simplistic, but absorption costing does not claim any high degree of sophistication. It attempts to analyse cost by products or departments, thereby providing management with a rudimentary guide for setting selling prices and determining costing and selling policies. Attempts have been made to take a more scientific approach to apportioning overhead costs to products, but they have often proved expensive and not significantly better than the 'rule of thumb' system. This is particularly true of selling and distribution costs.

Functional cost analysis can be used to analyse selling and distribution overhead by products or by product lines. Such costs as advertising, invoicing, warehousing, sales administration, and delivery could be apportioned to products in any one of a variety of ways. For example, delivery costs could be charged to products according to the weights of product units and the distances over which they are transported; advertising costs could be attributed directly or proportionately on a space basis to the products or lines being promoted. It is a difficult and tedious task. While statistical sampling techniques may be employed to reduce the time and effort spent on each such operation, there are any number of inherent difficulties. Nevertheless, it makes a challenging alternative to the simpler methods and could provide a useful means of establishing overhead burdens for each of a number of products.

Overabsorption and underabsorption

So far this discussion has concerned itself with the actual absorption of overheads into product costs. However, a further important aspect is the actual expense incurred. The overhead incurred in running a business is known with certainty, whereas the amount of overhead absorbed is based on prior estimates of the levels of production and overhead likely to be incurred during the period. Clearly, one of the most important factors to watch will be any difference between the budgeted overheads and the actual overheads incurred, and any departures from budgeted levels of expenditure should be investigated rigorously.

Overhead is absorbed or applied at a predetermined rate, and the resultant product cost consists of a mixture of essentially different elements: *actual* direct material cost, *actual* direct labour cost, *actual* direct expenses, and *applied* (or notional) overhead cost. To follow Horngren (1977), it is better that such a total product cost should be called a 'normal' product cost rather than an 'actual' product cost.

STOCKS

At the beginning of this chapter, the dispute between absorption costers and marginal costers was mentioned. That divergence is pointed up by stock valuation. The next chapter discusses the topic of marginal costing fully and at this stage it is sufficient to mention that while absorption cost includes overheads, marginal cost only includes those overheads which vary with output. Thus, when stocks of finished products and work in progress are being valued, notwithstanding the valuation method which is adopted (first in, first out or last in, first out, for instance), controversy arises as to whether this value should include a proportion of fixed overheads or exclude fixed overheads altogether.

Normally, stocks are described in one of three ways: raw materials, work in progress, and finished goods. No problem of overhead recovery arises in the valuation of raw material stocks although it would be tenable to argue for the apportionment of at least some warehousing costs. In the case of work in progress, the situation is quite different. Under an absorption costing system, production cost would be absorbed at each stage of the production process; stocks remaining at the end of a trading period will have been charged with an appropriate amount of production overhead. In some cases, administration overhead may have been charged to work in progress, but such a practice would not be in keeping with recommended accounting policies. Selling and distribution overhead should obviously not be charged to work in progress – unless, of course, some warehousing costs were apportioned.

Finished goods stock will have been charged with production overhead, may have been charged with administration overhead (even though this should not have been apportioned at this stage), and should not have incurred any selling and distribution overhead.

The problem of overhead recovery in stocks is concerned primarily with work in progress and attention should therefore be concentrated on that aspect of stock valuation. SSAP 9 explained that:

> In order to match costs and revenues, costs of stock and work in progress should comprise that expenditure which has been incurred in the normal course of business in bringing the product or service to its present location and condition. Such costs will include all production-related overheads, even though they may accrue on a time basis. The method used in allocating costs to stock and work in progress needs to be selected with a view to providing the fairest possible approximations to the expenditure actually incurred . . .

To illustrate the importance of stock valuation under both systems, Table 7.6 presents alternative profit and loss statements based on the essential principles of each system. The company works a 50-week year and produces one standard product at a normal level of 50 000 units a year. The product has a variable cost of £4 a unit and sells at £12 a unit. Budgeted costs per annum are: Production – £150 000; Administration – £80 000; Selling and distribution – £60 000. During Year 1, it is forecast that production will run at 100 per cent capacity but that sales will amount to only 60 per cent of production; in Year 2, production will only reach 60 per cent capacity, but sales will attain the target level of 50 000 units.

The question of which method has shown the operating position more fairly or more clearly is an open one, susceptible to subjective resolution. On balance, the marginal costing approach yields the better guide to what has happened and how the company stands at the end of each year. Consider, for example, the following. In Year 1, under the absorption costing approach profit was stated at £10 000;

Table 7.6
Alternative profit and loss statements (£000s)

ABSORPTION COSTING APPROACH				MARGINAL COSTING APPROACH		
Year 1				*Year 1*		
Sales			360	Sales		360
Marginal cost	200			Marginal cost	200	
less Stock	80			*less* Stock	80	
		—	120			— 120
			240			240
Fixed overheads:				Fixed overheads:		
Production	150			Production	150	
less Stock	60			Administration	80	
		— 90		Selling etc.	60	
Administration		80				— 290
Selling etc.		60		Loss		(50)
		— 230				
Profit		10				
Year 2				*Year 2*		
Sales			600	Sales		600
Marginal cost	120			Marginal cost	120	
plus Stock	80			*plus* Stock	80	
		— 200				— 200
			400			400
Fixed overheads:				Fixed overheads:		
Production	150			Production	150	
plus Stock	60			Administration	80	
		— 210		Selling etc.	60	
Administration		80				— 290
Selling etc.		60		Profit		110
		— 350				
Profit		50				

under the marginal costing approach a loss of £50 000 was reported. In Year 2, the absorption costing approach revealed a profit of £50 000; the marginal costing approach resulted in a profit of £110 000 being reported. When sales were low in Year 1, the marginal costing approach reflected the true position: when sales are lower than budgeted levels, profit is low. In Year 2, when sales recovered, profits under marginal costing were high. As Harris (1936) commented:

... a manufacturing company cannot realize a profit until its products have been sold. It cannot make a profit merely by producing goods for inventory.

That still holds good today!

PRICING POLICIES

Many firms still seem to base their pricing policies on absorption or total costing. Harvey and Thompson (1980), quoting a survey by Atkins and Skinner (1975), summarised as follows:

The main method of pricing appears to be adding a percentage to cost. A typical comment was, 'Though efforts are made to escape from the cost-based attitudes of pricing, we have no other starting points in most cases.' Costs are most often obtained by the use of absorption (or full) costing.

Absorption costing produces a means for determining selling prices, but in most cases accuracy cannot be achieved due to the nature of the overheads included in the calculations. Nevertheless, the method gives data which can help in decision making, and many firms operate such a system. The major alternative is marginal costing and this is considered in Chapter 8.

REFERENCES AND FURTHER READING

Anthony, R. N., 'The rebirth of cost accounting', *Management Accounting* (USA), October 1975.

Atkins, B., and Skinner, R., 'How British industry prices', *Industrial Market Research*, 1975.

Baxter, W. J., and Oxenfeldt, A. R., 'Costing and pricing: the cost accountant versus the economist', *in* Solomons, D. (ed), *Studies in Cost Analysis*, London: Sweet & Maxwell, 1968.

Demski, J., and Feltham, G., *Cost Determination: a Conceptual Approach*, Ames, Iowa: Iowa State University Press, 1976.

Dobson, R. W., *Distribution Cost Accounting*, London: Gee, 1950.

Grinnell, D. J., 'The product costing role of committed and discretionary fixed overhead costs', *Cost and Management* (Canada), March–April 1970.

Harris, J. N., 'What did we earn last month?', *NACA Bulletin*, 1936.

Hart, H., *Overhead Costs: Analysis and Control,* London: Heinemann, 1973.

Harvey, M., and Thompson, T., 'The cost pricing fallacy', *Accountancy*, August 1980.

Horngren, C. T., *Cost Accounting: a Managerial Emphasis,* 4th edn. Englewood Cliffs, N.J.: Prentice-Hall, 1977.

Owler, L. W. J., and Brown, J. L., *Cost Accounting and Costing Methods,* Plymouth: Macdonald & Evans, 1978.

Patterson, R., 'Stock valuation since SSAP 9', *Accountancy*, April 1979.

Shank, J. K., *Matrix Methods in Accounting*, Reading, Mass.: Addison-Wesley, 1972.

Thomas, A., *The Allocation Problem: Part Two*, Sarasota, Fla.: American Accounting Association, 1974.

8

Marginal Costing

J. Lewis Brown

Marginal or direct costing has been practised in one form or another for the past fifty years, having been introduced in the early 1930s. The controversy between marginal costing and absorption costing continues and looks set to continue for many years to come. It was only in the years after the second World War that interest in marginal costing developed to a significant level. Marginal costing (which might perhaps be better named 'variable costing') applies only the variable production costs to the cost of the product. One of the principal conceptual differences between the two systems – absorption and marginal – is that marginal costing treats fixed overhead as a period cost which is charged directly against revenue rather than as a product cost which is assigned to the units produced and thereby included in stocks. Notwithstanding the views of both the accountancy profession and the revenue administrations in the United Kingdom and the United States, which hold that direct costing is not a generally accepted method of stock valuation, the proponents of marginal costing argue strongly that to incorporate fixed factory overhead in product cost is incorrect and improper. The fixed part of manufacturing overhead, it is argued, is a function of the capacity to produce rather than of the production of specific quantities of product. As Amey and Egginton (1973) summarised:

> *Absorption costing involves the averaging of costs over units of output whether the costs are fixed or variable. The result is a product cost which is an average of costs at a particular level of output: the cost figure gives no indication of the short-run cost of producing additional units ... variable costing is used widely for internal management purposes, but rarely for product valuation in external reporting.*

As discussed briefly in Chapter 7, the alternative methods have widely divergent implications for performance and profit measurement. More important, perhaps, are the significant dangers of adopting too rigid an approach to the use of marginal costing. As the author concludes, the misuse of marginal costs could easily result in setting selling prices too low to allow the recovery of fixed overheads. Nevertheless, the growing interest and participation in marginal costing show an increasing awareness of the substantial advantages associated with this method and the concepts of the contribution approach to costing and the techniques of cost-volume-profit analysis.

There is a fair amount of controversy over the meaning of marginal cost. The prevailing accounting concept is that of 'variable cost'; that is those elements of cost which vary with output. Prime costs, such as direct material cost and direct labour cost, would be included, together with direct variable expenses. This accountant's concept is different from the economist's concept, which is that the marginal cost is the incremental cost of producing one additional unit of output. In comparing the economist's marginal costing model with that of the accountant, Sizer (1961) suggested that:

> the differences are not so great as is often implied – this is partly due to a lack of understanding and that the accountant's marginal costing techniques are a practical application of the economist's marginal cost and marginal revenue theory.

In 1961, following publication of two reports – one in the United States (National Association of Accountants) and one in the United Kingdom (Institute of Cost and Management Accountants) – professional interest in marginal or direct costing was heightened and the succeeding two decades have seen a considerable debate as to the merits or otherwise of marginal costing.

Wright (1962) has provided a succinct definition of marginal costing:

> Direct costing, then, is an accounting system that separates expenses that vary with volume from those that do not. In manufacturing companies, this requires that only direct manufacturing expenses be charged to inventory and then matched against revenue for the determination of realized income. Period expenses are charged directly to profit and loss for the period in which the money was spent.

This concept of charging period or fixed costs against profit, rather than absorbing them into products, is the central issue in the absorption costing versus marginal costing debate.

In marginal costing, overheads are classified as 'fixed', 'variable' or 'semi-variable'. From that approach, it is not possible to identify an amount of net profit per product but it is possible to identify the amount of contribution per product towards fixed overheads and profits. Contribution is an important component of a marginal costing system and it will be discussed more fully later, but a measure of its importance can be gained from a simple example. If a company manufacturing four products adopts an absorption costing approach, it might be seen that one of those products makes a net loss of £50 000 over a period. In that period fixed overheads totalled £835 000 and the aggregate profit came to £260 000. Adopting a marginal costing approach might reveal that the direct costs of that product were £200 000. If sales in the period of that product totalled £400 000, the contribution of that product would be £200 000.

In reviewing its product mix, the company might wish to abandon any loss making product. Then since it showed a net loss of £50 000 under the absorption costing method, the product described above would be a candidate for discontinuance. Consider, however, what would have happened in the period under review if that product had not been produced. The contribution of £200 000 would have been forgone and the total profit of £260 000 would have been reduced to £60 000.

It would be dangerous to give the impression that absorption costing gives the 'wrong' answers and marginal costing the 'correct' ones. Marginal costing is not a panacea for decision makers, but it can be argued that it provides a more appropriate base on which to found such decisions as pricing and volume levels.

COST CLASSIFICATION

Marginal costing has the essential task of grouping overhead costs into categories – fixed, variable, and semi-variable. In general terms, the semi-variable category costs can be analysed to separate its components into either fixed or variable elements; a simple example would be telephone charges, which are based on a fixed rental and a variable charge per call made. Costs can be represented graphically, as shown in Figure 8.1 which looks at the three categories of overhead cost on a total basis and on a unit basis. Those graphs illustrate a paradox of marginal costs, in that a fixed cost is fixed in total but is variable per unit, whereas a variable cost is variable in total but is fixed per unit. Of course, it has been assumed that a fixed cost is fixed, while a variable cost is variable with production. It is appreciated that this may be a little naive, in that a fixed cost may only be fixed in the short term. More plant may be required, for instance, which would increase depreciation charges, or more supervision may be called for; these developments would give rise to a 'stepped cost' situation, under which fixed costs are fixed for a certain range of production, rise markedly at some threshold point, and continue at a fixed rate for the next range of production, and so on. Similarly, a variable cost may change as economies of scale are gained, though seldom by any significant

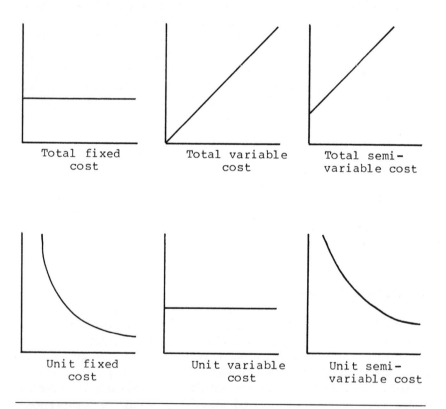

Fig. 8.1 **Total and unit cost graphs**

proportion. These refinements to the underlying concept will be discussed later.

The problem of analysing costs by category can prove difficult in practice, although a number of techniques have been adopted to effect such an analysis – the least squares method, the range method, the high–low value method, the scattergraph, and so on. At this stage it is not necessary to describe and discuss each of those methods, but consideration of the least squares method and the scattergraph will exemplify the analysis process. Both are based on the principle of the linear relationship represented by the equation

$$y = a + bx$$

where y is average total cost, a is the fixed element of that cost, b is the variable element, and x is a measure of activity. As an illustration, maintenance cost can be considered, in which the measure of activity, x, is machine hours.

An example

A company operates a number of machines of similar type and the budgeted operational data for a five-month period are shown in Table 8.1. Under the least squares method, the average total cost

Table 8.1
Maintenance costs

Budgeted data for five-month period	Feb	Mar	Apr	May	Jun	Total
Running hours	4 800	4 000	3 600	4 400	3 200	20 000
Maintenance costs (£)	21 600	20 000	19 200	20 800	18 400	100 000

Least squares analysis	Feb	Mar	Apr	May	Jun	Σ
Deviations from average hours (x)	+800	—	−400	+400	−800	—
Deviations from average cost (y)	+1 600	—	−800	+800	−1 600	—
x^2 (000s)	640	—	160	160	640	1 600
xy (000s)	1 280	—	320	320	1 280	3 200

would be calculated as follows. The least squares criterion is employed in statistics to determine whether a line through a number of points provides the best possible fit and a full description can be found in most statistical textbooks – see, for example, Freund and Williams (1982). The least squares formula for calculating b, the slope of the average cost line, is

$$b = \frac{\sum xy}{\sum x^2}$$

and Table 8.1 also gives the relevant variables for calculating those quantities. From the values in the table, it can be seen that b = 3 200 000/1 600 000 or b = £2. Average monthly cost is £20 000, and therefore the following calculation can be made:

$$£20\,000 = a + £2\,(4\,000)$$

where average monthly operating hours are 4 000. From that statement, it can be calculated that a = £12 000.

Those data could be presented in scattergraph form – as shown in Figure 8.2 – from which it might be seen that the 'best fit' line through the five points C_1 to C_5 intercepts the vertical axis at a point equivalent to £12 000.

The assumption that fixed costs are fixed and variable costs variable with production is fundamental to such basic graphical presentations of marginal costing data. It is particularly useful in that a series of graphs can be assembled, providing readily understood information to assist in decision making. The principal value of such information is the speed with which it can be used rather than its precision.

BREAKEVEN ANALYSIS

Traditional methods like the breakeven chart and its analysis can show quickly and simply the estimated results of trading at various levels of activity. Such charts show fixed and variable costs and sales revenue so that profit or loss at any given level of production or sales can be ascertained. From the graph, a breakeven point can be determined – at which neither profit nor loss is made – as can the safety margin – the amount by which sales could fall before a loss is

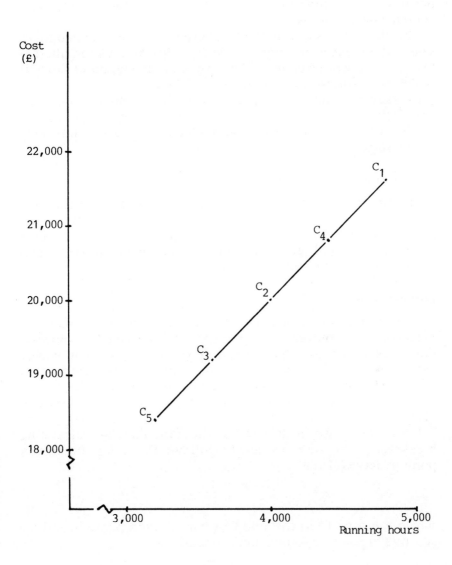

Fig. 8.2   Maintenance costs

experienced. The graph shown in Figure 8.3 is based on the following simple data: period fixed costs – £300 000; variable costs per unit – £5; selling price per unit – £15; production and sales volume – 40 000 units.

The chart shows clearly the breakeven point and the margin of safety; the breakeven point is at sales of 30 000 units (or, alternatively, breakeven revenue is £450 000), and the margin of safety is 10 000 units (or, in revenue terms, £150 000).

Breakeven points can be calculated by formula, also. Such calculations require the derivation of the contribution per unit of product and the profit–volume ratio, which can be discussed briefly at this stage.

Contribution

Contribution is the amount which a product generates towards total fixed overheads and profits. It can be described as either sales revenue less marginal cost or fixed cost plus profit. In the simple example shown in Figure 8.3, contribution is £10 per unit (£15 sales revenue less £5 marginal cost).

Profit–volume ratio

Profit–volume ratios reveal the rate of contribution per product as a percentage of turnover; while it might better be called a 'contribution-sales percentage', the term 'profit–volume ratio' is now widely used. In the simple example shown in Figure 8.3, total contribution is £400 000 for total sales revenue of £600 000, giving a profit–volume ratio of 66.7 per cent (or, taking unit figures, £10 as a percentage of £15).

From these two relationships, the formulae for calculating breakeven points are constructed as follows. The volume breakeven point is derived from:

$$B_v = \frac{F}{C}$$

where F is total fixed cost and C is contribution per unit, and the revenue breakeven point is derived from:

$$B_r = \frac{F}{PVR}$$

where F is total fixed cost and PVR is profit–volume ratio.

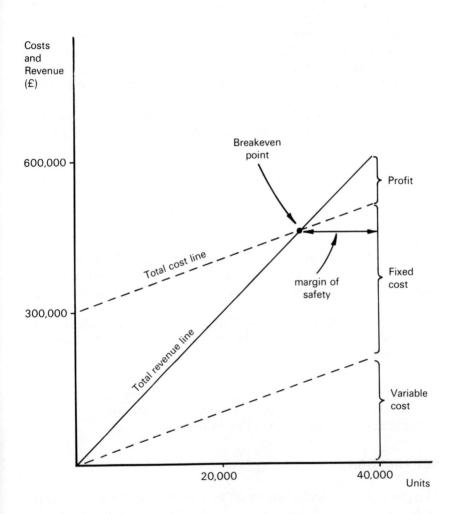

Fig. 8.3 Breakeven chart

For the earlier example, those two calculations would be as follows: $B_v = £300\,000/£10 = 30\,000$ units; $B_r = £300\,000/66.7\% = £450\,000$.

So far, the assumption has been that fixed cost remains fixed for any level of production. If that assumption is relaxed, a more realistic picture emerges. If fixed costs are assumed to rise at certain levels of activity, the 'stepped cost' approach could be used to produce a graph such as Figure 8.4, which includes the possibility that a selling price might have to be reduced to meet competition. Additionally, variable costs may be reduced in the long run.

It can be seen from the graph that complications arise with changes in the factor, and that there will be more than one breakeven point, with more than one margin of safety. This refinement of the breakeven chart imports more realism into the analysis by graphical techniques of marginal costs. A further development incorporates the 'relevant range' within which costs can be predicted with reasonable accuracy. Such a relevant range might be between the sales quantity points A and B indicated on the graph in Figure 8.4. The effect of such a narrowing of the field of concern is that it focuses the attention of management on particular levels of activity so that decisions can be taken more appropriately in a situation where predicted costs are more accurately portrayed.

Breakeven analysis has many limitations, but it provides a ready guide for decision making. The following limitations should be borne in mind:

1 fixed costs are not necessarily fixed in the long run;
2 variable costs are not necessarily strictly variable with output;
3 sales prices are not necessarily constant per unit;
4 capital employed is not taken into consideration.

KEY FACTORS

Marginal costing really shows its merit when scarce resources are being considered. Constraints or limiting factors inhibiting the production or sale of a product are key factors in a marginal cost analysis. Those factors can take a variety of forms – such as materials shortage, skilled labour scarcity, low sales demand, or insufficient capital. Where such scarce resources exist, the use of those key factors must be maximised so that contribution is as high

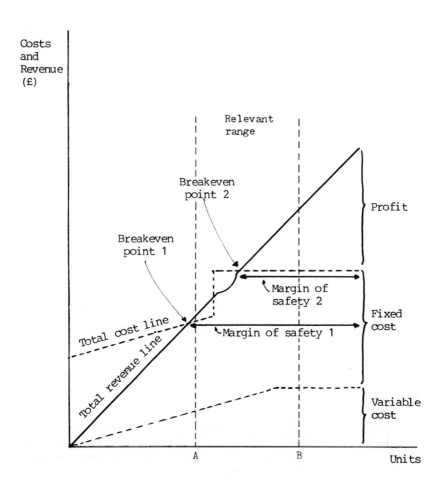

Fig. 8.4   Breakeven chart – stepped cost and relevant range

as possible. Where only one key factor is experienced, a simple marginal costing statement can show the level of activity which would optimise contribution; where two or more such key factors obtain, however, a mathematical approach is essential – linear programming, for example, as described and discussed in Chapter 5. Graphical solutions are possible, of course, but they may not always be sufficiently precise.

Single constraint

The data presented in Table 8.2 relate to a manufacturing company which produces four products and reveal the individual contributions and profit–volume ratios for each of those products.

Table 8.2
Four-product manufacturing company

	Product A	Product B	Product C	Product D
Sales price (£)	36	18	40	50
Variable cost (£):				
Direct materials	6	8	12	15
Direct labour	15	3	12	12
Variable overhead	3	1	1	5
	24	12	25	32
Contribution (£)	12	6	15	18
Profit–volume ratio	33.3%	33.3%	37.5%	36.0%

If the key factor or constraint were availability of direct materials, for instance, the appropriate criterion is contribution per direct material £; in the case of the four products, contributions per direct material £ are as follows: Product 1 – £2.00; Product 2 – £0.75; Product 3 – £1.25; Product 4 – £1.20. On that basis, Product 1 offers the highest contribution per limiting factor.

If the key or limiting factor were direct labour availability, the appropriate criterion would be contribution per labour £; in the example, those contributions are: Product 1 – £0.80; Product 2 – £2.00; Product 3 – £1.25; Product 4 – £1.50. On that basis, Product 2 offers the highest contribution per limiting factor.

If there are no scarce resources or limiting factors, the better product to concentrate on would be Product D, which offers the greatest contribution per unit. If, on the other hand, the criterion for measuring profitability (and thereby for concentrating production and effort) were the profit–volume ratio, the better product would be Product 3, which reveals a profit–volume ratio of £37.5 per cent.

Equally, of course, there may be upper limits on the quantities of any one product which can be sold in the market without altering the sales price and contribution relationships. In that situation, products would be ranked in order of their contribution, either in total or per limiting factor, or profit–volume ratio (whichever criterion was being employed). If, for example, sales demand is a further constraint, the problem moves from the relatively simple category of 'single constraint' to the more complex one of 'multiple constraints'.

Multiple constraints

When there are several limiting factors, the problem of contribution analysis and production level determination becomes very much more difficult. If only two products are manufactured and the number of constraints is also small, the optimal mix can be determined graphically. Three-dimensional graphs can cope with three products, but the complexities of that approach render the graphical solution impracticable; above three products, it is impossible to visualise graphical solutions and mathematical techniques are needed.

The simple graphical solution is illustrated in Figure 8.5, which represents the following data for a two-product manufacturing firm. Product A sells for £40.00 a unit; it requires 16 lbs of material costing £0.50 a lb; it takes 2 hours to go through the first stage of processing costing £3.00 an hour and 4 hours to go through the second stage costing £4.00 an hour. Product B sells for £48.00 a unit; it requires 19 lbs of material costing £1.00 a lb; it takes 3 hours in the first processing stage and 2 hours in the second.

In the coming period, the firm faces the following constraints. A maximum of 600 hours will be available in process stage 1 (P1) and 600 hours in process stage 2 (P2). There is a shortage of both types of raw material, so that only 1 920 lbs of material will be available for Product A (M1) and 3 420 lbs of material for Product B (M2).

These constraints may be plotted as shown in Figure 8.5, and a

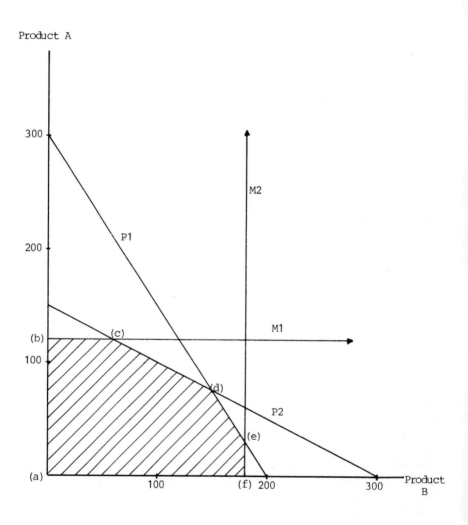

Fig. 8.5   Two-product manufacturing firm

feasible production area determined – the hatched portion of the graph. The parameters of the feasible area are delineated by the constraint lines, and the nodal points (a) to (f) represent the feasible limits of each constraint. The contribution at each nodal point can be calculated as follows:

(a) 0 units of A = £0 contribution; 0 units of B = £0 contribution; total contribution = £0.

(b) 120 units of A = £1 200 contribution; 0 units of B = £0 contribution; total contribution = £1 200.

(c) 120 units of A = £1 200 contribution; 55 units of B = £660 contribution; total contribution = £1 860.

(d) 75 units of A = £750 contribution; 150 units of B = £1 800 contribution; total contribution = £2 550.

(e) 25 units of A = £250 contribution; 180 units of B = £2 160 contribution; total contribution = £2 410.

(f) 0 units of A = £0 contribution; 180 units of B = £2 160 contribution; total contribution =£2 160.

The optimal contribution is obtained, therefore, at a production of 75 units of A and 150 units of B.

PRICING POLICY

As has been seen in Chapter 3, one of the most important functions of a marginal costing system is as an aid to pricing decision making. The marginal cost of a product is comprised of prime cost and variable overhead, so it is argued that marginal costs are relatively more accurate; perhaps it might be better to claim that, as marginal cost excludes all fixed overhead, it is less inaccurate than an absorption cost.

The application of marginal cost in the determination of prices can be exemplified by the familiar case of a special rail ticket. To attract football fans from Southbury to travel to Northbury to watch their team play in a cup match, the railway operators offer a return ticket at a special rate of £5, compared with the regular return price of £15. Clearly, the implications are that the marginal costs of providing an additional train will be covered; there may be some contribution also, but the fixed overhead would be recovered in the regular price of a ticket and there may be some shortfall there. The problem of basing selling prices on marginal cost is to make certain that sufficient contribution will be generated to recover all fixed overhead and to create an adequate profit. Pricing can be determined by considering what the market would pay or by calculations based on some profitability measurement, such as a profit–volume ratio.

In the former case, once the marginal cost is ascertained, it can be compared with the probable market price and the contribution determined. In the latter case, products would be appraised in terms of a desired profit–volume ratio.

A simple example may make the point clearer. A company produces six products, as illustrated in Table 8.3, which presents a pro forma profit and loss statement.

Table 8.3
Six-product manufacturing company

Forecast profit and loss statement (£000s)

	Product A	Product B	Product C	Product D	Product E	Product F	Total
Sales revenue	*1 500*	*833*	*2 333*	*1 667*	*1 000*	*2 667*	*10 000*
Marginal cost	900	500	1 400	1 000	600	1 600	6 000
Contribution	*600*	*333*	*933*	*667*	*400*	*1 067*	*4 000*

Fixed overhead 3 000

Profit 1 000

The company has forecast that it can produce the six items at the marginal costs shown and, at that level of output, fixed overheads are budgeted at the levels set out in the statement. If management determined that a minimum profit of £1 000 000 was required in the coming period, then a total sales revenue of £10 000 000 would be required. Those criteria would dictate a desirable profit–volume ratio of 40 per cent (£4 000 000 as a percentage of £10 000 000) and individual product sales revenue targets at levels consistent with profit–volume ratios of 40 per cent on average. Those targets and the forecast production levels will determine the individual product selling prices. The italicised figures in the pro forma statement represent these management estimates based on the marginal cost forecasts.

Obviously, in the real world, management would not aim at a uniform profit–volume ratio of 40 per cent for each of the six products, but would vary the individual ratios to suit market conditions, scarce resource usage, and so on. However, the average profit–volume ratio of 40 per cent provides a useful guide for setting individual product prices.

ADVANTAGES AND DISADVANTAGES

At various points, the advantages and disadvantages of marginal costing have been outlined as specific matters were discussed, and it may be helpful to summarise them briefly at this point. In most cases, because absorption costing and marginal costing are contrasting approaches rather than complementary ones, advantages of one approach are disadvantages of the other and vice versa.

The advantages may be summarised as follows:

1 Marginal costing provides management with more appropriate information for decision making.
2 The profit and loss statement is not distorted by changes in stock levels. Stock valuations are not burdened with a share of fixed overhead, so profits reflect sales volume rather than production volume.
3 Profit–volume analysis is facilitated by the use of breakeven charts and profit–volume graphs, and so on.
4 Pricing decisions can be based on the contribution levels of individual products.
5 The analysis of contribution per key factor or limiting resource is a useful aid in budgeting and production planning.
6 Responsibility accounting is more effective when based on marginal costing because managers can identify their responsibilities more clearly when fixed overhead is not charged arbitrarily to their departments or divisions.

Similarly, the disadvantages of marginal costing can be summarised as follows:

1 Difficulty may be experienced in trying to analyse fixed and variable elements of overhead costs.
2 Managers may find it difficult to adjust their thinking to profitability measurement in terms of profit–volume ratios.

3   Stock valuations (as, for example, under SSAP 9) may require the use of absorption costing methods.
4   The misuse of marginal costing approaches may result in setting selling prices which do not allow for the full recovery of overhead. This may be most likely in times of depression or increasing competition, when prices set to undercut competitors may not allow for a reasonable contribution margin.

REFERENCES AND FURTHER READING

Amey, L. R., and Egginton, D. A., *Management Accounting: a Conceptual Approach*, London: Longman, 1973.

Freund, J. E., and Williams, F. J., *Elementary Business Statistics: the Modern Approach*, 4th edn. Englewood Cliffs, N.J.: Prentice-Hall, 1982.

Hart, H., *Overhead Costs: Analysis and Control*, London: Heinemann, 1973.

Harvey, R., and Thompson, T., 'The cost pricing fallacy', *Accountancy,* August 1980.

Horngren, C. T., *Cost Accounting: a Managerial Emphasis,* 4th edn. Englewood Cliffs, N.J.: Prentice-Hall, 1977.

Institute of Cost and Management Accountants, *A Report on Marginal Costing,* London: ICMA, 1961.

National Association of Accountants, *Application of Direct Costing,* New York: NAA, 1961.

Owler, L. W. J., and Brown, J. L., *Cost Accounting and Costing Methods*, Plymouth: Macdonald & Evans, 1978.

Sizer, J., 'Marginal costing: economists v accountants', *Management Accounting*, April 1961.

Wright, W., *Direct Standard Costs for Decision-making and Control*, New York: McGraw-Hill, 1962.

9

Alternative Forms of Budgeting

John MacArthur

A pervasive theme of this handbook is that one of the most important functions of management is planning. In that planning process, budgeting plays a vital and varied role, and is a valuable tool in decision making. As the author recognises, budgeting and budgetary control lie at the very heart of the managerial planning and control processes. Significant advantages attach to budgets and their preparation, not least the heightened awareness among organisational members of the problems faced by their colleagues and of the different factors and elements involved in running a business. With a budget, people in the organisation become more conscious of the need to husband and preserve scarce and expensive resources. A budget provides management with an important measure for self evaluation and can be used to measure performance, efficiency and progress. 'Budget' is a generic term, covering many and varied types of planning document and proposal. All have the common feature of being quantified plans expressed in money terms. Budgets are designed to fulfil a variety of objectives: the planning and coordination of activities, motivation and evaluation of performance, identification and communication of corporate objectives and targets, authorisation of actions, and so on. Over and above those considerations, however, budgets fill another important managerial need: they bring planning to the forefront of operating and financing decisions. The main focus of this chapter is on short run budgeting for the day to day operational activities of an enterprise, and the author discusses the essential features of both planning and control budgets, introducing the important concept of opportunity costing (or a derived 'economic' cost) into the budgeting process. He covers often overlooked aspects of budgeting for non-production overheads, examining the incremental and zero-based approaches, and ends by examining the problems associated with uncertainty – one of the most difficult obstacles in the budgeting process.

As a ready guide, budgets can be classified conveniently into three groups that represent the different time spans or budget periods covered by the planning process.

Typically, the planning horizon for long-term budgeting stretches fives years or more into the future, and two main types of budget emerge from the long run planning process: strategic budgets and capital budgets. The strategic budget details the desired or planned profits and resources of an enterprise over its long term future. In broad terms, it puts money values on the enterprise's longer term objectives as perceived by senior management. Capital budgeting is concerned with the selection and financing of capital investment projects in the next budget period that are designed to lead the company towards the desired future states depicted in the strategic budget. Failure to identify suitable investment proposals for selection in those circumstances, of course, may lead to a revision of the long run objectives and the strategic budget.

As described in Chapter 4, the general consensus of the 'how to do it' sections of the extensive capital budgeting literature is that investment proposals should be prepared on a project by project cash flow basis and analysed using discounted cash flow models. This is appropriate if the boundaries of projects can be defined easily and where they are largely independent of each other, but is less satisfactory otherwise. More recent discussion has suggested dealing with the interdependence of projects by linking them together using the models of portfolio theory.

Budget items with planning horizons between one and five years away fall into the medium term category. Such items will be constrained by the long term capital budgeting decisions taken and by the objectives of the enterprise. Budgets falling within this time span will include those for advertising and promotion, research and development, and training. Such expense items will be directed towards influencing or determining behaviour in the medium term, whether of sales demand, product quality, or labour skill.

Many budget items have only short run impact, typically less than twelve months, but nonetheless form an integral part of the enterprise's planning to achieve long run objectives. The main focus of this chapter is on this essential area of budgeting. The concern is with budgeting for the day to day operational aspects of the business, and the budgeting process may be conducted in several alternative ways to help management plan and control the short term future of the enterprise. As with medium term budgeting, management's planning freedom is limited by the 'fixed' constraints – such as existing organisational structure or plant capacity. Figure 9.1 depicts some of the more traditional aspects of budgeting for the short term future.

Master budget

By definition, a master budget is the agreed master plan in money terms for the coming budget period, typically one year. It is the summation of all the separate budgets of an organisation's functional units and it represents the short run targets for a business. The master budget is considered to be the central short run planning document as it embodies the financial aspects of all the expected decisions during the year.

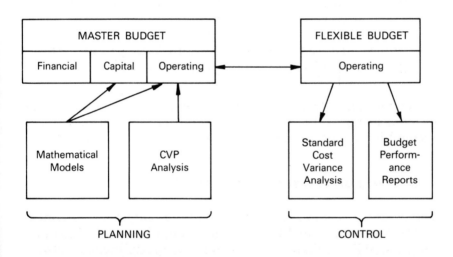

Fig. 9.1   Traditional short run budgets

Failure to achieve the master budget in any way will mean that the company has not realised its short run objectives, but this will not measure how efficient the company has been in producing its actual output. As discussed in Chapter 10, this requires a flexible budget, which is the operating part of the master budget adjusted to the revenues and costs expected for the actual level of production during the budget period. This the control budget. The arrows to and from the master budget and the flexible budget in Figure 9.1 represent these direct links between the costs and revenues of the master (planning) budget and the flexible (control) budget in a traditional budget system. They are essentially different views of the same budget since they represent the output of the same budgeting process.

Recent research into budgeting from a behavioural theory and systems theory viewpoint has indicated that such a single budgeting process is unlikely to produce an effective multi-purpose budget – see, for example, Amey (1979) and Otley (1977). An interesting hypothesis is that a 'good' planning budget is not necessarily a 'good' control budget because they serve different purposes. As Amey (1979) commented:

> Planning is . . . essentially an economic problem, which should be stated in economic terms. Control is concerned with quite different considerations, namely stabilization or regulation, which are not necessarily economic in character. The effectiveness of a control budget is measured solely by the results it produces, not by any relation the data it contains may have to economic reality.

As represented in Figure 9.1, traditional management accounting textbooks suggest that budgets based on the same principles can accomplish both purposes equally well.

PLANNING AND CONTROL BUDGETS

The essential features of both a planning budget and a control budget are outlined in Table 9.1, and a simplified worked example can be used to highlight those features and the differences between them. The traditional master and flexible budgets are examined in the light of that example. The example focuses attention on the production budget, ignoring budgeting for non-production overhead costs (which are considered separately later in this chapter).

A company is setting its production master budget for the coming trading period. The present output of products can be classified into three main groups – as suggested in Table 9.1 – and two new mutually exclusive alternative groups are being considered to replace the product lines in an existing group. The annual revenue and cost projections are given in Table 9.2.

Table 9.1
Essential features of planning budgets and control budgets

Planning budget	Control budget
Objective to facilitate choice between options, that is to aid decision making.	Objective to help keep the actual results within reasonable bounds, that is to help control the impact of decisions.
Problem of the allocation of, and claims on, resources.	Problem of stabilisation and regulation.
Consideration of costs and revenues in terms of programmes and outputs, that is to link inputs and outputs and indicate reasons for costs.	Consideration of items of expenditure and of functions, that is emphasising the inputs to the business.
Judged by its relation to reality.	Judged on its effectiveness in maintaining equilibrium.
Total business systems emphasis.	Individual partisan emphasis on responsibility and cost centres.

Table 9.2
Revenue and cost projections (£000s)

	Present product groups			Alternative product groups to replace C	
	A	B	C	D	E
Sales revenue	200	350	250	270	270
Production cost	160	320	289	215	216
Gross margin before non-production costs	40	30	(39)	55	54

Group C has been a stable product line for several years but is now experiencing a downward trend. The research and development department has proposed D and E as two equally profitable alternative product lines to replace C, either of which would involve minimal changes to the fixed production capacity charges since they could utilise plant and equipment currently used to produce

Group C products. The production budget proposal, therefore, is to combine D or E with A and B. A more detailed analysis of the cost projections for the three groups under review, based on conventional absorption costing principles, is given in Table 9.3. That analysis is subject to the following constraints and practices.

Table 9.3
Detailed cost analysis (£000s)

		Product C	Product D	Product E
Direct materials:	Type X	160	—	—
	Type Y	—	130	130
	Type Z	—	10	20
Direct labour:	Class I	10	10	5
	Class II	60	12	12
Prime cost:		230	162	167
Variable overhead:		5	5	5
Variable cost:		235	167	172
Fixed overheads:	Foreman's salary	6	6	6
	Rent and rates	5	5	5
	Depreciation	20	20	15
	Re-tooling	—	1	1
	Factory overhead	23	16	17
Total cost:		289	215	216

Existing stocks of direct material type X are sufficient to produce three-quarters of the projected annual output of Product C. There is no alternative projected use for this material within the company; it cost £128 000 but would only realise £50 000 if sold. The remaining one-quarter of the annual requirement of this material would cost an estimated £32 000 – making a total cost of £160 000 for Type X material. Direct materials type Y and Z are in common use for product groups A and B, as well as for proposed groups D and E. The costs shown in the analysis are those of expected average replacement cost for the coming period.

Class I employees are paid a set annual wage, irrespective of output produced. If proposal E were accepted, half the present workforce would be idle, without any alternative work, for at least twelve months. The current union agreement precludes the company from making those employees redundant during the coming budget period. If either proposal D or proposal E were chosen, only a fifth of the present Class II workforce would be required. One month's paid notice would have to be given to the others at a cost of £4 000; total redundancy payments, wholly payable within the first nine months after leaving the company, are estimated at a further £30 000.

The foreman's salary is a fixed annual sum, irrespective of the product group selected. However, if none of the proposed alternatives were selected, the foreman would be transferred to product group A to replace a temporary employee earning £4 360 a year. The net saving, after one month's paid notice to the temporary foreman, would be £4 000.

The depreciation charge is for multi-purpose plant and machinery purchased three years ago and suitable for either D or E, subject to relatively minor expenditure on re-tooling, estimated to cost £1 000 for either proposal. The net realisable value of the plant and machinery is currently £80 000 and is expected to have fallen to £50 000 by the end of the coming budget period. Proposal D would utilise existing equipment fully, but proposal E would require only three-quarters of it. It is considered that any machinery thereby left idle could be rented out for £2 000 a year.

An economic planning budget, based on the notion of opportunity cost, can be reconstructed for the three groups C, D, and E as shown in Table 9.4, and a brief explanation of some of the calculations will serve to make the concept clearer.

If the Type X material in stock is used to make Product C, the best future alternative opportunity forgone (measured in money terms) is the possible sale of that material outside the company for £50 000. The original cost of that material is clearly 'water under the bridge' – a past sunk cost about which nothing can now be done – and is irrelevant for planning future alternatives to aid decision making.

There is a fixed commitment to pay Class I employees for the whole of the budget period, irrespective of the availability of work. Class I wages are not, therefore, an economic cost under any of the three alternatives. The desirability of having such an underemployed workforce is, of course, a qualitative input into the decision process and other, non-monetary considerations may influence the final choice.

Table 9.4
Reconstructed economic cost analysis (£000s)

		Product C	Product D	Product E
Direct materials:	Type X (opportunity cost, 9 months)	50	—	—
	Type X (purchase cost, 3 months)	32	—	—
	Type Y (purchase cost, 12 months)	—	130	120
	Type Z (purchase cost, 12 months)	—	10	30
Direct labour:	Class I	—	—	—
	Class II (basic)	60	12	12
	Class II (paid notice)	—	4	4
	Class II (redundancy)	—	30	30
Variable overhead:		5	5	5
Fixed overheads:	Foreman's salary (opportunity cost)	4	4	4
	Rent and rates	—	—	—
	Economic depreciation	30	30	30
	Re-tooling	—	1	1
	Idle machinery rental	—	—	(5)
	Factory overhead	—	—	—
Total economic cost:		181	226	231
Sales revenue:		250	270	270
Net economic gain:		69	44	39

In terms of ranking the three alternatives, any future costs that are the same for all three proposals – such as the variable overhead –can be left out without harm. This is the procedure commonly proposed for 'decision' budgets. For a 'planning' budget, however, it is advisable to include all future costs so that the total economic cost of each alternative proposal can be compared with the total revenue. The full short term effect of each proposal can then be seen on the cash flows of the company. It is also the only sure way of determining that the best alternative is, in itself, acceptable by producing a positive net economic gain.

The foreman's salary is irrelevant as it will be paid whether any or none of the proposals is finally chosen. However, the company could save the salary of the temporary foreman if none of the proposals were accepted, and this salary represents, therefore, an opportunity cost for each of the three alternatives. This is an example of the 'total business systems emphasis' of the planning budget, as outlined in Table 9.1.

The rent, rates and factory overhead are future fixed commitments of the whole factory, irrespective of any choice between the three alternatives, and are not an economic cost to be included in the planning budget of any of the options. The allocation of such costs to product groups is decided by predetermined and arbitrary methods, which are always unnecessary for a planning budget.

The depreciation charge based on original cost does not involve any future expenditure and is clearly an irrelevant 'sunk cost'. The economic depreciation charge is the opportunity cost of deferring sale of the plant and machinery for one year, assuming that this is the best available alternative forgone if any of the three proposals is accepted. The initial re-tooling cost is an incremental cost, wholly included in the planning budget for the coming period.

The apparent decision to follow from the economic cost analysis in Table 9.4 would be to defer replacing Product C for at least one year, since C yields the highest net economic gain. This would be a mistake, stemming from the arbitrary choice of one year as the base period for the comparison of the three alternatives. In fact, the profitable first nine months projected for group C masks the final three months when the product group would make only a small gain, because of the need to buy new stocks of direct material X for this period. This is illustrated in Table 9.5 which examines the final three months of the year for Product C.

That analysis reveals that Product C would make a net economic gain of just £6 000 in that quarter of the period. By comparison, proposal D would generate a net gain of £11 000 (£44 000 × ¼) and proposal E would make a net gain of £9 750 (£39 000 × ¼). Product group C offers the worst alternative of the three.

Table 9.5
Economic cost analysis – Product C (final three months) (£000s)

Direct materials:	Type X	32
Direct labour:	Class II (£60 000 × ¼)	15
Variable overhead:	(£5 000 × ¼)	1
Fixed overheads:	Foreman's salary (£4 000 × ¼)	1
	Economic depreciation (£30 000 × ¼)	8
Total economic cost:		57
Total revenue:	(£250 000 × ¼)	63
Net economic gain:		6

The correct initial decision, then, is to retain product group C for nine months and thereafter to plan to adopt proposal D – if the current initial conditions still hold. This decision could not have been 'guessed' from the initial analysis of revenues and costs based on conventional absorption costing methods – which predicted a gross loss of £39 000 for Product C in the coming period. Yet this is the way in which a typical master budget is constructed. It fails to achieve the objective of a planning budget, which is to facilitate the choice between alternatives (that is to aid decision making) primarily because it does not model the organisation in terms of the short run future decision making opportunities available. Such a master budget is not designed to resolve 'what difference does it make' questions since it includes revenues and costs over which the organisation has no decision making power during the budget period (sunk costs and committed costs) and ignores other revenues and costs which are within its control (opportunity costs). The master budget of that type fails, therefore, by not representing fully the economic reality of the budget period.

These comments should not be taken to suggest that a conventional master budget is useless. Its preparation promotes communication between, and coordination of, the subunits of an organisation. For example, the sales management team must be in touch with production managers to ensure internal consistency between the sales and production budgets. A master budget is also the only comprehensive summary of all the projected revenues and costs, irrespective of the organisation's discretionary decision making power over those revenues and costs. That is essential for budgeting the financing requirements (the cash budget) for the forthcoming period. The master budget can, therefore, be considered as an intermediate step between the planning and control budgets.

Once a decision has been taken to adopt a particular alternative, the 'plan' becomes a 'decision'. A control budget is needed to monitor the effects of the decision, but this does not imply that the planning process ends as control of the actual output begins. There is also a need to monitor and control the planning budget.

Controlling the planning budget

Certain requirements must be met by a short run planning budget which embodies, in greater or less detail, the totality of the 'correct decisions' to be made for a specified period.

The long term and short term objectives must be defined explicitly so that plans can be prepared with a clear end in mind. This is easier in theory than in practice. The objectives of the budget planning process may be a profit level and growth pattern deemed satisfactory to top management rather than optimal, however simplistic and undynamic such aims might appear.

The critical planning variables and parameters must be identified and specified accurately. Such components will include the following:

1 the projected rate of inflation;
2 the effect of technological progress on products and production processes;
3 the demand function for each of the enterprise's products or services;
4 the availability and/or quality of capital, labour, and material resources, and their cost;
5 the expected actions and reactions of competitors;
6 the interaction of the short run with the longer run (a dynamic aspect) – the major concern being the long run success of the enterprise;
7 legal and statutory controls and regulations;
8 the needs of suppliers and customers (credit terms, service levels, and so on);
9 the speed and effectiveness of advertising impact on future demand;
10 productivity levels of the workforce;
11 the prices and supply of the factors of production.

Significant shifts in the objectives, parameters, or variables will require changes in the short term planning budget. If immediate and previously unplanned decisions are called for, there will have to be changes in the control budget as well. This is another dynamic aspect of real life budgeting.

It will be clear from the list of typical parameters and budget variables that the planning boundaries should be wider than the internal boundaries of the enterprise. Conventional budgeting tends to concentrate on identifying easily measurable endogenous (or internal) variables and to ignore exogenous (external) variables that interact with the endogenous variables. For instance, a company may require a certain component for one of its products. During the most recent peak production period, the quality of the components received from the supplier was lower than normal. An investigation reveals that this situation results from the supplier's recent difficulty in employing skilled labour of the required quality. On the surface such a labour difficulty seems to be solely the supplier's problem and completely exogenous to the company's planning concerns. However, further investigation reveals that part of the component supplier's problem derives from the irregular ordering pattern of the company's buyer. That pattern forces the supplier to experience widely fluctuating demand periods for the component. The supplier is not in a position to stockpile during the periods of low demand. Accordingly, the scarcity of temporary skilled labour (required by the supplier to meet high demand periods) is linked with the internal ordering procedure of the company and is, therefore, within the confines of its planning budget. Knowledge of that interaction may affect the company's operational behaviour. For example, the company might decide to change to a different supplier for all or part of its requirements, or it could change its ordering procedure and purchase stocks of the component on a regular basis; alternatively, it might do nothing at all, believing the supplier's labour problem to be temporary.

Control budgets

As mentioned, a control budget has a different purpose from a planning budget. A planning budget seeks to model the economic realities of alternative opportunities open to the enterprise, so as to help managers make the 'right' decisions, that is, choose the alternatives that best achieve the objectives of the enterprise. A control budget, in contrast, is designed to help make the selected decisions the 'correct' ones by providing warning signals so as to keep disturbances to a minimum. The intricacies of a control budget, outlined in Table 9.1, can be illustrated by examining the Class I and II direct labour budgets of the production discussed earlier (see Tables 9.3 and 9.4).

For control purposes, the product (output) groupings of the planning budgets should be changed to more detailed and conventional input classifications, as outlined in Table 9.1. Suppose the Class II direct labour of the company described produce products A and C and are physically based in four separate departments – two machining departments, an assembly department, and a polishing department. The total wages projection will be separated into four control budgets, each for a different foreman, responsible for the effectiveness and efficiency of the workforce in his own department. Making certain assumptions, such a four-budget structure would be as shown in Table 9.6, which depicts the two different classifications.

Table 9.6
Class II direct labour budget classifications (£000s)

Control Budget Classification	Product A	Product C	Total
Machining Department 1	3	30	33
Machining Department 2	3	12	15
Assembly Department	9	6	15
Polishing Department	15	12	27
Total	30	60	90

For the reasons advanced earlier, the cost of Class I direct labour was excluded from the planning budgets for products C, D, and E. This would, however, be inadvisable in a control budget for a number of fundamental reasons. Two such reasons are the need for internal consistency between the various parts of the total control budget, and behavioural considerations.

Internal consistency

Most management accounting textbooks give detailed illustrations of budgeting to show the underlying order of the budgeting process – sales budget, followed by production budget, and so on. This results from the view that a budget is primarily an aid towards coordination and implementation of the decisions taken by individuals within an organisation. From that standpoint, it is clearly necessary, for example, for the wages of Class I direct employees to be included in the cash budget as an outlay and in the production budget as a planned expense for an identical amount, subject to time lag adjustments.

Similarly, control budgets must be internally consistent to facilitate comparison with the actual results, which, in this term, should automatically be internally consistent. Deviations from the budget will then be meaningful as the control budget will be constructed along the same lines as the actual outcome is recorded and reported. It is interesting to note that the relationship of a control budget to reality differs from that of a planning budget – see Table 9.1. The equivalent criterion for a control budget is rather its effectiveness in giving 'signals' that indicate a need for action to maintain equilibrium.

Behavioural considerations

A planning budget including Class II direct labour at zero 'cost' may be a good thing from an economist's point of view for aiding decision making, but the inclusion of such a nil cost in a control budget may well have a marked demotivating effect. Class II employees may construe such a characteristic as reflecting a low value judgement of their 'worth' to the enterprise, especially when compared with the high positive 'value' included for Class I employees.

This is a simple example of the care needed when designing budgeting systems. It is dangerous to adopt a mechanistic view of budgeting – assuming that employees will automatically do their best to achieve a budget, irrespective of the way in which it has been prepared. Research into the behavioural aspects of budgeting (discussed further in Chapter 17 of this handbook) has revealed the fallacy of such a notion.

BUDGETING FOR NON-PRODUCTION OVERHEADS

The process of budgeting for non-manufacturing activities presents very different problems from budgeting for the direct costs of making a product or providing a service. The relationship between the input of resources and the final output of the organisation is much less clear cut. The number of employees and the quantity of direct material required to make a specified product can be measured physically, but the optimal size and composition of, for instance, a legal department may not be so easily or precisely determined. The tasks and output of a legal department cannot be linked directly with the organisation's physical output.

The traditional approach to budgeting for non-production costs is the incremental method. This deals very simply with the complexities involved in determining the total level of staff and support activities necessary to run an organisation effectively and efficiently; it ignores them. The focus of attention is limited to any proposed changes in the existing level of funding, rather than to the budget as a whole. Thus, inefficiencies in the existing arrangements may be carried forward year after year, unless management has other ways of identifying them. The incremental approach and an alternative, more comprehensive approach – the zero-based review or budget – are considered in this section, and they are represented diagrammatically in Figure 9.2.

Incremental and zero-base approaches

An incremental budget is presented by a manager to his superior in terms of total money required for the coming period. Except for any proposed increase, little explicit information is given about the activities covered by the total funds requested. By contrast, the starting point for developing a zero-base budget (ZBB) is, by definition, 'zero' activity – not taking existing levels of activity into account or for granted. ZBB describes in some detail the activities represented by both current funding and proposed increases. The focus of attention is, therefore, diverted from the required money input to a functional unit towards the activities and output of the unit in question. Accordingly, ZBB allows a far more critical and thorough analysis of the unit's total activities in the light of the needs and objectives of the organisation and it facilitates the consideration of alternative ways of providing the required service for the coming budget period.

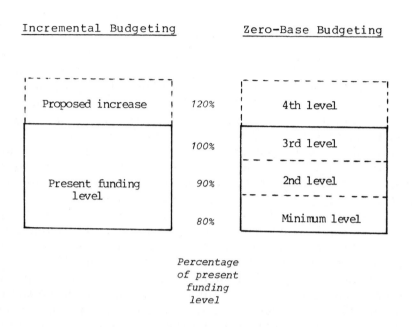

Incremental Budgeting   Zero-Base Budgeting

Proposed increase — 120% — 4th level

100% — 3rd level

Present funding level — 90% — 2nd level

80% — Minimum level

Percentage of present funding level

Fig. 9.2   Incremental budgeting for non-production overheads

Zero-base budgeting is one member of a 'family' of output-oriented budgeting systems which emphasise a programmed or systematic approach to budget setting and resource allocation. Other related budgeting systems are the Planning – Programming – Budgeting System (PPBS) and Management by Objectives System (MBO). Much of the pioneer work has been carried out in the United States in the public sector – in which, of course, output and program achievement is of far greater concern – and there has only been a limited attempt to introduce these systems into private sector budgeting. Dean and Cowen (1979) and Stonich (1977) have, however, described significant applications of ZZB in the private sector; Pyhrr (1973) pioneered the formalisation of ZBB as a practical management procedure.

Phare (1979) described zero-base budgeting as:

... comprehensive managerial planning and resourcing from the setting of specific goals for each project or activity through the setting of priorities on the basis of hard data – not emotion.

Six basic stages

In more practical detail, the ZBB process can be exemplified and described in six stages using the budgeting data of an hypothetical legal department of XY Limited. The legal department has three 'decision units': debtors' follow-up; litigation; estates.

Stage 1 is common to both ZBB and the traditional incremental approach. Senior management will decide the general assumptions regarding the state of the economy as a whole; within that framework, lower levels of management will determine the more detailed assumptions for each of the decision units (in Stage 2).

The planning assumptions for the XY legal department for 1983 are as follows:

1   proposed legislation will come into force by June 1983, giving customers wider statutory purchasing rights;
2   the average number of debtors and the repayment period allowed will remain unchanged from the current year;
3   planning permission for two additional factory buildings will be sought, requiring legal work in the Estates unit;
4   an outstanding claim against the company for damages will be settled by September 1983, entailing work in the Litigation unit.

Stage 2 identifies the 'decision units'. Decision units can comprise any groupings of activities which facilitates the analysis required later. The most convenient way to define the decision units is to make them synonymous with the traditional cost centre or budget unit, so that the responsible decision unit manager is easily identifiable. The legal department of the company can be considered as a single decision unit or, as is the case here, as a set of three decision units with distinctive functions – debtors' follow-up, estates work, and litigation work.

Decision units may be defined also by activity, such as travel or communication, or by special one-off projects or programmes. The choice of notional units should be based on the costs and benefits expected from the various alternatives.

Stage 3 calls for analysis of each decision unit. It is the stage at which incremental and zero-base budgeting part company. The ZBB of each decision unit can be considered in four convenient steps.

First, the decision unit manager identifies and states the objectives of his unit, following discussions with his superiors and subordinates. Identifying the reasons for the activities of a unit is an obvious first step – if it can be done sensibly and meaningfully. Policy makers often agree as to the activities of a unit much more easily than they can agree its objectives.

For example, a manager may wish to expand his unit so as to gain recognition and subsequent promotion, but his immediate superior may wish to maintain the status quo because he does not want to take unnecessary risks so near his retirement. The eventual agreed objectives for the unit in question would probably represent some compromise between the manager and his superior and reflect the relative influences of the parties involved in the bargaining process. Further agreement would then be required on the means of achieving those objectives.

Owing to the potential conflict problem, stated objectives are often concluded in bland, general and somewhat obvious terms, with very little operational significance. Furthermore, any quantified targets tend to give agreed activity levels, without any indication of the reasons why those levels were chosen.

Secondly, the current activities and resources employed are described in sufficient detail for a higher level manager to understand.

Thirdly, alternative ways of achieving the purpose of the decision unit are considered by the decision unit manager and his superior; the best one is selected. Reasons for acceptance or rejection are stated in respect of each alternative. This third step is the 'creative' part of the process and calls for an estimate of the costs and benefits associated with each of the alternative 'decision packages'.

Traditional incremental budgeting concentrates on changes and improvements to existing activities and ignores completely any new, potentially better, ways of achieving purposes. In real life limited numbers of viable alternatives are available and marked degrees of resistance to change exist in any organisation, so the traditional incremental approach may be a more amenable and practicable line to follow.

Fourthly, having decided upon the most appropriate alternative, the decision unit manager determines different possible levels of activity and expenditure from the minimum level upwards which provide varying degrees of specified service. This permits 'fine tuning' in the allocation of resources to the activities of decision units in the order of priority.

These steps are illustrated below for the Debtors' Follow-Up Decision Unit in the legal department of the company.

Decision unit analysis

The objectives of the unit are agreed as: to expedite the receipt of money from debtors who have failed to pay their debts within the due period, and to advise the chief accountant on all legal aspects of deferred terms and invoice sales. The minimum performance target is set at the recovery of money from defaulting debtors which is at least double the operating costs of the unit.

Within the unit, a legally qualified unit head and deputy head, jointly responsible for general supervision, monitor the follow-up of outstanding debts which are more than six months overdue and/or greater than £5 000 in value, and advise the chief accountant. Other personnel include six debt follow-up clerks, one secretary/filing clerk and two mobile debt collectors. Other major resources comprise three company cars (one each for the unit head and the two debt collectors) and rented letter addressing and franking machines for legal action warning letters and other correspondence. It has been customary to send two warning letters before initiating legal action against defaulting debtors.

The decision unit manager has considered three principal alternative ways of achieving the unit's objectives. These are summarised in Table 9.7. Alternative 2, the use of an outside debt collection agency at a cost of £80 000, is rejected because it does not meet the minimum performance requirement. Alternative 3, the use of an outside debt collection agency at a cost of £75 000, is rejected because, while it

Table 9.7
XY Debtors' Follow-Up Decision Unit – alternatives for 1983

	Cost	Money recovered	Margin	Money recovered as % of cost
Alternative 1:				
Current activities	£50 000	£150 000	£100 000	300.0%
Alternative 2:				
Use agency A	£80 000†	£150 000	£70 000	187.5%
Alternative 3:				
Use agency B	£75 000	£150 000	£75 000	200.0%

†includes consultancy fee for advising chief accountant on legal matters

Table 9.8
XY Debtors' Follow-Up Decision Unit – incremental levels of activity for 1983

Description	% of current service level	Incremental cost	Cumulative projections 1983			
			Cost	Money recovered	Margin	Money recovered as % of cost
Increment 1 1 supervisor, 2 debt clerks, 1 secretary	24%	£18 000	£18 000	£36 000	£18 000	200.0%
Increment 2 Add 2 debt clerks, 1 mobile debt collector, 1 car	47%	£12 000	£30 000	£70 000	£40 000	233.3%
Increment 3 Add 1 deputy supervisor, 2 debt clerks, 1 mobile debt collector, 1 car	87%	£15 000	£45 000	£130 000	£85 000	288.9%
Increment 4 Add 1 rented franking machine, 1 letter addressing machine	100%	£5 000	£50 000	£150 000	£100 000	300.0%
Increment 5 Add 1 mobile debt collector, 1 car	120%	£10 000	£60 000	£180 000	£120 000	300.0%

meets the minimum performance requirement, it is not as cost effective as the unit's current activities. In addition, the big problem of re-deploying existing tenured staff would arise.

The decision unit manager proceeds, therefore, to assess the incremental levels of activity possible within the unit. That analysis is shown in Table 9.8, which examines five incremental levels – of which the first is the bare minimum service, including the fundamental tasks necessary to fulfil the top priority needs of management. The identification of those needs is a difficult but useful exercise in its own right, and should include any services needed to fulfil legal requirements imposed on the company.

For simplicity, the column in the table labelled '% of current service level' is based on money recovered – but consequently does not measure the quality of the advisory service provided to senior management. The fourth level is the current level of operating.

The legal department manager and the decision unit managers will formulate a consolidated set of decision packages for submission to senior management, ranking each increment of service in order of importance. Table 9.9 presents such a ranked submission.

Such a ranking will have been determined between the department manager and the decision unit managers, who will have agreed between themselves on the level of service that will be funded during the coming period for each of the decision units.

In respect of the estates unit, incidentally, a cost reduction is proposed by cutting the present staffing level and using external legal services for some occasional legal estate work outside the scope of the reorganised unit. This cheaper alternative was identified through use of the zero-base approach.

As a final stage, after senior management has agreed the final selection of decision packages for the whole company, the conventional 'line-by-line' annual budget can be prepared. If the decision units are largely synonymous with the budget or cost centres of the organisation this will be a relatively straightforward conversion process.

Implementation of ZBB

At least one major international company has implemented a system that reports actual results in the same format and detail as the agreed decision unit budgets. As Phare (1979) has reported:

This has converted the zero-base process from a static, once-a-

Table 9.9
**XY Legal Department's ranking of decision units and funds
request for 1983**

Ranking	Decision unit	Incremental cost	Cumulative cost	Current year projection
1	Litigation	£25 000	£25 000	£20 000
2	Debtors' Follow-Up	£18 000	£43 000	£48 000
3	Estates	£10 000	£53 000	£19 000
4	Debtors' Follow-Up	£12 000	£65 000	
5	Estates	£6 000	£71 000	
6	Debtors' Follow-Up	£15 000	£86 000	
7	Litigation	£5 000	£91 000	
8	Debtors' Follow-Up	£5 000	£96 000	
		£96 000		£87 000

Summary of proposed expenditure

	Proposed	Current	Change
Litigation Decision Unit	£30 000	£20 000	+50.0%
Debtors' Follow-Up Decision Unit	£50 000	£48 000	+ 4.2%
Estates Decision Unit	£16 000	£19 000	−15.8%
	£96 000	£87 000	+10.3%

year budget-negotiating exercise into a dynamic vehicle for on-going management planning, control and performance improvements.

The successes and failures of the implementation of zero-base budgeting in the 1970s have been well documented – see, for example, Thomas (1979). The main area of application has been in the staff and support functions, although it has been used in budgeting manufacturing overheads (for example, quality control, plant maintenance, and so on). It may be advisable to introduce ZBB into an organisation's budgeting system over a period of years, gaining experience and confidence in it as a management tool. In any case, ZBB is only beneficial in departments when managers have discretionary decision making power over significant costs. Otherwise, the potential cost savings and resource optimisations are minimal and would probably not justify the increased expenses of more detailed zero-based analysis.

One of the principal advantages of the ZBB approach is the large amount of analysis provided to decision makers, enabling them to consider alternative ways of providing a particular service. As with any management technique, however, a zero-based system must be designed and adapted to suit the organisation and not vice versa.

UNCERTAINTY

An underlying problem common to all forms of budgeting is future uncertainty. A manager is unlikely to be sure of the precise outcome of any decision. He may be faced with a range of possible outcomes that can be predicted with varying degrees of accuracy.

There are a number of ways of dealing with uncertainty in budgeting. Some of the more common ways can be illustrated by using the hypothetical vehicle running costs budget for a sales branch of a manufacturing company. The costs for the period 1970–1980 are shown in Table 9.10.

The variable running costs are to be budgeted at £1 a mile for 1981. It is expected that vehicle mileage will follow the historical ten or eleven year pattern during 1981. The management accountant preparing the budget might choose one of the three commonly used methods: single value budget estimate; high, low and most likely value budget estimates; probability analysis budget estimate.

Single value estimate

A manager may explicitly or implicitly ignore uncertainty by preparing only a single budget estimate that is representative of the whole range. The budget value chosen would probably be either the average value (that is, the mean or expected value) or the most likely value (that is, the mode value). As shown in Table 9.10, the mean value is near enough 9 182 miles a year; the most frequent or modal value is clearly 10 000 miles. It is higher than the mean because of

Table 9.10
AB Sales Branch A – vehicle running costs 1970–1980

Mileage recorded:

1970	9 000	1974	10 000	1978	10 000
1971	10 000	1975	9 000	1979	7 000
1972	9 000	1976	11 000	1980	8 000
1973	8 000	1977	10 000		

Grouped frequency distribution:

Mileage (x_i)	Frequency (f_i)	$x_i f_i$
7 000	1	7 000
8 000	2	16 000
9 000	3	27 000
10 000	4	40 000
11 000	1	11 000
	11	101 000

Mean = 9 182 (101 000/11)

the unsymmetrical frequency distribution of annual miles travelled, which is biased towards the higher mileage numbers, as shown in Figure 9.3.

Which is the better number to choose? Viewed from an individual branch level, the mode has distinct advantages over the mean value. For one thing it is an actual value that has been experienced. The mode is also, by definition, the most likely outcome in any one year. However, a problem arises in aggregating all the 'lower level' branch budgets into a 'higher level' total budget when the budget estimates are based on modal values.

Budgets based upon mean values can be added together quite safely. A mode is not a truly representative number for all the values in the frequency distribution – it is simply one of the values, the most likely one. It has been demonstrated that unit budgets which show a relatively small deviation from the mean value can lead to such pronounced distortions when the budgets are aggregated that the total budget is wholly unrealistic (Otley and Berry, 1979).

For example, if there are eight other sales branches virtually identical to Sales Branch A and if the standard deviation for each branch is approximately 1 170 miles, the total budget based upon mean values would be 81 800 miles (9 200 × 9), with a standard

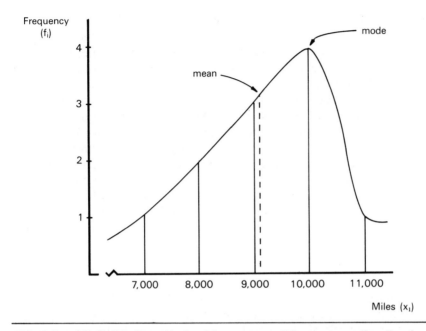

Fig. 9.3   AB Sales Branch A – histogram of frequency distribution (with an approximate continuous probability density function superimposed)

deviation of 3 510 miles; the distribution would be more symmetrical than each individual branch's frequency distribution.

The total budget based on modal values would be 90 000 miles ($10\,000 \times 9$). The individual branch modal budgets are less than one standard deviation away from the mean; $(10\,000 - 9\,200)/1\,170 = 0.68$ standard deviation. The total modal budget is over two standard deviations away from the mean; $(90\,000 - 81\,000)/3\,510 = 2.336$ standard deviations. It is a highly unrepresentative and slack budget for the nine branches considered together, with a very small probability of proving anywhere near the actual outcome.

The aggregation problem can arise whenever the unit budgets are not set equal to the mean value, whether or not the frequency distribution happens to be symmetrical. Budgets can be biased for a number of reasons other than inbuilt statistical skewness. For instance, an experienced and established manager may bias his cost budget upwards and/or revenue budget downwards to make attainment easier. A manager facing problems may do the opposite in order to create a favourable impression with his superiors.

Whatever the reasons for biasing lower level budgets, the aggregated budget has a much smaller chance of achievement than the individual lower level budgets. Obviously, there is as much need to control the budget setting process as the actual outcome of the period being budgeted. Otherwise comparisons between aggregated budgets and actual results are unlikely to be meaningful.

One way of monitoring the budget setting process for bias would be to prepare total budget estimates using alternative methods, as a rough check on the aggregation of lower level budgets. Using the earlier example, the total mileage expected by sales branch managers could be estimated by relating mileage to some other budgeted independent variable, such as budgeted sales volume, which might be expected to influence mileage, and this could be compared with the aggregated budget.

High, low and most likely value estimates

A relatively simple and straightforward way of indicating the uncertainty surrounding a budget estimate is to give the highest and lowest perceived values, in addition to a representative central value such as the mode or the mean.

Using the data in Table 9.10, the high budget value is £11 000 (at the running cost rate of £1 a mile) and the low value is £7 000; the most likely value is £10 000. These values give a feel for the skewness of the expectations, while also indicating the range of possible outcomes. Although this method has the disadvantage that it does not use all the available data, it may represent the most sensible compromise between a simple method, such as described earlier, and a more complicated method, such as described below, when the likely frequency of possible values is very uncertain.

Probability analysis estimate

The frequencies in Table 9.10 can be translated into probability form by dividing each one by the frequency total (that is, 11); for example, the probability of 7 000 miles occurring in any one year is near enough 0.09 (1/11). The frequencies or probabilities can be used to calculate an average measure of deviation around the mean, known commonly as a standard deviation (σ). The standard deviation for the sample values given in Table 9.10 is 1 168 miles (or £1 168) around a mean (μ) of 9 182 miles (or £9 182).

The standard deviation is a useful measure when it can be assumed that budget data are continuously and normally distributed, as depicted in Figure 9.4. In such cases, all that really needs to be known about the data are the average value (the mean) and the average dispersion (the standard deviation) in order to have a complete mathematical picture of the data. For example, it can then be confidently stated that just over 68 per cent of all possible budget values will lie within one standard deviation either side of the mean value, as is also depicted in Figure 9.4.

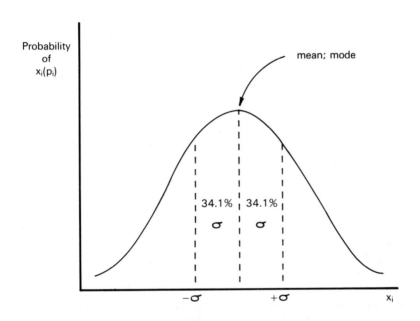

Fig. 9.4 Normal probability density function

The data in Table 9.10 are in discrete rather than continuous form, as represented by the vertical histogram lines in Figure 9.3, which also illustrates an approximate continuous probability function superimposed on the histogram – clearly showing the non-normal or skewed nature of the distribution of data. There is no justification for the use of a continuous approximation in this case, given the very few data points and the relatively large interval between them.

The calculation of the standard deviation involved the use of all the available numerical data, but it is important to make two significant reservations. First, the number actually obtained cannot be observed from the data themselves; the deviation between each possible value is constant at 1 000 and not the standard deviation of 1 168. This is perhaps intuitively strange and unsatisfactory. Secondly, the standard deviation gives no indication of the skewness inherent in the data.

In these circumstances, the standard deviation may not be a useful measure of uncertainty, and it might be better to adopt the second method – high, low and most likely value estimates. At least the 'high-low' measure of uncertainty points up actual numbers in the distribution and partially indicates the presence of skewness.

Alternatively, consider the coefficient of variation, which expresses the percentage relationship between the standard deviation and the mean. In the sales branch example, the coefficient of variation is 12.7 per cent (1 168/9 182). The higher the coefficient, the larger are the expected relative variations of likely outcomes around the mean – in other words, the greater is the perceived uncertainty. This is a relative measure rather than an absolute difference and can be usefully compared, for example, with the actual percentage variation from budget to gauge the latter's significance.

Whichever uncertainty measure is chosen, an important general point to bear in mind is that actual results can usually be expected to deviate from budget, simply due to 'random' fluctuations. Such deviations are not necessarily the 'fault' of any particular manager or controller. One of the main purposes for considering uncertainty during the budget setting process should be to establish the acceptable limits for deviations which are to be considered random and, as such, will not require investigation.

REFERENCES AND FURTHER READING

Amey, L. R., *Budget Planning and Control Systems*, London: Pitman, 1979.

Dean, B. V., and Cowen, S. S., 'Zero-base budgeting in the private sector', *Business Horizons*, August 1979.

Otley, D. T., *Behavioural Aspects of Budgeting*, London: Institute of Chartered Accountants in England and Wales, 1977.

Otley, D. T., and Berry, A., 'Risk distribution in the budgetary process', *Accounting and Business Research,* Autumn 1979.

Phare, G. R., 'Beyond zero-base budgeting', *Managerial Planning,* July–August 1979.

Pyhrr, P. A., *Zero Base Budgeting: a Practical Management Tool for Evaluating Expenses,* New York: Wiley, 1973.

Stedry, A. C., *Budget Control and Cost Behaviour,* Englewood Cliffs, N.J.: Prentice-Hall, 1970.

Stonich, P. J., *Zero Base Planning and Budgeting,* Homewood, Ill.: Dow Jones-Irwin, 1977.

Thomas, M. T., 'Another look at zero base budgeting', *The CPA Journal,* August 1979.

10

Variance Accounting

C. Stuart Jones

In this chapter, the author describes and discusses variance accounting techniques, demonstrating the presentation to management of periodic summaries of differences between actual results and predetermined budgets and standards. Such summaries are analysed by cause and responsibility. As the writer recognises, variances are most commonly associated with manufacturing industry, possibly because they were developed in that sphere of business activity, but variance analysis need not be confined to manufacturing activity. Any activity which is susceptible to definition and measurement before it takes place can be analysed for deviations. This is one of the attractive features of variance analysis, for it is sufficiently flexible for its principles to be applied to provide a great variety of variances to assist the managers of an enterprise to control its activities and plan future operations. The chapter concludes by discussing the use of variances in the processes of appraisal and decision making, and the writer draws attention to the problems associated with the use of variances derived from past performance to plan future outturn. Additionally, as Anthony and Reece (1979) and many others have emphasised:

> *. . . the terms 'favorable' and 'unfavorable' should be used with care; they denote the algebraic sign of a variance, not value judgments of managers' performance.*

Nevertheless, variance analysis is a welcome and straightforward technique for facilitating the better analysis of actual results, particularly when such analysis is conducted as promptly as practicable and reported as clearly and succinctly as possible.

The starting point for the analysis of variances is the standard cost for the product or service as derived from or used in the determination of the budget. The example in this chapter concerns a production department which constitutes a cost centre under the responsibility of a departmental manager. The department produces two products, A and B, using common resources and facilities, including two direct materials, X and Y, which can be partly substituted for each other. The standard cost for each unit of A and B is shown in Table 10.1 for the first three months of 1983.

Table 10.1
Standard sales and costs (per unit)

	Product A			*Product B*	
Standard sales price		6.00	Standard sales price		4.00
Standard costs:			Standard costs:		
Direct materials	2.00		Direct materials	1.50	
(6 lbs X @ £0.25;			(4 lbs X @ £0.25;		
1 lb Y @ £0.50)			1 lb Y @ £0.50)		
Direct labour	1.00		Direct labour	1.50	
(½ hr @ £2.00)			(¾ hr @ £2.00)		
		3.00			3.00
Contribution		3.00			1.00

Initially, it is assumed that a marginal or variable cost system is employed and, consequently, no fixed overheads are allocated to individual products. This approach simplifies the analysis and provides particularly useful information for management. The complications that arise when absorption costing is used are discussed later.

The agreed budget for the first quarter of 1983 consists of the budgeted sales and production quantities of each product multiplied by that product's appropriate standard cost for the period, as shown in Table 10.2; for simplicity, production for stock has been ignored at this stage.

Table 10.3 details the actual sales achieved for A and B in the period, together with the actual costs incurred by the department for the three-month period. The actual cost information is compiled from source documents (wages analyses, timesheets, stores requisi-

Table 10.2
Budgeted departmental sales and costs

	PRODUCT A	PRODUCT B
Sales and production units	2 000	3 000
	£	£
Sales	12 000	12 000
Direct materials: X	3 000	3 000
Y	1 000	1 500
Direct labour	2 000	4 500
Total direct costs	6 000	9 000
Contribution	6 000	3 000
		9 000
Fixed overheads		3 000
Budgeted departmental profit		£6 000

tions, invoices and so on), analysed in a form comparable with the detail given in the unit standard cost analysis (Table 10.1).

NAIVE ANALYSIS

A comparison of Tables 10.2 and 10.3 shows that the actual profit is £275 less than that budgeted for the period (£6 000 - £5 725). It is tempting to explain this difference by comparing each of the elements of the budget and actual results so that, for example, material X reveals a saving of £75 (budget £3 000 + £3 000 as against actual £3 125 + £2 800). Direct labour reveals overspending of £1 150, and so on. A little thought, however, will reveal that the departmental manager is unlikely to be happy with an unfavourable labour variance based on budgeted output of 5 000 units when his department has produced 5 300 units.

Comparison of the fixed budget with the results in this way is naive and unsatisfactory. Nonetheless, it cannot be denied that the actual profit is £275 below budget. The final result of any more sophisticated analysis should explain the causes of that variation.

Table 10.3
Actual departmental sales and costs

	PRODUCT A	PRODUCT B
Sales and production units	2 500	2 800
	£	£
Sales value	12 500	11 900
Direct materials: X	3 125 (12 500 lbs @ 25p)	2 800 (11 200 lbs @ 25p)
Y	1 120 (2 800 lbs @ 40p)	1 080 (2 700 lbs @ 40p)
Direct labour	2 925 (1 300 hrs @ £2.25)	4 725 (2 100 hrs @ £2.25)
Total direct costs	7 170	8 605
Contribution	5 330	3 295
	8 625	
Fixed overheads	2 900	
Actual departmental profit	£5 725	

FLEXING THE BUDGET

The next step is to revise the fixed budget by 'flexing' each variable cost to reflect the changes in output. This involves multiplying each variable cost by the multiple

(budgeted cost/budgeted output) $\times$ actual output

where all that is being done, in simple terms, is multiplying the actual output for the period by the standard cost for the period. Table 10.4 presents an analysis on that basis, wherein flexed budget costs are compared with actual costs to provide a meaningful overview.

An important stage in variance analysis has been reached, because Table 10.4 provides a structural framework to which all subsequent detailed analysis can be related. Column (d) reveals the

Table 10.4
Calculation of variances – marginal costing

		a	b	c	d = b − c
		Fixed budget	Flexible budget	Actual	Sales price & cost variances
		£	£	£	£
Unit sales:	Product A	2 000	2 500	2 500	
	Product B	3 000	2 800	2 800	
Sales revenue:	Product A	12 000	15 000 (2 500 × £6)	12 500	
	Product B	12 000	11 200 (2 800 × £4)	11 900	
		24 000	26 200	24 400	1 800(U)
Direct materials and labour:					
	Product A	6 000	7 500 (2 500 × £3)	7 170	330(F)
	Product B	9 000	8 400 (2 800 × £3)	8 605	205(U)
		15 000	15 900	15 775	125(F)
Contribution		9 000	10 300	8 625	1 675(U)
Fixed overheads		3 000	3 000	2 900	100(F)
Department profit		6 000	7 300	5 725	1 575(U)
Sales volume or activity variance			£1 300(F)		
Total profit variation			£275(U)		

Notes: F = Favourable   U = Unfavourable

unfavourable sales price variance of £1 800, the favourable direct cost variances of £125, and the favourable fixed overhead cost variance of £100. Together, those variances explain why the actual departmental profit of £5 725 is £1 575 less than what might have been expected for the level of output achieved. The flexible budget in column (b) shows that a profit of £7 300 might have been expected in the circumstances.

However, there is a further, and more important, aspect to Table 10.4; clearly, there has been a change in the level of activity in the department compared with that anticipated when the fixed budget was set, and this is significant. The activity level achieved is of considerable concern to management, which determined the production targets after considering the sales potential for each product. A budget of 5 000 units was fixed (2 000 units of Product A and 3 000 units of Product B), with a profit expectation of £6 000. Management would be pleased to see that a production total of 5 300 units was achieved and would have expected to see a profit of £7 300 on that output. That favourable variation of £1 300 – the sales volume variance – represents the opportunity cost of the additional output and is simply the budgeted contribution which the changed activity represents.

Alternatively, it could be calculated on the following basis. An extra 500 units of Product A were involved, each with a standard contribution of £3.00 a unit, implying a total extra contribution of £1 500; there were 200 less units of Product B, each with a standard contribution of £1 a unit, making a total lost contribution of £200; in total, an extra contribution of £1 300 should have resulted.

The departmental profit variation from budget – an unfavourable variance of £275 – can be explained by the favourable sales volume variance of £1 300 being offset by the unfavourable cost and price variances of £1 575.

DETAILED ANALYSES

It is now possible to prepare a more detailed analysis of the variances to reveal the causes, using the standard cost and actual cost data provided in Tables 10.1 and 10.3. In practice, the extent of the analysis depends upon the information needs of management and the ability of the cost accounting system to collect and retrieve the necessary information. For instance, a record of man-hours spent on each product would be required to enable the calculation of a labour efficiency variance; such recording might call for the introduction of a special job or product progressing system. In designing cost systems, the accountant must be aware both of the needs of management and of the cost involved in capturing the data. These needs and costs will alter from time to time as management faces new problems and new techniques become available, so a flexible approach is desirable.

There are many approaches to the detailed analysis of variances and perhaps the easiest is the mechanistic substitution of new periodic variables in pro forma statements. While not gainsaying the importance of a proper understanding of the principles of variance analysis, a practical and systematic framework has a lot to recommend it.

Some ground rules for variance analysis statements can be summarised at this point. First, as can be seen from Tables 10.5 and 10.6, it is convenient to record the actual costs or sales information in the left hand column (a) of the analysis tables. The final column on the right hand side of the tables will show the parallel information in terms of the flexed budget. The differences between the first column and the final column will represent the total variance for each cost item and their values will correspond with column (d) in Table 10.4. Between the first and the final column, one variable is altered at a time – from actual to standard – to isolate the variance. It is axiomatic that having once changed a variable from actual to standard it should remain at standard in subsequent columns; if this is not done, two variances will be confused.

Labour cost variances

Labour costs are analysed first because, for most production situations, they are straightforward. The analysis in respect of products A and B is presented in Table 10.5.

Two labour cost variances are calculated: a labour rate variance (reflecting the difference between the budgeted wage rate per hour and the actual wage rate per hour), and a labour efficiency variance (reflecting the increased or reduced cost because the actual hours taken to produce the output achieved were greater or lower than the standard hours specified for that level of output).

In the example, there is an unfavourable labour rate variance of £850, which might have occurred for a variety of reasons: a national

Table 11.5
Analysis of labour cost variances

	(a) Actual Cost Actual rate × Actual hrs	(b) Standard rate × Actual hrs	(c)* Standard rate × Standard hrs for actual output
	£	£	£
Product A	(£2.25 × 1 300 hrs) = 2 925	(£2.00 × 1 300 hrs) = 2 600	(£2.00 × 2 500 units = 2 500 × ½ hr)
Product B	(£2.25 × 2 100 hrs) = 4 725	(£2.00 × 2 100 hrs) = 4 200	(£2.00 × 2 800 units = 4 200 × ¾ hr)
	7 650	6 800	6 700

Labour rate variance   (Col. b – Col. a) = £850(U)
Labour efficiency variance   (Col. c – Col. b) = £100(U)
Total labour cost variances   (Col. c – Col. a) = £950(U)

*Column (c) is the flexed budget for labour costs and corresponds to the standard cost of labour for actual production wage award, or the award of increases in excess of standard, or the engagement of a more skilled grade of labour, or changes in an incentive or productivity scheme. There is an unfavourable labour efficiency variance, which might have been caused by a range of factors: excessive labour turnover and the need to train new employees, or changes in working methods, or inferior working conditions, or plant breakdowns, or short production runs.

If sufficient information is available, a portion of the labour variances can be attributed to each cause. This is important because some of the causes are outside the control of the departmental manager and should not affect adversely the appraisal of his performance, while others may be partly the result of a positive decision made by the manager – the engagement of more skilled workers, for example.

It is essential that the reasons for all variations are understood and the remedial action is taken and/or budgets and standards are revised.

Alternative labour variance calculation

As understanding of variance analysis is gained, the analyst will find that some of the simpler variances can be calculated without using any tabulation, thereby providing economy of effort and speed. For example, the labour efficiency variances can be approached as follows. The standard hours allowed to produce the actual output are compared with the actual hours taken and the difference is multiplied by the standard wage rate to produce either a favourable or unfavourable variance. For example, to produce 2 500 units of Product A should have taken 1 250 hours and to produce 2 800 units of Product B should have taken 2 100 hours, giving a standard total of 3 350 hours. The actual hours taken were 3 400 – a difference of 50 hours, which, at the standard wage rate of £2.00 an hour, gives rise to a labour efficiency variance of £100 (unfavourable).

Similarly, the labour rate variance could be calculated by comparing the standard rate of pay with the actual rate and multiplying the difference by the actual paid hours worked; for example, £2.00 was the standard rate, while £2.25 was the actual rate – a difference of £0.25 an hour for 3 400 hours, giving rise to a labour rate variance of £850 (unfavourable).

In formula terms, the labour variances may be represented as follows:

$$LRV = (SR - AR) \times AH$$

where LRV is labour rate variance, SR is standard rate, AR is actual rate, and AH is actual hours. In a similar fashion,

$$LEV = (SH - AH) \times SR$$

where LEV is labour efficiency variance, SH is standard hours, AH is actual hours, and SR is standard rate.

Material cost variances

The same approach is applied to the analysis of material cost variances as that used in analysing labour cost variances, and the variances themselves are also very similar. The material price variance is equivalent to the labour rate variance, while the material usage variance is equivalent to the labour efficiency variance.

The opportunity is now taken, however, to introduce two more advanced variances: the material mix variance and the material yield variance. These two variances are the two constituents of the material usage variance. Table 10.6 illustrates the analysis of material costs for products A and B.

The material price variance reflects the difference between the purchase price specified in the budget or standard cost statement and the actual price paid. For both products and both materials, the overall material price variance is £550 (favourable), but that total disguises the differences in type of material and product. For example, while the material price variance for material X used in Product A is £0, that for material Y used in Product A is £280 (favourable).

The material usage variance reflects the difference between the standard quantities of material allowed to produce the actual output achieved and the actual quantities used. Again, for both materials and both products, the overall material usage variance is £525 (favourable), indicating that the department has been efficient overall in the use of direct materials.

However, closer examination of Table 10.6 will reveal that the material mix variance for Product A is £153 (unfavourable), while that for Product B is £20 (favourable). The mix variance occurs because materials can be combined in different proportions to

Table 10.6
Analysis of material cost variances

	(a) Actual cost — Actual price × actual quantity at actual mix	(b) Standard price × actual quantity at actual mix	(c) Standard price × actual quantity at standard mix	(d)* Standard price × standard quantity at standard mix
	£	£	£	£
PRODUCT A:				
Material X	25p × 12 500 lbs = 3 125	25p × 12 500 lbs = 3 125	25p × (6/7 × 15 300) = 3 279	25p × 2 500 units × 6 lbs = 3 750
Material Y	40p × 2 800 lbs = 1 120	50p × 2 800 lbs = 1 400	50p × (1/7 × 15 300) = 1 093	50p × 2 500 units × 1 lb = 1 250
	4 245	4 525	4 372	5 000
	15 300			
PRODUCT B:				
Material X	25p × 11 200 lbs = 2 800	25p × 11 200 lbs = 2 800	25p × (4/5 × 13 900) = 2 780	25p × 2 800 units × 4 lbs = 2 800
Material Y	40p × 2 700 lbs = 1 080	50p × 2 700 lbs = 1 350	50p × (1/5 × 13 900) = 1 390	50p × 2 800 units × 1 lb = 1 400
	3 880	4 150	4 170	4 200
	13 900			
Total	8 125	8 675	8 542	9 200

Material price variance (Col. b − Col. a):
Product A   280(F)
Product B   270(F)   550(F)

Material mix variance (Col. c − Col. b):
Product A   153(U)
Product B   20(F)   133(U)

Material yield variance (Col. d − Col. c):
Product A   628(F)
Product B   30(F)   658(F)

£525(F) material usage variance

Total material cost variance (Col. d − Col. a)   1 075(F)

*Column (d) corresponds to the standard cost of material for actual production manufacture the product. In the example used, materials X and Y are partial substitutes for each other and discretion can be exercised during production.

The mix variance becomes particularly important when several ingredients are combined, as in steelmaking for example. To obtain a certain quality of steel, adjustments would have to be made to the mix of molten metal because of variations in the grade of scrap, pig iron and other ingredients. The possible combinations to produce a particular quality of steel are numerous and it would be impracticable to calculate a standard cost for all of them.

The material yield variance is a portion of the material usage variance and is due to the difference between the standard quantities of materials allowed to produce the actual output and the actual quantities used, other than that difference attributable to mix. Table 10.6 shows that the material yield variance for Product A is £628 (favourable), suggesting that considerable economy has been achieved during manufacture, which may have been aided partly by a more expensive mix of materials.

Alternative material variance calculations

Material variances can be calculated also in the more direct fashion described earlier for labour variances. The material price variance can be represented as follows:

$$MPV = (SP - AP) \times AQ$$

where MPV is material price variance, SP is standard price, AP is actual price, and AQ is the actual quantity of material. Similarly, the material usage variance can be represented as:

$$MUV = (SQ - AQ) \times SP$$

where MUV is material usage variance, SQ is standard quantity, AQ is actual quantity, and SP is standard price.

The material mix variance may be calculated as:

$$MMV = (AQ_s - AQ_a) \times SP$$

where MMV is material mix variance, AQ_s is actual quantities of material inputs in standard proportions, AQ_a is actual quantities of material inputs in actual proportions, and SP is standard price.

In like fashion, the material yield variance can be represented as:

$$MYV = (AQ_s - AQ_o) \times SP$$

where MYV is material yield variance, AQ_s is actual quantities of material inputs in standard proportions, AQ_o is actual quantities of material outputs in standard proportions, and SP is standard price.

Direct cost variances

The main variances calculated so far can be recapitulated as follows: LRV £850 (unfavourable), LEV £100 (unfavourable), giving an overall labour cost variance of £950 (unfavourable); MPV £550 (favourable), MMV £133 (unfavourable), MYV £658 (favourable), giving an overall material cost variance of £1 075 (favourable).

As shown in Table 10.4, there is a total direct cost variance of £125 (favourable), but that variance masked important information which needed to be made available to management. Furthermore, the analysis of the detailed variances raised many more points meriting managers' attention. Some of those were within the control or responsibility of the departmental manager, while others were

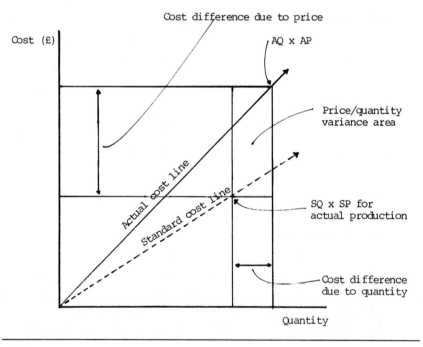

Fig. 10.1   Cost comparison graph

clearly outside his control – and, indeed, outside the control of the company.

A diagrammatic illustration of the procedure of variance analysis is given in Figure 10.1, which presents a graphical comparison of actual and standard cost for either direct material or direct labour. The graph is drawn on the assumption that the actual cost is greater than the standard cost for actual production and all variances are unfavourable.

Direct expenses and variable overhead variances

For clarity of illustration, neither direct expenses nor variable overhead was included in the earlier statements for products A and B. In practice, both categories of cost are likely to be present and will occasion two types of variance.

First, an expenditure or spending variance, which is very similar to the material price variance and is calculated in the same way, is calculated to reflect changes in the price paid. Second, where an expense varies with man-hours or machine-hours instead of unit output, an efficiency or usage variance can be calculated. It indicates the standard cost value of any difference between the standard number of man-hours allowed for the actual output produced and the actual number of man-hours worked, or machine hours where appropriate. The method of arriving at the variance in hours worked was explained earlier, and this variation is multiplied by the standard cost of the particular expense to provide a value for the variance.

A simple addition to the data provided earlier in connection with products A and B will make this explanation clearer. The budget variable overhead for the three-month period was estimated at £1 625; on the basis of a total labour utilisation of 3 250 man-hours (for 2 000 units of A and 3 000 units of B), variable overhead per man-hour was budgeted at £0.50. The actual variable overhead expenditure was £1 870, and 3 400 man-hours were worked.

On that basis, the variable overhead expenditure variance can be calculated as follows:

$$VSV = (SR - AR) \times AH$$

where VSV is variable overhead expenditure variance, SR is standard variable overhead rate per man-hour, AR is actual variable overhead rate per man-hour, and AH is actual man-hours worked. In this instance, the calculation would be:

$$VSV = (£0.50 - £0.55) \times 3\ 400$$

giving a variable overhead expenditure variance of £170 (unfavourable).

Similarly, the variable overhead efficiency variance can be calculated by:

$$VEV = (SH - AH) \times SR$$

where VEV is variable overhead efficiency variance, SH is standard man-hours for output produced, AH is actual man-hours worked, and SR is standard variable overhead rate per man-hour. In this case,

$$VEV = (3\ 350 - 3\ 400) \times £0.50$$

giving a variable overhead efficiency variance of £25 (unfavourable).

The flexed budget for variable overhead would have been calculated at £1 675 (being £0.50 an hour for the standard 3 350 man-hours for the actual production output achieved – 2 500 units of A and 2 800 units of B); the difference between actual variable overhead and flexed budget variable overhead is, therefore, £195 (that is, £1 870 − £1 675).

Sales variances

Sales variances may be calculated in two ways: related either to the effect on turnover or sales revenue or to the effect on contribution. In explaining the change in profit between budget and actual (see Table 10.4) from £6 000 to £5 725 as an unfavourable variance of £275, the latter basis must be used.

Three variances arise under either method, but with different values depending on the approach. Sales managers tend to think in terms of turnover or revenue and this approach is perhaps the more appropriate for them.

The three variances that can be calculated are: sales price variance, sales mix variance, and sales volume variance. Table 10.7 illustrates the calculation of these variances as related to turnover and it can be seen that the approach is similar to that adopted for material variances. Two points should be noted, however. First, each column is deducted from the immediately preceding left hand column in order to give the correct 'sign' for the variance; this is

Table 10.7
Turnover-based analysis of sales variances

	(a) *Actual Sales* Actual price × actual quantity at actual mix	(b) Standard price × actual quantity at actual mix	(c) Standard price × actual quantity at standard mix	(d) Standard price × budgeted quantity at standard mix
		£	£	£
Product A	£5 × 2 500 = 12 500	£6 × 2 500 = 15 000	£6 × 2 120* = 12 720	£6 × 2 000 = 12 000
B	£4.25 × 2 800 = 11 900	£4 × 2 800 = 11 200	£4 × 3 180* = 12 720	£4 × 3 000 = 12 000
	5 300 24 400	26 200	5 300 25 440	24 000

Sales price variance (Col. a − Col. b):

Product A	2 500(U)	
Product B	700(F) }	1 800(U)
Sales mix variance (Col. b − Col. c)		760(F)
Sales volume variance (Col. c − Col. d)		1 440(F)
Total sales turnover variance		400(F)

*Actual sales unit of 5 300 split in the ratio budgeted:

$$\text{Product A} \quad 5\,300 \times \frac{2\,000}{5\,000} = 2\,120 \text{ units}$$

$$\text{B} \quad 5\,300 \times \frac{3\,000}{5\,000} = 3\,180 \text{ units}$$

$$\underline{5\,300}$$

opposite to the procedure for deriving cost variances. Second, the resultant total sales turnover variance of £400 (favourable) cannot be related to the analysis in Table 10.4 since the variance explains turnover rather than profit changes.

Table 10.8 illustrates the sales variances calculated on a contribution basis. Because Table 10.4 adopts a marginal cost presentation, the analysis of the sales variances is related to contribution rather than profit. The changes in contribution provide extremely useful tools for management decision making because they approximate opportunity cost; their significance is discussed later in this chapter. Suffice it to say at this point that if absorption costing is used, then a proportion of fixed overhead is included in the direct product costs and sales variances are then calculated using profit rather than contribution. The methodology is the same, but the variances will be smaller.

The sales price variance of £1 800 (unfavourable) is the same under either turnover or contribution or profit calculation methods. The sum of the sales mix and sales volume variances in Table 10.8 is £1 300 (favourable), which is, of course, the sales volume variance or activity variance shown in Table 10.4.

A sales volume variance can be analysed further, into a market size variance and a market share variance. Again, a simple example will serve to demonstrate the calculation and interpretation of the variances. Taking the earlier illustration, for products A and B, it is assumed that the market for products A and B has grown during the period from an expectation of 50 000 units demanded to 54 000 units demanded, and that the company's share of the market has fallen from 10.0 per cent to 9.815 per cent. The change in turnover due to the increase in market size is calculated as follows:

$$MTV = MT_c \times MS_b \times BP_b$$

where MTV is market size variance, MT_c is change in total market size, MS_b is budgeted market share, and BP_b is budgeted price at budgeted mix, giving

$$MTV = 4\ 000 \times 10\% \times £24\ 000/5\ 000$$
$$= \text{favourable variance of £1 920.}$$

Similarly, the change in turnover due to reduced market share is calculated as follows:

$$MSV = MS_c \times MT \times BP_b$$

Table 10.8
Contribution-based analysis of sales variances

	(a) Standard contribution × actual quantity at actual mix	(b) Standard contribution × actual quantity at standard mix	(c) Standard contribution × standard quantity at standard mix
	£	£	£
Product A	£3 × 2 500 = 7 500	£3 × 2 120 = 6 360	£3 × 2 000 = 6 000
B	£1 × 2 800 = 2 800	£1 × 3 180 = 3 180	£1 × 3 000 = 3 000
	5 300 10 300	5 300 9 540	9 000

Sales price variance
Product A 2,500(U)
B 700(F) 1 800(U)

Sales mix variance (Col. a − Col. b) 760(F)
Sales volume variance (Col. b − Col. c) 540(F) } £1,300(F)

Total sales variance 500(U)

where MSV is market share variance, MS_c is change in market share, MT is total market size, and BP_b is budgeted price at budgeted mix, giving

$$MSV = -0.185\% \times 54\,000 \times £24\,000/5\,000$$
$$= \text{unfavourable variance of } £480.$$

Those two variances combine to give a favourable sales volume variance of £1 440 (as shown in Table 10.7). They can be calculated also on contribution basis, by multiplying the variance expressed in turnover terms by the budgeted contribution per £ of sales at budgeted mix.

For the market size variance, the calculation is:

$$£1\,920 \times £9\,000/£24\,000$$

giving a variance of £720 (favourable). For the market share variance, the calculation is:

$$£480 \times £9\,000/£24\,000$$

giving a variance of £180 (unfavourable). Aggregated, the £540 (favourable) variance corresponds with the sales volume variance on a contribution basis (as shown in Table 10.8).

Fixed overhead expenditure variance

This variance is sometimes called the budget or spending variance, and is calculated as follows:

$$OSV = AFO - BFO$$

where OSV is fixed overhead spending variance, AFO is actual fixed overhead expenditure and BFO is the flexed budget fixed overhead expenditure. The £100 (favourable) variance shown in table 10.4 may mask several significant but compensating variances. In practice, therefore it is important to calculate and report variances for each classification of expense.

The important question of fixed overhead variances is considered in more detail later in this chapter.

STANDARD COST ACCOUNTS

The departmental operating account shown in Table 10.9 is the

Table 10.9
Departmental operating account

	£	£		£	£
Opening work-in-progress valued at standard marginal cost incurred		Nil	Finished production valued at standard marginal cost:		
			Product A 2 500 units @ £3 = 7 500		
Actual costs incurred:			B 2 800 units @ £3 = 8 400		15 900
Direct material X	5 925		Closing work-in-progress		Nil
Y	2 200	8 125	Budgeted fixed overheads debited to profit and loss account		3 000
Direct labour		7 650	Unfavourable variances debited to profit and loss account:		
Controllable fixed overheads		2 900	Labour rate	850	
Favourable variances credited to profit and loss account:			Labour efficiency	100	
Material price	550		Material mix	133	1 083
Material yield	658				
Fixed overhead expenditure	100	1 308			
		19 983			19 983

pivot of standard cost accounts and is introduced at this juncture to reinforce the analysis described so far. A separate account is opened for each cost centre which is the responsibility of a manager. It is debited with the value of direct materials used, actual labour cost incurred, actual overhead costs incurred, and, if absorption costing applies, with apportioned overheads from service departments and general overhead accounts. It is credited with the standard cost of production, consisting of both finished production and any work-in-progress; both are valued according to the standard cost of the work performed. If marginal costing is used, the standard cost credited excludes any fixed overhead, whereas with absorption costing fixed production overhead and certain administration overhead are included.

The balance of the account should represent variances which are under the control of the departmental manager. At the end of the period, variances are transferred out of the operating account to the profit and loss account, and thereby written off in the period in which they are incurred.

Table 10.10 illustrates the format of the profit and loss account used for internal purposes when a standard costing system operates. It supports the principle of 'management by exception' by highlighting the impact of variances in changing the profit from that budgeted to that achieved. All the figures used can be traced to the analyses described in this chapter, and it is interesting to note how the sales variances on both profit and turnover bases are included in an informative manner.

FIXED OVERHEAD VARIANCES UNDER ABSORPTION COSTING

When an absorption costing system is used, the analysis of fixed overhead variances, with the exception of the spending or expenditure variance, becomes more complicated and the sales volume variance alters also. The reason is that absorption costing includes fixed overhead in the valuation of stock and work-in-progress – the method prescribed by SSAP 9. This leads to an underrecovery or overrecovery of budgeted fixed costs as production levels vary from those budgeted, giving rise to a fixed overhead volume variance which may be further split into an efficiency variance and a capacity variance.

Table 10.10
Profit and loss account

	Sales	Margin
	£	£
Budgeted sales and margin	24 000	6 000
Add (subtract) sales variances:		
Price	(1 800)	(1 800)
Mix	760	760
Volume	1 440	540
Actual sales	24 400	
Subtract standard cost of actual sales	15 900	
Subtract fixed overheads	3 000	
Standard profit of actual sales		5 500
Add (subtract) cost variances:		
Labour rate	(850)	
Labour efficiency	(100)	(950)
Material price	550	
Material mix	(133)	
Material yield	658	1 075
Fixed overheads spending		100
Actual profit for period		5 725

Table 10.11 is a revision of Table 10.4 to reflect the adoption of an absorption costing approach. The first important difference is the flexing of fixed overhead in column (b) to reflect the recovery of fixed overhead (£3 093) included in the valuation of the actual output. It is assumed that the fixed overhead is recovered in product costs on the basis of hours worked. The budgeted fixed overhead rate per hour is thus £0.923 (that is, £3 000/3 250 hours) and the fixed overhead standard cost for Product A is £0.462 (£0.923 × ½) and for B £0.692 (£0.923 × ¾).

This step increases the total fixed overhead variance to £193 (favourable) by introducing the volume variance of £93 (favourable); at the same time, the sales volume variance is reduced by £93 because this is now calculated at the profit level and not the

Table 10.11
Calculation of variances – absorption costing

		a Fixed Budget	b Flexible Budget	c Actual	d = b − c Sales price & cost variances
		£	£	£	£
Unit sales:	Product A	2 000	2 500	2 500	
	Product B	3 000	2 800	2 800	
Sales revenue:	Product A	12 000	15 000	12 500	
	Product B	12 000	11 200	11 900	
		24 000	26 200	24 400	1 800(U)
Direct materials and labour:	Product A	6 000	7 500	7 170	330(F)
	Product B	9 000	8 400	8 605	205(U)
		15 000	15 900	15 775	125(F)
Fixed overheads		3 000	3 093*	2 900	193(F)
Total cost of production		18 000	18 993	18 675	318(F)
Department profit		6 000	7 207	5 725	1 482(U)

Sales volume or activity variance £1 207(F)

Total profit variation £275(U)

*Actual output @ standard fixed overhead cost per unit:
Product A £0.462 × 2 500 units = £1 155
B £0.692 × 2 800 units = £1 938
3 093

contribution level. The calculation of the detailed variances is shown in Table 10.12.

A volume variance can be calculated for any category of fixed overhead, but it is customary to restrict it to fixed factory or production overhead. Most administration, selling, distribution, and research and development fixed overheads are normally written off to the profit and loss account in the period in which they are incurred and so receive treatment similar to production overhead under the marginal convention.

Table 10.12
Analysis of fixed overhead variances

		£
(a)	Actual expenditure	2 900
(b)	Budgeted expenditure	3 000
(c)	Actual direct labour hours worked @standard cost per hour $(3\,400 \times \frac{£3\,000}{3\,250})$	3 138
(d)	Actual man-hours produced @ standard cost (3 350 hrs @ £0.923)	3 093
Fixed overhead expenditure variance b − a		100(F)
" " capacity c − b		138(F)
" " efficiency variance d − c		45(U)

volume variance £93(F)

Total fixed overhead variances	193(F)

Alternative approaches

The calculation of overhead variances can be conducted in a number of different but essentially cohesive ways, and several writers have advocated alternative approaches – the three-part or four-part overhead variance analysis, for example. Amerman (1953 and 1954) gave several examples of using a number of reference points to produce alternative combinations and subdivisions of fixed overhead variances. Solomons (1968) provided a further analysis of the variation of fixed overheads.

By way of illustration, Figure 10.2 presents a taxonomy of sales, production and overhead variances.

Difficulties

If management by exception is to be useful, the significance

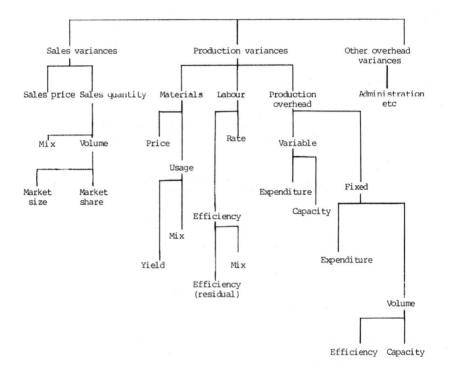

Fig. 10.2   Standard cost variances

attached to variances must be clear and unambiguous. Management must have confidence that the majority of figures which are not emphasised in reports are correct and that the reported variances have been calculated from reliable information. If credibility is to be maintained, the underlying cost accounting systems must be of a high order. Frequently, when challenged because of unfavourable variances, a manager will criticise the information recording system.

Obviously a balance has to be struck between the cost of analysis and the provision of reliable management information. This problem is heightened if the firm is in a turbulent environment with quickly changing information requirements.

The manner in which costs vary is a further problem. For illustration purposes it has been easy to assume that direct material, direct labour and direct expense costs vary directly with output; in practice, separating costs to reflect their true relative variability is extremely difficult. However, this has to be attempted if meaningful variances are to be reported. To illustrate the point further, it is customary for variable overhead to be regarded as a function of a single variable such as machine hours, whereas the facts of cost behaviour belie any such single assumption. The introduction of several bases of cost behaviour greatly increases the complexity of analysis, although the general principles remain unchanged.

INTERPRETATION AND ACTION

The manner in which variances are interpreted and acted upon is important if they are to be valuable for management control. Unfortunately, the cause of a particular variance may not be obvious. Material price variances may be caused by errors in forecasting price movements or by shifts in world prices following political changes in supplier countries or because ordering patterns have become uneconomic or because of the substitution of higher priced materials. Clearly, some reasons are within the control of the firm with the responsibility being borne by different managers, but many are outside the firm's control.

The reasons for variations are complex. It is vital that they be researched thoroughly, understood clearly and acted upon in a reasonable manner. The temptation to use unfavourable variances as a 'weapon' for criticising subordinate managers must be resisted. Such unwise use of variances would have a distinct demotivating and suboptimising effect on most managers.

It is possible for management to define limits for variances, within which no action is needed – in a similar manner to statistical quality control. In practice, such an approach is rare and investigation is usually arbitrary. Some firms leave it to each manager to investigate his 'own' variances as he feels necessary to improve future performance. Other firms favour more formal arrangements, with managers meeting to discuss variances and determine remedial action.

Generally, it is less than helpful to prescribe rigid limits (such as variations of more than £X or X per cent), since some variances will be persistently over the limit for the same reason every period. Other variances may be small but herald increasing problems.

There can be no substitute for an intelligent and flexible approach to variances if they are to be used effectively to control critical areas of a business. The same applies to the frequency with which variances are reported.

Variances are reported normally in money terms, although back-up statistical data are often very useful. For instance, a production foreman may find an awareness of man-hours gained or lost more meaningful than a simple statement of the money value of the labour efficiency variance. Efficiency, activity and capacity ratios can be used effectively alongside the money variances. An efficiency ratio can be constructed as the percentage relationship between the standard hours for the output and the actual hours worked; an activity ratio may be calculated as the percentage relationship between the standard hours for the actual output and the budgeted standard hours; a capacity ratio may be calculated as the percentage relationship between the actual hours worked and the budgeted standard hours.

SIGNIFICANCE OF VARIANCES

Most variances have economic significance, since they represent a real gain or loss to the enterprise, but the variance analysis of fixed overhead volume cannot be commended on that ground. Many writers have attacked the real significance of the overhead volume variance – notably Dopuch et al. (1974), who argued that the variance is meaningless for management in the short run. The variance merely balances the books when absorption costing is used. When the variance is expressed in non-financial terms, such as actual departmental or direct labour hours compared with budget, or production units compared with budget, the difficulties of interpretation do not arise.

The loss of a unit of production has an immediate and tangible meaning for operational managers and implies the loss of all the benefits that could have derived from that unit. The measurement of capacity utilisation has to be much wider than a simple consideration of volume variance.

The fixed overheads which comprise capacity costs represent important resources which management should seek to use in the most efficient manner possible. Since these are, by definition, largely a function of the passage of time rather than of output, it follows that their efficient use should take the form of maximising contribution in the time available to the stated objective of the firm. Jones (1980) and others have emphasised this opportunity cost approach to variance analysis. A close approximation to that opportunity cost of the change in the use of production capacity can be derived from the sales activity variance calculated at the contribution level – see Tables 10.4 and 10.8, for example, where such a variance is set at £1 300 (unfavourable).

If, however, absorption costing operates, the sales volume variance of £1 207 (favourable) – see Table 10.11 – will be calculated at the profit level, and this no longer measures the opportunity cost. However, if that variance is combined with the fixed overhead volume variance of £93 (favourable) in Table 10.12, the total is £1 300 (favourable), which is an approximation to the opportunity cost.

It will be an approximation provided the opportunity exists to sell the output or it makes economic sense to produce for stock in anticipation of future sales. Also, it will only be an approximation in the sense that the contribution used represents existing product contributions which may not reflect the optimal mix or optimal opportunities that really exist for that capacity. Nevertheless, for planning purposes at a senior level in the firm, the contribution measure of opportunity cost represents a useful starting point.

The significance of variances for decision making must be considered also. Variances relate only to past events and nothing can be done about them; they are sunk costs or benefits. Furthermore, the standards used to produce such variances are at best only *ex ante* estimates which represent the dynamic business situation by a static model and ignore the decision alternatives implied by the actual conditions encountered. Such estimates are likely to include random errors and slack, and they can quickly become irrelevant. A dynamic environment will tend to frustrate comparison.

A partial solution to some of these drawbacks may lie in superimposing actual prevailing conditions on to the standards, thereby providing a more realistic measurement of performance. Such an approach was used, for example, in introducing market size and market share variances based on the actual market size for the period under review.

Because traditional variance analysis relies upon comparisons of actual experiences with *ex ante* standards, it generally ignores decision alternatives implied by the actual conditions encountered. A more comprehensive solution proposed by Demski (1967), using linear programming techniques, extends the traditional analysis to include all inputs to the decision model by revising the original decision based on deviations encountered. That enables an *ex post* optimum to be determined from additional information acquired during implementation of the *ex ante* programme.

The difference between the *ex ante* and the *ex post* situations is a crude measure of the firm's forecasting ability, while the difference between the actual results and the *ex post* optimum reveals the opportunity cost to the firm of failing to use available resources to their fullest advantage. The difference between the *ex ante* budget, actual performance, and the *ex post* optimum can be analysed using traditional or conventional variance analysis techniques.

The prime intention of this approach is that the provision of the opportunity cost impact of deviations facilitates learning and taking remedial action. The system is not without its critics – see, for example, Amey (1973) – because of the difficulty of determining an *ex post* optimum for the complicated operations of a typical firm. Additionally, that optimum cannot be calculated until all the events anticipated in the original decision model have occurred. The longer the decision period, the more difficult it becomes to attach any meaning to the *ex post* optimum.

REFERENCES AND FURTHER READING

Amerman, G., 'The mathematics of variance analysis', *Accounting Research,* July 1953, October 1953, January 1954.

Amey, L. R., 'Hindsight v expectations in performance measurement', *in* Amey, L. R. (ed), *Readings in Management Decision,* London: Longman, 1973.

Anthony, R. N., and Reece, J. S., *Accounting: Text and Cases,* 6th edn. Homewood, Ill.: Irwin, 1979.

Bromwich, M., 'Standard costing for planning and control', *The Accountant,* 19 April 1969, 26 April 1969, 3 May 1969.

Dearden, J., *Cost and Budget Analysis,* Englewood Cliffs, N.J.: Prentice-Hall, 1962.

Demski, J. S., 'An accounting system structured on a linear programming model', *The Accounting Review,* October 1967.

Dopuch, N., Birnberg, J. B., and Demski, J. S., *Cost Accounting,* 2nd edn. New York: Harcourt Brace Jovanovich, 1974.

Dyckman, T. R., 'The investigation of cost variances', *Journal of Accounting Research,* Spring 1969.

Jones, C. S., 'Fixed overhead volume variance: an opportunity cost approach', *Management Accounting,* May 1980.

Kaplan, R. S., 'The significance and investigation of cost variances: survey and extension', *Journal of Accounting Research,* Autumn 1975.

Solomons, D., 'The analysis of standard cost variances', *in* Solomons, D. (ed), *Studies in Cost Analysis,* London: Sweet and Maxwell, 1968.

11

Responsibility Accounting

David Fanning

Preceding chapters have emphasised the importance of control, not only from the point of view of controlling actual costs incurred but also from that of controlling the cost management behaviour of responsible managers. Three principal devices are available to senior management to control the behaviour of subordinate managers and to ensure the optimisation and congruence of their activities. Budgeting has been discussed at length, performance measurement has been touched upon and is discussed in more detail in Part Four; the third tool, responsibility accounting, is described and evaluated in this chapter. A proper system of management control employs three complementary reporting frameworks: full cost accounting, differential accounting ('what if' accounting for a number of alternative courses of action), and responsibility accounting. The essence of responsibility accounting is that it traces costs – and revenues and/or assets, if needed – to separate, individual decision units or organisation units, each under the direct control of a manager. These units are commonly called responsibility centres. A system of responsibility accounting is of tremendous value for many management purposes, especially in that it enables the identification of individual managers responsible for satisfactory or unsatisfactory performance. The chapter argues that, if managers are to be held responsible for costs or revenues, they should only be responsible for those items which are within their direct control. The notion of controllability is central to the concept of responsibility accounting. Equally important, considerable motivational benefits can accrue from implementing a system of responsibility accounting. The author describes and discusses the identification of 'responsibility' costs and the preparation and interpretation of responsibility reports.

The main distinguishing dimensions of cohesive organisations are formalisation and standardisation, format, authority and power, responsibility and accountability, roles and tasks, and hierarchy. Structuring of activities is the central phenomenon of organisation, covering such concepts as the amount of documentation and written rules, the prevalence of routine and standard procedures. Organisations can be designed or evolve along definite lines, with four notable types of format – functional, product, territorial, and matrix (with vertical and horizontal authority flows). Organisations are characterised by the nature and extent of the centralisation or decentralisation of authority and by the span of control and management. Individuals within the organisation are accountable for the exercise of power or the execution of tasks, and they are required to conform to expected modes of behaviour. Hierarchy is a pyramidal, unbroken and clearly defined dimension. The horizontal differentiation of an organisation's elements is seen by most writers and managers as conducive to optimising behaviour and achieving organisational goals.

The system of management control reporting that coincides most closely with the dimensional structure of the modern organisation is the system called responsibility accounting. As Horngren (1977) has observed:

> To work optimally, top managers subdivide processes and stipulate an organizational hierarchy of managers, each of whom is expected to oversee a sphere of responsibility and ordinarily has some degree of latitude to make decisions within that sphere. . . . Some form of responsibility accounting system usually accompanies this subdivision of decision making.

Responsibility accounting, then, is a system or mechanism for controlling the wider freedom of action that executives – decision centre managers, in other words – are given by senior management and for holding those executives responsible for the consequences of their decisions.

The discussion in this chapter will concentrate upon a simple form of organisational responsibility hierarchy, and Figure 11.1 presents a schematic representation of that structure. The functional or service departments are omitted, for the sake of clarity, and the chart illustrates only one production director's field of authority – two production divisions, five departments, and fifteen departmental sections. These line managers and their departments are

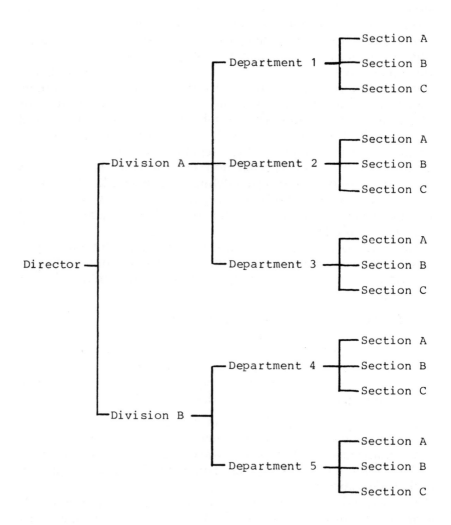

Fig. 11.1   Responsibility hierarchy chart

directly concerned with achieving the goals of the organisation. In practice of course, there would also be service (or staff) units and other line directorates. Additionally, there would be executive committees, boards of directors, and so on to whom line directors would report in terms of their responsibilities.

All the units in the diagram are operational units, or decision centres. In the context of this chapter, they can be better labelled 'responsibility centres'.

PRINCIPLES

The purpose, and the technique, of responsibility accounting is to trace costs (or revenues or returns) to the individual managers who are solely or principally responsible for making decisions about the costs (or revenues or returns) in question. Many similar definitions abound in the literature; Horngren (1977) defined the system's quintessential practice:

> ... revenues and costs are recorded and automatically traced to the individual at the lowest level of the organization who shoulders primary day-to-day decision responsibility for the item.

To identify and trace costs is not as easy as it might appear, and those matters are discussed later in this chapter.

Three principles can be stated at this stage, however. It is necessary to determine certain groundrules attributing responsibility for a cost. The greatest benefit of a system of responsibility accounting will be an improved motivation of managers to conduct their department's affairs in the best interests of the enterprise as a whole. That end will only be achieved if a departmental manager cannot shrug off the responsibility for a particular cost by passing it over to a second department. For example, if Department A fails to order sufficient materials to enable it to complete the production of an urgent order within the planned time and if Department B as a consequence has to work overtime to complete the assembly and packing of that order, which departmental manager should bear the responsibility for the cost of that overtime? Clearly, a system that allows the production department to avoid the consequences of its own inefficiency is not desirable. The first principle of responsibility accounting, therefore, is that costs and revenues should be traced directly to the unit responsible for them. In the case mentioned, Department A should be charged with the cost of the overtime worked by Department B.

Equally, innumerable situations arise in which two or more departments work together and incur a cost or attract a revenue which could be held to be 'joint'. For example, Department C might win an important order from an overseas customer who expects delivery as soon as possible. Department D is the unit responsible for transporting and shipping all the enterprise's products. Department D decides that, since time is of the essence, the goods should be sent by air rather than the customary sea freight. The extra shipping charge is fairly high. Who should bear the cost? The manager of Department C accepted the order with a time constraint, and the manager of Department D handled the order in that light. But should the costs of that order be classed as transport selling costs (of Department C) or distribution costs (of Department D)? The responsibility lines are clearly drawn, but further guidance and action are needed.

The second principle is that costs should be traced directly to the department which has the power to accept and pay for them. In this case, that would be the distribution department. However, such a treatment could be said and seen to be unfair, in that the cost was dictated by the conditions on which Department C accepted the order. There needs, therefore, to be an awareness of these relationships, and the enterprise would institute some kind of 'transfer pricing' mechanism for charging-on such costs incurred by 'agent' departments.

The value of a system of responsibility accounting derives from its identification of variations between budget costs and revenues and actual costs and revenues, as will be demonstrated later. It follows, therefore, that there must be a high degree of comparability between budgets and actual results, which calls for uniformity in the preparation and reporting of budget forecasts and actual period outcomes. This, then, is the third principle: variances from budget and comparisons between budget and actual results must be grounded firmly in a discernibly uniform and clearly comparable system of budgeting and reporting. It should also be possible to distinguish between the responsibility for adhering to standards and the responsibility for any deviations from those standards.

Costs may be authorised by one responsible manager, and in that sense they are controlled by that manager. However, in almost any organisation other managers will be able to influence the amount of such costs or affect their incurrence. No individual manager will have absolute control of costs and the feasibility of a system of responsibility accounting will depend very largely on its modification as required to meet the special circumstances or activities of an organisation.

RESPONSIBILITY COSTS

Subject to the reservations entered above, the determination of departmental responsibility costs is relatively straightforward. A simple example will serve to illustrate this point. Using the production structure shown in Figure 11.1, it can be assumed that three products, A, B, and C, are manufactured, finished and assembled by Departments 1, 2, 3, and 4. Costs for these activities can be reported in several ways; perhaps the easiest to visualise are calculated by full product costing and departmental costing. Table 11.1 presents a full product cost report for these activities for a trading year; Table 11.2 presents a departmental cost report for the same period and the same activities.

From the information in Table 11.1, it is impossible to identify the

Table 11.1
Full product costs (£)

	Product A	Product B	Product C	Total
Direct material	75 000	40 000	10 000	125 000
Direct labour	60 000	120 000	30 000	210 000
Direct production overhead	30 000	25 000	15 000	70 000
	165 000	185 000	55 000	405 000
Indirect production overhead	40 000	80 000	20 000	140 000
Other overhead	11 000	9 000	7 000	27 000
	216 000	274 000	82 000	572 000

individual departmental managers' cost responsibilities. Departmental costs, particularly in the cases of Departments 3 and 4, have been allocated to the three products, as have overhead costs. The information in Table 11.2, showing departmental costs, forms the main ingredient of a responsibility accounting system, revealing, as it does, the amount of costs for which each departmental manager is responsible. The two tables represent alternative arrangements of the same data, collected and recorded differently in each case.

Table 11.2
Departmental costs (£)

	Dept 1	Dept 2	Dept 3	Dept 4	Total
Direct material	85 000	40 000	—	—	125 000
Direct labour	150 000	60 000	—	—	210 000
Other labour	5 700	7 500	14 300	17 500	45 000
Supplies	11 500	8 000	18 000	12 500	50 000
Other costs	43 000	37 000	27 000	35 000	142 000
	295 200	152 500	59 300	65 000	572 000

Table 11.2 does not, however, reveal the separate costs of each of the three products. To be really useful, the report needs to reveal both individual product costs and individual departmental or centre costs. Such a format is presented in Table 11.3, which shows a responsibility matrix for the four departments' involvement in the production of the three products.

The analyses in the tables proceed along fairly naive lines, assuming that it is possible to classify costs along three dimensions: the amount of the cost; the purpose of the cost (that is, the product or programme cost); the location of the cost (that is, the responsibility cost). While such a 'perfect' categorisation is feasible in respect of direct material and direct labour costs, it becomes less practicable as one enters the realms of direct and indirect overhead costs.

Controllability

The notion of controllability was introduced into the definition of

Table 11.3
Responsibility matrix (£)

	Dept 1	Dept 2	Dept 3	Dept 4	Product costs
Product A	111 456	57 656	22 364	24 524	216 000
Product B	141 384	73 032	28 408	31 176	274 000
Product C	42 360	21 812	8 528	9 300	82 000
Responsibility costs	295 200	152 500	59 300	65 000	572 000

first principles for a responsibility accounting system, and it is a concept which bears very much closer attention.

Figure 11.2 presents a diagram of three broad cost groupings: controllable or non-controllable; variable or fixed; direct or indirect. The illustration makes a number of fundamental points. What is direct is not always controllable; what is variable is not always controllable. Equally, what is controllable is not always variable, although it is always direct. Some simple examples may serve to make the distinctions clearer.

Departmental costs are either direct or indirect; by definition, indirect costs are those which are allocated to the department and are, therefore, not wholly controllable by the department. All controllable costs must, accordingly, be direct costs; however, not all direct costs are controllable. The cost of maintenance supplied to a department, occupying one rented factory on its own, is a direct cost but is not controllable by that department. Similarly, the rent for the factory is direct but non-controllable. 'Controllable' in this context is perhaps best defined by Solomons (1965), who distinguished three main situations:

1 the department is completely free to choose the quantity and source of the good or service in question;
2 the department is not free to choose the source of the good or service but is free to decide upon the quantity taken;
3 the department is not free to choose either the source or the quantity of the good or service taken.

In the first situation, the cost of the good or service is wholly controllable – or at least as controllable as any other direct cost

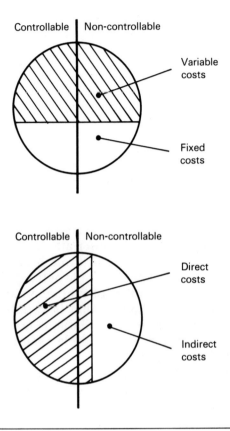

Fig. 11.2   Cost categories

incurred by the department. In the second situation, the quantity factor of the cost is controllable, the price factor is not. In the third case, the cost is non-controllable. The notion of 'wholly controllable' advanced above is a theoretical precept and is not sustainable in practice. A manager or decision taker exercises little control over the cost of most goods or services he buys. The actual unit cost of raw materials will be determined and controlled by market forces outside his control; the wage rate for direct labour will be negotiated and monitored by market forces outside his control. The quantities of those goods and services which he decides to take will be much more within his control, but again not wholly. The condition of 'absolute' controllability must be relaxed, therefore; in its place is substituted the suggestion of 'significant influence' over costs.

Departmental costs can be classified also as either fixed or variable; by definition, variable costs are those that vary proportionately with the volume of output. Controllable costs are not necessarily the same as variable costs, although most variable costs are controllable. For example, the cost of direct labour is usually regarded as an archetypal variable cost, but that cost may be well outside the control of the departmental manager. Wage rates, work periods, job security, and so on – all will combine to lessen the influence of the individual manager on the cost of direct labour. Equally, the cost of raw material is seldom within the absolute control of the departmental manager. On the other hand, many costs regarded as fixed, not varying proportionately with the volume of output, are clearly controllable by the departmental unit manager. Charges for electricity supplies or security services, for example, are fixed but controllable.

The concept of controllability is examined more closely in Chapter 18, which discusses wider categories of costs or expenses which can be taken into account in calculating results by which to judge departmental managers' performances.

The underlying principle remains, however. A departmental manager, a decision unit manager, should only be judged by the consequences of his decisions where those decisions or their outcomes are susceptible to his control or significant influence.

RESPONSIBILITY CENTRES

The discussion so far in this chapter has proceeded along the lines of responsibility for costs, but there are other dimensions. Decision units, or responsibility centres, can be described in a very straightforward way. Figure 11.3 represents a responsibility centre in a diagrammatic way. Responsibility centres use assets or resources to turn inputs into outputs. Inputs such as raw materials, labour and various services are used to perform work, and fixed and current assets are needed to permit those tasks. The results of the work are outputs, whether goods or services, which can be sold to customers, whether internal or external.

All these items can have monetary values, whether they are monetary items or not, and it is those values which responsibility

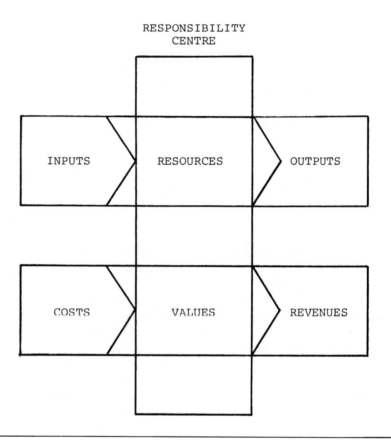

Fig. 11.3   Responsibility centre

accounting uses to provide information about the inputs and outputs of a responsibility centre.

Four types of responsibility centre can be established for management control purposes: a cost or expense centre; a revenue centre; a profit centre; or an investment centre. These different types can be explained briefly as follows.

Cost or expense centre

If a responsibility centre has no directly measurable output, or if management decides to ignore its output, and if it is judged by the extent and level of its operating costs or expenses, then it is an expense centre. (The use of the term 'cost centre' in full cost accounting procedures makes it sensible to use the expression 'expense centre' in this context.) Such an expense centre might be the company secretariat or the legal department. If the duty of the unit is to produce a given quantity of articles or a certain level of service at the lowest feasible cost, then there seems little need to consider the value or money equivalent of any output. Categorisation as an expense centre would meet management's need and enable a sufficient degree of responsibility reporting to be undertaken.

Revenue centre

Conversely, if a responsibility centre manager is held accountable for the outputs of his unit, the unit is termed a revenue centre. If the duty of the unit is to generate a sufficient or target level of revenue, without the requirement to do so at the lowest feasible cost or where that cost is not directly reportable, then the centre is a revenue centre. Most sales offices, for example, are considered revenue centres.

Profit centre

In general terms, most responsibility centres are viewed as profit centres, taking the difference between revenues and expenses as profit. Significant advantages accrue from recognising decision units as profit centres. Each is a business in miniature, and can be measured and judged along those lines. Income (or profit and loss) statements can be generated for such profit centres, even incorporating notional tax charges, so that the profitability of each unit may be judged more clearly. The managers of such centres are encouraged to act as if they were running their own separate business, of course, and this may have adverse effects on the enterprise as a whole. This aspect of responsibility accounting is examined later in this chapter while a number of other related problems, such as transfer pricing and managerial motivation, are discussed in other chapters in this handbook. Nonetheless, the development of profit centres is a desirable one for most organisations.

Investment centre

In many cases, departmental managers are held accountable for the use of assets as well as the level of costs and revenues; such centres are called investment centres. In such centres, the manager is held responsible for the return earned by the assets under his control. The return can be measured in a number of ways, and this measurement is discussed in Chapter 18. Two popular methods are the 'return on investment' approach, whereby profits are calculated as percentage of either total assets or net assets, and the 'residual income' approach favoured by Solomons (1965) and others, whereby profits are subject to certain charges for the use of capital and are then calculated as either percentages of the assets (investment) in the centre or surpluses or shortfalls above or below a specified level of return. The use of the investment centre method is best reserved for 'stand alone' divisions or departments in which managers are responsible for a distinctive range of goods or services, or where the decision unit in question is a subsidiary of a holding company or a foreign branch of an enterprise. More than any other categorisation, the investment centre differentiation has the advantage of increasing the manager's identification with his own sphere of influence and making him responsible for its activities and its profitability in a much wider sense than, say, the profit centre differentiation.

Several problems arise from the investment centre concept. As Tomkins (1980) has argued, the investment centre distinction

> ... implies that the divisional manager has discretion over investment as well as production, marketing, etc. In investment centres, the manager has therefore to be evaluated on the basis of how well he uses the volume of investment he decides to employ and returns must be related to the volume invested. ....
> Divisional managers need to be motivated to search for new investment opportunities and evaluated upon their success in so doing. The investment for the year may be finally approved by top management, but that does not mean that divisional performance in seeking out investment opportunities need not be evaluated.

Tomkins went on to argue against the simplistic use of a 'return on investment' measure or a 'residual income' measure – in essence, because of the general irrelevance of past costs for decision making and on the premiss that incremental cash flows make a better appraisal yardstick.

RESPONSIBILITY REPORTS

Leaving aside, for the moment, the important issues of the measurement of divisional (departmental) performance, the following sections concentrate on the format of responsibility reports and their interpretation in broad terms.

Using the examples presented earlier, in Tables 11.2 and 11.3, and making certain assumptions about monthly levels of costs and about the controllability or otherwise of certain costs, an illustrative responsibility report for Department 1 can be constructed as shown in Table 11.4. Total controllable costs for the year have been calculated at £264 000 (leaving a non-controllable total of £31 200), as against a budget total of £253 000 for controllable costs, giving an unfavourable variance of £11 000. Monthly controllable cost levels ran at £22 425 in the final month of the year, as against a budget level of £21 200, giving an unfavourable variance of £1 225.

Table 11.4 Responsibility report – Department 1 (£)

	Budget		Variances	
	This month	This year	This month	This year
Direct material	7 300	87 500	150	2 500
Direct labour	11 400	136 500	(1 200)	(13 500)
Other labour	400	4 800	25	300
Supplies	1 000	12 000	200	500
Other costs	1 100	12 200	400	(800)
Total controllable costs	21 200	253 000	(1 225)	(11 000)

The figures adduced in the table, show that the department's labour cost experiences have been the principal causes of that apparently 'poor' performance. While partially offset by 'savings' on direct material expenditure, the effects of the 'increased' labour expenditure have been fairly significant. Such increases may, however, have been almost entirely outside the control of the departmental manager. Company-wide rate rises may have been imposed or resulted from national rate rises. Equally, the available labour force may have been less effective in skill or productivity terms than expected, and the manager may have been forced to implement more overtime working or longer shifts than forecast.

On the other hand, the variation from budget may have resulted from the manager's failure to act speedily to rectify an adverse situation. For example, it might have been possible for the manager to substitute less skilled workers, on a lower wage rate, for more skilled workers earning much higher wages. The manager may have failed signally to monitor productivity and effectiveness; he may have estimated wage rates inaccurately at the beginning of the period; or he may have based his budget levels on an inappropriate period in the department's past.

Whatever the underlying reasons, the significant variations from budget revealed in the responsibility report will give cause for concern. The departmental manager, and his divisional superiors, will want to isolate and identify the cause of such adverse variances and act to rectify the situation. It is important, however, that such responsibility reports and their information are interpreted carefully. In broad terms, little of value can be gained from the simple attribution of 'blame' for a specific variance or perceived 'misbehaviour'. Admittedly, the purpose of responsibility accounting is to reveal the quality of a manager's discharge of his responsibilities and the apportionment of blame may form part of this process. However, the variances reported will not, of themselves, give the solutions; rather than identifying the person to whom blame should be attached, the reports should be used to identify the person to whom questions about the variances should be addressed. There may then be cause for blame and radical remedial action, but the responsibility report itself should not dictate such action.

Table 11.5
Responsibility report – Department 1 – direct labour costs (£)

Budget		Actual		Variances	
This month	*This year*	*This month*	*This year*	*This month*	*This year*
11 400	136 500	12 600	150 000	(1 200)	(13 500)
				(10.5%)	(9.9%)

The format of report shown in the table is not the only one used in practice, of course. Often the report form uses a further set of figures giving actual results and perhaps presenting variances as both actual variations from budget and as percentage variations from budget. In that case, the direct labour element line from Table 11.4 would appear as shown in Table 11.5. As variance from budget is running at an annual rate of 9.9 per cent, but the past month's variation is 10.5 per cent, the situation may well be worsening steadily. Comparison with the responsibility reports for previous months would reveal whether there had been a steadily rising trend in direct labour costs over and above budget.

Table 11.6
Responsibility report – Division A (£)

	Budget		Variances	
	This month	*This year*	*This month*	*This year*
Department 1	21 200	253 000	(1 225)	(11 000)
Department 2	13 900	118 000	(760)	(7 200)
Department 3	3 500	37 500	(45)	500
Total controllable costs	38 600	408 500	(2 030)	(17 700)

Similarly, using the figures estimated earlier, and assuming that Divisional Manager A is responsible for Departments 1, 2, and 3, a responsibility report can be constructed for his division, as shown in Table 11.6, in which assumptions have been made about the controllable cost levels and variances for the other two departments. In general, the division has performed less well than budgeted, with an adverse variance of £17 700 for the year. The cost experiences of Department 1 have contributed significantly to that unfavourable outturn, although Department 2 has also turned in a markedly unfavourable report. Viewed in percentage terms, which may be a better yardstick than absolute variances, Department 1 has performed slightly better over the year than Department 2, but markedly worse than Department 3. Over the final month of the year, Department 2 performed better than Department 1, while Department 3 performed better than either. 'Performed' in this sense must be taken as a rough and ready measure, implying nothing more than an apparent ability to keep actual costs in line with budget. Table 11.7 presents the percentage variations from budget for each of the three departments. Further comparison with monthly reports for each of the preceding eleven months would be necessary before any long run trend estimates could be made, but matters appear to be getting worse as far as Departments 1 and 3 are concerned, and slightly better in the case of Department 2. However, all these qualitative comments carry little weight; much deeper and more structured analysis would be needed before reliable criteria for decisions or changes could be determined.

Table 11.7
Responsibility report – Division A – departmental variances from budget

	This month	*This year*
Department 1	(5.8%)	(4.3%)
Department 2	(5.5%)	(6.1%)
Department 3	(1.3%)	1.3%

The divisional reports – say for Divisions A and B in the organisation shown in Figure 11.1 – would be amalgamated into a higher level responsibility report from the Director in charge of Divisions A and B, addressed to either a chief executive or a board of directors, as the case may be. Such reports would be in summary, supported where necessary or appropriate with full or extracted subordinate reports. For example, in presenting the results of his division to his director, the manager of Division A would wish to demonstrate the contributory causes of the adverse variance of £17 700; that might best be done by submitting the departmental responsibility reports as supporting documents.

The precise format chosen will depend, of course, on the nature and needs of the enterprise concerned. However, there is considerable merit in selecting a format which directs attention to important deviations from budget levels. This is the essence of management by exception; it saves executive time being misapplied to those items which reflect smoothly running parts or sections of the enterprise.

In general terms, a manager should receive a report on the costs (or revenues or profits) that he incurs or generates personally, together with a summary report on the controllable costs for each subordinate manager and a report of those controllable costs broken down by 'natural' classification into their various elements (direct materials, direct labour, supplies, and so on). A structured network of responsibility reports will extend across the whole enterprise, from the chief executive's office to the lowest level of managerial unit.

These reports form a valuable part of the feedback process referred to in Chapter 6 (see Figure 6.1, for example) and are central to the control aspects of management accounting and the systems view of the organisation, as discussed at length in Chapter 22. They are not, however, self-activating; unlike the thermostat in a central heating system, which reacts positively to temperature levels and initiates corrective action of its own volition, responsibility reports are only part of the feedback loop. Positive management action is needed, either to revise the standards for future operations or to correct the causes of deviations from appropriate standards. There are three steps in the control process: identification of the items or areas requiring investigation; investigation to determine whether or not action is needed, and of what kind; action when necessary.

DIFFICULTIES

As with any control system based on apparently simple and straightforward techniques, a number of problems or difficulties occur with the responsibility accounting system. Some of these have been touched upon already in this chapter. For instance, the complexity of cost groupings and the nature and variety of costs sometimes preclude their firm classification as either controllable or non-controllable. For that reason, the notion of 'significant influence' has been advanced as the most appropriate criterion for inclusion or exclusion.

For instance, it may be more economical to have one enterprise-wide service contract for repair and maintenance, rather than to allow each departmental manager to negotiate and conclude his own service contract. In that case, one of the departmental managers may be given the responsibility for seeking and engaging repair and maintenance services for all departments. The other departmental managers will seek to have some say in the terms and conditions of that contract; equally, their requirements may sometimes exceed the estimated levels used to determine the budget cost of the contract. Their budget levels will be exceeded. The fault cannot be laid at the door of the manager negotiating the original contract. On the other hand, to allocate the actual costs to individual departments violates the concepts of responsibility accounting; individual departmental managers would then be held accountable for costs that they did not incur personally.

Problems will also arise in handling the charges of service departments. A legal department may undertake contract formulation, debt recovery, and patent registration for all the departments of an enterprise. The requirement of one department – say for a complicated manufacturing agreement to be prepared, drafted and concluded in a very short period – may force the legal department to work overtime to fulfil its other duties. As a consequence, the costs of the legal department will be higher than budget, and an allocation of those costs in proportion to work done for departments may be inequitable. In any event, the principles of responsibility accounting will be violated.

It is possible to argue, of course, that managers should be held responsible for all the costs of their departments, particularly since they could reasonably be expected to be aware of the probable incidence of allocated costs from other departments. They should, therefore, be more careful in requesting services from other departments and in the timing of those requests likely to involve extra work.

The most amenable solution to these kinds of problems is to establish billing rates for the service departments – akin to transfer prices for processed goods, for example – and for each serviced department to be charged for work done on its behalf as if it were an 'external' customer.

A further set of problems relate to the motivational aspects of any form of accountability. By concentrating attention on the individual performance of departments and their managers, there is a considerable danger that responsibility reporting will encourage dysfunctional behaviour. The pursuit of separate departmental targets – even at the level of minimising costs – will frequently take precedence over enterprise goals. Managers will tend to act in their own best interests, and a disadvantageous spirit of competition will emerge between departments and divisions. The design of a management control system, which will include a framework of responsibility reporting, must therefore be such that individual managers are encouraged to take only such actions in their own interests as are also in the best interests of the enterprise. Goal congruence should be achieved so that the aims of individual managers are consistent with, and lead towards, the goals of the organisation as a whole.

Equally, as discussed in Chapter 22, there are obvious dangers in relying on a system of responsibility reporting as the definitive mechanism for appraising performance and the principal means of motivating 'good' behaviour. Responsibility accounting plays an important role in coordinating and motivating departmental performance, but it serves only to direct attention to those areas of performance requiring further investigation.

Difficulties may be occasioned by the timing and duration of responsibility reports. On an intuitive level alone, if something is going awry, the quicker it is reported and investigated the better. The time period covered by such reports should be the shortest in which management can usefully intervene, reports being prepared and issued as soon as practicable after the end of the period to which they refer.

There should be a cost-benefit-analysis approach to responsibility reports. Obviously, the cost of such reports should be lower than their perceived benefit, and the difficulties of preparing them should be fewer than the advantages gained from their use.

Finally, as with all reporting systems, and particularly with accounting reports, there is a danger of information overload. Responsibility reports must tell their story clearly and succinctly. There is little merit in a reporting system which generates masses of computer printout covering each and every aspect of a department's or a division's activities. As mentioned, the essence of a responsibility report is to highlight instances of deviation from budget. Relevant and significant information must be included in such reports, rather than all available information.

The behavioural problems arising from any form of management control system have been summarised neatly by Horngren (1977), who listed:

> overemphasis on short-run goals, presence of slack, failure to pinpoint responsibility, cooperation versus competition, inaccurate source documents, and faulty cost analysis.

CONCLUSION

The overwhelming benefit of a system of responsibility accounting is in its formalisation of information provision. The nature and format of responsibility reports offer ready vehicles for the transmission and interpretation of relevant cost or revenue data.

Responsibility accounting has a number of significant and valuable uses. It provides a mechanism for presenting performance data, which can be used both to motivate managers to act in the best interests of the enterprise and to establish the framework of a managerial performance appraisal system. Additionally, and in many ways more important, responsibility reports provide relevant and up-to-the-minute information on which to base future estimates of cost or revenue behaviour and by which to formulate standards for departmental budgets.

The information derived from responsibility reports is intended to be helpful for management control purposes; equally, it is essential for planning the enterprise's future. While specifically designed for the management control process, responsibility accounting forms a fundamental part of the total management accounting network of systems, providing pertinent information for planners and decision makers at all levels in an organisation.

One of the most difficult tasks facing senior management is to delegate responsibility while retaining control. Responsibility accounting systems play a valuable role in reconciling those twin objectives.

REFERENCES AND FURTHER READING

Anthony, R. N., and Dearden, J., *Management Control Systems: Text and Cases,* 3rd edn. Homewood, Ill.: Irwin, 1976.

Anthony, R. N., and Reece, J. S., *Accounting: Text and Cases,* 6th edn. Homewood, Ill.: Irwin, 1979.

Horngren, C. T., *Cost Accounting: a Managerial Emphasis,* 4th edn. Englewood Cliffs, N.J.: Prentice-Hall, 1977.

Lawler, E., and Rhode, J., *Information and Control in Organizations,* Pacific Palisades, Ca.: Goodyear, 1976.

Solomons, D., *Divisional Performance: Measurement and Control,* New York: Financial Executives Research Foundation, 1965.

Tomkins, C., 'Financial planning and control in large companies', *in* Arnold, J., Carsberg, B., and Scapens, R. (eds), *Topics in Management Accounting,* Oxford: Allan, 1980.

Tomkins, C., *Financial Planning in Divisionalised Companies,* London: Haymarket, 1973.

Vancil, R. F., *Decentralization: Management Ambiguity by Design,* New York: Financial Executives Research Foundation, 1979.

PART THREE
SELECTED
MANAGEMENT
TECHNIQUES

OVERVIEW

The contributions in this section are designed to draw attention to a selected number of specialised applications of management accounting techniques, and, by highlighting those examples, illustrate the ways in which management accounting can play an extended role in the modern enterprise.

In the first chapter in this section, Major Anthony Hollis of the Army's Management Accounting and Costing Services describes a variety of ways in which cost reduction can be achieved. The competitive situation forces attention to costs, and the effective application of management accounting techniques will secure a significant measure of cost reduction. The static approach, with concern being expressed at the level of costs in a previous period and with slow responses to perceived problems, must be replaced by the dynamic approach, encompassing, above all, a speedy reaction to adverse developments. The editor, in the second chapter, deals with the prevention of loss, covering such topics as risk measurement and management, insurance, health and safety at work, and taking a cost-benefit analytical approach to lessening the incidence of loss. While such matters have generally been regarded as the preserve of insurance specialists and risk managers, the management accountant's traditional skills and wider view of the enterprise are valuable tools in any systematic appraisal of the enterprise's exposure to risk and loss.

Dr Richard Pike and Dr Richard Dobbins of the Management Centre of the University of Bradford describe and discuss the difficulties associated with the planning and control of capital projects, drawing special attention to the strategic planning processes involved and to the decision making stages of investment planning. They argue that the evaluation of projects is only one part of their management and they direct attention to the processes of implementation and control.

Monitoring the management process is reviewed by Jan Santocki of the Department of Accounting and Finance at the City of Birmingham Polytechnic in his chapter on management auditing. He describes management audit as an objective, independent, informed and constructive appraisal of the effectiveness of managers or teams of managers, with particular reference to their achievement of company objectives. The identification of existing and potential weaknesses and strengths in an organisation is a managerial function; in its practice, however, with considerable need for quantification and analysis, the management accountant is a vital member of a management audit team. Differing from a financial audit in many respects, the management audit is a most effective way of determining the performance and achievements of a management team. While not strictly a management accounting technique, the management auditing process calls for practical implementation of most of the management accountant's skills and methods; as such, management auditing forms a useful part of the management accounting repertoire.

The chapters in Part Three offer a representative sample of management techniques with particular reference to the management accountant's role in the modern enterprise. They emphasise, both explicitly and implicitly, the importance of the 'team' approach to the management of organisations. No less than other managerial specialists, management accountants cannot stand alone in the execution of their tasks and responsibilities. As discussed in these chapters and many others in the handbook, the processes of planning and control call for a multidisciplinary team approach to the management problems and constraints of a modern enterprise. It has been argued by several commentators that perhaps the time has come to drop the name 'management accountant' and to recognise the wider concerns of today's management controllers. The concluding chapter in the handbook returns to this theme; meanwhile, the chapters in this section present examples of the wider ranging responsibilities of the professional management accountant.

12

Cost Reduction Techniques

Anthony Hollis

Over the past decade, several economic factors have combined to promote cost reduction techniques to a position of importance in the management of industrial and commercial businesses. The energy crisis has severely strained company profitability, the continuing recession has eroded business margins, the development of competition on an international scale has worsened trading conditions. It has been argued that the growth in the employment of management accountants by private and public sector enterprises reflects their increasingly fierce struggle for survival. Management has been provided with vital information on the costs of business operations. Faced with increasing problems in external markets, companies have been forced to concentrate on cost reduction as a means of maintaining profitability. The success or otherwise of those efforts, at a time when there is little scope for businesses to increase prices, has been and remains crucial to the viability of industry. The author recognises that there must be a firm and continuing determination to operate effectively and efficiently at the minimum cost, and he discusses the varied techniques which can be employed to reduce costs. Describing such factors as value engineering and variety reduction, the chapter deals with a broad range of cost areas, not least the reduction of labour costs, and presents valuable guidelines and checklists for ascertaining suitable areas for action. The importance of staff motivation and organisational communication are recognised, and the author suggests that 'cost reduction' may be a discouraging label for a vital function. A positive approach is called for; in that case, perhaps it would be better to talk about 'profit maintenance' or 'profit improvement'.

The process of cost reduction has been defined by the Institute of Cost and Management Accountants (1959) as follows:

The achievement of real and permanent reductions in the unit costs of goods manufactured or services rendered without impairing their suitability for the use intended.

The definition sets the parameters for any study of cost reduction techniques and underlines the importance of qualitative information. Particular emphasis is placed on the lasting nature of any cost reduction, it should be 'real and permanent', indicating that any technique employed should be judged on the following criteria:

1 It must be appropriate to the organisation or activity under consideration.
2 Its introduction and implementation must be planned soundly on a participative basis.
3 Its effects must be monitored regularly.
4 It must result in genuine, identifiable, reductions in unit costs.

The definition indicates also that the scope for the use of cost reduction techniques ranges across the entire spectrum of an enterprise's operations – from design to production, from distribution and marketing to financing and administration. Particular emphasis must be placed, however, on the importance of retaining the essential purpose of the good or service; its suitability for the purpose intended must be preserved. Clearly, any reduction in the unit cost of a product brought about by the elimination of wasteful and unnecessary resources employed in its design, manufacture, sale and distribution can properly be regarded as cost reduction. Equally clearly, reductions in the quality of a product or the range of its uses cannot be regarded as fitting cost reductions.

FACTORS FOR CONSIDERATION

For the purposes of this chapter, detailed study of specific cost reduction techniques will be illustrated by the selection of some of the more important methods within each area of management control. It should be recognised at an early stage, however, that cost reduction schemes can affect many aspects of a business, and that the use of categories to identify them is largely a matter of convenience.

It must be stressed also that the success of these techniques depends upon the cooperation of all those involved, whether directly or indirectly. The motivational implications of cost reduction schemes are discussed later in this chapter, but suffice it to say here that such schemes must be planned thoroughly and their effective implementation and results monitored closely. The mechanics and operations of such schemes must be communicated clearly and concisely to organisational members – preferably in a written form. Those required to operate a cost reduction scheme must be convinced of the personal benefits to them.

Monitoring and assessment systems must be understood by all participants in the scheme. Where any cost reduction scheme includes monetary or staff appraisal aspects, its introduction and working must be by agreement – both as to the nature of the scheme and its appraisements.

Finally, there is a continuing requirement for management to assess the schemes in the light of experience, ensuring that:

1 There is no overlap between schemes, or 'double counting' of reductions or savings.
2 Success in one area is not severely hindering or damaging other aspects of the business, or that success in one area is not being eroded by failure in another area.
3 The measures have no undesirable effects on external parties, for example suppliers or customers.
4 The schemes are within the letter and the spirit of national or local legislation and regulation, for example in the areas of health and safety standards.

A number of factors should be considered by senior management when designing or implementing a cost reduction scheme; some have been outlined above. First, the degree of skill or efficiency of operational management has a direct effect on costs. Inefficient management will invariably lead to extra costs being incurred or to projects being abandoned, with costly severance payments. When the enterprise is facing difficult trading conditions, the attention of managers will be forced to focus on costs; when conditions improve, there may be less inclination to control costs and their impacts.

Secondly, it has to be recognised that even the most efficient business incurs unnecessary costs. The skill of management is tested in identifying those unnecessary costs and acting to eliminate or reduce them. Thirdly, it is vital that costs are examined and restrained at source. The sources of costs and the areas within which reductions can be achieved are examined at length later in this chapter.

Fourthly, it is essential for the enterprise's wellbeing that cost reductions should be maintained. There is little long term benefit in a short term reduction which is not sustained. Executive attention to cost items – such as telephone charges or stationery costs – will typically last for a fixed period, during which such attention will occasion marked reductions in those costs. Once executive attention is directed elsewhere, those cost levels will increase again. There is, therefore, a need for continuous monitoring and control of costs.

Cost reduction schemes depend for their success on the participation of organisational members, at whatever level, and will nearly always call for changes in managerial behaviour. Thus, the fifth factor we must list is the recognition of the reluctance of managers and workers to change their patterns of behaviour. The need for consultation and participation is vital to the success of a cost reduction scheme.

Sixthly, it must be appreciated that a perfect scheme covering all eventualities will be both expensive and complicated to implement. This calls for realistic appreciation of the costs and benefits involved in any such scheme. Complex refinements to eliminate unnecessary costs may be more expensive than the underlying costs themselves. There is no point in spending £1 000 a year to eliminate stationery wastage running at £5 a week. Equally, the motivational expense of a scheme must be considered fully. For example, keeping all the stationery in a central locked cupboard, with access restricted to departmental secretaries, might not involve much additional cost and might generate significant savings. But if managers and executives have to ask every time they want an envelope or a scrap pad, the demotivating effects of such a procedure may be more expensive in the long run than having an open, easy access cupboard.

COST AREAS

The following areas have been selected for more detailed consideration in this chapter: design; purchasing; production; marketing; distribution; finance. That order does not necessarily reflect the degree of individual importance of cost reduction to the profitability of an organisation, but it does present a logical sequence of events in the life of a product and serves to illustrate the benefits which can accrue across the board.

Design

The design function offers management the greatest potential for cost reduction. Designers are concerned with the aesthetic values of their product and are usually determined to achieve their objectives of style, quality and serviceability. They wish to see their ideas translated into a finished product, without enduring too many constraints. Management must find a balance between the quest for reductions in unit design costs and the requirement to develop a marketable product. In areas of high technology, it will be necessary to plan to restrict design costs to a level commensurate with the expected life cycle of the product and its derivatives. A key factor in the control of design costs is the involvement of management accounting specialists at the very earliest stage. Costs must be estimated with great care. A number of relevant factors must be taken into account: alternative materials, production techniques, production sites, market size and proximity, and so on.

A programme of design cost reduction should not be restricted solely to new products, but should include critical analysis of all products within the enterprise's range. There should be awareness of the possibility of introducing cheaper materials, of changing production methods, and of responding to consumer preferences. This will inevitably include competition intelligence appraisal, involving a thorough analysis and understanding of competitors' products.

The technique of value analysis or 'value engineering' involves the systematic evaluation of materials, components, design features, and so on. The process involves asking the following questions (Institute of Cost and Management Accountants, 1959):

1 Does the use of the product contribute value?
2 Is the cost proportionate to its usefulness?
3 Does it need all its features?
4 Is there anything better for the intended use?
5 Can a usable part be made by a lower cost method?
6 Can a standard product be found which will be usable?
7 Is it made on proper tooling, considering the quantities used?
8 Do material, reasonable labour, overhead and profit total its costs?
9 Will another dependable supplier provide it for less cost?
10 Is anyone buying it for less?

The British Productivity Council (1964) issued a valuable series of case studies in value analysis, incorporating most of the above features.

Directly linked to value analysis is the quest for standardisation and simipfication of the materials, equipments and methods involved in design, production and distribution. Competition analysis involves examining and evaluating a competitor's product, and aims to assess the materials and other costs of production of that rival item.

Pre-production purchase analysis entails detailed analysis of all design work with a view to identifying areas for cost reduction before materials are purchased and machines set up. It involves the close cooperation of designers with other managers and production personnel. All departments should be conscious of the time factors influencing design and production. Product introduction pro-grammes should be established to match the availability of materials and other resources to production plans, thereby reducing the possibility of 'missing the market'.

Purchasing

The purchasing function provides a most important link in an enterprise. This link, between the design function and the production process, is vital to profitability and is fundamental to any programme of cost reduction. The technique of value analysis, mentioned above in relation to design, can usefully be employed throughout the purchasing function.

Benefits from the efficient selection of materials have been mentioned, and its success will depend to a great extent on the skills of the purchasing department. The aim should be to provide a material of sufficient specification to meet requirements at the minimum cost.

Capital equipment analysis involves the evaluation of potential investment in equipment. The analysis is designed to determine the cost effectiveness of investing in new equipment compared with that of retaining existing equipment. The operating costs and enhanced benefits from technological improvements should be identified where possible, and a cash flow approach taken to the appraisal of the potentialities.

If full value is to be gained from the purchasing function, the following additional factors must be considered. Deliveries must correspond to production requirements, storage capacity, cash flow, and the level of short term capital investment in stocks. Ordering practices must follow the economic order quantity approach. There must be an efficient system of monitoring the receipt of goods from suppliers, checking both the quantity and the quality of goods accepted.

Production

The production function is a very large area for cost reduction scrutiny. Covering planning, plant layout, stock control, material handling and usage, and production, the function offers considerable scope for cost savings. The four principal elements of cost are: materials, labour, overheads, and capital. Hundreds of techniques exist for reducing production costs; for the purposes of this chapter, the more important methods are summarised below.

In terms of production planning, the Institute of Cost and Management Accountants (1959) defined the problem in a precise manner:

> Production planning and control are so established that they exert their influence upon the business from the receipt of orders to the final dispatch of the product to the customer. . . . There is no doubt that the high output per man and the apparent smooth flow of work from start to finish were in no small measure due to careful planning and effective control, [that is] having the right material at the right place at the right time.

The effective arrangement of plant and equipment is a major factor in production planning. A successful plant layout will have the following features: optimal use of space; efficient control of work flows; minimal materials handling; minimal waste; effective built-in flexibility; worker satisfaction and productivity enhancement.

A sound system of stock control is a fundamental requirement. Among the possible areas for cost reduction would be the following:

1   the storage location and its associated costs;
2   the indirect services involved in the system, for example, administration and its costs;
3   the incidence of stock losses and write-offs, whether due to pilfering, deterioration, obsolescence, or other causes;
4   the requirements for inspection and stocktaking.

Material handling, usage and yield offer further significant opportunities for cost reduction. One method of assessing the effectiveness or otherwise of material handling procedures is through the use of a ratio, where the quantity of material handled is related to the quantitative output of finished product. Establishment of comparative standards for material usage and yield are important for cost reduction in terms of unit costs. Those standards must reflect acceptable levels of usage and waste. Adverse variances may reflect faults or inefficiencies in the materials themselves or in the machinery used or in the inspection processes. They may also point to the need for increased or improved training of labour.

The control of production overheads is an important factor in costs minimisation. A system of budgetary control and standard costing provides the most effective framework for monitoring and controlling such overheads. The quest for voluntary reductions through incentives, or enforced reductions through imposing cash spending limits, helps management to restrict the overhead cost content of unit costs. Individual investigations will delve into the effectiveness of factory and plant layout, of inspection and maintenance of plant and equipment, and of normal controls on utilities and services.

In most manufacturing enterprises, and in all service undertakings, the cost of labour is the largest single element in total prime cost. Thus, the cost reduction programme finds its best opportunities in the areas of direct and indirect labour. The factors affecting labour costs have been studied and debated for many years, and the following summaries of typical techniques and their applications indicate the possible areas for intervention. They are considered in no particular order, other than partially alphabetical which is no reflection of their respective importance.

Absenteeism is an increasing problem for industry, and one solution might be to make bonus payments for regular attendance. Labour turnover is one of the more expensive factors in labour cost behaviour, and the reduction of turnover rates is essential to the maintenance of cost effectiveness, particularly where recruitment, induction and training costs are comparatively high. Provision of suitable and amenable working conditions is extremely important to the maintenance of morale and motivation. Improvements will be possible in both factory environment (heating, lighting, ventilation, and so on) and in operating conditions (noise, heat, dust, and so on); they may also be possible in welfare and leisure facilities.

The effects vary, as many contradictory studies have indicated, but as a corporate strategy such improvements will help to create an environment in which productivity and loyalty will be enhanced.

In addition, the application of such scientific techniques as ergonomics and operations research, will aim to establish a working environment which matches the needs of the workforce as closely as possible.

Any programme of cost reduction must take into account the legal and moral requirements of health and safety legislation and other occupational regulations. Proper attention to these factors will serve to create marked non-financial incentives.

A variety of monetary incentives can be considered. These range from direct wage schemes, productivity agreements, bonus payments and the like to 'perks' and ancillary benefits. Again, these factors can boost labour motivation.

Payroll costs can be reduced markedly, through the use of computerised payroll services or through the introduction of direct transfer pay schemes, whereby wages and salaries are transferred direct to bank or building society accounts. For most small companies, such a change in payment patterns offers a fruitful area for cost reduction.

Performance rating is an effective technique for comparing employees with a view to ranking, and a system of job evaluation (matching pay and skills on a comparative basis) may have significant cost saving implications.

Careful selection and training of employees are key factors in the creation of an harmonious and efficient working unit in which the cost-effective use of resources can be promoted. Non-productive or wasted labour time is a principal cause of high product costs and is a prime target for cost reduction strategies.

Workforce specialisation, by the use of the comparative advantage technique, will give the maximum advantage over other workers or enterprises and should result in beneficial cost reductions.

Marketing

The selling aspect of marketing covers salesmen and their sales office support and administration, market research and advertising, and after sales service. The marketing function does not lend itself so readily to cost reduction as other business functions. Nonetheless, a number of techniques exist for reducing costs, and it is important to recognise the opportunities for making economies in marketing.

Clearly, the success of an enterprise hinges on how well its products or services sell, and management must have access to detailed analyses of sales and markets. Those analyses are valuable in themselves, of course, but they are even more useful when conducted in terms of trends and deviations. The establishment of sales targets is an important strategy in marketing a product, and analysis of individual performance – on either a personal or a departmental basis or both – will reveal areas for further examination. There may be a lack of, or inefficiencies in, training in sales techniques and product knowledge. An awareness of competitive products and their comparative advantages or weaknesses may be absent. There may be a marked lack of motivation and incentive. There may be poor or disabling 'support' from sales office personnel. More important there may be serious errors in market potential assessment and customer demand. Proper attention to such weaknessses will pay rich dividends.

Selling expenses – commissions, travelling expenses, and the like – can be examined and a number of areas isolated for further scrutiny. A reorganisation of sales regions or territories, for example, might lead to a substantial reduction in travelling times and associated costs.

Market research and advertising are obvious areas for both the better expenditure of money and the closer examination of costs. The technique of value analysis can be most aptly applied to these considerations. Pricing strategies have been discussed in Part One of this handbook and they offer effective ways of improving and maintaining profits. On this aspect of a business enterprise's activities, the management of value added tax receipts and payments offers a most useful mechanism for cost and cash flow control. The impact of VAT might be reduced, for example, by eliminating processes in which value is added or by reducing the value-adding steps through which a product goes before reaching its final consumer.

Distribution

Distribution management is discussed in Chapter 19 of this handbook, but a brief word may be in order here to maintain the sequence of this overview. The distribution function includes the method of disposition of the product (wholesale, retail or direct), the method and location of warehousing, the packing and transport of the finished product. There can be considerable scope for comprehensive reorganisation of existing methods and concomitant reductions in cost.

The chosen method of disposition will tend to be influenced by trade customs, by tradition, and by the nature of the business. There is scope for improvement, either by changing the method or changing the agency. Either solution is extreme, of course, and should only be chosen after careful consideration.

The general principles applying to the storage and safekeeping of stocks are no less relevant to the warehousing of finished goods. Physical layouts are obvious candidates for scrutiny. The access to and handling of stored goods can be improved by such techniques as palletisation, mechanical handling procedures, and so on.

Packaging requirements are integral to design function, but the method of storage and of distribution will impose further conditions – most of which will be susceptible to examination as part of a cost reduction programme.

There are many factors to consider when reviewing the transport arrangements in an enterprise. The means used can vary from road, rail, sea, canal or air; the method from own fleet, leased fleet, contract hire, casual hire, contracted carriage, *ad hoc* carriage, freightliner or any number of variants thereon. In broad terms, there are three principal considerations:

1   Is the present method the most suitable, and can it be adapted for higher volumes if necessary?
2   Is the type of transport used the most appropriate in terms of customer satisfaction, damage incidence, cost effectiveness, distances covered, and so on?
3   Is the method chosen most efficient in terms of factory and warehouse locations, distributor and customer locations, and so on?

Finance

The effective employment of capital in a business is of paramount importance. The investment in the right machinery at the right time, for example, can yield significant cost advantages.

The capital equipment and investment programmes of a business can be appraised and analysed in a variety of ways (see Chapter 4, for example) and the control of projects and their expenditures is vital to the proper monitoring of costs (see Chapter 14, for example). The methods of funding capital expenditure should be examined from the point of view of cost effectiveness and the likely requirement for replacement or refurbishment.

APPROACHES

In general terms, most managerial approaches to cost reduction founder on one or more of three fundamental barriers.

The first failing is to issue a directive calling for an organisation-wide 'pulling up of socks' or some such emotive phrase. The general reaction to falling profits and rising costs is one of modified panic! If senior management orders that costs must be cut across the board by a given percentage or by an absolute amount, it ignores the fact that some costs cannot be cut or that costs in other areas must be cut drastically to protect further areas. The workforce, whether shop floor workers or middle managers, is not impressed with such a 'shotgun' approach to the task in hand and reacts apathetically – or even negatively.

Secondly, an isolationist approach is often taken to cost reduction. The managers of individual departments are singled out for reprimand. On their part, this prompts a demotivating awareness that other departments are not being asked to cut costs and that there is a lack of team spirit. Equally, of course, such a departmental approach may have serious effects on the level of service provided to other, non-reprimanded departments.

The third shortcoming of most cost reduction exercises is that they are conducted in a routine and almost nonchalant fashion. Instructions to reduce costs are issued in an unexceptional way, with no apparent enthusiasm or commitment on the part of senior management. In those circumstances, the bulletin or memorandum is filed and very little action is taken.

The burden of this section is that it is vital to motivate all those responsible for the incurrence of costs. Without the full and committed cooperation of all participants in the enterprise's operations, any cost reduction programme is doomed before it starts.

It can be argued that the use of terms such as 'cost reduction' or 'cost cutting' has significant negative motivational impacts, introducing notions of waste and extravagance and ineffective management. Nobody relishes being told that he is performing badly or less well than he might.

In those circumstances, it might be better to employ a more positive term – say, for example, 'profit maintenance' or 'profit improvement'. These have connotations of betterment and greater effectiveness, and would generate more positive reactions to a cost reduction programme.

As mentioned earlier, any programme of cost reduction must include marked changes in the behaviour of managers and workers. Given that most managers and workers are reluctant to change their behaviour significantly, incentives will be needed to engineer essential changes, and to involve responsible employees in the processes of determining and designing the cost reduction exercises. Communication is vital – good communication, that is. The introduction of a cost reduction or profit maintenance programme must be accompanied by clear and agreed explanations of every aspect involved, how it will be assessed, and – perhaps most important – how it will be rewarded. Unless the means of implementing and appraising such a programme are clearly understood by those responsible for the underlying activities, the programme will not be effective, and there may well be dysfunctional consequences as workers and managers act to frustrate what they perceive as 'unfair' or 'meaningless'.

Notwithstanding the organisational theorists who predicate the 'organisational loyalty' of workers and managers, the success of any organisational program designed to enhance or change employee behaviour will frequently be frustrated by the human nature of those employees. Current organisational theory is naive, it has been argued (Ramos, 1981), because it is predicated on 'rationality' and implies loyalty to the organisation. Cost reduction programmes will only succeed if supported by incentives and if introduced after a process of negotiation and consultation at all relevant levels in the business.

Ad hoc 'one off' approaches are less likely to succeed than structured and integrated programmes. To ensure effective cost reduction, the exercise must be implemented throughout the organisation. The cost behaviour of one functional department may be dictated by individual, selfish needs – speed of delivery or long production runs, for instance – which conflict with other departments' needs. While each functional departmental manager acts in the best interests of the enterprise in respect of his own function, the aggregate effect of such individual efforts may prove disharmonious rather than cohesive. There is, therefore, a clear need for an integrated and comprehensive plan for the entire enterprise.

REFERENCES AND FURTHER READING

British Productivity Council, *Sixteen Case Studies in Value Analysis,* London: BPC, 1964.

British Productivity Council, *Variety Reduction,* London: BPC, 1961.

Gage, W. L., *Value Analysis,* New York: McGraw-Hill, 1967.

Institute of Cost and Management Accountants, *Cost Reduction,* London: ICMA, 1959.

Kotler, P., *Marketing Management: Analysis, Planning and Control,* 3rd edn. Englewood Cliffs, N.J.: Prentice-Hall, 1976.

Lockyer, K. G., *Factory and Production Management,* 3rd edn. London: Pitman, 1974.

Ramos, A. G., *The New Science of Organizations,* Toronto: Toronto University Press, 1981.

Ross, J., *Productivity, People and Profits,* Englewood Cliffs, N.J.: Prentice-Hall, 1981.

Schmenner, R. W., *Making Business Location Decisions,* Englewood Cliffs, N.J.: Prentice-Hall, 1982.

Solomons, D. (ed), *Studies in Cost Analysis,* London: Sweet and Maxwell, 1968.

13

Loss Prevention

David Fanning

In many enterprises, risk management and loss prevention have still to make any significant impact. While firms insure against possible loss or damage and decide against carrying large amounts of risk themselves, it would make far better sense for them to introduce extensive programmes of loss prevention. Loss prevention is the most logical path for a firm to follow; expenditure on preventive measures and equipment is an essential capital investment. As such, loss prevention measures are susceptible to rational investment appraisal, just like any other capital project or opportunity. This chapter examines the benefits and costs of such measures and discusses the areas in which loss prevention techniques can have the greatest impact. Medium sized and smaller firms, at least, show marked reluctance to enter into a full scale programme of risk management and to take an organisation-wide view of their whole exposure to loss and damage. In the author's opinion, it makes good sense for any business, be it large or small, to mount as extensive a programme of loss prevention as its resources allow. The processes of evaluation in risk management are exemplified by a number of simple yet revealing cases. On balance, the most attractive strategy for the greater number of businesses combines a suitable loss prevention system and the purchase of adequate insurance cover. In assessing its exposure to possible loss and damage, a firm needs to know and consider many wider responsibilities – to its employees, to the local community, to suppliers and customers, and so on. Crockford (1980) has argued strongly that

> *the days when a company and its risks were its own affair are gone. It is part of the community and the community will increasingly demand a say in how it is managed. . . . Risk management will then become more and more obviously a matter of charting a path for a*

company which avoids it getting so far out of line with what these various forces require of it that it incurs crippling penalties. . . . The danger is, of course, that risk management may then be seen to be almost exclusively concerned with variable risks . . . and neglect what is now its main preoccupation – the constant risks.

This chapter examines the ways in which modern business organisations can manage both these constant risks and the variable, societal risks. Dealing with constant risks (fire or pilferage, for instance) may be more mundane and less theoretically arcane than the intellectually challenging task of identifying and controlling variable risks, but it is a more rewarding process. Constant risks will not go away and their disastrous consequences will not be lessened. The author covers a wide range of risk management applications in this chapter, taking the broad view that loss and risk control and prevention are crucial to the well being of the organisation and regarding 'loss' and 'risk' as synonymous in these contexts.

While the term 'risk management' has come into business parlance only in the past decade or so, the practice is as old as commerce itself. Carter and Doherty (1974) reported that:

> From time immemorial mankind has sought ways of avoiding the unpleasant consequences of uncertain events: the merchants of the ancient world who gathered together in caravans to cross hostile deserts and mountain passes were practising loss prevention, and insurance dates back at least to the Middle Ages. Coming more up to date, several large firms recognized fifty or more years ago the importance of dealing effectively with their pure risks by appointing full-time specialist staff . . .

Nonetheless, insurance against future possible loss is often the only measure taken by a firm to minimise the damaging effects of, say, fire or theft or product liability.

Insurance provides compensation for damage and loss, and frequently for consequential loss – although that loss may be difficult to quantify and insurance companies interpret such outcomes fairly restrictively. Insurance does not provide, however, for the longer term effects of business interruption or loss, such as contraction of market share or diminution of customer loyalty, or loss of production momentum and future profits. Additionally, a firm will generally be penalised by its insurers for any claim made; future premium rates will be higher, for one thing, and full cover may be difficult to obtain. The classic example of the accident-prone, 23-year-old driver of a sports car has its business equivalents – the small construction firm losing tools and equipment from building sites, or the poorly policed city centre hotel with wealthy, cash-carrying guests.

Loss prevention measures will provide the most sensible steps for most companies to take; it is better to assess the probability of an event and seek to avoid it than to face actual loss and then act to prevent its recurrence. The identification of potential threats and the analysis of their probable consequences are fundamental parts of the processes of risk management and loss control.

BUSINESS RISKS

Risk and uncertainty are preconditions of business activity. It is in the management of those risks and uncertainties that firms differ, and it is in those differences that profitability and stability lie. As depicted in Table 13.1, two distinct types of risk or loss face a business enterprise.

Table 13.1
Risk in business

DYNAMIC RISKS	STATIC RISKS
Economic and financial	Natural and physical
Political	Socially deviant
Social and marketing	Personal
Technical and production	Technical

Dynamic risks, or economic risks, are those which affect the whole business community and have no physical effect on persons or property. They arise from changes in economic or social environments, changes in demand or supply conditions, changes in price levels or currency exchange rates, and so on. In general terms, these are speculative risks and the concern of general management. Events occasioning economic losses can also give rise to economic gains; it may be that one firm's loss is another firm's gain, one country's loss is another country's gain.

The other class of risk or loss is that labelled 'static', or pure risks. These are losses occasioned by physical acts or omissions; the cause or the effect is peculiar to the firm or person concerned. These hazards are the concern of risk managers and the focal point of this chapter. A clearer idea of the distinctions between the two categories may be gained from a description of some of the typical causes occasioning certain types of effects. It should be understood, however, that the distinctions between dynamic and static risks are not absolute or mutually exclusive. Risks from one class may have significant impacts on risk levels in another class. Risk management cannot, therefore, be seen in a rigid, categorised way. As Carter and Doherty (1974) have commented:

> The way in which an organization responds to its business risks can have important repercussions on its pure risks. Moreover it is the task of top management to ensure that not only is everyone concerned with the handling of all types of risk informed of the organization's corporate objectives but that decisions taken regarding both business risks and pure risks are equally consistent with those objectives.

Dynamic risks

Business or dynamic risks arise in four principal sectors: economic, political, social and technical. Additionally, these four primary sectors can generate risks in secondary sectors: financial, marketing and production.

Economic risks will encompass changes in the economic environment, alterations to monetary and fiscal policies, increases in price levels, competitive movements in markets, and related events. Political risks include threats of nationalisation or indigenisation, of industrial unrest, of worsened international relations or even war, and of trade restrictions. Monopoly and merger policies, securities industry regulations, consumer protection legislation, and so on, all add to the political risks facing the corporation. In the social sector, changes in customer tastes or in product acceptability, union militancy, equal opportunity regulations, or community changes will pose risks for the business. Technical threats can result from technological backwardness and lack of knowledge of new developments or from difficulties associated with new processes.

Those four areas of risk combine in different ways to produce threats in the financial, marketing and production sectors.

Financially, the economic environment may occasion a greater incidence of bad debts and harder credit terms. Banks may be reluctant to make loans or overdraft facilities as freely available as in the past and suppliers may require payment more promptly. In marketing terms, changes in social and economic conditions and alterations to supply and demand patterns may reflect in the loss of market share or markets to competitors. Earlier estimates of sales levels will be in error, and the risk of loss through insufficient cash flow or reduced profit will be increased. Political, economic and technical factors can affect production. Interruptions to production runs and schedules can arise from strikes, machinery inefficiencies, cash shortages, and a variety of other reasons. All those factors can have a powerful effect on production costs, with concomitant risk of cash and profit shortfalls. Materials and labour may be in short supply due to any number of combinations of primary factors.

These risks are the proper concern of general management; they are the strategic or dynamic risks facing all businesses in a modern economy. As such, they are susceptible to avoidance or minimisation by the application of the science or art of management.

Static risks

Pure or static risks arise in four principal ways: from the natural environment and the effects of breaking natural laws or relationships; from the effects of socially deviant behaviour; from the effects of events occasioning bodily harm; from the technical environment. Such risks arise typically from combinations of factors, and causal chains can be difficult to construct.

The physical effects of nature and of interference with it can include such events as floods, earthquakes, storms, soil erosion, fire, and so on. Expected codes of conduct will be violated and such socially deviant actions can include theft, rioting, negligence, disobedience, and so on. Fraud is a clear example of such deviation from acceptable behaviour.

Risks in the personal sector can occasion death, injury, sickness and disability; each of those events gives rise to substantial further risk of financial liability, interrupted production, labour unrest, and so on. On the technical front, pure risks arise in the areas of plant breakdown and malfunctioning, of hazardous processing of dangerous materials, of safety device failure, and of plant and material unsuitability.

These risks are the concern of risk management; they are the static or pure risks facing individual firms and they are susceptible to avoidance or amelioration in one of four ways, as discussed later in this chapter. Pure risks can be handled by either risk avoidance techniques or risk transference techniques or risk retention techniques or risk reduction techniques. Figure 13.1 illustrates the various ways of handling static or pure risks, and the individual methods will be examined later in the section 'Risk management techniques'.

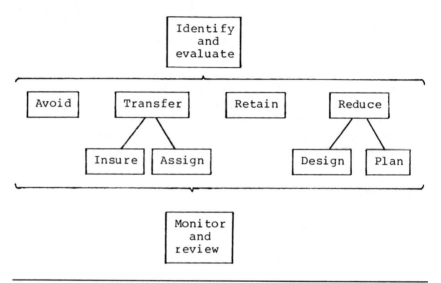

Fig. 13.1   Handling static (pure) risks

Whatever the chosen method of dealing with the perceived hazard, two procedures are essential for effective risk management. First, comes the process of identifying, analysing and evaluating the pure risk exposure of the firm. Second, there is the process of monitoring and reviewing the whole risk management operation. These processes and the techniques involved are examined further in the following sections.

RISK IDENTIFICATION AND EVALUATION

In any analysis of the environment in which a business operates, it is fairly easy to link causes and effects without taking full notice of the events which occur as a result of those causes and which give rise to those effects. The dangers in that approach, one of identifying perils to which the firm is exposed and trying to assess the consequences, are that some perils may be overlooked and sources of potential loss ignored. A better approach is that exemplified in Figure 13.2.

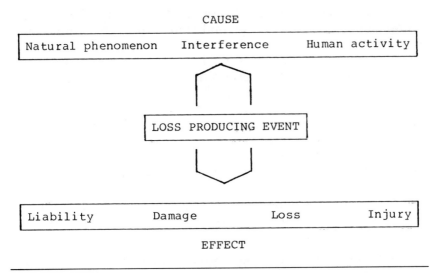

Fig. 13.2 **Risk identification**

Loss producing events are identified and categorised, and a thorough analysis undertaken of the possible causes. The possible outcomes are evaluated and their effects analysed and quantified where feasible.

The significant advantage of this approach is that, by identifying loss occasioning events and working backwards and forwards to identify causes and effects, the possibility of overlooking either causes or effects is markedly reduced. A simple example of the alternative approaches may serve to illustrate the differences between the two. A factory is dependent upon a steam boiler, which has the obvious potentiality of exploding. Such an explosion could cause damage and loss in a variety of ways: to the premises in which it is sited; to the premises and property of adjoining factories or residential accommodation; to other equipment and goods in the factory. An explosion could also cause the death or injury of employees and bystanders. Production would be seriously disrupted, and good customer relations impaired. An explosion could be caused by either the physical effects of nature (lightning damaging an external safety valve, for instance) or the effects of interfering with natural laws (by installing a release pressure pipe of insufficient capacity) or the effects of human activity (negligence or sabotage, for instance).

That approach serves only to confuse the situation. The method shown in Figure 13.2, however, makes the process of identification and evaluation much easier. A loss producing event is identified; in the case of the boiler, that event is the loss of steam generating capacity. That loss could be occasioned by any of a numer of perils, of which exlosion is but one; fire, flood, earthquake, faulty design, bad water pressure, and so on, are some of the range of causes. Each cause would need to be evaluated on the grounds of its probability of occurrence; each effect would need to be evaluated and quantified. Such an approach is a more comprehensive one than the simple linking of cause and effect, and it should ensure that no possible cause and no probable outcome are overlooked.

A similar approach has been advanced by Crockford (1980), who has argued that any risk is comprised of four components, which he classified as follows:

1 Threats – forces which could produce an adverse or disadvantageous result.
2 Resources – the physical and human assets and profits which could be affected by the threats.
3 Modifying factors – the particular features which could increase or reduce the likelihood of the threat becoming a reality or the severity of its consequences.
4 Consequences – the manner in which, or the extent to which, the threat affects the resources.

That approach to risk analysis is illustrated in Figure 13.3, which is based on Crockford's appraisal. He argued in favour of the formulation of risk checklists, broadly arranged under each of the four headings listed above. While the figure shows the four-stage approach in a vertically linked relationship, the use of checklists would encourage the 'ripple' approach exemplified in Figure 13.2.

Under 'Threats', for example, would be entered broad classifications of the type of risk facing the enterprise in its operations: natural forces, human forces, artificial forces; or, such threats as fire,

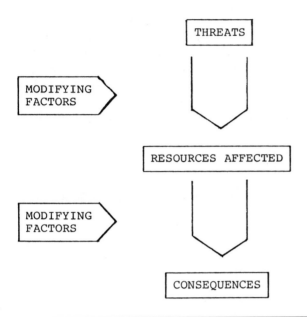

Fig. 13.3 Risk analysis

flood, human error, sabotage, nationalisation, profit restriction, and so on. Crockford listed 'progressive deterioration' as an important category of threat to the continued efficient operation of a business:

> ... operations can be interrupted just as severely because a piece of equipment is worn out or because it, or an organizational process, has ceased to operate as efficiently as it should.

The 'Resources' category would include the fixed and current assets owned by the business and those assets owned by others for which the firm was responsible or with which it might be involved. People affected by the business, whether employees, customers, or neighbours, would be included in this category.

'Consequences' would include the different situations in which the business might find itself – liability, damage, loss, injury, and so on. Under 'Modifying factors', categories such as plant location, factory construction, legislation, and so on, would be entered.

Risk measurement

The qualitative identification of potential risks or threats is perhaps the easiest part of the whole risk management process. The evaluation of those risks is less straightforward, involving as it does quantitative assessment of qualitative estimates of causes, events and effects of varying probabilities. Nevertheless, the process of evaluation has to be undertaken scientifically and systematically if the process of management is to be at all effective.

There are three major stages in the risk measurement process:

1   collection of data;
2   estimation of probability of occurrence;
3   evaluation of the cost of damage or loss.

Generally, these stages are self-explanatory but it will be useful to discuss first a simple example and then to examine the general points raised by those stages and their execution.

As an example, consider the problems of computer fraud. The following discussion and analysis relies on figures and conclusions reported by the Department of the Environment (1981) in the results

Table 13.2
Computer frauds – value of losses

Range of financial losses (£)	Number of reported cases	Value of ascribed losses (£)
Nil	17	–
Less than 250	8	1 055
251 – 500	6	2 681
501 – 1 000	4	3 164
1 001 – 1 500	2	2 600
1 501 – 2 500	6	12 403
2 501 – 5 000	3	11 100
5 001 – 7 500	3	16 491
7 501 – 10 000	3	26 888
10 001 – 15 000	3	33 767
15 001 – 20 000	4	80 000
20 001 – 50 000	4	152 000
50 001 – 100 000	2	133 000
100 001 – 250 000	2	430 000
More than 250 000	0	–
	67	905 149

of a survey of the largest users of computers in the public and private sectors in the United Kingdom. Of the 319 replies to that survey, 79 per cent of the respondent organisations said that they had not suffered a computer fraud in the previous five years. A total of 67 cases of computer fraud was reported, of which 17 had no financial loss ascribed to them, being concerned with the use of an organisation's computer for private purposes. Those 67 cases are summarised in Table 13.2, which shows the range of financial losses, the reported number of cases, and the total values ascribed to those losses.

The survey reported that the types of fraud could be broadly classified in one of four categories: unauthorised alteration or theft

Table 13.3
Computer frauds – type

Category of fraud	Number of reported cases	Value of losses (£)
INPUT:		
Purchases	6	401 225
Payroll/expenses	16	61 487
Sales	5	97 458
Personal accounts	10	41 703
Stocks	5	256 297
	42	858 170
OUTPUT:		
Cheque/cash theft	2	3 600
PROGRAM:		
Alteration of program	1	26 000
RESOURCES:		
Private work	12	16 339
Time theft	2	500
Software theft	2	500
Output theft	2	40
Sabotage	3	–
Invasion of privacy	1	–
	22	17 379

of input data or master file; destruction, suppression or mis-appropriation of output data; theft, alteration or misuse of programs; theft or misuse of computer time and/or resources. Those categories and their subsets are reported in Table 13.3.

The majority of frauds were discovered through internal control procedures (51 per cent), combined occasionally with external audit procedures or accidental discovery; external audit procedures uncovered relatively few cases (4 per cent); accidental disclosure or outside information or voluntary confession accounted for the discovery of a considerable number of cases (45 per cent).

While admittedly a small sample, the response rate to the survey was high. The big problem with these figures and percentages is that they only included instances of computer fraud which had been uncovered by the respondents. The real value of computer fraud may never be known. However, the results can be used by management to assess the likelihood of loss through computer fraud. There is a 79 per cent chance of escaping frauds – or at least not discovering frauds – and a complementary 21 per cent chance of suffering at least one fraud. Given the occurrence of a fraud, it is possible to estimate the probability of its severity in terms of financial loss; that information is presented in Table 13.4, from which it can be seen for example, that there is a 25 per cent chance that the fraud will occasion no financial loss and a 3 per cent likelihood that the loss incurred will be greater than £100 000.

The probability of occurrence and the probability of loss severity

Table 13.4
Computer frauds – frequency and probability of losses

Value of losses	Frequency	Probability
Nil (£0)	17 (25.4%)	0.254
Negligible (less than £250)	8 (11.9%)	0.119
Small (£251 – £1 000)	10 (14.9%)	0.149
Moderate (£1 001 – £10 000)	17 (25.4%)	0.254
Medium (£10 001 – £100 000)	13 (19.4%)	0.194
Large (more than £100 000)	2 (3.0%)	0.030
	67	1.000

can be combined into a matrix representing their discrete joint probability distribution function. That matrix is given in Table 13.5. In both tables, the original monetary ranges have been replaced by a sixfold qualitative classification, each of which categories has a representative value, set below the midpoint value to allow for the positive skewness of the distribution.

Table 13.5
Computer frauds – probability matrix

	Probability of loss	Representative value (£)	Expected cumulative loss (£)
No fraud	0.000	0	0.00
Fraud			
Nil	0.0533	0	0.00
Negligible	0.0250	100	2.50
Small	0.0313	600	18.78
Moderate	0.0533	5 400	287.82
Medium	0.0408	54 000	2 203.20
Large	0.0063	150 000	945.00
	0.2100		3 457.30

Having arrived at the probabilities in Table 13.5, the manager will then proceed to estimate the expected cumulative loss over the next five years, by multiplying each probability in Table 13.5 by the corresponding representative loss value. The expected cumulative loss is calculated at £3 457.30 over the next five years.

That measurement of computer-related loss through fraud would be added to other computer-related loss measurements to provide an aggregate estimated loss. Management could then take a considered decision about that likely level of loss and choose the most appropriate method of handling that perceived risk.

Similar exercises could be conducted for each part of a firm's operations; theft by employees, for instance, or loss through fire, or loss through industrial accidents, or loss through strikes and stoppages. In all these cases, external data would have to be considered alongside internal data relating to the firm's own experiences. Where necessary, either type of data would be modified to take account of the risk manager's personal assessment of the firm's probable future risk profile in respect of the hazard being measured. The statistical principles and practices used in the measurement of data and the establishment of likely outcomes are discussed in most textbooks on statistics and business forecasting – see, for example, Freund and Williams (1982).

Care must be taken not to interpret the data in just one way, as the computer fraud problem demonstrates. The measurement of risk in that example focused on the value of probable financial loss. The analysis in Table 13.3 shows that 63 per cent of reported frauds were in respect of input items and 33 per cent in respect of resources. Equally, 95 per cent of the loss by value was in respect of input items. Given that the probability of fraud was estimated at 21 per cent or 0.210, the joint probability of fraud arising from input alteration or theft can be calculated at 0.1316; from output destruction, misappropriation or suppression, at 0.0063; from program theft, alteration or misuse, at 0.0032; and from resource theft or misuse, at 0.0690. If the average loss through alteration or manipulation of purchases inputs is calculated at £66 870 and the probability of such an occurrence is estimated at 0.0188, the expected loss could be forecast at £1 257. Taking that approach to the calculation of a total expected cumulative loss for the firm would indicate a total expected loss of £2 840 or so over the next five years.

Data collection and use

The collection of data for risk measurement can present serious problems, not least of which are the lack of much directly useful data and the generally unsatisfactory nature of that which is available. Obviously, where both internal and external data sources are accessible it would be foolish to ignore them. The cost of gathering data and qualitative information can be extremely high and a careful judgement needs to be made between the need for accurate data and the consequences of relying on intuition or less sound information. Available figures may derive from a large number of observations; will any gain result from extending the area of collection? They may be limited in supply; is there any benefit in widening their availability? Data from a small number of observations may be more appropriate than data from a larger sample.

The nature of the available data must also be considered. For risk measurement purposes, there are obvious dangers in not having sufficient information; there are equal, if not greater, dangers in having too much! As a simple guide, data should be gathered on three principal aspects:

1 the number of losses which occur in a given period, classified by size and, if possible, cause;
2 the frequency of loss producing events in the same period of time;
3 the maximum possible loss for each cause.

To be useful, data must be classified and should be collected so that all losses or potential losses associated with a particular event can be ascertained or estimated.

Internal loss data are, potentially, the most valuable and will typically be those relating to past insurance claims or write-offs against profits. Other internal data and information will be available – such as the fire resistance qualities of raw materials used in production processes. External loss data, derived from the experiences of other firms or from the insurance companies' loss statistics or from nationally collected and aggregated data (such as vehicle accidents or crimes or strikes), will be of considerable use – provided there is a clear understanding of their nature. External data to be useful must be accessible, relevant and timely.

Loss valuation

Losses can be divided most easily into two categories: direct or indirect. Their evaluation poses significant problems for risk managers. One of the more comprehensive treatments of this difficult area has been provided by Carter (1974) and the following outline derives from his analysis.

The calculation of the total, direct and indirect, loss attributable to any event must be augmented by an evaluation of the level of resources needed after such an event to ensure the continuance of the enterprise's activities. The first element tells the firm the amount it stands to lose if provision is inadequate or incorrectly planned; the second element shows the level of financing the organisation will need to have available if the event occurs.

Direct losses occasioned by a loss producing event are generally easy to quantify; most such losses have a unique cost about which there is no doubt. Theft, for example, or liability claims for fixed sums and agreed legal costs can be identified readily. Other direct costs are not so easily traceable. If an item of plant is destroyed, there are several ways of arriving at a cost for that event. Is the cost the same as the original cost of the plant or its written down book value? Or is the cost the current replacement cost of a similar item? Is it the price someone would have paid for the item before its destruction? Or, more sensibly, is it the opportunity cost of the loss – the forgone amount of future net earnings attributable to use of the item?

Indirect costs are even more difficult to assess. Damage to, or destruction of, production plant has an obvious effect on production time and quantities, but would also affect sales and continuing market demand. Planning and building regulations can also have a marked incremental effect on indirect costs. If a factory is burnt down, it may not be possible or permissible to rebuild in the previous way on the same site. Heavy additional expenditure may be incurred. Equally, a number of extended interruptions to production time, and consequent temporary lay-offs of production workers, may result in employee dissatisfaction and increased labour turnover, which could have adverse long run impacts on future labour manning levels or workforce availability.

Losses of the second 'type' – that is, considerations of the value of resources needed after a loss producing event – can be classified in the following ways:

1 Property losses – the destruction, damage, loss, theft or con-
   tamination of the fixed and current assets of an enterprise, valued
   by the potential loss if the business were deprived of those assets.
2 Liability losses — injuries to employees, customers, members
   of the public, loss of income or earnings for organisations and
   individuals, damage to other owners' property and interests.
3 Personnel losses – losses suffered by members of the organisation
   or their dependents, as the result of death or disablement for
   which the organisation has no direct legal liability, and non-legal
   losses facing the enterprise arising from the death or disablement
   of key employees, customers, agents, and so on, and business
   liquidation losses (such as loss of goodwill) arising from the death
   or disablement of business partners or controlling shareholders.
4 Financial losses – credit losses and fraud losses.
5 Business interruption losses – losses arising from the other
   classes of loss discussed above and representing additional
   expenditure to replace lost facilities or lost income.

Cost-benefit analysis

The consideration of the benefits and costs associated with a particular loss prevention measure can be facilitated by a systematic approach, such as that illustrated in Table 13.6, which presents the various components of a cost-benefit analysis *pro forma* – say for an automatic fire alarm system installation. The constituents of such an analysis can be varied to suit the particular situation in hand, but the value of a structured approach cannot be gainsaid.

Table 13.6
Cost-benefit analysis

BENEFITS	
Direct benefits:	Tax savings on capital expenditure
	Insurance premium reductions (net)
	Government or local authority grants
Indirect benefits;	Loss reduction – property
	Loss reduction – personnel
	Loss reduction – public liability
	Loss reduction – interruption
	Labour relations improvement
	Community relations improvement
	Productivity improvement
COSTS	
Direct costs:	Capital equipment or system costs
	Installation and construction costs
	Recurrent maintenance costs
	Training and supervision costs
	Back-up systems or service costs
Indirect costs:	Interruption during installation
	Production curtailment
	Labour relations impairment

The evaluation of benefits and costs can be a complicated process and will require a careful assessment of all relevant factors. The analysis itself may be relatively straightforward once all the under-lying assumptions have been made and all the alternatives considered.

The criterion for acceptance may be the simple one of payback (seeing how long it will take for the increase in net cash flow to equate the estimated cost of the preventive measures) or the slightly more sophisticated one of internal rate of return (using discounted cash flow techniques to establish the return being earned by the capital investment). The chapter concludes with some simple examples of the employment of these techniques.

RISK MANAGEMENT TECHNIQUES

As illustrated earlier in Figure 13.1, there are several ways of handling risk, once it has been identified and evaluated. Four strategies are available to managers, and these will be used more often than not in combination. The four strategies are: risk avoidance; risk transference; risk retention; risk reduction.

Risk avoidance

The avoidance of risk is perhaps the easiest strategy to adopt – in principle, that is. Generally the avoidance of a particular risk will involve abandoning a project or an activity which the organisation wishes to pursue. It may be better to give up manufacturing a product which relies on hazardous processes, even though such an action entails forgoing substantial profits.

Other instances of risk avoidance are less costly to implement, such as the avoidance of payroll losses by introducing a bank transfer system for the payment of wages and salaries.

Generally, to be effective, risk avoidance measures must be implemented at an early stage in the life of a product or process; at later stages, the avoidance of risk is likely to involve substantial costs.

Risk transference

The technique of transferring the liability can take two forms: the transfer to another of the activity occasioning or enhancing the risk; the transfer to another of the financial loss arising from the occurrence of the risk. The most common instance of action under the first strategy is the sub-contracting of hazardous or complicated work to a specialist firm. In return for agreeing a fixed contract price, the firm gets rid of an uncertain amount of potential cost.

The most common form of the second strategy is insurance.

Policies generally guarantee compensation to the insured party in accordance with an agreed set of contractual rules; many policies also include indemnity clauses under which the insured will be fully compensated for monetary losses caused by the insured event. Nonetheless, insurance policies tend to cater for the most probable, and they neglect to provide cover for the many consequential, longer term losses flowing from a loss producing event. In certain cases, outside the scope of insurance policies, portions of risk may be assigned to others by contracts or agreements; for example, losses through theft from motor vehicles parked in public multistorey garages are specifically disclaimed by the proprietors or managers of such garages.

Risk retention

Risk retention or assumption can arise in one of two principal ways. If part of a risk is insured, then part remains with the insured party; for instance, motor insurance policies typically expect the insured to carry the first part of any claims or insured losses. On the other hand, risk retention may arise through neglect or ignorance, where a risk is not identified or where its magnitude is underestimated.

Essentially classified as 'active' and 'passive' risk retention strategies, they may also be labelled 'self-insurance' and 'non-insurance'. Managements may decide, of course, that the likelihood of loss is so small that the value of insurance is negligible and may decide to carry all the risk. In the second category, negligence includes the failure to appreciate the underlying value of the asset being insured, particularly in times of inflation.

Risk reduction

The reduction of risk can take several forms, and the technique is aimed at either reducing the probability of a loss producing event or lessening the effects of its occurrence.

Broadly, there are six basic approaches to risk reduction, as follows:

1 Safety and security measures and devices – fire alarms, security officers, window bars, sprinkler devices, safety guards, flame-proofing, cut-out devices, and so on.
2 Safety and security procedures – working procedures, plant

layout, security patrols, employee checks, supervision of safety guard use, and so on.
3   Employee training.
4   Interruption planning – back-up systems, alternative sources of supply, stockpiling, contingency plans, and so on.
5   Recovery – salvaging, for instance, and prompt reaction to loss producing events.
6   Financial planning – contingency planning in cash budgeting, proper insurance cover, access to support capital, and so on.

In simple terms, risk reduction techniques concentrate on loss prevention measures. The following section examines a number of typical instances of loss prevention planning.

LOSS PREVENTION

In the management of risk reduction, loss prevention plays a central role and can be classified in a number of ways. Essentially, the main classification is into the six categories mentioned above, but there are a further four ways of looking at loss prevention in a 'secondary' or 'subsidiary' way. The first is the elimination of the preconditions for a loss, or at least their recognition and evaluation. Secondly, there are possibilities of preventing losses arising from those preconditions – through the use of safety fuses or cut-out devices, for example, or security locks on outside doors. Thirdly, it is important to recognise the incidence of loss producing events at an early stage – through alarm systems, regular internal checks and audits, and so on. The fourth category covers the limitation of losses. Once an initial event has occurred, it is essential to limit the loss – by installing fire doors, for example, or by locking internal doors or by the availability of skilled medical assistance.

Each of these classifications can be considered in each of the three principal categories mentioned earlier – physical devices; procedural devices; and educational and training devices. Table 13.7 presents such a matrix of loss prevention devices. The following sections give summarised studies of some practical instances of such procedures.

Fire prevention

Hyflam Products is considering the installation of an automatic

**Table 13.7
Loss prevention matrix**

	Physical devices	Procedural devices	Educational & training devices
Pre-conditions for loss	Venting of fumes	Security checks	Safety courses
Prevention of loss	Security locks	Security officers	Safety manuals
Discovery of loss	Fire alarms	Night patrols	
Limitation of loss	Automatic sprinklers	First aid officers	Safety procedures

sprinkler system in its factory and offices. It pays an annual insurance premium of £15 000 to cover fire damage and consequential loss. The sprinkler system it plans to install will cost £45 000 and will have an estimated effective life of ten years, with no residual or scrap value at the end of that time.

The company's insurers have said that they will allow a discount of 55 per cent on the annual premium if the system is installed to their satisfaction. The firm's probable annual loss through fire and smoke damage, based on previous experience, is estimated at £2 500 if the factory and offices are left as they are. The company pays corporation tax at the rate of 52 per cent on taxable profits.

The relevant calculations are set out in Table 13.8, and it can be seen that the system will pay for itself in just over five years. Alternatively, using discounting techniques, the internal rate of return on the initial expenditure has been calculated at 10.6 per cent. The choice of discount rates is largely governed by intuition in this example. Alternatively, the company might have established a required rate of return for capital expenditure of this sort.

In the absence of the automatic sprinkler system, Hyflam would continue to pay annual premiums of £15 000 and to incur probable annual losses of £2 500.

Table 13.8
Hyflam Products – fire prevention

		£
Increased net cash flows (savings)		
Year 1	First year allowance (£45 000 @ 52%)	23 400
	Reduced insurance cost (net of tax relief) (£15 000 @ 55%)	3 960
		27 360
Year 2 and after	Reduced insurance cost	3 960

Discounted annual net cash flows

	15%		10%	
	Discount factor	Present value £	Discount factor	Present value £
Year 1	0.870	23 803	0.909	24 870
2	0.756	2 994	0.826	3 271
3	0.658	2 606	0.751	2 974
4	0.572	2 265	0.683	2 705
5	0.497	1 968	0.621	2 459
6	0.432	1 711	0.565	2 237
7	0.376	1 489	0.513	2 031
8	0.327	1 295	0.467	1 849
9	0.284	1 125	0.424	1 679
10	0.247	978	0.386	1 529
		40 234		45 604
Cost		45 000		45 000
Net present value		−4 766		604

Rate of return: 10% + [5 × (604/5370)]% = 10.6%

Theft prevention

Hyval Trading has changed its product mix and now needs increased cover against theft. Its insurance company has said that the cover will only be increased if the firm installs a sophisticated burglar alarm system. The firm pays £2 500 a year in insurance premiums, which the insurers propose to raise to £3 500 for the increased cover. The firm pays corporation tax at the rate of 52 per cent of taxable profits.

Its probable losses through theft and intruder damage will run to some £2 500 a year on average, but may be considerably higher as the value of stocks held increases in line with the changed product range. The alarm system recommended by the insurance company will cost £8 000 and is expected to last for ten years, with no residual or scrap value at the end of that time.

Table 13.9
Hyval Trading – theft prevention

		£
Increased net cash outflows		
Year 1	Burglar alarm	8 000
	First year allowance	(4 160)
	(£8 000 @ 52 %)	
	Increased insurance cost	480
	(net of tax relief)	
	(£1 000 @ 48%)	
		4 320
Year 2 and after	Increased insurance cost	480

The various calculations are set out in Table 13.9, and it can be seen that the firm will have increased net expenditures of £4 320 in the first and £480 in each of the succeeding nine years. Against this has to be set the likely cost of losses which, even at the firm's lowest estimate, will run at some £2 500 a year.

While that amount would be recovered from the insurers, experience-related premiums would mean that the firm has to expect an increase in premium demands after each successful claim.

Fraud prevention

Hyway Distributors is engaged in the wholesale trade of motor spares and accessories. Annual turnover in the past year ran at £7 500 000 and is expected to increase by 14 per cent this year. Recently, the company has been badly hit by bad debt and fraud losses. Together, such credit losses accounted for 2 per cent of turnover on average, and losses through fraud are estimated at a quarter of that total.

The company has been advised by management consultants to appoint a credit controller and to employ one extra secretary/clerk to support the controller. It is estimated that a salary of £12 500 would be paid to the controller and £4 500 to the secretary/clerk. Additional office and administrative costs have been estimated at £3 000 a year.

Table 13.10
Hyway Distributors – fraud prevention

	(£)
Annual outflows	
Credit controller's salary (net of tax)	6 000
Secretary/clerk's salary (net of tax)	2 160
Office and administration costs (net of tax)	1 440
Reduced fraud losses (net of tax)	(12 312)
Reduced annual outflow	2 712
Annual inflows	
Increased debtor payments (net of tax)	9 234

Based on experiences in similar firms, it is estimated that the credit controller would be able to reduce the incidence of fraud losses by around 60 per cent; additionally, his activities would have a 'spin-off' effect on other credit losses, perhaps saving some 15 per cent or so of those deficiencies.

The relevant calculations are summarised in Table 13.10, from which it can be seen that the additional staff would involve an annual expenditure of £20 000. According to the estimates presented above, there would be an additional annual income of around £19 238, subject to tax at 52 per cent; there would be a reduced fraud loss write-off of £25 650, again subject to a deduction in respect of tax now payable on that 'released' amount of profit. The net effect of the appointments, assuming the estimates prove accurate, would be an additional annual profit of around £12 000.

CONCLUSION

Loss prevention programmes can be treated just as any other investment programmes or projects. The costs and benefits of loss prevention measures can be ascertained, and the discounting techniques of capital investment appraisal can be applied to loss prevention projects. If the discounted net present value of a loss prevention scheme is positive, then the investment is worthwhile. Obviously a lot hinges on the discount rate chosen.

In the case of Hyflam (Table 13.8), for example, the discounted present value of the investment needed was calculated at £604 (at 10 per cent) and −£4 766 (at 15 per cent). If Hyflam's cost of capital, or the rate of interest at which it could borrow, was around 18 per cent, the project would clearly not be worthwhile in the short term. The value of future savings or net cash flows would be enhanced, of course, as the insurers raised successive annual premium rates as claims were made; that would increase net present value.

Hyval's increased annual cash outflows would have a present value of £5 750 (at 15 per cent), whereas the likely annual incidence of theft (£1 300 a year, net of tax) would have a present value of £6 525 (at 15 per cent). Clearly, a real saving can be made.

Following the discussion in this chapter, it can be seen that a firm wishing to pursue a programme of loss prevention is faced with four possible avenues of approach:

1   carrying all the risk itself, without insurance and without instal- ling any special equipment;
2   insuring against expected risks;
3   installing a suitable system or equipment, without insurance;
4   installing a suitable system or equipment and insuring against expected risks.

An analysis of alternative strategies will be influenced heavily by the circumstances and needs of the firm itself, but it is possible to generalise and recommend that the fourth path outlined above is the most suitable one for most firms. Installation of a suitable loss prevention system and purchase of adequate insurance cover, at a reduced or not-increased premium, offer the most attractive strategic choice for the greater number of firms.

Additionally, the wider responsibilities of the modern firm must be considered fully. The firm's managers have a duty to minimise losses and to prevent them if at all possible; the maximisation of shareholder wealth enjoins that duty, in monetary terms if in no others. However, a firm has responsibilities to its employees and the community. Fire can have effects which are much further-reaching than the immediate or consequential losses occasioned to the firm. Individuals' lives may be affected by serious injury, employment prospects may be jeopardised, neighbours' properties may be endangered, and so on.

The evaluation of the merits of a loss prevention programme cannot be limited, therefore, to the cost-benefit analysis described in this chapter. That analysis does provide, however, an essential and structured starting point for a general evaluation.

(Editorial note: Parts of this chapter rely on ideas in the author's article in Management Accounting *in November 1979; the permission of the Institute of Cost and Management Accountants to reproduce parts of that article is gratefully acknowledged.)*

REFERENCES AND FURTHER READING

Carter, R. L., 'Valuation of potential losses', *in* Carter, R. L., and Doherty, N. A., (eds), *Handbook of Risk Management,* London: Kluwer-Harrap, 1974.

Carter, R. L., and Doherty, N. A., (eds), *Handbook of Risk Management,* London: Kluwer-Harrap, 1974 (with updatings).

Crockford, N., *An Introduction to Risk Management,* Cambridge: Woodhead-Faulkner, 1980.

Crockford, N., 'The systematic identification and measurement of risk', *Foresight,* April 1976.

Department of the Environment, *Computer Fraud Survey,* Bristol: Local Government Audit Inspectorate, 1981.

Doherty, N. A., *Insurance Pricing and Loss Prevention,* Farnborough: Teakfield, 1976.

Fanning, D., 'Loss prevention: a cost-benefit approach', *Management Accounting,* November 1979.

Freund, J. E., and Williams, F. J., *Elementary Business Statistics: the Modern Approach,* 4th edn. Englewood Cliffs, N.J.: Prentice-Hall, 1982.

Hickmott, G. J. R., *Principles and Practice of Interruption Insurance,* London: Butterworth, 1970.

Mehr, R. I., and Forbes, S. W., 'Risk management decision in the total business setting', *Journal of Risk and Insurance,* September 1973.

Mehr, R. I., and Hedges, R. A., *Risk Management: Concepts and Applications,* Homewood, Ill.: Irwin, 1974.

Rosenbloom, J. S., *A Case Study in Risk Management,* New York: Appleton-Century-Crofts, 1972.
Williams, C. A., and Heims, R. M., *Risk Management and Insurance,* New York: McGraw-Hill, 1964.

14

Project Planning and Control

Richard Pike and Richard Dobbins

The authors of this overview chapter point out correctly that most of the capital budgeting literature is concerned with the evaluation of capital investment, ignoring the vital stages of implementation and control. The message conveyed in this chapter is that sound investment decisions and investment programmes require sound capital project planning and control processes. That some projects will fail is an inevitable consequence of risk-taking and a fact of business life. The proportion of failed projects could be substantially reduced, however, by an effective capital budgeting system embracing all facets of the investment planning and management process. The underlying principles and techniques have been discussed at length elsewhere in this handbook, and the authors concentrate their arguments on identifying the approach needed to ensure effective planning and control. To support their arguments and to show the relevance of the accounting and financial management aspects of the problems of capital budgeting and planning, the chapter includes a case study of one real-life company faced with alternative investment and financing strategies.

Capital budgeting has been described by Myers (1976) as

> the art of finding assets that are worth more than they cost.

This may look deceptively simple in concept, but it is, arguably, the most difficult of all the tasks facing the manager. Those who have worked on large scale projects know well the frustrations and difficulties entailed in capital investment planning, decision making, budgeting and controlling. Primarily, this is because those activities demand the approval, cooperation, enthusiasm and coordination of a variety of people, corporations, financiers and, possibly, local authorities and governments.

STRATEGIC PLANNING

Investment planning is an integral part of the wider processes of strategic planning and budgetary control. Investment proposals should not be generated on an *ad hoc* basis but should be viewed in relation to the existing and possible future investment programmes based on underlying corporate objectives and strategies. The capital investment planning process and its relationship with the overall planning process is outlined in Figure 14.1 and discussed below.

Financial decision making involves purposeful behaviour, which implies the existence of a goal or, rather more likely, some combination of goals. In the absence of any objective, the firm

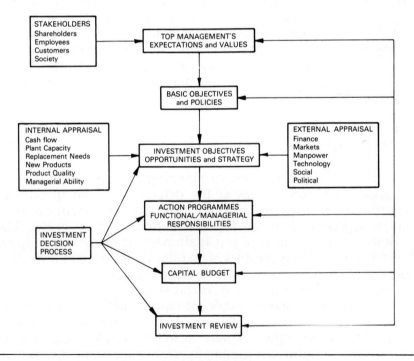

Fig. 14.1 Capital investment planning process

would have no sound criterion for choosing among alternative investment strategies and projects. In recent years a wide variety of goals has been suggested for a firm – from the traditional goal of profit maximisation to the survival of the firm, maximisation of sales, achievement of satisfactory profits, or attainment of a target market share. Modern financial management asserts that directors should seek to maximise the market value of the firm. Empirical studies suggest that firms have at least a minimum profit target and seek long run profitability and stability, rather than maximising market value (see for example Lowes and Dobbins (1978)).

Following the formulation of basic objectives and policies, specific objectives would be established to ensure that a balanced investment programme is obtained which achieves financial and other goals. As part of the decision process, investment opportunities will be generated in line with the developed strategy adopted to achieve defined objectives. Action programmes specifying responsibilities for carrying out the investment programme turn hopes and forecasts into achievable plans. They break down the investment strategy into specific tasks, dates and, sometimes, costs, which if fulfilled, will ensure that investment objectives are achieved. The capital budget is then compiled as a financial model which describes the planned activities and goals. It provides a framework for management control by the comparison of actual and budget performance.

INVESTMENT DECISION PROCESS

At the heart of any investment planning process is the decision process which commences at the perception of an investment opportunity or problem, concludes with the investment decision, and is represented in the implementation of the decision. The various stages between idea and attainment are many and complex, but a procedure along the lines of that shown in Figure 14.2, whether formalised or not, should exist in every organisation.

The first, and probably most crucial, stage in the process involves the recognition of opportunities. Economic theory regards investment as the interaction of the supply of capital and the flow of investment opportunities. Rarely, however, does a regular flow of investment opportunities present for evaluation. Some investments are recurrent, of course, such as the need to replace existing plant or

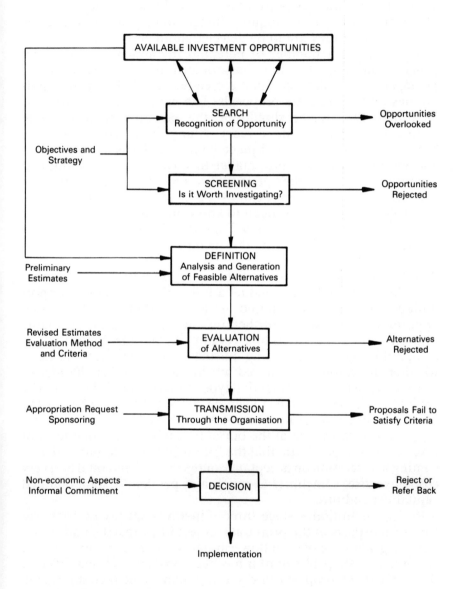

Based on a diagram by King (1975)

Fig. 14.2   Investment decision process

equipment, but even here, recognition will often be too late. Typically, profitable opportunities do not throw themselves on the manager's desk. They require imagination and diligence by management if they are to be detected at an early stage.

At any time, a number of potential investment opportunities which would satisfy the firm's basic objective(s) will be feasible. It is management's task to conduct a creative search for such opportunities and to generate proposals. The earlier an opportunity is identified, the greater should be the potential returns before competitors and imitators react. Many large companies are obviously aware of this and place heavy emphasis on innovation and research, but even the smaller firm can – at little additional expense – place a higher priority throughout its organisation on encouraging early identification of investment opportunities. Naturally enough, it is difficult to know quite how much attention should be given to this vital area. The costs of ignoring opportunities do not show up directly in the income statement; the costs of searching do.

In the second stage – that of screening proposals – it is neither feasible nor desirable to conduct a full scale evaluation of opportunities. All that is required is to determine whether such opportunities are worth further investigation. Readily available information must be used to ascertain whether the opportunity is compatible with the existing business and corporate strategy, whether the resources required are to hand, whether the idea is technically feasible, whether that type of investment is known to be profitable elsewhere or has been so previously, and whether the likely returns compensate for the risk involved. In the case of major projects, it is advisable at the outset to establish the total level of investigatory expenditure that the firm is prepared to put at risk in coming to a decision on acceptance or rejection. This could be a very costly exercise; sometimes as much as 5 per cent of total planned capital expenditure.

Project definition – stage three – involves specifying both the technical aspects of the proposal (project life, capacity, and so on) and the generation of cash flow estimates. An investment proposal is vague and shapeless until it has been properly defined. Even at this early stage, proposals are gaining management commitment. As information is being gathered, a number of people are beginning to give backing and tacit promises, and minor decisions are being made – such as incurring expense on a feasibility study.

Evaluation

Much of the literature on capital investment decision making is concerned solely with the evaluation of projects. While such evaluation is fundamental, it is only one stage of a complex investment process. The evaluation stage in the decision process involves the assembly of information in terms of inputs and outputs and the application of specified investment criteria to produce the optimum capital project mix. In line with the objective of maximising shareholders' wealth, it is important that inputs and outputs are measured by cash flows rather than profit flows. The main differences between the two are that cash flows make no distinction between capital and revenue items and ignore accounting concepts and policies such as the accruals and realisation concepts and depreciation. In addition, only incremental after tax cash flows should be considered, that is those cash flows that arise as a result of a specific decision. However, those cash flows are not always easily determined.

The assumed objective implies consideration of the timing of cash flows. The two better known discounted cash flow techniques are net present value (NPV) and internal rate of return (IRR), as described in Chapter 4 of this handbook. Only net present value is wholly compatible with the objective of maximising market value. The internal rate of return criterion is less likely to give correct solutions where mutually exclusive projects differ significantly with respect to the size of investment, pattern of cash flow, or length of project life.

Uncertainty surrounds the future returns from any capital investment. Over the past few decades a variety of techniques has been developed in an attempt to evaluate the risk dimension; these include, among others, sensitivity analysis, simulation techniques, decision-tree analysis, and certainty equivalent factors. Nonetheless, the evaluation of risk is not an optional extra. It is fundamental to the appraisal of any investment opportunity or proposal.

Companies vary widely in the extent to which evaluation systems are formalised and sophisticated. Simple models such as payback period are still popular today, and have the merit of being easy to understand and interpret. One reason given for the use of payback analysis is that its strong emphasis on the early years of a project's life is wholly appropriate to recent economic conditions under which long run forecasting has been extremely difficult and hazardous.

Other reasons advanced for the reluctance of many firms to adopt more sophisticated approaches are that managers are still not fully aware of the usefulness of the 'new' techniques, and that managers are wary of making probability estimates which, if proved incorrect or markedly inaccurate, would bring their judgement into question. Additionally, there is no evidence to suggest that firms using more advanced evaluation techniques consistently produce better investment decisions, and the costs of improving the evaluation system may well outweigh the benefits.

Project review and approval

Once the evaluation stage has been completed, the investment proposal moves through the various levels of the organisational hierarchy until it is eventually approved or rejected. It is well to remember that this process, like the whole of the capital budgeting operation, is not an abstraction from reality, considered theoretically in an academic setting. It takes place in an active organisation with all the attendant problems of human relations, ambitions and motivations and of political manoeuvring. The willingness of a manager to sponsor a project often depends not so much on the intrinsic merits of the project as on the possible enhancement of his own standing as a manager. It is for that reason that some economically viable projects ultimately founder and never reach the approval stage. Middle management may well be more risk-averse than senior management, in which case very few projects with high rewards and moderate or high risk will ever be sponsored. In most organisations, a decision maker appraises the sponsor as much as the project.

For most firms, the approval stage is little more than a formal endorsement of commitments already given or pledged. However, this stage performs a vital quality control service. If the earlier stages have been executed correctly and if established criteria are met, there is little reason to reject proposals at this late stage. Senior management should review the proposal and ask the following questions. Are the estimates well based and reasonably accurate? What is the likelihood (and cost) of failure? Have all available alternatives been explored fully? Are there any unquantified aspects to be considered? No matter how sophisticated the evaluation techniques employed, the effectiveness of a capital budgeting process is dependent largely upon the accurancy of cash flow

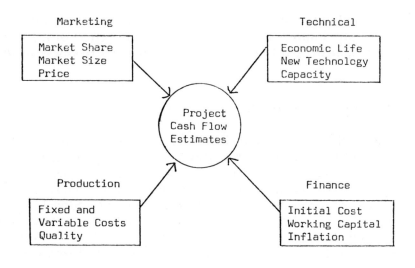

Fig. 14.3   Economic assumptions influencing cash flow estimates

estimates. These estimates are, in their turn, dependent upon the validity and soundness of the assumptions concerning a number of economic variables, as depicted in Figure 14.3.

Over the past decade the problem of estimating inflation has caused great concern. A recent survey by one of the authors revealed that, although firms have improved their approach to the inflation problem over the past five years, only 29 per cent of the largest organisations surveyed specified separate rates for costs and revenues. The most popular approach was to specify cash flows in constant prices and to apply a real rate of return (that is, excluding inflation) to these figures. While it was clear that some firms were very careful in their calculation of the real rate of return, many had given little thought to the full implications of excluding the impact of inflation in hurdle rates and cash flows.

The senior management review should examine also the likelihood of project failure and the associated costs. Although the main reason for failure is usually poor estimation of economic variables, it could also result from such problems as delays in project construction and implementation. A formal assessment of those risks should be conducted, to explore ways of reducing the probability and cost of failure. Wherever possible, an abandonment option (that is, an opportunity at specified times to abandon the project and liquidate the investment) should be built into the project's programme. This can have the double effect of reducing the anticipated cash outflows and reducing the riskiness of the project.

PROJECT COST CONTROL

The main difference between investment in fixed and current assets is that, unlike investment in current assets, it may be many years before the success or failure of a long term capital investment is fully appreciated. In the meantime, the decision maker will have judged many investment options with little informational feedback on the profitability of earlier profits. Learning by trial and error is a slow and costly business with fixed investments, and some form of project control and review is necessary. Figure 14.4 outlines the

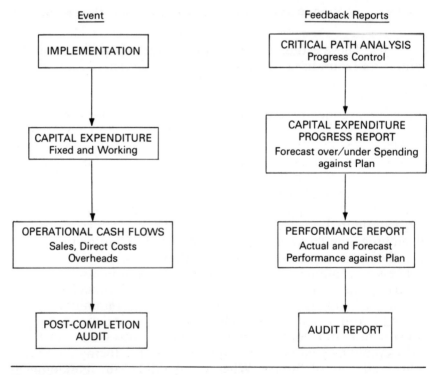

Fig. 14.4   Implementation and control

stages and information requirements for such a control and review system. It includes the use of critical path analysis, which provides a systematic approach to the planning and control of project implementation, and regular capital expenditure progress forecasts of over or underspending against plan. Review information will include feedback on investment performance against plan and, where appropriate, a post-completion audit review.

The primary purpose of these reports is to furnish management with information on the success or otherwise of the investment, so that the quality of future investment decisions will be improved. It may become apparent, for example, that sales estimates are consistently higher than actual results. That kind of information could be used to improve the quality of the marketing data input into the evaluation process.

Potential for cost control exists in the early stages of implementation – such as in the design, tendering and procurement stages. Figure 14.5 shows the relationship between project life and cost control potential. As projects move towards completion and become fully operational, the potential for cost control diminishes rapidly.

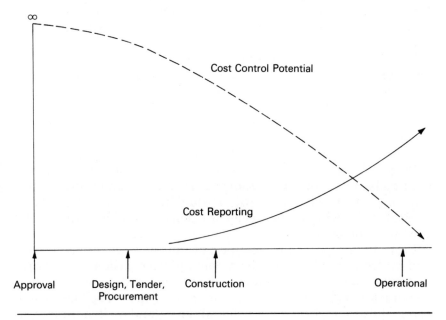

Fig. 14.5 Cost control potential

Typically, nonetheless, cost reporting increases in inverse ratio to cost control potential.

Sound investment decisions require a comprehensive capital investment planning and control process. Investment control and review should, as far as possible, control the cost and timing of project implementation and improve the planning of future investments.

CAPITAL BUDGETING – AN EXAMPLE

As an exemplification of a capital investment decision process, the following case study describes the opportunities facing a family-owned transport firm and the appraisal of those opportunities.

Heaton Transport Limited is a family business, owned by three brothers, Matthew, Mark and Luke Cuthbertson. The son-in-law of the eldest brother, Matthew, has recently joined the firm as financial controller. A qualified accountant, John Reynolds has the primary responsibility of controlling the firm's financial management and overseeing the management accounting function. Additionally, however, he has been given the responsibility for identifying and evaluating capital investment projects and for reviewing the firm's capital structure.

Four projects are being analysed for the coming year; these are the four main capital investment proposals available to Heaton Transport for that period. Table 14.1 gives details of costs and cash flows for each of those four projects.

Project A proposes the construction of additional warehousing space at the firm's Northern depot; the extra space would provide four new loading bays and additional storage accommodation.

Project B proposes the addition of four new loading bays to the existing building; the extra storage space created under Proposal A is not urgently needed. The project would have the same capital cost as Project A owing to the need for extensive modifications to the existing structures.

Project C proposes the purchase of four new articulated tractor and trailer units. Owing to heavy demand from customers, the firm had been forced to rely on independent freelance drivers, using their own tractor and trailer units, on a short term basis. The high cost of using those temporary drivers and units makes it desirable to discontinue that practice, or at least not to use their services too

Table 14.1
Project costs and cash flows

	Project A	Project B	Project C	Project D
Cost (£)	300 000	300 000	600 000	300 000
Cash inflows (£)				
Year 1	61 500	210 000	133 500	83 220
2	61 500	150 000	133 500	83 220
3	61 500	45 000	133 500	83 220
4	61 500	30 000	133 500	83 220
5	61 500		133 500	83 220
6	61 500		133 500	
7	61 500		133 500	
8	61 500		133 500	
9	61 500		133 500	
10	61 500		133 500	

often. Project C would resolve that problem and would also ensure better maintenance programs for all Heaton equipment in service.

Project D proposes the purchase of special handling equipment for use at the Southern depot, to facilitate the loading and unloading of chemical drums, the freightage of which is likely to increase significantly over the next few years, owing to Heaton's expertise in

Table 14.2
Forecast profit and loss account – present year

	£
Sales	10 800 000
less Variable expenses	8 100 000
Gross profit (25% on sales)	2 700 000
less Operating expenses (including depreciation £576 000)	1 775 000
Net profit before tax	925 000
less Tax (@ 52%)	481 000
Net profit after tax	444 000
less Dividends (@ 10%)	120 000
Retained earnings	324 000

the handling, storage and transportation of awkward and potentially dangerous cargoes. Government agencies are, however, considering plans to restrict the carriage by road of such hazardous loads.

Projects A and B are mutually exclusive. On the basis of a forecast profit and loss account for the present year, with sales expected to run at £10 800 000, Reynolds expects around £900 000 to be available from internally generated sources (retained earnings plus depreciation charges) for investment in capital projects. The firm has used a cost of capital of 10 per cent in previous evaluations and Reynolds accepts that rate as being reasonable in the current circumstances. The forecast profit and loss account for the present year and the forecast balance sheet at the year end are given in Tables 14.2 and 14.3, respectively.

As a preliminary step, Reynolds calculates the net present values of the four projects, their respective internal rates of return and profitability indices. Those calculations are summarised in Table 14.4. The incidence of any first year allowances or subsequent tax equalisation charges has been ignored for the purposes of those calculations.

On the basis of the calculations in Table 14.4, Reynolds proposes that Projects C and A be approved for implementation. He prefers to use the net present value criterion, although previous decisions in the firm have been made on the basis of a required rate of return of 16 per cent, which would argue for the adoption of proposals B and C.

Notwithstanding the reported moves to restrict the road move-

Table 14.3
Forecast balance sheet – present year

		£
Net fixed assets		3 045 000
Current assets	1 350 000	
less Current liabilities	825 000	
Net current assets		525 000
		3 570 000
Share capital		1 200 000
Retained earnings		2 370 000
		3 570 000

Table 14.4
Project evaluation criteria

	Project A	Project B	Project C	Project D
Net present value (@ 10% discount factor)	£77 918	£69 075	£220 358	£15 487
Internal rate of return	15.8%	25.4%	18.0%	12.2%
Profitability index (cost-benefit ratio)	1.26	1.23	1.37	1.05

ment of hazardous cargoes, Reynolds has taken advice from the firm's traffic manager, and from other firms engaged in the industry, and it is thought unlikely that effective controls could be brought in for another six years or so. Arguably, the cash flows for Project D could be extended for some time beyond the five-year life selected. In Reynolds' view, it would make good sense to invest the further £300 000 in Project D; it reveals a positive net present value and is likely to continue to generate sizable incremental cash flows for some years beyond the deadline date chosen in the appraisal.

The Cuthbertsons' personal investments yield an average annual return of 16 per cent; the opportunity cost of those 'outside' investments. In other words, funds are available over and above the £900 000 expected to be generated from this year's operations, but the marginal cost of those additional funds is 16 per cent rather than the 10 per cent cost of internal funds.

Reynolds expects to present further investment opportunities over the coming five years and he expects to be able to demonstrate that a much higher level of capital investment can be undertaken at higher rates of return. Under the existing capital structure, any extra capital for investment purposes would have to come from the Cuthbertsons, who would have to liquidate other investments and so would expect to earn at least 16 per cent on those further injections of capital into Heaton Transport. The company has a policy of not using long term debt, with which Reynolds does not agree, and he is anxious to change the brothers' minds in that respect. He believes that debt financing has significant advantages and would have marked beneficial effects on the capital structure of the company and on its capital budgeting.

To that end he prepares a forecast profit and loss account for the

Table 14.5
Forecast profit and loss account – coming year

	£
Sales	13 000 000
less Variable expenses	9 750 000
Gross profit (30%)	3 900 000
less Operating expenses (including depreciation £621 000 and debt interest £240 000)	2 328 125
Net profit before tax	1 571 875
less Tax (@ 52%)	817 375
Net profit after tax	754 500
less Dividends (@ 10%)	120 000
Retained earnings	634 500

coming year, based on the implementation of Projects A, C and D, and assuming a long term loan of £1 500 000 could be negotiated at an annual rate of interest of 16 per cent. That forecast profit and loss account is shown in Table 14.5, and the resultant forecast balance sheet as at the end of the coming year is given in Table 14.6. Reynolds expects an underlying growth of 10 per cent in the sales

Table 14.6
Forecast balance sheet – after inclusion of long term debt

		£
Net fixed assets		4 998 000
Current assets	1 636 500	
less Current liabilities	930 000	
Net current assets		706 500
		5 704 500
Share capital		1 200 000
Retained earnings		3 004 500
Shareholders' funds		4 204 500
Long term debt		1 500 000
		5 704 500

revenues and he estimates that the implementation of the three projects will generate a further gross revenue of £1 120 000 in the coming year. Again, those estimates ignore any first year tax allowances.

In his discussions with the Cuthbertsons, Reynolds will demonstrate that the inclusion of long term debt will reduce the company's cost of capital from its present 10 per cent to around 9.4 per cent, as shown in Table 14.7. The calculation of the weighted average cost of capital for the geared firm (that is, with long term debt in its capital structure) is relatively straightforward: the after tax cost of the annual interest payment is £115 200, representing an effective cost of 7.7 per cent for the long term debt. The weightings are arrived at by calculating the proportionate presence of each class of fund in the total capital employed in the firm.

Table 14.7
Capital structure and the cost of capital

	Capital employed	Weighting	Cost	Weighted cost
No long term debt				
Shareholders' funds	£3 570 000	1.00	10.0%	10.0%
Long term debt	£0	0	0%	0%
	£3 750 000	1.00		10.0%
Long term debt				
Shareholders' funds	£4 204 500	0.74	10.0%	7.4%
Long term debt	£1 500 000	0.26	7.7%(a)	2.0%
	£5 704 500	1.00		9.4%

(a) after tax cost – nominal interest 16% p.a.; tax rate 52%.

The ratio of long term debt to total assets for the geared firm would be 26.3 per cent, against a current industry average of 50 per cent. Other significant financial ratios would alter beneficially. The present relationship of current assets to current liabilities is 1.64:1; in the geared company, that ratio would increase to 1.76:1. The acid test or quick ratio is currently 1.27:1, and it would rise to 1.33:1. The

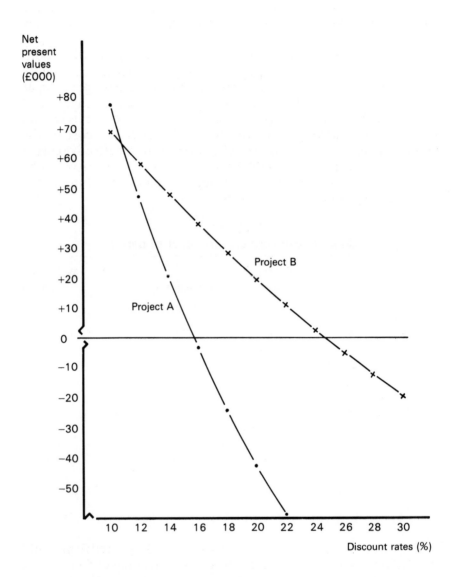

Fig. 14.6   Project A v Project B – net present value curves

rate of return on capital employed (expressed as earnings before interest and tax as a percentage of capital employed) would fall from 42 per cent to near 32 per cent, but the rate of return on shareholders' funds (expressed as net earnings attributable to shareholders after tax as a percentage of shareholders' funds) would rise from just over 12 per cent to near 18 per cent.

On the basis that Projects A and B were mutually exclusive, and since Project A had the higher net present value, Reynolds decided that whatever else was approved, Project A was to be preferred to Project B. However, the two projects bear further examination. Project A provides storage space which is not immediately required. If Project A were adopted, a new warehouse would be constructed in five years' time to supplement the present facilities. If Project B were adopted, a new warehouse would be built in one year's time, with the existing Northern depot structure becoming a maintenance and repair shop.

It is often of assistance to the capital investment decision to plot the returns on a graph. Figure 14.6 depicts the returns (that is, net present values) of Projects A and B plotted against various discount rates. Positive discounted returns are shown above the horizontal 'zero return' line; negative discounted returns are shown below that line. If the curves of the two proposals are examined and interpreted, it can be seen that Project A is a better investment candidate only when the lowest acceptable rate of return is below 11 per cent or so; in all other circumstances, Project B is better. The discounted internal rate of return for each alternative is at the point where the present value line crosses the zero axis on the chart (15.8 per cent for A and 25.4 per cent for B). The cost of the investment is balanced by the discounted returns at the rate indicated at the point of crossover.

If Reynolds accepts the apparent total capital budget constraint of £900 000 in the coming year, he has to choose between two possible combinations, assuming that the projects are indivisible and on the basis that Project D is well out of line and should be ignored at this stage. A further assumption is that the full £900 000 would be invested, although that condition might well be relaxed. Since Project C offers the highest net present value, it would be a pre-eminent candidate for adoption; the question remains as to whether Project A or Project B should be adopted in addition.

Table 14.8 compares the two alternative sets of projects: C + A, and C + B. It can be seen that the first combination generates a present value cash flow totalling £1 198 276, the second a total of

Table 14.8
Project combinations

	£
Alternative One	
Project C: present value (@ 10%)	820 358
Project A: present value (@ 10%)	377 918
	1 198 276
Cost of investments	900 000
Net present value	298 276
Alternative Two	
Project C: present value (@ 10%)	820 358
Project B: present value (@ 10%)	369 075
	1 189 433
Cost of investments	900 000
Net present value	289 433

£1 189 433. There is a net difference between the two combinations of £8 843 in net present value terms. However, as detailed in Table 14.1, Project B generates high cash flows in the first two years of its life. A realistic view of Heaton Transport's present and likely future situations might lead to the recommendation of Project B for adoption, with a fresh look being taken at the Northern depot in three years' time.

It is argued by the elder Cuthbertson brother that some account should be taken of the possibility of error in Reynolds' estimates. The cash flows predicted by Reynolds are thought to be the most likely, but what would be the situation if they were wrong by a factor

Table 14.9
Project A v Project B

	Project A	Project B
	£	£
Most likely outcome's net present value (@ 10%)	77 918	69 075
Pessimistic outcome's net present value (@ 10%)	2 334	−4 740
Optimistic outcome's net present value (@ 10%)	153 501	142 890

of 20 per cent either way? Reynolds prepares a comparison between Project A and Project B of the most likely, the pessimistic, and the optimistic net present value outcomes, as shown in Table 14.9, from which it could be seen that Project A was consistently better than Project B.

CONCLUSION

In making any investment decision with a long range impact, there is always the risk that the estimates will be rendered useless by economic or social changes, within the company, the industry or the community. The problem can be approached by the use of 'what if' modelling and the incorporation of probabilities in the evaluation.

After implementation, a project must be watched closely. Its performance, from a technical and an economic point of view, must be audited or reviewed regularly and particularly at the end of the initial 'shakedown' or settling-in period. That audit or review will reveal whether things are going to plan, and whether the project is meeting expectations.

Project evaluations may be made more carefully if those evaluations are to be given a performance test at a later date. Over and above that benefit, however, project audits will reveal information and behaviour patterns which can be applied in future investment planning.

The strategic importance of capital investment decisions demands a proper system of planning and control. Capital investment decisions usually involve the commitment of substantial sums of money for long periods of time. Plans must be made well into an uncertain or parlous future. The prosperity or continued existence of a company may depend upon the results of a single or relatively few investment decisions. Above all, it may be impossible or disastrously expensive to reverse the effects of a poor decision.

Systematic monitoring and performance measurement procedures are vital to a firm's capital budgeting programmes.

REFERENCES AND FURTHER READING

Bierman, H., and Smidt, S., *The Capital Budgeting Decision,* 4th edn. New York: Macmillan, 1975.

Cyert, R. M., Dill, W. R., and March, J. G., 'The role of expectations in business decision-making', *Administrative Science Quarterly*, 1958.

King, P., 'Is the emphasis of capital budgeting theory misplaced?', *Journal of Business Finance and Accounting*, Spring 1975.

Levy, H., and Sarnat, M., *Capital Investment and Financial Decisions*, 2nd edn. Englewood Cliffs, N.J.: Prentice-Hall, 1982.

Lowes, B., and Dobbins, R., 'Objective setting: a corporate planning approach', *Managerial Finance*, 1978.

Merrett, A. J., and Sykes, A., *The Finance and Analysis of Capital Projects*, 2nd edn., London: Longman, 1973.

Myers, S. C., *Modern Developments in Financial Management*, Hinsdale, Ill.: Dryden, 1976.

Solomon, E., *The Theory of Financial Management*, New York: Columbia University Press, 1963.

Van Horne, J. C., 'Capital budgeting decisions involving combinations of risky investments', *Management Science*, October 1966.

Van Horne, J. C., *Financial Management and Policy*, 5th edn., Englewood Cliffs, N.J.: Prentice-Hall, 1980.

Weingartner, H. M., *Mathematical Programming and the Analysis of Capital Budgeting Problems*, Englewood Cliffs, N.J.: Prentice-Hall, 1963.

Weingartner, H. M., 'The excess present value index – a theoretical basis and critique', *Journal of Accounting Research*, Autumn 1963.

15

Management Auditing

Janusz Santocki

The author of this contribution argues that the philosophy of management audit deems every organisation capable of improvement and recognises that managers are made and not born. Management audit is a constructive appraisal of the strengths and weaknesses of a management team, accompanied by recommendations as to the best ways of improving the team's performance, achieving corporate objectives and implementing corporate policies. To be effective, management audit 'must be and be seen to be an outside function'. The author discusses the correct approach to be adopted and distinguishes between the conventional duties of the financial auditor and the different concerns of the management auditor. The management auditor appraises the business structure of an organisation, examining the use of the human and material resources employed, and reviews the management team's processes for determining, planning and controlling organisational objectives and policies. Holding that there are five essential elements in the management auditor's method of work – information, knowledge, techniques, analysis, and report – and describing the nature of each item, the author argues for the creation of a multi-disciplinary management audit team. Managers now have greater accountability to wider interest groups than ever before and a properly conducted management audit is a most effective way of determining the performance and achievements of a management team and focusing attention on the real problems in an organisation. Management audit is more than just an accountancy function, but it is a process in which the management accountant has an important role to play.

Management audit is not a new concept. What is new is the greatly increasing interest in the techniques and function of a management audit shown during the past two decades. The earliest recorded evidence of the concept seems to be that given by de Roover (1963), who described how an auditor was sent to the London branch of the Medici Bank in 1948.

> with instructions to audit the books to ascertain whether the manager had made wise investments and operated within the scope of the policies established by the managing partners.

As a further example of early interest in management audit, a leading work was published in London in the early 1930s (Rose, 1932). Empirical research in management auditing was being conducted in Europe and the United States during the 1950s and early 1960s.

The description of the Medici Bank auditor's brief sets out well and simply the objective of management audit. The assumption is that the manager's duty is to make 'wise investments' and that it is for the auditor to check whether or not that duty has been discharged efficiently and to report accordingly. It is accepted that the manager has the duty not only to operate within the scope of the policies and rules of an organisation, but also to attempt to make the optimal use of resources under his control.

The philosophy of management audit refuses to accept that the management of an organisation cannot be improved. Equally, it is false to hold that directors are born with the qualities required for successful management and that those qualities cannot be developed. Acceptance of these tenets means that directors and managers are prepared to open their managerial process and the resulting performance to somebody else's appraisal. That appraisal should comprise two elements: the review, and the recommendations. These should assist management through reporting on weaknesses in performance and recommend ways of minimising, if not eradicating, those weaknesses.

MEANING OF MANAGEMENT AUDIT

Several definitions have been advanced in attempts to set out the meaning of the management audit function. The Dutch accountants' institute (Nederlands Instituut van Registeraccountants, 1979) saw management audit as a:

recurrent comprehensive investigation into apparently healthy organisations with the object of achieving an insight into the state of the organisation – and also its environment – so as to be able to form an opinion on future prospects whereby specific action can be taken to arrive at a better control of the operations of the organisation.

Another definition was provided by Dombrower (1972), who saw management auditing as:

a concept which will assist management in developing its own resources more effectively by adopting an independent and objective analytical approach to (a) the organization, (b) the controls, and (c) the functions of the entire operation. The results of this review are then compared to the objectives and standards of the organization with specific reference to generally accepted management and operational concepts. Usually a sound operational audit department will be preventive in its approach, since it will attempt to detect problem areas while they are in their early stages of development.

Campfield (1967) defined management audit as follows:

Management auditing is an informed and constructive analysis, evaluation, and series of recommendations regarding the broad spectrum of plans, processes, people and problems of an economic entity.

These definitions share a marked degree of common ground. Santocki (1976) defined management audit as an objective, independent, informed and constructive appraisal of the effectiveness of managers or teams of managers in their achievement of corporate targets and objectives, identifying existing and potential strengths and weaknesses at all levels in the organisation and in all functions and operations of the organisation. Presentation of recommendations designed to rectify weaknesses and potential weaknesses featured prominently in this context.

Probably the most important aspect of management auditing is the intention to assist management to improve performance. Through that assistance, the management auditor can help to increase productivity and profitability. The function is advisory, however, in the management consultancy tradition, and not executive. The management audit draws management's attention to what needs to be done to make the best use of the resources available. Management audit is intended neither to replace management nor to curtail its responsibility for decision making and control. The role of management auditing is to provide relevant and timely information on the basis of which management can make decisions.

The management auditing process is a system of investigation, analysis and appraisal. It is not the 'doing' function; its objective is to conduct the audit and produce the recommendations that will lead to the 'doing'. The description of management auditing as 'preventive medicine' is an apt one. It is important for management auditors to report in the early stages of each project, before problems have the chance to get out of hand.

The management auditor must be independent and his function must be, and be seen to be, 'external'. A management audit team must not form part of the management team of the department which is being appraised. The team must be independent of those being audited – and this happens in most organisations, where the management audit team is responsible to a chief executive or controller.

Confusion has arisen in the literature as to the meanings of apparently synonymous names for the process. Among others, the terms 'management audit', 'performance review', 'operational audit', and 'efficiency audit' have been used interchangeably. The distinction between an operational audit and a management audit, advocated by some writers, deserves a brief discussion. The former is said to be a purely internal function to serve the needs of an organisation's management; the latter is an 'external' function serving the needs of a wider audience – such as the shareholders, for instance. Those refinements seem unnecessary. Management auditing is the more popular term, and it can be for management (the internal role) and for shareholders (the external role). There seems little point in labouring what is a relatively unclear distinction.

THE APPROACH

'An auditor is a watchdog' is an apt description of the role of the statutory financial audit, and still represents the legal view of the auditing function. An outsider checks the administration of an entity for a period, with a view to detecting errors or omissions in financial statements. Mistakes could be either intentional or accidental. Intentional errors include such actions as the falsification of accounts or the embezzlement of property. Unintentional errors arise from incompetence of staff or imperfection of systems and controls.

The watchdog is the guardian of conventions and orderliness, and this is accepted as an important function. The role of the statutory financial auditor can be described as essentially protective, that is ensuring that the rules are observed. The limitations of such a function are that its main contribution to the wealth of an organisation and its owners is to minimise losses incurred through dishonesty or negligence, and that it attests only to the reliability and accuracy of certain kinds of published financial information. With the adoption of auditing standards by the main professional bodies, those limitations are reinforced by the narrowing field of relevance of the auditor's opinion. Considerable disquiet has been expressed about the value of the financial auditing process – and, let it be said, the increasing cost of that process (see, for example, Briston and Perks (1977)).

The fundamental philosophy in the auditing process should be to increase the wealth of an organisation, as well as to protect it. That requires a more constructive and dynamic approach. The underlying assumption is that an organisation's management has not yet reached its optimum performance, realises that fact, and is open to suggestions as to how to improve performance and attain the optimum.

Both kinds of auditor – financial and management – may use the same or similar techniques. The ways in which each uses those techniques will differ, however, because the objectives differ. Management auditing is a comparatively new 'philosophy' and, as such, requires a different attitude of mind in its implementation. A description of some typical questions will illustrate and explain the differences in approach of the two kinds of auditor. Table 15.1 presents examples of financial auditing and management auditing questions.

The difference between the two groups of questions is fundamental and demonstrates that the need for a management audit is derived from the extended meaning of management's accountability. Attention turns from the verification of the compliance of management with regulatory frameworks and of the accuracy and reliability of the financial information to the assessment of underlying causes, related management practices, and resulting managerial perfor-

Table 15.1
Financial audit *v* management audit

Financial audit	Management audit
Has the entity kept proper accounting records?	Is the data provided to management accurate and timely and relevant?
Was the transaction properly authorised and is there acceptable evidence?	Has management satisfied itself that the price paid was the most economical, and how did it do so?
Are salaries paid to key employees within the limits imposed by the entity's regulations?	Is there a staff development programme adequate to replace retiring key employees and to cater for future likely requirements?
Do the balance sheet and profit and loss account show a true and fair view?	Is management well informed of existing and potential weaknesses and limitations in planning and budgetary controls?
Have decisions been made within the formal powers of the directors?	Can the processes leading to decision making be improved?

mance. Public demands for improved accountability continue to grow and the legalistic approach of the statutory financial auditor is inadequate for the discharge of the extended accountability of management.

Scope of management auditing

The areas of management auditors' involvement described and discussed here are those for which there is reasonably good evidence of practical application and resulting benefits.

First, there must be an appraisal of the business's organisational structure, with special reference to the effective use of all the resources employed, physical and financial and human, and to the degree of support for the aims and objectives of the business. The management auditor reviews the organisation's structure by analysing its components and relating those to the corporate aims. Too elaborate a structure is cumbersome, ineffective and costly; idle capacity is wasteful; shortages and bottlenecks are expensive of time and resources; and so on.

Second, there is the appraisal of management's processes and procedures for determining organisational objectives and policies. Frequently better and more effective ways will be available, and a thorough analysis and evaluation of existing processes will lead to the identification of aspects susceptible to improvement.

Third, there is the appraisal of management systems of planning and control, with a view to determining whether those systems are adequate, whether they are reviewed and updated regularly, and whether they are understood and used continuously by all employees. To be effective, any system must be clearly understood by those using it and must be reviewed regularly to ensure its continued relevance and feasibility.

Fourth, there is the appraisal of management control techniques, to determine whether relevant, timely and accurate information reaches all levels of management, whether such information is acted upon, and whether the information contains budgetary control and standard costing data. The importance of relevant information being available to management at the right time has been emphasised by other contributors to this handbook and there can be no substitute for timely and useful information.

Fifth, there is the appraisal of technical competence, to determine the abilities of staff to achieve the organisation's objectives and to examine the scope and effectiveness of staff development and training schemes and the nature and extent of staff recruitment. The management auditor is concerned to discover whether the organisation possesses the resources necessary to achieve its objectives efficiently and effectively. Does management appreciate the technical and resource environment in which it operates, and is it aware of the problems and dangers ahead? Proper management requires an appreciation of both short term and long term needs and opportunities.

Sixth, there is the appraisal of management planning and control systems in the terms of the communication systems which they incorporate, so that effective systems transmit relevant and timely information. This aim of management auditing goes further than the appraisal of management control techniques, and it refers to the effectiveness of the entire communication system throughout the organisation. The question to decide is whether a proper monitoring procedure ensures that all concerned receive timely, accurate and adequate information. Intuition and hunch are not the best foundations for decision making and control; relevant information is crucial. A management auditor with experience and skill can make a significant contribution to the resolution of any problems in this area.

Seventh, there is the appraisal of results, with a view to determining whether or not the firm's objectives and policies are appropriate to the business and its environment, are attainable, and are being met. Ideal objectives and policies are easy to proclaim, but the frustration caused by failing to achieve such ideal targets can be most demotivating and dysfunctional. The management auditor's review and assessment will bring a sense of reality to the process of determining objectives and policies. Once appropriateness and feasibility are established, the determination of actual attainment levels can follow smoothly.

Management training and performance

Management auditing can contribute markedly to the management training scheme of an organisation. Typical responses to a survey conducted by the author included the following:

> The most difficult problem at present is retaining the people in the [management audit] team and recruiting suitable replacements. We had over 100 per cent labour turnover last year due to members of the team moving into operating companies as line managers ...

and other respondents indicated that a period with the management audit team was an integral part of managerial training programmes.

It is perhaps a high commendation for the management auditing process that it contributes significantly to the development of line managers, even to the extent of forming a pool of managerial talent from which line managers can be recruited.

Management auditing contributes also to the development of standards for the evaluation of managerial performance. Teach-ins and staff seminars conducted by a management audit team can assist greatly in the acceptance by managers of a system of managerial assessment. Performance standards must be both properly based in the organisation's activities and clearly understood by those to be evaluated; management auditing helps markedly in those respects.

AUDITING ASSIGNMENTS

The typical management audit assignment is not a single 'problem' or area; of routine, a management audit takes full account of all facets of an organisation's activities. Table 15.2, however, presents some specific areas of concern, drawn from the management audit programme of a leading UK public company.

Table 15.2
Typical management auditing assignments

To review and report upon labour turnover at a number of different locations

> An imposed assignment from the board of directors, deriving from a realisation that turnover rates at certain locations were very much higher than at others.

To review and report upon certain cost centres

> Part of a regular random audit assignment.

To review and report upon the distribution methods and procedures of a regional depot

> An audit assignment from line management, concerned that one regional depot was out of line with other depots.

To investigate and report upon all aspects of operations at a specific location

> A comprehensive audit assignment from senior management.

To review the staffing position of the production planning department

> An assignment prior to the decision whether or not to approve a request for additional staff in the production planning department.

They are examples of an audit programme for one period of three months, and are drawn from Santocki (1979). The management audit programmes of many companies have life cycles of three or four years, during which all aspects of operations are reviewed more or less automatically. Additionally, from time to time a number of further assignments are imposed or requested.

Once an established management auditing function exists within an organisation, access to it is generally available to senior and line management, as the examples in the table demonstrate.

Method of working

There are three fundamental questions which the management auditor will pose in connection with most, if not all, assignments, and which will influence the chosen method of fulfilling the assignment:

1 Does the organisation know what it wants to achieve? The ambiguity of objectives and policies should be resolved before other aspects can be examined properly.
2 Is the organisation capable of achieving what it wants to achieve? Targets which are too demanding or unrealistic are worse for staff motivation and optimising behaviour patterns than no objectives at all.
3 Are the organisation's structure and methods efficient and effective enough to allow it to pursue those objectives and policies? This aspect of the investigation requires the greatest amount of effort in a management audit.

Answers to those three preliminary questions will lead to two further questions:

4 Are there any ways in which the management auditor can assist management in its pursuit of the organisation's objectives and policies?
5 Can the management auditor assist management to improve processes and procedures for the attainment of those objectives and policies?

There are five essential elements of the management auditing process: information, knowledge, techniques, analysis, and report.

Information

Information plays a key role in any management audit. The past affects the present and the two together influence the future; for each phase, information is needed. The management auditor may face two particular problems in respect of information provision. First, staff may volunteer information, and the management auditor should be conscious of the motives behind such voluntary disclosure. Second, staff may be too guarded in their dealings with the management auditor and reveal little information or make its acquisition difficult. A more careful explanation to staff, describing the need for a management audit and the scope of its findings and recommendations should go some way towards alleviating that problem. Above all else, a management auditor should try to collect information objectively, reducing the impact of subjective personal judgements.

Knowledge

The management auditor should get to know the available management methods and practices which are appropriate to his work. Managerial planning and decision making processes should be understood clearly, and the management auditor should be able, when necessary or appropriate, to see matters as a practising line or functional manager would.

He must also possess a sound knowledge of the particular organisation or department and its operations. This knowledge will ensure that he will begin his work from a favourable position; it may also, of course, impart a degree of prejudice, in that the auditor will not be wholly impartial, but an experienced management auditor will be sufficiently skilful to discount any such special bias.

Techniques

Among the management auditing techniques in common use are the following. A well-conducted interview is unavoidable since other techniques of eliciting information are unlikely to be so effective. Such an interview must be planned and structured, and the interview must be conducted in a disciplined and professional manner.

Direct observation is a further essential technique for management auditing, and it will generally disclose information which is difficult to recover or collect by other means. Staff relationships, for example, can best be assessed by observation; attitudes can be discerned; operational styles and preferences can be appraised. The study of internal documentation – staff manuals, organisation charts, operational memoranda, and so on – will reveal a great deal more about an organisation and its management than might be thought likely. The management auditor will need to familiarise himself with the budgets, forecasts and internal accounting reports of the subject entity.

In some instances, a questionnaire approach may be followed with good effect, especially where an anonymous response can be elicited on various otherwise sensitive topics. As in any other use of questionnaires, the management auditor needs to satisfy himself about the validity, truthfulness and relevance of both questions and answers.

Ratio analysis and trend analysis are two commonly used

techniques which the management auditor will use to evaluate the performance and status of the unit being audited.

Analysis

Analysis can be considered in two ways: from the point of view of the adequacy of the information available, and from that of the interpretation of the information.

A management auditor does not need to know all the facts; sufficient relevant information is all that is required. Total and absolute data are expensive, both in their collection and in their interpretation. The management auditor should seek out significant and relevant information, rather than accept all that is offered or available.

The interpretation of that information must be conducted sensibly and in a structured way. The first important task will be to separate facts from opinions. The measurement of management performance is discussed elsewhere in this handbook (see Chapter 17 for example), and there are a number of popular and apposite standards by which to judge managerial performance – for instance, return on capital employed or rate of growth. Other measures may be more or less apposite, depending on the nature of the audit assignment – for instance, profit per employee or labour turnover or direct material cost. As discussed in Chapter 11, responsibility centres and responsibility accounting practices will go a long way towards assisting in the evaluation of managerial performance.

Statistical sampling techniques and other quantitative methodologies have a role in the management audit processes, although care must be taken not to overlook the vital qualitative aspects of an audit of this nature.

Report

Reporting completes the assignment and the management auditor, as explained earlier, is not concerned with the actual implementation of his recommendations. The report should figure largely in the management auditor's mind throughout the whole audit process. In that way, a more disciplined investigation may be undertaken with constant attention to the purpose of the assignment.

Management auditors usually report to management, though sometimes reports are made to shareholders or employees' representatives. The report always features the management of the enterprise, but the emphasis and detail may vary from one type of recipient to the other. Typically, reports to management are more comprehensive and more detailed than those to other parties. It should be noted that management auditing for third parties is not legally required or enforceable in the United Kingdom, and it is essential that the terms of reference for such a reporting task should be determined clearly at the beginning of the investigation. In general terms, also, reports for management are prepared by internal teams, whereas reports for outsiders are prepared by external auditors.

One of the cardinal rules of management audit reporting is that – unlike, say, the consultants' report on the London Transport undertaking – the final report should not be a surprise to those being audited. The discussion and appraisal of a draft report, involving those reported upon, will have beneficial effects, and at the very least appropriate managers should receive copies of the management audit report.

PROCEDURES AND PROBLEMS

Santocki (1975) reported the results of an examination of the ways in which typical management audits were conducted, and the following description exemplifies the general approach:

> It is not stereotyped but is adopted according to the nature of the audit. However the most frequent procedure [is]: (i) initial informal interviews with senior management (after a general review of accounting information available at H.Q.); (ii) then development of a questionnaire, usually sectionalized, eg marketing, finance, production, etc; (iii) this is followed by visits to units where appropriate and other interviews with relevant personnel; (iv) audit reports are then developed from the above and the principal points are discussed with the unit, before a report is submitted . . .

The view is almost unanimous that a successful management audit team must be a multidisciplinary one, and the strong (but not dominant) presence of accountants is supported almost as vigorously. The legalistic approach of statutory financial auditors diminishes their effectiveness as members of a management audit team. Equally, the preoccupation with costs and budgets may lessen the effectiveness of 'traditional' management accountants. Nevertheless, each has the potential for making a worthwhile and crucial contribution to the management audit team. Other specialists and professionals to complement the accountant in a team would include economists, psychologists, engineers, personnel managers, data processing experts, marketers, and so on.

The greatest difficulty facing the management auditor is ignorance – that is, the ignorance of management at all levels in an organisation. Senior management must understand and believe in the value of management auditing for it to have a good chance of success. There is ample evidence, especially from North America, of the successful application of management auditing, and there are many instances of quantifiable benefits arising from its endeavours. What is needed is the effort to adopt the practice and work from its results. An understanding of management audit processes and their implications will remove unjustified fears of its adverse effect on line managers and their subordinates. Some critics argue that the process of management auditing curbs managerial initiative and removes individual manager's decision making and controlling functions. For that reason and others, the introduction of management audit to an established business must be undertaken carefully and in a planned fashion, preceded by initial discussions and explanations throughout the organisation.

CONCLUSION

Management auditing is neither a new nor a purely academic concept. It is an essential and practicable component of a sensible organisation structure. The Dutch institute's report (Nederlands Instituut van Registeraccountants, 1979) demonstrated the need for management auditing:

> The demands being made on the enterprise by the many parties involved are no longer of a financial nature only. . . . During a period of frequent bankruptcies, supervision of payments and business closures, it is to be expected that interested parties will take a more critical attitude towards management. . . . The following questions then arise: why were we not earlier involved in the problems; was this unavoidable? . . .

The need for management audit is always present; it becomes more acute at a time of economic pressure or constraint.

The importance of management audit is that it directs senior management to constantly appraise the effectiveness and efficiency of their areas of operations, whether or not they are currently the subject of management audit. In many cases an early indication or warning of bad management or potential difficulties has resulted in remedial action being taken to good effect.

The quality of the management auditor is vital to the success of the practice, rather than his professional orientation or training. Management auditing is primarily an attitude of mind; the knowledge and the techniques are available, waiting to be employed.

REFERENCES AND FURTHER READING

American Institute of Management, *The Appraisal of Management,* New York: Harper, 1962.

Briston, R. J., and Perks, R. W., 'The external audit – its role and cost to society', *Accountancy,* November 1977.

Campfield, W. L., 'Trends in auditing management plans and operations', *Journal of Accountancy,* July 1967.

de Roover, R., *The Rise and Decline of Medici Bank,* Boston: Harvard University Press, 1963.

Dombrower, D., 'The professional accountants' formula for survival – operational auditing', *Canadian Chartered Accountant,* December 1972.

Greenwood, W. T., *Management and Organizational Behavior Theories: An Interdisciplinary Approach,* Cincinnati: South-Western Publishing, 1965.

Greenwood, W. T., *A Management Audit System,* Rev. edn., Carbondale, Ill.: Southern Illinois University, 1967.

Leonard, W. P., *The Management Audit,* Englewood Cliffs, N.J.: Prentice-Hall, 1962.

Nederlands Instituut van Registeraccountants, *Management Audit,* (English translation), Amsterdam: NIVR, 1979.

Rose, T. G., *The Management Audit,* London: Gee, 1932.

Santocki, J., *Auditing: A Conceptual and Systems Approach,* Stockport: Polytech, 1979.

Santocki, J., *Case Studies in Auditing,* 2nd edn., Plymouth: Macdonald and Evans, 1978.

Santocki, J., 'Management audit from the inside', *The Accountant,* 28 March 1974.

Santocki, J., 'Management audit – is it myth or reality?', *Management Accounting,* September 1973.

Santocki, J., 'Management performance – how the British measure their managers' efforts', *Accountants Weekly,* 13 June 1975.

Santocki, J., 'Meaning and scope of management audit', *Accounting and Business Research,* Winter 1976.

Secoy, T. G., 'A CPA's opinion on management performance', *Journal of Accountancy,* July 1971.

PART FOUR
SPECIAL ASPECTS
OF MANAGEMENT
ACCOUNTING

OVERVIEW

This section of the handbook contains seven chapters, each by a specialist, examining particular areas of interest to the management accountant engaged in the planning and controlling of modern business organisations. The emphasis of these chapters is on the enhancement of those planning and controlling processes by the adoption of special techniques and approaches to the management task.

Professor Roger Groves of the Department of Business Administration and Accountancy at the University of Wales Institute of Science sets the scene for the section by highlighting the importance of organisational and behavioural insights. He draws together the components and framework of a contingency theory approach to management accounting. In his view, and in that of many other recent writers on management accounting and its modern role, the implementation of an information system will be more effective and more efficient if a wider understanding is achieved of the implications for management accounting of insights from the organisational, decisional and behavioural sciences. The Editor draws on those insights in discussing the fundamental area of the control of divisional performance and the problems associated with its measurement. The notion of controllability is central to the writer's approach to the problems of divisionalisation and he argues for a more structured and realistic yardstick for the measurement of divisional performance. There is a considerable need for further research in this area and the continued concern of managements with decentralised and divisionalised operational units renders that need ever more pressing.

The divisional manager's particular problems are discussed

further in the succeeding chapter. Jeffrey Davies of the Welsh Regional Management Centre at the Polytechnic of Wales examines the problems and practices of transfer pricing. By contrast to most writers in this area, the author takes a straightforward and clear look at the difficulties and drawbacks of transfer pricing systems. Badly used, such systems can have a deleterious and debilitating effect on the firm as a whole, and the dangers of suboptimisation and dysfunctionalism are clearly spelled out by the author. Again, there is a call for management accounting information systems which are timely, relevant and clear cut. Systems are crucial to planning and control, and as the author demonstrates and stresses, transfer pricing is an integral part of the planning and controlling processes.

The next chapter in this section examines the application of management accounting approaches to one specific managerial problem – the physical distribution of goods. Gordon Hill, a Vice President of A. T. Kearney Limited, an international firm of management consultants, discusses the problems arising from road transport of manufactured goods. His contribution represents the practical exemplification of the theoretical concepts and approaches discussed throughout the handbook; in particular, the behaviour of different types of cost or elements of cost is a fundamental factor in any structured analysis of a costing operation.

Bernard Cox, Technical Director, Research, of the Institute of Cost and Management Accountants, describes and discusses the application of value added analysis to management accounting problems, singling out two specimen areas of interest – value-added ratio analysis, and incentive or productivity schemes. In his opinion, value added concepts have particularly important implications for the management acountant – and for the financial accountant as well. The emotive associations of the notion of profit are avoided, and it is argued that employees and others take a more kindly view of such phrases as 'value added' or 'wealth created'. Certainly, the author's studies in the field of incentive or bonus schemes founded on value added precepts indicate that many strong advantages can accrue from successful and thoughtful incorporation of value added into the enterprise's measurement, evaluation and decision making processes.

It has been suggested by a number of commentators that the not-for-profit sector is a burgeoning one – and one which is badly in need of the management accountant's skills and experiences. The tools and techniques of management accounting in profit oriented companies are being transferred wholesale to the planning and controlling of nonprofit organisations, no matter how inappropriate they might seem. In the penultimate chapter in this section, Colonel Duncan Bennett of the Army's Management Accounting and Costing Services presents an overview of the nature and characteristics of management accounting in the not-for-profit sector and supports his discussion by a number of valuable and illuminating examples. A significant part of the economic activities of most countries is accounted for by the not-for-profit sector and it is timely for increased attention to be paid to planning and controlling the activities of participants in that sector. Generally, there is thought to be less awareness of modern management techniques among executives of not-for-profit organisations and less concern for the market place and the consumer. The proper application of the concepts and approaches of management accounting to entities in that sector can only lead to improved performance and greater benefits.

The final chapter of this section, and of the handbook as a whole, is contributed by the Editor, who draws together some of the persistent themes of other chapters and argues for the more wholehearted adoption of a systems approach to the management and control of modern business organisations. He introduces the elements of control theory and examines ways in which modern control theory can assist management in its more difficult tasks and guide the development of management accounting as a modern and forward looking discipline. He discusses the components of a structured and systematic approach to the formulation of a normative theory for management accounting, arguing that management accounting in its present form has come to include everything in which the management accountant is interested, almost without any logical or sensible rationale for that inclusion. There is a clear need for the development of strengths and skills consonant with the size and complexity of the modern business organisation; equally, there is little real evidence of the first stages of any progress towards that development.

16

Organisational and Behavioural Concepts in Management Accounting

Roger Groves

The author emphasises the importance of taking an organisational view of the planning, control and decision making aspects of management accounting, and argues that management accounting must be part of the larger management information system which is for the benefit of managers and a prerequisite of good management. In that context, the chapter begins by discussing the three theories of, or approaches to, management which have influenced modern thinking: the scientific management model, which sees management as based on formal models and bureaucratic systems; the participative or behavioural model, which views management and organisations as based on coalitions of individuals; and the contingency model, which sees management as being 'situation specific' in its systematisation and frameworks. The author develops a contingency framework for management accounting and examines in detail the many variables involved, both exogenous (such as technology and the economic and social environments) and endogenous (such as organisation structure and climate and individual behaviour). Drawing attention to the numerous problems encountered in building and operating a management accounting information system, the writer claims that such a system may be both 'considerable' in its size and complexity and 'dangerous' in the effects on the organisation and its individual members. In Professor Groves' view, the better the management accountant's appreciation of the organisational and behavioural implications of designing and operating an accounting information system, the greater the improvement in that system's effective operation and the wider the benefits to be derived from its use.

It is unfortunate that the emphasis in most textbooks on management accounting is on the technical procedures and mechanisms involved. That emphasis is manifested by the vast majority of the texts which set out the rules and methods for calculating accounting information designed to aid managers in budgeting their resources or controlling their staff. For instance, the mechanisms for budget formulation and review are usually described at length and the reader is left in no doubt about how to identify and measure variances from the targets formulated so mechanically in most texts. Just as faithfully, the computational methods necessary for deriving accounting information for use in management decisions – such as 'make or buy' – are described and explained in detail.

Regrettably, in the detailed description and discussion of those techniques, there is usually no more than a mention of the organisational, behavioural and political processes underlying their production and use. This detachment of the technical processes from the settings in which they are employed helps to maintain the emphasis on the accounting procedures once the reader attempts to practise what he has learned. In reality it is not possible to dissociate the organisational and technical aspects of budgeting, because not only did the organisation's structure help form the budgetary process, but that same budgetary process aided and influenced the evolution of the organisation's structure.

After all, a decision to market a new product could result in several organisational changes: a salesman could be promoted to product manager to oversee the new product's successful introduction, while the techniques of selling that new product might require changes in existing methods, including the hiring of new sales personnel. However, it is doubtful if the organisational costs and benefits accruing from that one decision were included in the technical accounting analysis which led up to the marketing decision.

In every aspect of management accounting – planning, control, and decision making – it is necessary to take an organisational view and to highlight the social, political and economic structures as well as the technical processes in order to arrive at the most appropriate outcome. As it derives from numerous arguments and debates involving all the appropriate personnel, and takes account of their social and political positions, the budget reflects the socio-economico-political structure of the organisation, and it is foolish to ignore that fact. A management accountant cannot exist on knowledge of technique alone.

Chandler and Daems (1979) felt that management accounting had developed primarily to enable activities in disparate and diverse organisations to be coordinated, so as to ensure that all sub-groups' performances are properly monitored, while securing an efficient allocation of funds to those sub-groups. Management accounting must be part of the wider management information system which is designed for the benefit of managers and to promote good management. It is therefore useful to consider three theories of management which have been in or out of vogue since the turn of the century. Each in its own way will help to indicate the most appropriate accounting techniques to adopt in different circumstances.

SCIENTIFIC MANAGEMENT

The early theory of scientific management is based on the assumption that an individual's motivation is governed by economic rewards and penalties, and that man's goal is to maximise his economic welfare. Taylor (1947) is regarded as the 'father' of this approach.

Many of the accounting texts fit this model, suggesting that the accounting system is a 'goal allocation' device which not only permits management to select, divide and distribute its operating objectives throughout the firm but also provides a control device aimed at identifying and correcting undesirable performance. The belief was held that there was sufficient certainty, rationality and knowledge within the system to permit accurate comparisons of results, thus identifying both responsibility for performance and the ultimate benefits or costs of that performance. The accounting 'system' was felt to be neutral in its evaluation mode: the system was assumed to be objective and thus personal bias was eliminated.

Within that theoretical framework, the essence of management control is authority and the management accounting systems and techniques found in the textbooks and offered as prescriptions for success could easily be placed within the context of the scientific management model; for instance, optimal production plans, stock models, investment strategies, and formal systems for recording information, such as standard costing, job or process costing. These are all impersonal techniques designed to ensure the achievement of the corporate goals of top management.

PARTICIPATIVE MODEL OF MANAGEMENT

The second model that has influenced research in management accounting is the participative model, or, as Caplan (1966) and others described it, the behavioural model.

Whereas the scientific model is based on formal systems and bureaucratisation, the participative or behavioural model is based upon the concept that organisations are coalitions of individuals. The underlying assumption is that individuals are not 'mindless', though organisations are, and so they get together formally or informally. It is through the coordination of those groups and the individuals within them that the corporate objectives are set and the entity managed.

Coordination comes about through the participative approach to goal selection, planning, control and review. For example, Likert (1967) suggested dividing organisations into 'group structures' so that those smaller groups might support their individual members. Thus, it was argued, participation can be encouraged through the use of small groups. Those small groups can be coordinated further in a participative way without reducing the benefits of decentralised decision making. This argument was based on the notion that participative management is in the long run interests of the organisation (see McGregor's (1960) explanation of 'theory X' versus 'theory Y'). The participative approach is almost the antithesis of the bureaucratic formality of the scientific management approach.

The participative approach tries to obtain an organisational structure susceptible to participation while maximising the individual's and the group's autonomy and power of discretion. This is not an easy task. On the one hand, there is the attempt to decentralise decision making as much as possible, while on the other, coordination between autonomous sub-groups is still necessary to ensure the achievement of corporate goals. Thus, it is still necessary to have some of the trappings of bureaucracy, such as rules, plans, forms, etc, which make for scientific management! Remembering that management accounting systems are part of the larger management information system, it is pertinent to note the need to retain frameworks and formal structure to a limited extent, even when the process view of management information systems is being advocated rather than the structural view (Earl and Hopwood, 1980).

Formal management accounting systems based solely on the participative model of management are not well developed. Even those management accounting systems established for decentralised ventures, and intended to encourage departmental or divisional independence, require flows of information back to head office and usually impose rigid rules to help maintain both the system and head office's ultimate authority. It is in sections or stages of the information system, however, that the participative approach has proved most helpful. Evidence of its benefits through informal information systems is provided by Galbraith (1973) and Clancy and Collins (1979) and in the budgeting process, by Hofstede (1967) and Swieringa and Moncur (1975). The fact that neither the scientific nor the participative model provided anything like a complete answer led to the emergence of an alternative approach in the 1960s.

One result of the overemphasis on the 'humanistic' approach has been to direct organisers to make decisions in terms of the behavioural system, leading to serious imbalances. Model builders forget that the behavioural system in an organisation is part of a much larger system network, which also incorporates the technological system and the economic system. The move away from the 'one line of approach' analysis of organisations and organisational strategies gained momentum in the 1970s, with writers turning to contingency or situational designs and eschewing the narrow perspectives and biased analyses that restricted earlier approaches.

CONTINGENCY MODEL OF MANAGEMENT

This approach assumes that no one optimum type of management system exists or can be formulated. Contingency theory includes all situational factors comprising the technical, political, social, financial and personal environment within which the firm operates. It concerns itself with the interaction of environmental forces, technology, formal structures, behavioural forces, and decision making processes. Dermer (1977) argued that planning and control systems should be 'situationally specific'; different environments require different organisational relationships for optimum effectiveness. The challenge is to discover the appropriate model for a given situation.

Contingency theory, then, has moved towards an open systems approach to organisation theory, away from the universalism of the scientific and participative models of management. The academic literature has put an increased emphasis on the effective design of systems to achieve specific organisational objectives – see, for example, Otley (1980) or Waterhouse and Tiessen (1978).

Many practising management accountants would argue that their management information systems had been designed in this way. However, they might also be prepared to agree that their systems, while technically adequate, might not be organisationally or environmentally satisfactory. The normative appeal of contingency theory is that it provides a framework which facilitates the choices between alternative management theories and varying information system designs.

A contingency framework for management accounting

The map of the accounting network of divisions, cost centres, profit centres, and so on, illuminates the roles that the financial planning mechanisms have to play, and have played, in building the corporate organisation. A framework for a contingency theory of management accounting can be constructed, as shown in Figure 16.1. Otley (1980) prescribed a 'minimum necessary contingency framework' and Likert and Bowers (1968) presented valuable suggestions for such a framework.

The primary causal relationships start from the contingent variables through organisational control packages and the intervening variables; those two sets of factors are interactive, with the intervening variables pertaining to the individuals who comprise the groups, sections, and so on, which constitute the systems of the control packages. From the efforts of individuals are produced the outputs which are measured by the end result variables. The dynamic process is continued through the feedback loops which operate in the interactions between organisational members and between the organisation and the external environment. The figure depicts the skeleton of the contingency framework for management accounting; the following discussions flesh out that skeleton by describing the elements in the framework and analysing relevant empirical findings.

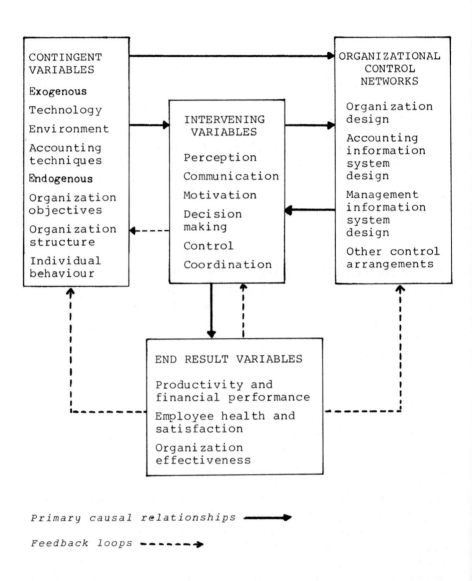

Fig. 16.1   A contingency framework for management accounting

CONTINGENCY VARIABLES

Many of the empirical writings enquiring into the behavioural aspects of accounting have presented conflicting results, which have not been susceptible to resolution within either the scientific or participative frameworks. For instance, Otley (1978) presented findings on the manner in which budgetary information was used, conflicting with earlier findings by Hopwood (1972). The conflict was due to situational differences in the two organisational structures observed. Nonetheless, both results were valid in their own contexts; they could not be generalised, however, without substantiation by other findings from other organisational situations. In each case, there is a crucial need to identify the contingent variables and appraise their likely effects before the organisational control networks are investigated and before the intervening and end result variables are analysed. It is easiest to examine those contingent variables in two categories – the exogenous variables external to the organisation, and the endogenous variables internal to the organisation. As detailed in Figure 16.1, the exogenous variables include technology, the environment, and accounting techniques; the endogenous variables include the organisation's objectives and structure and the behaviour of individuals within the organisation.

Technology

Differences in the production technology have long been recognised as having a bearing on accounting information systems. Woodward (1965), for example, reported differences in recording and reporting costs under unit production, small or large batch production, and mass production and processing. In process costing, the bulk of the costs are incurred jointly by a mix of products and may require considerable financial processing according to arbitrary allocation rules determined by an accountant with particular biases and interests – another contingent variable. In job-costing situations, the production measure is well defined and will call for only limited allocation and processing since the majority of the costs incurred are due to the specific job.

The complexity of the technology used in production has a bearing on the financial control structure to be adopted (see Piper (1978)), and Daft and MacIntosh (1978) showed how knowledge of a task and the variety of tasks performed affected the design of the information system.

Where there are little or few changes in an organisation's technological environment, control is probably best exercised through an application of scientific management precepts. Organisations mass producing standard products using well defined technology, and in an unchanging market, should try to build similarly stable organisational structures. Standard procedures, clearly defined lines of communication, and clear cut allocations of responsibility can be implemented, and managerial performance can be judged against consistent and clearly stated standards. That would not gainsay the opportunities for participation and representation within the system, but changes within the system would not be frequent and the system would not be subject to continued review by management.

On the other hand, when an enterprise operates in situations of high variety or volatility, where technical and economic conditions are unpredictable or even novel, a different kind of management system is needed. This calls for an 'organic' system, within which creativity and commitment would be crucial factors. If producers are faced frequently with unexpected requests, either in terms of product types or production volumes, or if the product market is changing rapidly, or if the technological base of the enterprise is altering, a rigid adherence to defined standards and processes will lead to inflexibility and an inability to react appropriately to change. Examples, such as companies engaged in high technology industries or areas, come readily to mind. By introducing a participative control system, management can encourage increased productivity and job commitment and enhanced product or service quality. Not surprisingly, empirical results in this area have been somewhat contradictory – see, for example, Hofstede (1967) or Morse and Reimer (1965) or Vroom (1960). Nevertheless, the consensus is that commitment is enhanced, both to the specific task in hand and to the organisation.

The above comments indicate that neither the scientific nor the participatory approach is universally successful. It is better to take the contingency approach, setting management's main task as the interpretation of the organisation's situation in terms of its predictability. Lawrence and Lorsch (1967) suggested that management should attempt to identify the rate of change of environmental conditions, the certainty of available information concerning conditions at any time, and the speed of feedback on the outcomes of decision implementations. Their view was that the greater the rate of change, the more uncertain the conditions and the slower the feedback experienced, the greater the need to develop an organic organisation, which would be reflected in a similar style of accounting information system.

Environment

The concluding paragraphs of the foregoing section show how difficult it is to isolate specific influences on the organisation and on the accounting information system. Certainly all firms face markedly different economic, social and political environments, and those different environmental constraints determine the choice of accounting systems. Otley (1978) found that if a requisite feature of an accounting system was the accuracy of its budgets, different budget styles were needed for the differing levels of competition faced by the organisation. He researched a large firm, with several physically separate operational units managed and controlled as individual entities and facing significantly different trading conditions. He found that a flexible style of budget use provided the most accurate budget estimate in a liberal environment; in a tough environment, however, the most accurate estimate came using a more rigid style.

In an earlier study, Khandwalla (1972) found that different types of competition, price, product and marketing factors had markedly diverse impacts on the use made of accounting controls within a manufacturing organisation.

The social and political facets of the external environment affect the budgetary style also; for example, it may be acceptable to run a corporate unit at a loss in one or more geographical regions because of political or social expediency or obligation. The accounting information system adopted, and management's actions and outputs, seek to ensure that all regions are as efficient and effective as possible. If political pressures allow for the continued operation of uneconomic or unprofitable activities because of the social and political consequences of remedial or termination action, the enterprise has to accept those constraints and act accordingly.

Accounting techniques

Usually a manager can choose between a fair number of alternative accounting techniques to measure, record, analyse and report an event. As Hofstede (1967) pointed out, managers soon learn to play the game of budgetary control, padding budget estimates to provide negotiating leeway or safety margins against overspending or underperforming. Similarly, they learn how to provide for 'anticipated' expenditure to increase 'actual' expenditure or to relinquish provisions for expenditure no longer needed so as to improve reported profit positions.

Currently, one of the complex choices facing organisations is that of using historical cost accounting or current cost accounting as a basis for budgets. Management has to select from different inventory valuation methods, alternative depreciation charging practices, and so on. Even so, however, there is no conclusive evidence that the choice of one accounting method rather than another leads to different managerial decisions – as witness studies reported by Dyckman (1964), Jensen (1966), and others.

Amigoni (1978) tried to assess the appropriateness of a range of accounting control tools, and concluded that, by adding new accounting tools to those already in use, organisations could adapt to increasing structural complexities. In situations of high environmental discontinuity, old accounting methods were losing their force and there was a pressing need for the introduction of 'new' accounting techniques and tools to deal with complex situations and environmental disturbances.

Organisation objectives and structure

The objectives of an organisation are clearly vital to the formulation of a sound accounting information system and determine the targets used to assess organisational effectiveness. Non-profit organisations (charities, government bodies, and so on) have clearly different needs from profit oriented enterprises; public sector organisations have a different set of objectives to those in the private sector. The detailed plan of the enterprise's future course of action – the budget, in other words – should enshrine, reflect and develop the corporate objectives. The reflection of those objectives in the budget will depend upon organisational members' belief in and commitment to those objectives and upon those members' political and decisional strengths. Debate and deliberation will have taken place in the production and refinement of both the objectives and the budget plans, and the results will have arisen from the political processes permeating organisational life and from the particular structure of the individual concern.

Bruns and Waterhouse (1975), for example, argued that the budget-related behaviour of a manager depended upon aspects of the organisation's structure – such as the amount of autonomy or decentralisation, or the degree to which activities were structured. Hayes (1977) concluded from his investigations that three variables affected the performance of sub-units within an organisation: sub-unit interdependence, environmental relationships, and factors internal to the sub-unit concerned. He produced evidence relating to production, marketing and research and development units, but his conclusions have been criticised by Waterhouse and Tiessen (April 1978).

Hopwood (1972) and Otley (1978) investigated the impact of organisational structure on the way in which budgetary information is used. Hopwood perceived three stylistic variations of subordinate evaluation by managers; he labelled them 'budget-constrained', 'profit-conscious', and 'non-accounting'. The budget constrained approach saw meeting the budget as the single most important factor in performance evaluation; the profit conscious approach took a longer term view of performance; the non-accounting approach appraised non-financial criteria as well as financial yardsticks. Hopwood concluded that managers with rigid, short term, budget-constrained approaches were associated with high degrees of job-related tension, dysfunctionalism, data manipulation, interpersonal disharmony, and so on. The longer term and wider perspective 'profit conscious' or 'non-accounting' approaches were taken by managers who were free from such problems. Otley, on the other hand, used comparable measures but found dissimilar results; he reported, for instance, a strong association between good performance and the rigid, budget-constrained style. There were, however, important differences in the two situations investigated. Hopwood examined an American integrated steelworks, split into cost centres but with considerable interdependence. Otley investigated profit centres in the British coalmining industry, each virtually independent of the others. The discrepancies can be readily explained, therefore, by the contingent variables involved; thus, the studies cannot be used to postulate generalisations.

Individual behaviour

If they are to be effective, financial practices cannot operate in isolation from management practices; each is dependent upon the other, and each reinforces the other. Managerial leadership style influences organisational climate, which in turn affects individual subordinate and peer relationships. Vroom (1960) found that managers with high authoritarian needs responded less favourably to high participation levels than did managers with low authoritarian needs; Tosi (1978) disputed that finding, however. Nonetheless, managers do affect the performance and behaviour of subordinates and peers.

House (1971) argued that the motivational functions of a leader or supervisor should include maximising the personal 'pay-off' of the subordinate. That can be done by increasing opportunities for personal satisfaction or by smoothing the path the subordinate has to thread to achieve his organisational goal (by reducing or removing obstacles, for example). If the leader's behaviour produces positive motivational responses, the subordinate's view of his role will be less ambiguous. A leader's behaviour will change over time, depending on whether he is dealing with a new recruit, a tried and trusty worker, or a difficult character. Equally, the job or activity being undertaken will affect the leader's behaviour – if it represents a new challenge, for example, or is a standard task of long standing.

Leadership styles and behaviour, peer relationships, subordinate/ superior relationships, and the like will be affected by the feedback through the intervening variables within the framework or the control networks or the end result variables – such as employee satisfaction or organisation effectiveness.

INTERVENING VARIABLES

Individuals respond to cues and stimuli, and their actions or responses are based on their perceptions of those cues and stimuli. In the work environment, the budgetary process and the budget itself are sets of stimuli. Individuals' perceptions are affected by the environment (the contingent variables) and take into account the communication mode used and individual motivation in a particular decision making or control situation. Individuals' responses will be influenced by the combined interaction of all those and other relevant factors.

This fact has been stressed by many writers – by Argyris (1952), for example. Swieringa and Moncur (1975) reported that individuals realised 'budget pressure', affected their behaviour on the job.

Budget pressure was defined as the consequence of the perception by a person of the frequency of stimuli coming directly or indirectly from budgeting activities. This main pressure was occasioned by general discussion of budget matters. Next in importance was pressure from higher management, followed by pressure from active involvement in supervision. The final budget pressure was generated by the investigation and control of budget/actual variances. Each of those pressures are broad descriptions derived from sets of individual stimuli.

The stimuli include such events as the discussion of budget variances with an immediate supervisor or direct action by others to correct budget variances or managerial investigation of an individual's ability to perform to budget levels. Naturally, the individual's perceptions of such stimuli will affect his performance (the end result variables) and the design and continued operation of organisation control networks. Those perceptions will also affect feedback and contingent variables.

It is appropriate at this point to mention human information processing and the understandings advanced by various writers of the ways in which individuals process information. The results of research in this area have been varied and of little value to a systems designer. Researchers in the psychological disciplines have examined the cognitive processes of individuals, the extent to which heuristic approaches have been used in processing information, and other aspects of information handling styles. Libby and Lewis (1977) have provided a good review of the area, and Churchman (1980) argued forcefully for the acceptance of the truism that:

> managers must use intuition in every decision no matter how complete the [management information system] and no matter what degree of confidence they have in it. . . . If intuition plays a major role in the manager's decision, then how can we design an 'aid' if we do not have the foggiest idea what intuition is, how it occurs, whether it is reliable, whether it ought to be used, and so forth.

It has been argued that information systems can be designed to match individual decision making styles. This theory like many others is easier to formulate than to implement.

The motivational levels of individuals vary, both in respect of what is desirable and of what can be achieved. Many writers have found that – up to a point – setting higher goals or aspirations led to the achievement of higher targets. Stedry and Kay (1966) pointed out, however, that there was a threshold or perceived level of difficulty of attainment above which an individual tended to give up. That 'switch-off' point depends on the work environment as much as on the individual. Combining individuals into an organisation produces different interests, motivations, and perspectives on life. Since objectives and targets tend to emerge through the organisational interactions, rather than being provided ready-made, it is useful to analyse the decision making process and deduce guidelines for the design and implementation of the organisational control networks.

ORGANISATIONAL CONTROL NETWORKS

Determining the goals towards which individuals are working within the organisation may have involved lengthy and discordant debates and negotiations leaving uncertainty and disquiet as to the desirability and feasibility of the objectives. The greater the instability in the external environment and the greater the instability within the organisation, the greater the degree of uncertainty about the objectives. A similar scale of uncertainty exists regarding the consequences of the actions prescribed to achieve the objectives.

Earl and Hopwood (1980) developed a simple matrix, based on the theoretical approach of Thompson and Tuden (1959) designed to identify the decision making processes for the different combinations of uncertainty levels for the organisation and action consequences. Different types of processes require different inputs of information and the Earl and Hopwood approach can help to define the roles of the information system and the control system in the organisation.

In a stable environment, where the objectives and the consequences of the necessary actions to achieve those objectives are known with reasonable certainty, decision making will usually be effected in a computational manner. That is to say, it will be possible to compute easily and accurately the consequences of actions and decide whether or not the goals will be attained. As the degree of uncertainty grows, either about the objectives or the consequences of enabling actions, the process becomes more complex. Where organisational objectives are not clear cut, but the consequences of organisational actions are certain, decision making will be achieved through a bargaining process. On the other hand, if objectives are clear but the consequences of actions are not, a judgemental process will be employed. If both the objectives and the consequences of actions are unclear, inspiration is called for in the decision making processes. Sometimes, in this latter case, the objectives become clearer during the decision making processes; they may even clarify while the actions are taking place.

A wide variety of managerial practices and information system designs have been devised to aid management in these differing decisional environments. In a relatively stable environment, the structural techniques of management accounting are most useful. For instance, integrated in the formal budgetary process, stock models and production models can facilitate the coordination of organisational activities. Financial models for short and long term plans can be incorporated into that process linking the objectives with the organisational strategies.

Where bargaining is part of the process of arriving at a decision, there is a need for 'information ammunition' to help the participants. The management accounting mechanisms will provide information for effective bargaining. Similarly, where decision making is conducted on the basis of judgement, probability analysis and risk evaluation can be introduced with good effect.

The build up of budgetary processes, in addition to other management accounting mechanisms, will help to cement relationships and reduce organisational uncertainty. It does tend, however, to work in a downwards direction, because that is the direction of the power and visibility. Subordinates do not get many opportunities to review their leaders and this tends to reinforce the centralised coordination of activities. Where the decision making is predominantly by inspiration the information system will be geared towards producing information that will help managers rationalise their decisions.

From this it is possible to see that the technical practices of budgeting and other procedures can be adapted to meet particular circumstances in specific organisations. The uses and sources of budgetary control and management accounting are diverse and complex, although this may not become apparent until attempts have been made to probe the underlying organisational processes; insights into aspects of budgetary practices in public organisations, exemplifying those circumstances, can be gained from Wildavsky (1974) or from Rosenberg et al. (1980).

END RESULT VARIABLES

The standard performance measures used by organisations have tended to be financially-oriented – profit, return on capital employed, and so on. However, it is worth questioning whether those measures are appropriate ones to use when monitoring organisational effectiveness in achieving goals. Profit and return on capital are not directly related to the satisfaction of human needs, except in the narrow and restricted sense of the owners' dependence on dividends or share prices.

The question of organisational effectiveness has been addressed by several writers, but with little useful result – as summarised by Campbell (1976) who argued that:

> ... searching for so-called objective measures of organisational effectiveness is a thankless task and virtually pre-ordained to fail in the end ... it is probably a mistake to concentrate scarce resources on attempts to discover results-oriented measures, that is, measures of the more technical outcomes of organisational functioning, such as return on investment, productivity and the like.

Perhaps the present measures should continue in use until better ones can be substituted!

CONCLUSION

Building an accounting information system is a considerable and dangerous task. It is considerable owing to its complexity and size and dangerous because of its effects on the organisation and its members. This chapter has drawn attention to the intricate relationships between the practices of budgeting, financial planning and control of the organisation. The budgetary processes of an enterprise may have been introduced to enhance the economic efficiency of that entity, but their functions will undoubtedly ensure the creation and maintenance of particular patterns of political and social power in addition to economic influence. Such a development will reinforce and legitimise the present organisational practices – which may not be a good thing.

This uncertainty concerning the benefits of changing organisational practices through the introduction of financial planning or management accounting mechanisms is a measure of the need for further research in these areas. The complexities should not deter continuing attempts to improve accounting information systems in use or to design better programmes. What is clearly needed is a closer integration of the organisational and behavioural implications of the financial and management accounting crafts with the traditional understandings of those crafts. In that context, it is fitting to conclude with the comments of Schoenfeld (1980):

> ... a great deal of conceptual research is needed first before a coherent theory of managerial accounting may emerge and before empirical research for verification purposes can be undertaken on a large scale. It is, however, obvious that the continuation of randomly adding pieces of knowledge to our field without examining their position in an overall framework is not likely to accelerate the development of managerial accounting.

REFERENCES AND FURTHER READING

Amigoni, F., 'Planning management control systems', *Journal of Business Finance and Accounting,* 1978.

Anthony, R. N., *Planning and Control Systems: A Framework for Analysis,* Cambridge, Mass.: Harvard Business School, 1965.

Argyris, C., *The Impact of Budgets on People,* New York: The Controllership Foundation, 1952.

Bruns, W. J., and DeCoster, D. T. (eds), *Accounting and its Behavioral Implications,* New York: McGraw-Hill, 1969.

Bruns, W. J., and Waterhouse, J. H., 'Budgetary control and organizational structure', *Journal of Accounting Research,* Autumn 1975.

Campbell, J. P., 'Contributions research can make in understanding organizations' effectiveness', *in* Spray, S. L. (ed), *Organizational Effectiveness: Theory-Research-Utilization,* Kent, Tex.: Kent State University, 1976.

Caplan, E. H., 'Behavioral assumptions of management accounting', *The Accounting Review,* July 1966.

Chandler, A., and Daems, H., 'Administrative coordination, allocation and monitoring', *Accounting Organizations and Society,* 1979.

Churchman, C. W., 'Intuition and information', *in* Holzer, H. P.

(ed), *Management Accounting 1980,* Urbana-Champaign, Ill: University of Illinois, 1980.

Clancy, D., and Collins, F., 'Informal accounting information systems: some tentative findings', *Accounting Organizations and Society,* 1979.

Cooper, D., 'A social and organizational view of management accounting', *in* Bromwich, M., and Hopwood, A. G. (eds), *Essays in British Accounting Research,* London: Pitman, 1981.

Daft, R. L., and MacIntosh, N. B., 'A new approach to design and use of management information', *California Management Review,* Fall 1978.

Dermer, J., *Management Planning and Control Systems,* Homewood, Ill.: Irwin, 1977.

Dyckman, T. R., 'The effects of alternative accounting techniques on certain management decisions', *Journal of Accounting Research,* Autumn 1964.

Earl, M. J., and Hopwood, A. G., 'From management information to information management', *in* Lucas, H. J. et al. (eds), *The Information Systems Environment,* Amsterdam: North-Holland, 1980.

Galbraith, J., *Designing Complex Organizations,* Reading, Mass.: Addison-Wesley, 1973.

Gordon, L. A., and Miller, D., 'A contingency framework for the design of accounting information systems', *Accounting Organizations and Society,* 1976.

Hayes, D. C., 'The contingency theory of management accounting', *The Accounting Review,* January 1977.

Hofstede, G. H., *The Game of Budget Control,* Assen: Koninklijke Van Corcum, 1967.

Hopwood, A. G., 'An empirical study of the role of accounting data in performance evaluation', *Journal of Accounting Research,* Supplement, 1972.

Hopwood, A. G., 'Towards an organizational perspective for the study of accounting and information systems', *Accounting Organizations and Society,* 1978.

House, R. J., 'A path-goal theory of leader effectiveness', *Administrative Science Quarterly,* September 1971.

Jensen, R. E., 'An experimental design for a study of effects of accounting variations in decision-making', *Journal of Accounting Research,* Autumn 1966.

Keen, P. G., and Scott Morton, M. S., *Decision Support Systems,*

Reading, Mass.: Addison-Wesley, 1978.

Khandwalla, P. N., 'The net effect of different types of competition on the use of management controls', *Journal of Accounting Research,* Autumn 1972.

Lawrence, P. R., and Lorsch, J., *Organization and Environment,* Cambridge, Mass.: Harvard Business School, 1967.

Libby, R., and Lewis, B. L., 'Human information processing research in accounting: the state of the art', *Accounting Organizations and Society,* 1977.

Likert, R., *The Human Organization, Its Management and Value,* New York: McGraw-Hill, 1967.

Likert, R., and Bowers, D. G., 'Organizational theory and human resource accounting', *American Psychologist,* September 1968.

Livingstone, J. L. (ed), *Managerial Accounting: the Behavioral Foundations,* Columbus, O.: Grid, 1975.

March, J. G., and Simon, H. A., *Organizations,* New York: Wiley, 1958.

McGregor, D., *The Human Side of Enterprise,* New York: McGraw-Hill, 1960.

Morse, N., and Reimer, E., 'Experimental change of a major organizational variable', *Journal of Abnormal and Social Psychology,* 1956.

Otley, D. T., 'Budget use and managerial performance', *Journal of Accounting Research,* Spring 1978.

Otley, D. T., 'The contingency theory of management accounting: achievement and prognosis', *Accounting Organizations and Society,* 1980.

Piper, J., *Determinants of Financial Control Systems for Multiple Retailers – Some Case Study Evidence,* Loughborough: the author, 1978.

Rosenberg, D., Tomkins, C., and Day, P., 'The accountant in a social service department: values and interpretations of work role', *Working Paper,* University of Bath, 1980.

Schoenfeld, H-M. W., 'Management accounting: discernable future directions', *in* Holzer, H. P. (ed), *Management Accounting 1980,* Urbana-Champaign, Ill.: University of Illinois, 1980.

Stedry, A. C., *Budget Control and Cost Behavior,* Englewood Cliffs, N.J.: Prentice-Hall, 1960.

Stedry, A. C., and Kay, E., 'The effects of goal difficulty on performance: a field experiment', *Behavioural Science,* 1966.

Swieringa, R. J., and Moncur, R. H., *Some Effects of Participative*

Budgets on Managerial Behavior, New York: National Association of Accountants, 1975.

Taylor, F. W., *The Principles of Scientific Management,* New York: Harper & Row, 1947.

Thompson, J. D., and Tuden, A., 'Strategies, structures and processes of organizational decision', *in* Thompson, J. D. (ed), *Comparative Studies in Administration,* Pittsburgh, Pa.: University of Pittsburgh Press, 1959.

Tosi, H., 'A re-examination of personality as a determinant of the effects of participation', *Personnel Psychology,* 1978.

Vroom, V., *Some Personality Determinants of the Effects of Participation,* Englewood Cliffs, N.J.:Prentice-Hall, 1960.

Waterhouse, J. H., and Tiessen, P., 'A contingency framework for management accounting systems research', *Accounting Organizations and Society,* 1978.

Waterhouse, J. H., and Tiessen, P., 'The contingency theory of management accounting: a comment', *The Accounting Review,* April 1978.

Wildavsky, A., *The Politics of the Budgetary Process,* Boston, Mass.: Little Brown, 1974.

Woodward, J., *Industrial Organisation: Theory and Practice,* Oxford: Oxford University Press, 1965.

17

Divisional Performance and Control

David Fanning

One of the fastest growing forms of decentralisation in modern business affairs is divisionalisation, defined by Child (1977) as the:

> *assignment of profit responsibility to divisional managers; the establishment of a central headquarters mainly concerned with strategic planning and control; and the commitment of corporate managers to organisational performance rather than the performance of any specific division.*

The concepts of profit and investment centres were discussed earlier in this handbook (see Chapter 11), and it is clear that an operating centre can only be classified and seen as a division if its manager has clear and considerable control over profits; that is, over controllable revenues and controllable expenses. Given that the activities of divisions are crucial to the welfare of the firm, it is essential that such activities should be measured, reported and controlled in the best interests of the firm as a whole – and in the best interests of the divisional managers and their colleagues. The measurement of divisional performance is undertaken in terms of accounting yardsticks: return on investment, for example, or residual income. This chapter discusses these two approaches, which are the principal ones in general use, and examines their appropriateness to the modern business situation. Return on investment has significant shortcomings as a mechanism for assessing managerial effectiveness; in particular, it can lead to confusion between divisional and corporate objectives, with marked dysfunctional impacts on the achievements of both. Residual income, on the other hand, concentrates on controllability and offers a better assessment of divisional performance. Both measures share the failings of all such accounting measures – dependence on historic cost accounting principles and practices, concentration on short run results and conditions, exaggeration of one bottom line figure, and so on. There is a clear, and pressing, need for developing other techniques for the appraisal of divisional performance; an undue concern with one-number yardsticks leads to a lack of concern with other vital measures, such as marketing, training, employee productivity, and long run viability. This chapter discusses the criteria to be applied to a system of divisional performance measurement, the problems associated with such measurement processes, and the advantages and disadvantages of the two most popular yardsticks. It highlights the areas in which further research and development is needed if divisionalisation is to continue to be the boon it is thought to be.

In many textbooks on managerial accounting, decentralisation and divisionalisation are regarded as synonymous labels for the same process. However, clear and important distinctions must be made between the two processes. Decentralisation implies the delegation of decision making and relaxation of the constraints and strictures governing managerial freedom. Both benefits and costs associate with decentralisation, and the extent to which any firm adopts the process is dictated by the perceived net difference between those costs and benefits. The benefits of decentralised management have been well described by many writers – see Horngren (1977), for example – and can be summarised as follows: the optimisation of decision making, the dispersal of the burden of decision making, the heightening of managerial freedom and motivation, the better development of managers, and the closer monitoring of transfer prices and effective activities. On the other side of the equation, the costs include the dangers of suboptimisation and dysfunctional behaviour, the additional costs of gathering, presenting and analysing performance data, and the likelihood of duplication of activities in separate divisions.

Divisionalisation is one form of decentralisation, in which a divisional manager is given responsibility for all the operations and outcomes of a division – planning, implementation, production, marketing, costs, revenues, profits. Such a division may be an operating unit of a company, a subsidiary company of a holding company, or a group of operating companies within a conglomerate. Divisions can be delineated on product or market lines, by geographical criteria or in any way beneficial to the establishing corporation.

The process of divisionalisation gives rise to two major problems. First, as Child (1977) and others have argued, the very process of divisionalisation is divisive in organisational terms. The creation of operating divisions leads to the dilution of corporate loyalty. A divisional identity develops instead; managers belong to, and owe allegiance to, a division. Decisions may not be taken in the best interests of the organisation as a whole, particularly where divisional and corporate interests conflict. There are strong pressures on divisional managers to act in their own best interests – given greater strength by the adoption of accounting yardsticks as measurement devices.

Secondly, and perhaps more fundamental, full divisional autonomy is virtually impossible to achieve. There can be no such thing as a fully independent division. The corporation is formed, owned and judged as a whole; central management and corporate directors are held responsible for group performance, in which divisional performances play a crucial role. The concept of full responsibility has to be replaced, if a realistic view is to be taken and realistic judgements made of managerial performance, and the most amenable substitute is the notion of controllability, as discussed later in this chapter.

The test of a skilful central management is the extent to which its decentralisation and divisionalisation practices succeed. Control must be maintained, despite the force of motivational freedom; divisional contribution to corporate wealth must be maximised, despite the spur autonomy gives to profit making for divisional benefits alone. These are daunting obstacles in the path of any organisation wishing to decentralise and divisionalise its operations, and overcoming them is one of management's most difficult tasks.

PERFORMANCE MEASUREMENT

Most yardsticks used to judge managerial performance are founded on accounting information, and those used to appraise divisional performance offer easy and attractive measures of the success or failure of divisional activities. The strengths and weaknesses of such accounting yardsticks have been described and discussed by many writers in recent years – notably Solomons (1965) and Tomkins

(1973). Two methods of appraisal or measurement have been adopted by companies, although other less attractive and flexible tests have been advanced. It can be argued that neither method is wholly acceptable, but the fact of their widespread use makes it sensible to present their main characteristics and discuss their implications. The two most common methods are: return on investment and residual income. Each is examined in turn.

Return on investment

The most common form of performance evaluation in divisionalised companies is the return on investment method (see Mauriel and Anthony (1966) for a discussion of the identification of responsibility centres and methods in a sample of divisionalised companies). In this context, return on investment is calculated as a ratio of net divisional profits (before tax) to the net assets (at book values) employed in the division.

Table 17.1
Divisional income statements and balance sheets

	Division A	Division B
	£	£
Sales revenue	858 000	236 050
less Cost of goods sold	405 000	101 500
Gross profit	453 000	134 550
less Operating expenses (including allocated overheads	167 000	53 820
Net profit before tax	286 000	80 730
Net fixed assets	630 000	139 550
Net current assets	95 000	21 250
Net capital employed	725 000	160 800

By employing such a simple yardstick, the assessor concentrates on the percentage return: the divisional objective is to maximise that percentage return, and little attention is given to absolute values. Table 17.1 presents the income statements and summarised balance sheets for two operating divisions in a multiproduct company. Adopting the simplistic return on investment approach (that is by expressing net profit before tax as a percentage of net capital employed in the division) the return on investment for Division A can be calculated at 39.4 per cent, and that for Division B at 50.2 per cent. Taking a slightly more realistic approach, by making a notional charge against each division for corporation tax (say at a rate of 52 per cent), would reduce each division's profits to £137 280 and £38 750 respectively. On that basis, the return on investment for Division A would be calculated at 18.9 per cent and that for Division B at 24.1 per cent.

The next step in appraisal is to relate those calculated returns on investment to the company's cost of capital or some other measure of required rate of return for divisional profits. Even where firms use an investment hurdle rate or internal rate of return for appraising capital investment projects, the rates will be determined in very different ways from the calculated rate of return on investment – a point discussed below. A comparison between the two will be misleading, as will the view that the highest rate of return is always the best. A better approach is to compare the rate of return after tax for each division with the excess of those earnings over different costs of capital. Solomons (1965) applied this technique to the evaluation of the alternative merits of various investment opportunities, but the procedure can be used just as effectively to appraise divisional operating results.

Table 17.2 illustrates this procedure, where the firm's cost of capital has been set at 12 per cent, 16 per cent and 20 per cent, respectively. It can be seen that a straightforward appraisal of Division B as being more profitable, as measured by its superior rate of return on investment, will not be the better judgement for all costs of capital. If the firm's cost of capital is 20 per cent, for example, then Division B is clearly the better performer. However, for costs of capital of 12 per cent or 16 per cent, Division A generates greater excess returns. The actual cutoff point between the divisions is, of course, close to 18.9 per cent as a cost of capital.

This analysis highlights one of the major drawbacks to the adoption of a return on investment criterion. The manager of Division B, aware that his activities are earning a return of 24.1 per cent on investment and rewarded on that basis by central management, will act to ensure the continued 'superiority' of his division. For circumstances where the firm's actual cost of capital is less than

Table 17.2
Divisional earnings

	Division A	Division B
Net capital employed	£725 000	£160 800
Net profit after tax	£137 280	£38 750
Rate of return on capital invested	18.9%	24.1%
Excess of net profit after tax over cost of capital		
at 12%	£50 280	£19 454
at 16%	£21 280	£13 022
at 20%	(£7 720)	£6 590

18 per cent or so, the manager of Division A is performing better in the interests of the firm as a whole, although his division's rate of return on investment of only 18.9 per cent will lead, on this approach, to an unfavourable comparison with the manager of Division B.

A further problem with the straightforward return on investment approach is that it is constrained by accounting practices and procedures. Simply by the imposition of depreciation charges, a manager's return on investment will increase over time, even if his actual profitability remains static or declines slightly. For instance, if the manager of Division B depreciated his fixed assets by some 15 per cent per annum on a straightline basis, and if the average life of those assets is 6 years or so and if the assets in the balance sheet in Table 17.1 are three years old at that balance sheet date, the depreciation charge for the next period will be around £38 000. If the division's profits decline to some £32 000, the calculated rate of return on investment will be 26.1 per cent (£32 000/£122 800) – an apparent increase in divisional profitability, but in the absence of any real improvement.

Allied to that problem is the further one that such rates of return are calculated in relationship to balance sheet book values – whether opening, closing, or average values. The values may bear little or no relation to real underlying values, especially in the absence of any adjustments to take account of changing prices or replacement costs.

The rate of return on investment is calculated on short run fixed period returns, ignoring any consideration of the time factors involved. Hurdle rates and internal rates of return are calculated in respect of capital investment projects over the lifetimes of those projects and have considerable regard for time factors. Flower (1971) has proposed a mechanism for overcoming the problems generated by picking balance sheet values at a fixed point in time, and there are obvious mechanisms for overcoming the disparate approaches of the rate of return on investment and the internal rate of return for projects or capital investment opportunities – as discussed above and illustrated in Table 17.2.

Table 17.3
Divisional project

Initial investment:	£20 000	Required return:	20.0%
Cash flows: Year 1	£3 000	Return:	15.0%
2	£3 300		16.5%
3	£3 600		18.0%
4	£11 000		55.0%
5	£12 100		60.5%
6	£13 310		66.6%
Net present value (at 20%)	£1 499	Internal rate of return:	22.3%

For the group as a whole, the rate of return on investment criterion lends itself to short term judgements and will act as a dysfunctional influence on divisional managers so judged. If, for example, a divisional manager is required to obtain a rate of return on capital employed of greater than 20 per cent and if he is presented with an investment opportunity such as that outlined in Table 17.3, his short run decision will be to reject the proposal. The rate of return in the first three years is less than his required rate of return and his immediate reaction will be to avoid the possibility of being judged adversely. The short run view of what should or should not be undertaken will ignore the real benefits to be gained over the lifetime of the project.

Residual income

According to Mauriel and Anthony (1966), about one-third of the companies they surveyed used the residual income approach, either on its own or in combination with the return on investment yardstick, to measure divisional performance. The residual income technique deducts a charge for the use of assets from divisional profits, and bases this charge on the company's cost of capital. The emphasis of the residual income approach is to determine an absolute value for divisional income, as adjusted, rather than a percentage value.

Table 17.4
Divisional income statement

		£
Sales revenue		858 000
less Variable cost of goods sold	405 000	
Variable divisional selling and administration expenses	27 300	
		432 300
Variable profit		425 700
less Controllable divisional overhead		62 700
Controllable profit		363 000
less Fixed non-controllable divisional overhead		41 700
Contribution margin		321 300
less Allocated extradivisional fixed non-controllable expenses		35 300
Net profit before tax		286 000

The significant feature of the residual income method, as exemplified by Solomons (1965), is the notion of controllability – one of the criteria for divisional performance measures discussed later in this chapter. If a division is to be charged for the use of capital and some measure of residual income derived, it is reasonable to expect that the profit figure adjusted for that capital charge should be one which reflects all items subject to any substantial degree of control or influence by the divisional manager – and that items over which the divisional manager has little control should not be included.

Such an approach can be applied to the income statement for Division A given in Table 17.1; adjusted to distinguish between controllable and non-controllable items of expenditure, the income statement would appear as in Table 17.4. It can be seen that such a statement reveals three possible measurements of divisional profit: net profit before tax; contribution margin; controllable profit. Which should be used? The arguments advanced by Solomons (1965) and later writers held that divisional income statements should clearly reveal a figure of controllable operating profit against which would be set a charge for use of capital in the division during the period, based on the corporate cost of capital. Such a statement, described as a divisional residual income statement, is presented in Table 17.5. The corporate cost of capital has been estimated at 18 per cent, and the division employed a net capital of £725 000 during the period (see Table 17.1), leading to a charge on controllable investment of £76 500 – calculated on the basis that net current assets represented controllable capital invested in the division and that controllable fixed assets had a net book value of £330 000 (being plant and equipment), whereas non-controllable fixed assets had a net book value of £300 000 (being land and buildings). Accordingly, as shown in the table, controllable residual income for Division A was calculated at £286 500, representing a rate of return of 67.4 per cent on controllable capital invested in the division; net residual income before tax was calculated at £155 500, representing a rate of return of 21.4 per cent on capital invested in the division. Taking a similar approach to the activities of Division B produced a controllable residual income figure of £92 300 (after a charge of £29 700 on controllable investment), representing a rate of return of 55.9 per cent on controllable capital invested in the division; net residual income before tax was calculated at £31 230, representing a rate of return of 11.4 per cent on capital invested in the division.

The most obvious outcome of such a revision of divisional earnings measurements is that the relative positions of Divisions A and B are reversed. Division A is estimated to have the higher rate of return, by either definition of capital invested, as shown in Table 17.6. From being significantly 'worse' than Division B, Division A is now seen to perform much better. The figures derived can be adjusted further, by making a notional tax charge (based on a rate of 52 per cent), as shown in the table – there Division A's rate of return on capital employed is 10.3 per cent and Division B's is 5.5 per cent. Taking the further refinement shown in Table 17.2, those rates of

Table 17.5
Divisional residual income statement

		£
Sales revenue		858 000
less Variable costs		432 300
Variable profit		425 700
less Controllable divisional overhead		62 700
Controllable profit		363 000
less Interest on controllable investment		76 500
Controllable residual income		286 500
less Interest on non-controllable divisional investment	54 000	
Fixed non-controllable divisional overhead	41 700	
Allocated extradivisional fixed non-controllable expenses	35 300	
		131 000
Net residual income before tax		155 500

return can be compared for different costs of capital. In those circumstances, both divisions have significant shortfalls at all rates of cost of capital.

A number of writers – notably Amey (1969) – have criticised the inclusion of a charge for interest on capital employed in the calculation of residual income. Amey's criticism was founded on

Table 17.6
Divisional residual incomes

	Division A	Division B
Controllable capital employed	£425 000	£165 000
Controllable residual income	£286 500	£92 300
Rate of return on controllable capital invested	67.4%	55.9%
Net capital employed	£725 000	£275 000
Net residual income before tax	£155 500	£31 230
Rate of return on capital invested	21.4%	11.4%
Net residual income after tax	£74 640	£14 990
Rate of return on capital invested	10.3%	5.5%

the belief that operating divisions have little actual control over capital investment in their divisional activities. Nonetheless, the evidence that the measure is used, as adduced by Mauriel and Anthony (1966), tends to negate Amey's criticism. He argued also that the inclusion of a charge for interest did little to encourage the maximisation of the rate of return on capital and, if it was designed to encourage the maximisation of divisional profits, would have a marked dysfunctional effect since managers would be instructed to maximise residual income. The arguments against these criticisms have been marshalled by Samuels (1969) and by Mepham (1980), and as Solomons (1965) demonstrated clearly, residual income has marked beneficial effects as a divisional performance measurement yardstick.

Amey considered that the firm's corporate objectives would be served best if divisional managers had no control over their own capital investment. The cost of capital in Amey's argument was a fixed cost, and as such should play no part in either divisional investment decision making or, more important, in divisional performance measurement. Emmanuel and Otley (1976) reviewed these arguments and criticisms and came down conclusively in favour of residual income as a measurement tool. That divisional managers are knowledgeable in matters of investment for their own areas of responsibility is one of the more cogent arguments for divisionalisation. Equally, capital invested in a division includes working capital, or net current assets, and so comes under the close, day to day control of divisional managers. Any charge for interest will be comprised of two elements, therefore, and will tend to act as a powerful motivational force in the improvement of divisional performance.

The residual income approach, like the return on investment method, concentrates on short run results in fixed periods, but the calculation of residual income after levying a charge for the use of capital takes account of the cost of capital and involves consideration of the time value of money and present values. In such circumstances, divisional decisions are likely to be more in keeping with corporate decisions. The data in Table 17.3 ignore depreciation, and it might be useful to bring that into this discussion. Charging depreciation would reduce book values (that is, capital invested) and would result in a reducing charge for interest on capital invested in the division. Under the residual income approach, there would be a positive increment to residual income in each year of the project's life and this factor would aid its acceptance by the divisional manager, with concomitant long run benefits.

A beneficial effect of the employment of the residual income approach is that it encourages divisional managers to be take more notice, and even to become aware of, the real costs of using capital. The motivational impact of the inclusion of an actual charge for capital use is likely to be far greater than the recognition of a percentage rate of return on capital. Arguably, if managers have to pay for the use of capital, that capital will be used more effectively and efficiently. The appreciation of the actual cost of retaining under used capital resources will prompt a rationalisation of capital requirements, thereby releasing funds or assets for use elsewhere.

MEASUREMENT CRITERIA

Having examined the two leading measurements and discussed their advantages and disadvantages, we can now compile a list of the criteria by which such measurement devices should be judged. Shillinglaw (1961 and 1962) suggested that there are three criteria against which divisional profit measurements must be judged before they are considered acceptable:

1 Divisional profit should not be increased by any action that reduces total company profit.
2 Each division's profit should be as independent as possible of performance efficiency and managerial decisions elsewhere in the company.
3 Each division's profit should reflect all items that are subject to any substantial degree of control by the division manager or his subordinates.

The first rule is clearly in the best interest of the firm as a whole. It can be shown convincingly in any dicussion of transfer pricing, for example, as in Chapter 18 of this handbook, that 'selfish' profit seeking actions by divisional managers will reduce overall contribution. Central management will take action to restrain divisional managements found to be price cutting or operating suboptimising transfer pricing practices. The various accounting practices followed in a firm – for instance, in relation to depreciation or absorption costing – may induce conflict between divisional interests and those of the firm as a whole. Dearden (1960 and 1961) has discussed a number of these related problems, and Solomons (1965) has provided the simplest solution:

> . . . unwise rules of divisional profit measurement may cause a division to act against the best interests of the company. They are really all manifestations of a single defect. In every case there is a failure to make a division bear the true cost to the company of the division's action – the true cost of using capital, of administrative services, of scrapping equipment and so on.

Once those defects are recognised, there is every chance of devising a system which will rectify matters.

The second and third criteria advanced by Shillinglaw are concerned with the independence of divisions and with the contention that divisional managers should be judged only on the results of those activities over which they have full control. As discussed before (in Chapter 11, for instance) the notion of absolute control is not realistic; a more acceptable criterion is that of significant influence. Shillinglaw's view of divisional performance reports was that they should only include those items over which the manager had control. To include and identify controllable items is one thing, and thoroughly commendable at that, but to exclude and thereby ignore other aspects of divisional performance is clearly naive and undesirable.

Alongside Shillinglaw's criteria, it is valuable to examine the purposes for which divisional reports will be drawn up. They have three principal roles:

1 the guidance of divisional management in making decisions;
2 the guidance of corporate management in making decisions;
3 the appraisal of divisional management by corporate management.

Those three roles have two different orientations. Decision making guidance relates to the future, whereas appraisal relates to the past. In the one case, profit figures, however derived or defined, have limited value for forecasting future outcomes and making decisions. In the other, profit figures may be the only information available for assessment of managers' endeavours and the appraisal of their results.

In those circumstances – and it must be remembered that all classes of profit figure are surrounded with qualifications and misgivings as to their accuracy, usefulness and relevance – the residual income approach seems to offer better and more appropriate information to both divisional and corporate management.

For divisional managements in the process of taking decisions, the controllable residual income before tax figure (see Table 17.5, for example) offers the better guide; for corporate managements in the process of making decisions concerning investment, the net residual income figure before tax offers a more appropriate guide, although the incidence of tax and its allocation to divisions may make the after tax figure a better criterion in certain circumstances.

For corporate managements wishing to appraise the performance of divisional managements, the controllable residual income figure represents the more effective and amenable yardstick of divisional performance. No account should be taken of factors outside the divisional manager's control or influence when appraising that manager's performance. For that reason, the measurement of controllable residual income, free of all cost elements outside the divisional manager's control, offers the better yardstick for performance measurement.

DIVISIONAL CONTROL

As discussed elsewhere in this handbook, control is best exercised through the use of budgets; controllable residual income will form a part of any divisional operating budget or profit budget, if that is the yardstick adopted. Divisional managers report the congruence, or lack of congruence, between budgeted results and actual outcomes, and support such reports with explanations and analyses of variances, current plans and proposed actions to rectify or eliminate shortcomings.

Corporate management can take action as appropriate on the basis of those budget reports, as described and discussed in the chapter dealing with responsibility accounting (Chapter 11), but special problems inhibit the effectiveness of budget reports as control mechanisms or evaluatory devices.

These have been described by Anthony and Dearden (1976) as falling into three principal categories:

1 the degree of discretion available to divisional managers;
2 the degree to which critical performance variables can be controlled by the divisional manager;

3   the degree of uncertainty associated with the critical performance variables.

The greater the degree of discretion allowed to a divisional manager, the harder it becomes to set precise goals or targets. The greater the number of choices available to a divisional manager, the more difficult it is to decide which of those choices will be best for the firm in the long run.

The greater the degree of control of the divisional manager over the critical performance variables by which he is to be judged, the easier it is to set quantified and effective budgetary control systems.

The greater the degree of uncertainty surrounding those critical variables, the harder it will be to set satisfactory goals and to measure subsequent performance. In general terms, the higher the level of uncertainty associated with a division's operations, the lower the controllability of the divisional manager, especially where the greater proportion of any uncertainty will surround variables external to the division and the firm.

Additionally, the problem of the time span of both managerial activities and performance measures becomes acute when divisional managers are engaged in making decisions regarding long term projects. Managers of innovative or experimental divisions may not be fairly judged in such cases. Equally, however, the results of current performance are influenced by the impacts of previous decisions, so substantial compensating influences may be at work.

Delegation – tight or loose?

Control devices are needed over and above the profit budget, and their importance will vary with the degree of delegation adopted by corporate management. That aspect of divisional control can be examined by considering the two extremes: tight delegation and loose delegation.

It is frequently said that one of the marks of a 'bad' manager is his inability to delegate efficiently. Such a manager delegates only routine tasks, maintains a close watch over their progress and participates in the planning and execution of any delegated tasks which he considers important or attractive. In much the same way, corporate managements practise tight delegation procedures, taking the view that divisional managers work best within a clearcut and short period, and when corporate management shares important decision making exercises. Advocates of tight delegation argue that managers work better when they are committed to a relatively short term role – that is, for example, within a one-year budget period. Equally, it is argued that although divisional managers make day to day decisions, the participation of corporate management in those decision processes will increase the scope for making better and more profitable decisions.

Under conditions of tight delegation, it is necessary to augment the budget control process by two further control mechanisms. There will need to be a much closer involvement of corporate and divisional management in the budgeting and reporting system, encompassing regular meetings, systematic analyses of divisional reports, and much deeper insights into the detailed facets of divisional operations. Additionally, the existence of a structure of tight delegation will call for a competent, experienced and alert infrastructure of accounting and budgeting staff. In other words, the management accounting team's role becomes crucial.

In conditions of tight delegation, the divisional manager will be judged by his adherence to budget plans, and that process of evaluation by proximity to targets will lead to some of the dangers discussed earlier in this chapter: the encouragement of uneconomic actions and the subsequent incorrect evaluation of the manager. The control devices built on to the budget system can help to alleviate those weaknesses. Corrective actions can be discussed and evaluated more logically and in greater detail, and appraisals of divisional managements will be made more in terms of personal observation than report interpretation.

Loose delegation practices use the budget as a planning and communication device, rather than as a measurement and performance appraisal device. The philosophical tenet of loose delegation is that divisional managers are good managers, experienced and efficient, and should be left to get on with their delegated tasks. In such circumstances, central management would be negligent if it took the naive view that such divisional managers could be left completely to their own devices. Some kind of early warning system must give clear signals when divisional managements are performing unsatisfactorily or ineffectively. In complex organisations, such as most business enterprises, the accounting and budgeting systems offer only limited assistance in that direction. By their nature, such systems depend on historical data, and evaluations of past performance, and fail to offer sufficiently early warnings of poor managerial performance. Personal observation by experienced managers is probably the only sensible way of operating such an early warning system; Stewart and Stewart (1982) gave valuable insights into detecting, understanding and remedying poor performance.

Non-financial control measures

There seems to be general agreement that profitability alone is inadequate to measure the performance of divisional managers. The General Electric Company adopted eight measures of divisional performance when it decentralised in the 1950s:

1 profitability;
2 market position;
3 productivity;
4 product leadership;
5 personnel development;
6 employee attitudes;
7 public responsibility;
8 balance between short range and long range goals.

Anthony and Dearden (1976) argued that, as a minimum, divisional managements should be judged by market and product performance and development, employee performance and development, and social or public responsibility. Those measurements can be formalised and incorporated in a structured system of management by objectives, or they can be informal and unstructured.

CONCLUSION

Notwithstanding the very large problems associated with both the return on investment and residual income approach to divisional performance measurement, the two methods underlie any system of divisional measurement and control. As such, the main task for the coming years is to refine those methods and tailor their structure more closely to the enhanced measurement of divisional performance.

Fundamental difficulties must be overcome to design and implement control systems which will recognise the influences and impacts of accounting, behavioural, decisional and organisational differences on divisional performance, and there is a clear need for wider research into these areas from the viewpoint of divisional performance measurement and evaluation.

In appraising a divisional manager, there is a danger that the importance of the profitability yardstick will overshadow other, and perhaps equally crucial, yardsticks and measurement devices. Corporate management must take a balanced but realistic view of divisional performance, and there is a need for researchers and practitioners to develop suitable mechanisms and approaches to make that realistic view more accessible. The ability of central management to control divisional operations depends on its ability to recognise, encourage and reward 'good' performers and to identify, understand and cure 'poor' performers.

REFERENCES AND FURTHER READING

Amey, L. R., 'Divisional performance measurement and interest on capital', *Journal of Business Finance*, Spring 1969.

Anthony, R. N., and Dearden, J., *Management Control Systems: Text and Cases*, 3rd edn. Homewood, Ill.: Irwin, 1976.

Child, J., *Organisation: A Guide to Problems and Practice*, London: Harper & Row, 1977.

Dearden, J., 'Problem in decentralized profit responsibility', *Harvard Business Review*, May–June 1960.

Dearden, J., 'Problem in decentralized financial control', *Harvard Business Review*, May–June 1961.

Emmanuel, C. R., and Otley, D. T., 'The usefulness of residual income', *Journal of Business Finance and Accountancy*, Winter 1976.

Flower, J. F., 'Captim – a bright idea from Bristol', *Accountancy*, December 1971.

Horngren, C. T., *Cost Accounting: A Managerial Emphasis*, 4th edn. Englewood Cliffs, N.J.: Prentice-Hall, 1977.

Mauriel, J. J., and Anthony, R. N., 'Misevaluation of investment center performance', *Harvard Business Review*, March–April 1966.

Mepham, M. J., 'The residual income debate', *Journal of Business Finance and Accountancy*, Summer 1980.

Samuels, J. M., 'Divisional performance measurement and interest on capital: a contributed note', *Journal of Business Finance*, Autumn 1969.

Shillinglaw, G., *Cost Accounting: Analysis and Control*, Homewood, Ill.: Irwin, 1961.

Shillinglaw, G., 'Toward a theory of divisional income measurement', *The Accounting Review,* April 1962.

Solomons, D., *Divisional Performance: Measurement and Control,* New York: Financial Executives Research Foundation, 1965.

Stewart, V., and Stewart, A., *Managing the Poor Performer,* Aldershot: Gower, 1982.

Tomkins, C., *Financial Planning in Divisionalised Companies.* London: Haymarket, 1973.

18

Transfer Pricing

Jeffrey Davies

In the calculation of divisional profits and the measurement of divisional performance, particular problems arise when divisions are not wholly independent. If one division supplies goods or services to another, a transfer price must be established to help to determine the buying division's costs and the selling division's revenues. There are obvious opportunities for suboptimising and dysfunctional behaviour. The concepts of divisionalisation were discussed in the preceding chapter, and attention was drawn to the dangers from divisional managers acting in their own best interests at the expense of the firm's advantage. This chapter examines the setting of transfer prices and discusses the many problems associated with intracompany pricing.

As merger activity continues and concentration increases, industrialised business systems are increasingly composed of multiproduct, multiprocess companies. It has been shown that to facilitate greater efficiency, and hence profitability, a divisionalised organisation is advantageous for such firms, each such division being regarded as a profit centre.

There is a danger that, when each division is seen as a profit centre and each manager knows that his performance is being appraised on the basis of divisional profit, divisional managers will attempt to increase such profits by maximising transfer prices or other intracompany differentiations. The effect of such selfish behaviour will be that the firm's contribution will fall, even though the individual division's profits may rise. All relationships between profit centres are, therefore, compromises between the allowance of independence in decision making and the facilitation of optimal corporate decision making.

SUBOPTIMISATION

In economic theory, maximum profit will be earned where marginal revenue is equal to marginal cost. In practice it is not always possible to measure such costs and revenues precisely, but the logic is correct. The example of a divisionalised company, Croeso Cycles, can be used to illustrate the various points for discussion. Croeso Cycles has three operating divisions; the Wheels and Gears Division supplies, among others, the Frame and Assembly Division which, in turn, supplies completed but unpainted cycles to the Marketing Division.

Subject to the constraint that the firm feels for strategic reasons that it must produce the majority of its own components in order to maximise profits, the following problems must be resolved:

1 the output to be achieved;
2 the method for determining transfer prices between divisions;
3 the level of profits to be earned by each division.

Pursuing the economic approach, the best joint level of output will be determined at that level of output where total marginal cost (TMC) is equal to marginal revenue (MR). To obtain that output, each divisional manager should prepare a schedule of respective processing costs for various levels of output. That will give the marginal cost (MC) of producing each additional unit. These marginal curves can be aggregated to produce a total marginal cost curve; by comparing that total marginal cost curve with the marginal revenue curve, the optimum production level can be determined.

Figure 18.1 shows the marginal cost and revenue curves for the three divisions, although only the Marketing Division has a marginal revenue curve. The costs OX, MY, and NZ are the fixed costs incurred by each division respectively. Figure 18.2 shows the total marginal cost curve for the company and indicates that its profit will be maximised where total marginal cost equals marginal revenue – at point J with output at a level of OQ_1.

By looking at each divisional marginal cost schedule, the cost of producing the output quantity can be determined and transfer prices between each division can be built up in the following manner.

For output OQ_1, the Wheels and Gears Division has incurred a total cost of $OXDQ_1$ (in Figure 18.1) and it will use as a transfer price

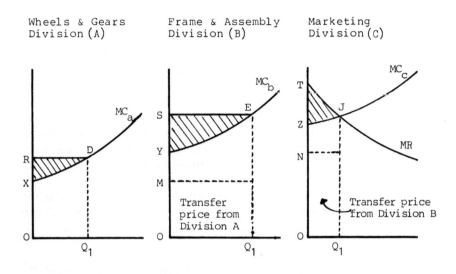

Fig. 18.1   Divisional costs and revenues

the marginal cost of producing the OQ_1th unit. Price charged will be, therefore, OR and total revenue obtained will be $ORDQ_1$; divisional profit will be represented by the triangular area XRD. The Frame and Assembly Division adds the transfer price to its own processing costs, and determines a transfer price at which to charge the units handed over to the Marketing Division. In this case, the transfer price will be 'OS' and the division will make a profit of 'YSE'. The Marketing Division sells the finished product on the open market, earning a profit of 'ZTJ'.

The overriding aim of the firm's endeavours should be to maximise its profits as a whole, or its aggregate contribution towards fixed costs and profits. As shown in Figure 18.1, different levels of profit are earned by each division. It is vital that managers responsible for decision taking should understand the importance of the firm's interests; it is not necessary for each division to earn the same profit. It is the maximisation of total company profits which is important, and any attempt by a divisional manager to increase his own division's profits at the expense of another division will lead to a shortfall in total company profits – suboptimisation, in other words.

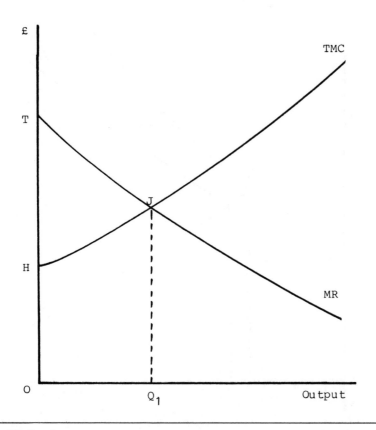

Fig. 18.2   Company costs and revenues

Figure 18.3 shows the situation that would obtain if the manager of the Wheels and Gears Division overstated his costs deliberately so as to increase the transfer price he charged to the Frame and Assembly Division, and therefore boost his own divisional profit.

The result of this falsification is that central management will derive a different total marginal cost curve for the firm as a whole – labelled TMC (false) in the figure. The result of that false impression will be that the apparent total marginal cost curve intersects the marginal revenue curve at the point J_2 rather than the true point of intersection, J_1. The output is determined at Q_2, to the left of the optimal production point Q_1. As a direct result, total company profits fall from HTJ_1 to HTJ_2K, a loss of profit of KJ_2J_1.

The firm as a whole will be convinced that the profit maximising

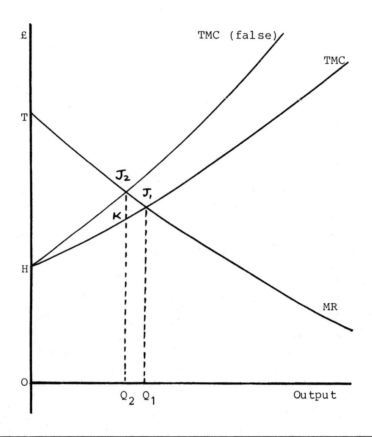

Fig. 18.3   Company costs and revenues

output is Q_2 and that could have serious repercussions on other aspects of the firm's business operations – the loss of sales to other manufacturers, for instance.

Research into transfer pricing practices proves that there is inevitably a tendency to act in divisional interests and pursue suboptimising policies – unless the calculation of transfer prices is integrated into the group planning and budgeting system and unless managers are fully aware of the effects of their activities on other divisions and on the attainment of the short and long term objectives of the firm.

For example, it is commonplace for the manager of a buying division not to be concerned about the fixed and variable cost elements of an intracompany transfer price; the whole transfer price is a variable cost in his opinion, since the actual price charged will vary with the quantity bought. However, as far as the selling division is concerned, the amount of fixed cost included is dependent on the number of units sold, so that a change in the number of units will have a significant effect on the profitability of the selling division. Full cost can never make a satisfactory foundation for the establishment of transfer prices, and full information must be transferred to the purchasing division on the costs of the product quantity transferred.

Second, a transfer pricing system which uses marginal cost to the supplying division, and therefore does not permit that division to earn a profit, will ignore the divisional performance measurement aspect. It cannot be employed, therefore, without damaging the decision making autonomy of divisional management. As long as marginal cost transfer pricing is in operation, the fixed costs of the supplying division will not be absorbed in the transfer price. A loss will be shown and divisional managers will be reluctant to determine transfer prices at levels which will affect head office assessment of their effectiveness and may even prefer to eschew intracompany trade in favour of selling their products on the external market. In situations where marginal costs increase with volume, marginal cost will vary according to the total demand of the buying division plus the demands of the selling division's external customers. In those circumstances, neither division can make its decisions independently and divisional autonomy is endangered, if not impossible to maintain.

Third, because accounting systems seldom record the opportunity costs of the best alternative rejected, an important aspect of the transfer pricing problem is overlooked in practice. Where excess operating capacity can be eliminated by a small decrease in the selling price of the intermediate product to outside buyers, the opportunity cost of selling the intermediate product internally becomes significant, and the profits accruing from existing sales of the finished product must be reviewed. Each time the forecast of opportunity cost is changed, the optimal decision relating to the volume of interdivisional trading must be revised.

There is also the problem of determining the validity of the price at which the intermediate product is available from outside suppliers. Where this price can be interpreted as a 'distress' price (offered by the outside supplier in a desperate effort to retain business), it can hardly be a valid guide for establishing transfer price. Whether or not a price can be interpreted as a distress price depends on the circumstances obtaining at the time, of course. Where the question arises of a division ceasing to produce an intermediate – as a result of that product being available at a cheaper price on the external market – careful attention must be paid to the probable costs of seeking to re-enter the market at a later date if the external supplier raises his 'distress' price to a more acceptable level.

Finally, it has to be realised that the existence of a market price arrived at by arm's length competitive bargaining between an independent buyer and an independent seller does not always guarantee the best price for the optimum benefit of the organisation as a whole. Transfer prices agreed in those circumstances can motivate divisional managers to take decisions which are not in the best interests of the firm as a whole.

If the determination of transfer prices causes so much difficulty and is so surrounded by snags, why are such prices necessary? It could be argued that they are not really necessary in a vertically integrated firm. Products could be passed from one division to the other, it might be said, and profit could be calculated for the firm as a whole. Such a practice cannot be recommended.

The abolition of transfer prices would prevent the meaningful measurement of the profits of individual operating units. It would also prevent the accurate estimation of likely earnings on proposed investment projects. Further, transfer prices give divisional managers an economic base and incentive for correct decision making. Finally, transfer pricing is a means of facilitating decentralisation.

There has been an unfortunate tendency among managers and practitioners to see transfer pricing as a problem in isolation and to ignore its role in the total planning and control system.

TRANSFER PRICES AND BUDGETARY PLANNING AND CONTROL

A comprehensive budgetary planning and control system should exist in all firms, and multidivisional firms have a particular need for such a system to draw together the disparate and diverse elements within the group and to ensure the appropriate pursuit of the firm's long run objectives.

Transfer pricing practices and techniques must form an integral part of that budgetary system and transfer pricing plays a vital role in interdivisional relations. That role can be examined under four headings: establishing transfer pricing policies and administrative procedures; selecting transfer prices; reconciling divisional and corporate interests; and measuring profit performance of divisional units.

Policies and procedures

Policies must be clearly stated and communicated to those concerned. However, a degree of flexibility must be present to accommodate the complexities and fluctuating nature of the transfer pricing problem. There is no single universal rule for establishing transfer prices; each company needs to devise transfer pricing policies and practices that are consonant with its own affairs and characteristics.

The task of communicating policies and procedures is crucial, and their incorporation in some form of company manual is probably the most efficient way of conveying their characteristics. As a minimum, such procedures should include the following:

1 formulae for setting transfer prices;
2 sources to be used when determining market prices;
3 price lists;
4 price ceilings;
5 lists of transfer pricing units and the price formula applicable to them;
6 statement of corporate policy regarding purchases from extra-company sources;
7 procedures to be followed in the case of a dispute.

Selecting transfer prices

The actual transfer price chosen will depend upon a number of factors:

1 the existence or not of an external market price for the product;
2 the market structure in which the company operates;
3 the degree of interdependence or independence existing between divisions.

Transfer prices have been established, therefore, by the following methods: some concept of cost; some appreciation of market cost; some assessment of negotiated or bargained market price.

Among the reasons given for using costs as the determinants of transfer prices have been the following considerations. First, the selling division is regarded as a cost centre and not a profit centre. Second, emphasis has been placed on the profitability of products rather than the profitability of operational units. There are advantages, of course, in using costs as determinants of transfer prices. Data are readily available and easily interpreted. Prices based on costs are usually more acceptable to buying divisional managers – and to certain government departments!

The use of costs as a base has disadvantages as well as advantages, of course, as has been recognised by many managers. It weakens the authority of a divisional manager, and it can interfere with the evaluation of divisional performance. It becomes more difficult to decide the profit contribution of each division when freedom to operate is limited to costs over which divisional managers have less than complete control.

More important perhaps, there are alternative criteria for determining cost – full cost; standard cost; marginal cost. Actual full cost is not a good base to use because it is seldom known until the end of a trading period, and is never available in sufficient detail at the time at which a decision has to be made. Standard cost is preferable to full cost but suffers from the problems associated with standard costs of any type. There is a danger of carrying forward the last period's inefficiencies. Direct or marginal cost is rarely used in practice.

A common practice is to base transfer prices on some assessment of cost augmented by a mark-up derived in one of a number of ways: a percentage on cost; a percentage of some notional return on capital employed; a percentage of some estimate of aggregate group profit; a fixed amount per item. The actual mark-up chosen will probably be determined by custom and practice, and its impact on divisional performance and managerial motivation will be hazardous and haphazard. Such a procedure will not provide valid guidelines for the efficient allocation of resources between divisions.

Transfers at market prices are generally recognised to be correct – if a market price exists and if the market is competitive. The use of a market price will create the actual market conditions facing divisions if they were operating as separate businesses rather than as divisions. Furthermore, to the extent that they can be established as dependent on outside forces of supply and demand, they form an excellent performance indicator because they cannot easily be manipulated by individual divisional managers with personal interests in the resultant profits.

Ascertaining market prices is not always as easy as might appear, and care has to be taken to ensure product comparability, to account for handling or distribution costs, to obtain up-to-date prices, and to make sure that there is ready access to the external market without damaging side effects. The appearance of a former internal buyer in an external market might drive market prices up or alter trading conditions.

Market prices used for transfer price determination must be adjusted for the above factors, and internal transfers are frequently negotiated at market price less a discount to compensate for cost savings – marketing or debt collecting expenses, for instance.

Dean (1955) suggested that provided each division of a firm is a profit centre and divisional managers have relative autonomy it would be preferable to determine transfer prices through a process of negotiation. Three simple procedures must then be followed:

1   Transfer prices into and from a profit centre should be determined by negotiation between buyers and sellers.
2   Negotiators should have full access to all data on alternative sources and markets.
3   Buyers and sellers should be free to deal in external markets.

Such a scheme has considerable advantages over calculating transfer prices on a market price formula, particularly where it is difficult to establish a market price. The process of negotiation takes account of such matters as reduced selling costs or handling costs. The drawbacks are that such a negotiation system is expensive of time and is subject to manipulation by stronger divisional managers.

There has been a move towards the establishment of a 'general rule' for transfer price setting, so that the chosen transfer price should:

1   be consistent with decentralised profit responsibility;
2   permit a valid comparison of divisional performance;
3   identify unprofitable or inefficient operations;
4   provide greater incentive for cost reduction.

The general rule is discussed further in a later section of this chapter.

Reconciling divisional and corporate interests

Management must prevent the interests of a particular division from interfering with the achievement of corporate goals. Corporate interest must always take precedence over divisional interests. The management processes for setting transfer prices must ensure that such prices are scrutinised and validated to remove the possibility of dysfunctional special interests affecting the optimum corporate behaviour.

Measuring profit performance

As discussed in the preceding chapter and elsewhere in this handbook, the evaluation of divisional performance depends on a number of factors, of which profit is the most important in many measurement models. Transfer pricing plays a critical role in the determination of divisional profits and management must ensure that a spirit of fairness and realism permeates the transfer price setting processes.

THE GENERAL RULE

Transfer pricing must assist in the process of allocating scarce resources, and it does this by breaking the tendency to suboptimise. A series of requirements must be satisfied if the firm is to achieve its maximum potential.

First, the intracompany pricing method must generate a competitive price; this concept is central to the whole notion of decentralisation. Profits are the more commonly used yardsticks for the measurement of managerial effectiveness and if intracompany transfer prices are not competitive, an important tool in management evaluation is lost.

Senior management must use divisional income statements to arrive at policy decisions concerning the profitability of divisional ventures. The decision on whether to make various components or to sub-contract their production will be greatly influenced by the apparent performance of a division. At one extreme, the continuance of a division might be influenced by operational results affected by intracompany transfer prices.

The intracompany pricing system must therefore be realistic and prices must be designed to foster a healthy interdepartmental spirit of competition, to provide an adequate profit yardstick against which departmental managers can be judged, and to provide reliable figures and information for central management decision making.

Benke (1980) argued for the establishment of the general rule to help create an efficient pricing system.

The general rule can be expressed as follows: The transfer price (TP or, more conventionally, p^*) should equal the standard variable cost (SVC) plus the lost contribution margin (LCM). The lost contribution margin is the contribution margin per unit on an external sale which is forgone when that unit is sold or transferred internally.

There are, therefore, two separate costs to a firm when a product is transferred internally rather than sold on the outside market. The first is the cost of the product itself, the standard variable cost of manufacturing the product and selling it internally. The second is the opportunity cost of carrying out the transaction as an internal transfer rather than an external sale. The standard variable cost in this general rule will not always be the same as the standard variable cost of products manufactured and sold in external markets. Internal transfers or sales will allow cost savings on selling and distributing expenses, advertising and promotional expenses, financing and collecting charges, and so on. The standard variable cost in the general rule application will usually be lower than the standard variable cost of goods sold in external markets.

The lost contribution margin depends on the ability of the selling division to place the product in the external market, and the quantity released to the external market has a significant impact on that ability. Also, if a supplying division is operating at full capacity, any internal transfer will reduce external sales. The full contribution margin is forgone in respect of each unit transferred rather than sold externally. On the other hand, if the supplying division is operating at less than full capacity and cannot sell any further units in the external market without cutting the unit selling price, the full contribution margin is not forgone.

Most large firms organised on divisional lines produce a number of items that require many different components. The market supply and demand conditions for each of those components vary enormously and may range from widespread competition to near-monopoly. The relevant market conditions must be considered in each case, and products can be divided into four broad categories for that purpose.

Category 1 products

These are products transferred between divisions that are never likely to be produced outside the company. For reasons of quality control, secrecy, relative value or patent protection, management wishes to produce some products within the company – irrespective of any economic considerations. Competitive market prices are not available, therefore, for products of this type; the common practice is to set a 'phantom' market price, based on standard variable cost plus a contribution allowance. The contribution allowance will be a negotiated figure based on capital employed or some other measure, on similar products' contributions, and on the firm's general contribution experience.

Category 2 products

These are products which management may be willing to buy from outside sources, but only on a relatively long term basis. Their manufacture will generally require a considerable investment in manufacturing skills and facilities. Here, the lost contribution margin should be calculated on estimated long run competitive prices. Short term fluctuations should be ignored, since the source of such products would be changed infrequently owing to the special manufacturing technologies and expertise required.

Category 3 products

These are products that could be produced outside the company without any significant disruption to current operations. They will be relatively small in volume and capable of being produced with general purpose equipment and facilities. No problems arise in pricing because a ready market exists.

Category 4 products

These are products that can be bought and sold readily within and without the company. With the existence of an established outside market, there are no problems in arriving at a transfer price based on standard variable cost and lost contribution margin.

Practical application

The example of Croeso Cycles can be used again to illustrate the

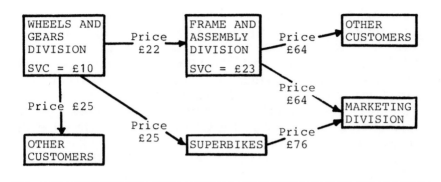

Fig. 18.4   Croeso Cycles – alternative opportunities

application of the general rule. Figure 18.4 represents the alternative situations facing the divisions of the company.

The Marketing Division not only sells and distributes cycles but also paints them and applies transfers, flashes, and so on. Until recently, it has obtained all its unpainted assembled frames from the Frame and Assembly Division. However, it has been offered a similar unfinished cycle by Superbikes. The Frame and Assembly Division makes the frame and the brakes, but purchases the wheels and gears from the Wheels and Gears Division before final assembly. The Frame and Assembly Division is currently operating at 90 per cent capacity.

The Wheels and Gears Division sells wheels and gears to a number of outside firms and is currently operating at full capacity. Superbikes plans to purchase wheels and gears from the Wheels and Gears Division. The net cost to the company of the unfinished cycles from Superbikes is therefore £61 – calculated on the basis of a sales price to the Marketing Division of £76 less the contribution earned by the Wheels and Gears Division of £15 (£25 selling price to Superbikes less the standard variable cost of £10). This is a significant alteration to the cost and revenue pattern shown in the figure, where the Frame and Assembly Division appears to have a price advantage of £12 (£64 as against £76).

Should the Marketing Division purchase its unfinished cycles from Superbikes? Only a calculation of the transfer prices based on the general rule can tell. The transfer price from the Wheels and Gears Division to the Frame and Assembly Division is £22, but the application of the general rule reveals that the transfer price should be £25: standard variable cost = £10; lost contribution margin = £15 (£25 selling price to external customers less £10 standard variable cost). The Wheels and Gears Division is operating at full capacity and the full opportunity cost is therefore applicable.

The transfer price from the Frame and Assembly Division to the Marketing Division should be £58: standard total variable cost = £48 (£25 plus £23); lost contribution margin = £10 (see below for an explanation of this estimate). The £58 transfer price is less than the net cost of £61 for cycles purchased from Superbikes, so the Marketing Division should purchase its cycles from the Frame and Assembly Division.

The apparent lost contribution margin derived from a selling price of £64 and a standard total variable cost of £48 is £16. However, the Frame and Assembly Division is operating at 90 per cent capacity (producing 9 000 assembled but unpainted cycles) and to increase production to 10 000 cycles, say, would call for a price reduction of £0.60 per cycle. Table 18.1 shows the contributions derived from outputs (and sales or transfers) of 9 000 cycles and 10 000 cycles. The additional or incremental contribution from each of the extra 1 000 cycles is £10. Because of the excess capacity, the current selling price and its contribution of £16 are not relevant to the calculation of the lost contribution margin; the appropriate lost contribution margin is the £10 derived in Table 18.1.

Table 18.1
Lost contribution margin – Frame and Assembly Division

	£
9 000 cycles	
Revenue (9 000 @ £64)	576 000
less Standard variable cost (9 000 @ £48)	432 000
Contribution	144 000
10 000 cycles	
Revenue (10 000 @ £63.40)	634 000
less Standard variable cost (10 000 @ £48)	480 000
Contribution	154 000
Net increase in contribution	10 000

By calculating the transfer price using the general rule, the true economic cost of trading within and without the company is established. With a transfer price of £58, the Frame and Assembly Division is indifferent to selling the 1 000 extra cycles internally or externally. Sales of 10 000 cycles at £63.40 will generate a total contribution of £154 000; selling 9 000 cycles at £64 will generate a total contribution of £144 000 and selling 1 000 cycles at £58 would generate a further total contribution of £10 000, making an aggregate total contribution of £154 000.

CONCLUSION

Studies of transfer pricing systems indicate that there is often considerable disparity between the practical applications of transfer pricing mechanisms and what might be reasonably expected from a study of the theoretical analyses of the subject. In some instances, special circumstances account for this disparity. Where, for example, an organisation supplies a range of finished products to the outside market and the sales of each item are largely dependent on the availability of other products in the range, transfers of intermediate products or sub-assemblies will continue to take place internally, although external sales might be more profitable. Similarly, there may be some justification, in isolated cases, for sanctioning economically unviable transfer prices in the short term, where central management is anxious to support a division as a vital part of the firm's long run structure.

There are still many instances, however, in which the chosen transfer price cannot be justified on any logical grounds. There is considerable evidence that managements are influenced by a variety of factors other than economic considerations. Many managements are unaware that suboptimising behaviour is occurring in their companies or that a change in transfer pricing policies could markedly affect their group profitability.

For the general rule to be applied effectively, the management accounting system must be efficient and capable of producing the necessary relevant information. As always in any consideration of management planning and control, systems are crucial and rules and procedures have little value in the absence of timely, relevant and clear information. Transfer pricing is an integral part of the budgetary planning and controlling system for divisionalised companies and there are many problems still to be solved. The scope for empirical research is considerable.

REFERENCES AND FURTHER READING

Benke, R. L., *Transfer Pricing: Techniques and Uses,* New York: National Association of Accountants, 1980.

Davies, J. R., 'How to determine transfer prices', *Management Accounting,* October 1978.

Dean, J., 'Decentralization and inter-company pricing', *Harvard Business Review,* July–August 1955.

Emmanuel, C. R., 'Transfer pricing: a diagnosis and possible solution to dysfunctional decision-making in the divisionalized company', *Management International Review,* 1977.

Finnie, J., 'Transfer pricing practices', *Management Accounting,* December 1978.

Hirschleifer, J., 'On the economics of transfer pricing', *Journal of Business,* July 1965.

Institute of Cost and Management Accountants, *Management Accounting Guidelines No 1: Inter-unit Transfer Pricing,* London: ICMA, 1981.

Manes, R. P., 'Birch Paper Company revisited: an exercise in transfer pricing', *The Accounting Review,* July 1970.

Solomons, D., *Divisional Performance: Measurement and Control,* New York: Financial Executives Research Foundation, 1965.

Tomkins, C., *Financial Planning in Divisionalised Companies,* London: Haymarket, 1973.

Watson, D. J. H., and Baumler, J. V., 'Transfer pricing: a behavioural context', *The Accounting Review,* July 1975.

Young, A., *Pricing Decisions: A Practical Guide to Interdivisional Transfer Pricing Policy,* London: Business Books, 1979.

19

Physical Distribution Management

Gordon Hill

In this contribution, the author examines the costing and management of the physical distribution function, with respect to one aspect – the costing of road transport. Measurement and control of freight costs are vital elements of the distribution operations of industrial and commercial enterprises. The objective of effective physical distribution management is to optimise the relationship between distribution costs and service to customers. According to figures emerging from a recent survey conducted by the Centre for Physical Distribution Management, transport now accounts for almost 30 per cent of total distribution costs, representing more than 3.5 per cent of sales value on average. On another aspect, the author reported, at a 1980 Institute of Cost and Management Accountants seminar on freight costing, that drivers spent 34 per cent of their working time actually driving, around 25 per cent directly making deliveries (including waiting time and parking, etc), and the balance taking meals, waiting at the depot, and so on. A further instance quoted by the author at that seminar was that of a typical depot servicing 2 800 accounts with a fleet of 29 vehicles. In respect of 28 per cent of the accounts, the direct cost of distribution exceeded the gross margin on the business transacted; 38 per cent were contributing to fixed costs and profit, but not adequately, and the remaining 34 per cent were profitable in every sense. The concept of physical distribution management is important to the management accountant in practice. Many businesses fail to appreciate the true cost of distribution operations and thereby lose the opportunity of controlling the escalating costs of the distribution process. That failure can be explained in part by the conventional practices in organisations: different departments are often responsible for separate aspects of physical distribution and the calculation of some 'total' physical distribution cost is often difficult. Distribution costs are high, both in absolute terms and proportionately; currently, such costs represent around 12 per cent of selling price. Those costs are rising at a greater rate than other production and marketing costs and are likely to run at around 15 per cent of selling price by 1985 or so. External transport of goods has a literature of its own, of course, as do the other aspects of distribution (storage, materials handling, and so on), but the literature on total physical distribution management is scanty by comparison. In this chapter, the author concentrates on just one part of that process, but his approach and analysis can be applied just as effectively to other facets of distribution management. Significant economies can be achieved by a proper application of management accounting concepts and practices to the costing of freight and delivery operations.

In this chapter the principles of management accounting are applied to the costing of road transport. Emphasis is given to the costing of transport operations associated with the physical distribution of manufactured goods. Essentially, such distribution involves two types of transport operation: that known as trunking, and that known as local delivery. Trunking involves, typically, the point-to-point movement of relatively large consignments over long distances. Local delivery, on the other hand, is concerned with the delivery of relatively small consignments to such outlets as private dwellings, retail shops and institutions. Such consignments could consist of just one parcel or of several packages weighing several tons. There are both similarities and significant differences between the two types of transport operation and the way in which they are costed.

COST ELEMENTS

The objective of a well managed physical distribution function is to deliver the goods to the customers in such a manner as to minimise cost, so far as this is consistent with predetermined customer service standards. It is essential, therefore, that the behaviour of each element of cost, and the factors influencing that behaviour, are understood clearly. Particular attention is paid in this chapter to the costing of road transport, but the points made are of general significance and other aspects of physical distribution are considered.

Conventionally, transport costs tend to be quoted in terms of tons carried or tons delivered. From the viewpoint of the manufacturing company, this is convenient because the cost per ton can be converted into the cost per unit product. Thus, the transport element of the total cost of goods sold can be established. However, such calculations can be extremely misleading, since only average transport costs can be used. Such averages disguise the range and magnitude of the actual costs associated with transport and delivery. For example, a vehicle which undertakes a 250-mile round trip to make an urgent delivery to a customer would incur almost exactly the same actual transport costs whether the order delivered weighed 10 tons or 100 kgs.

To say that transport costs are independent of tonnage would be inaccurate. Equally, to say that there is a simple relationship between tonnage carried and cost would be grossly misleading. In order to understand transport costs more clearly, we must examine the cost elements and the factors affecting their behaviour.

Vehicle operating costs

The costs of operating a vehicle fall into two groups which, consistent with conventional management accounting principles, are fixed costs and variable costs. The fixed costs are referred to as the 'standing charges'; these are time-dependent costs which will be incurred whether the vehicle is driven or not. The variable costs are referred to as the 'running costs'; these can be related directly to the distance the vehicle is driven.

Nine elements of cost constitute the range of standing charges for a vehicle. An operator's licence fee must be paid annually for most goods vehicles over 3.5 tonnes maximum permissible gross weight. Additionally, excise duty is payable on all goods vehicles. The rate of duty payable depends on the way in which the vehicle is used, its unladen weight, and the way in which it is constructed.

Insurance premiums are influenced by such factors as the nature of the cover contracted and the insured person's claim record. The operators of small fleets of vehicles usually seek comprehensive insurance cover, whereas the larger fleet operator may choose to bear some or all of the costs of accident repair charges. The cost of such repairs would be set against the saving on insurance premiums. While it could be argued that the vulnerability to accidents is directly related to the mileage travelled, insurance is an annual cost, independent of the extent to which the vehicle is used. Most goods vehicles are required to be tested annually at an approved heavy goods vehicle testing station to ensure that they meet the legal requirements for mechanical condition and safe operation.

It is now common to treat the wages of the driver (together with associated employment costs) and any crew as an annual cost. In the event that no work is available, it may be possible to allocate the crew of a vehicle to other duties. In that case, proportionate recognition would need to be taken of the extent to which that occurred.

The operation of a fleet of vehicles will incur overhead costs

Table 19.1
Standing charges and running costs

	Rigid van	Articulated tractor and trailer
Carrying capacity	10 ton	21 ton
Gross vehicle weight	16 ton	32 ton
Capital cost	£19 000	£28 000
Residual value (after 5 years)	£1 900	£2 800
STANDING CHARGES (annual):		
Depreciation (20%)	£3 420	£5 040
Excise duty	£620	£1 580
Operator's licence	£20	£20
Insurance	£715	£1 095
MOT	£15	£15
Interest	£1 570	£2 310
Driver's wages	£8 840	£8 840
	£15 200	£18 900
RUNNING COSTS (pence per mile):		
Fuel	14.30	20.43
Lubricants	0.50	0.60
Tyres	3.36	5.04
Maintenance	16.84	17.93
	35.00	44.00

which cannot be attributed directly to any specific vehicle. Such costs will include the costs of transport management, traffic management, parking and garaging space, and so on. It is important that these additional costs are recognised and taken into account when operating costs are being calculated.

Financing charges accrue also: leasing, for example, gives rise to specific charges. Depreciation should also be included in the 'standing charge' category. It could be contended that depreciation is a running cost, on the basis that the decline in value of a vehicle is influenced greatly by the intensity of its use. However, the value of a vehicle is as much dictated by its age as by any other factor. The treatment given to depreciation must be decided in the light of experience, but it is more common for this element of cost to be included as a fixed cost or standing charge. Typically, the value of a new vehicle can be expected to decline by some 90 per cent or so over the first five years of its life.

Interest should be included, either as the actual expense of interest paid on capital borrowings to finance the purchase of the vehicle or as the opportunity cost of capital. This cost is overlooked more often than not, even though it represents a large portion of realistic standing charge totals.

By way of illustration, Table 19.1 presents the estimated standing charges and running costs of two typical vehicles – a 16-ton van and a 32-ton articulated tractor and box trailer. From the examples, an impression can be gained of the relative significance of each element of cost; generally, the costs quoted are those obtaining in late 1981.

Standing charge per journey

The decision as to the proportion of the annual standing charges of the vehicle that should be attributed to each journey made merits some attention. It is influenced by several considerations.

1 *Availability of the vehicle:* Routine servicing is undertaken normally during the day, with the result that the availability of the vehicle for operation is limited. Additionally, it is prudent to anticipate that the vehicle will be off the road for some of its working life as a result of accidental damage or breakdown. Experience will indicate the extent to which maintenance requirements reduce the availability of the vehicle; a conservative estimate would be between 10 per cent and 12½ per cent over its working life. This estimate

implies that a fleet of nine vehicles would be needed to ensure the availability of eight operational vehicles each day. In such a circumstance, the standing charges of the eight operating vehicles should be increased by one-ninth to cover the standing charges of the other vehicle.

2 *Availability of the driver:* Unless provision is made to cover for the driver in the event of holiday or sick leave absence, the operational availability of the vehicle will be reduced. The extent is likely to be of the order of 8 per cent to 10 per cent. It is unlikely that the driver's absence could be precisely coordinated with the non-availability of the vehicle for maintenance reasons. It would be prudent to plan on the assumption that those two considerations will not coincide. If a fleet operator finds that the annual holidays of the drivers cannot be staggered appropriately, it might prove necessary to make special provisions for relief or temporary drivers. As an example, the effective standing charge for each vehicle in a company fleet could be calculated as follows. The company regularly operates 14 articulated tractors and trailers; it has a fleet of 16 such vehicles and employs 17 full-time drivers. The standing charge, excluding driver's wages, for each vehicle is calculated at £10 060 a year; drivers' wages average £8 840 each a year. The effective standing charge for each vehicle operated each day is £22 231: standing charge excluding driver's wages = £10 060 × 16/14 = £11 497; driver's wages = £8 840 × 17/14 = £10 734.

3 *Availability of transport work:* If there are some days, or even longer periods, during which no transport work offers, a correspondingly greater standing charge must be attributed to the days on which work is undertaken. An example of such a situation might be that of a fleet of ice-cream distribution vans, of which hardly any would be used in the winter months. The effect of such an additional loading could be offset to some extent by careful scheduling of vehicle maintenance and drivers' holidays. The provision of stand-by vehicles and drivers could further increase the standing charges if such slack period scheduling were not practicable.

4 *Intensive vehicle use:* In accordance with EEC rules, the time and (for some vehicles) the distance that a driver may drive between appropriate periods of rest are defined precisely. The vehicle, on the other hand, is available for twenty-four hours each day. In some circumstances, it may be possible to use the vehicle intensively by employing several drivers on a shift basis. The effect would be to increase the overall cost of drivers, but there would be a significant

reduction in the standing charge attributable to each hour of operation and to each journey. Another way in which it is possible to use vehicles intensively is by articulation. For instance, the use of articulated vehicles enables trailers to be switched speedily and easily at the end of a journey, thus avoiding the expense of waiting time during the unloading/reloading process. An example of a situation where that arrangement works well is between a company's factory and its finished goods warehouses. In this particular case, storage space at the factory is limited and goods are loaded direct from the production line on to a trailer; when the trailer is fully loaded, a tractor is coupled up and the goods are taken ten miles away, to the company's warehouse. This arrangement calls for one tractor and three trailers – one being loaded at the factory, one being unloaded at the warehouse, and one on its way between the two points. Under such arrangements, the standing charges for the vehicles involved can be spread over a significant amount of activity and, as a consequence, the cost of transport is kept to a relatively modest amount.

Running costs

Table 19.1 gave details of the estimated running costs per mile for the two typical vehicles described; those costs fall into four main categories – fuel, lubricants, tyres, and maintenance. Maintenance refers to both mechanical and bodywork maintenance. In addition, there is a periodic need to clean the vehicle, since a clean appearance is taken by many operators to indicate corporate effectiveness – or at least to reflect corporate image.

JOURNEY COSTING

The cost of a journey is the aggregate of the standing charges for the period of the journey and the running costs for the distance of the journey. Two simple examples will serve to illustrate the points made earlier.

The articulated tractor and trailer unit referred to in Table 19.1 was used on 225 days in the year. On one of those days, it made a round trip of 210 miles to make a delivery of 14 tonnes to a customer. The journey cost was computed as follows: standing charges = £18 900/225 = £84.00; running costs = 210 × £0.44 = £92.40; journey cost = £176.40.

The unit was used later on to make a round trip of 490 miles to make a delivery of 10 tonnes to a customer; the journey took two days and the cost was computed as follows: standing charges = £18 900/225 × 2 = £168.00; running costs = 490 × £0.44 = £215.60; driver's overnight allowance = £12.00; journey cost = £395.0.

In evaluating the cost of local delivery, it is again necessary to take account of both standing charges and running costs. A local delivery journey could involve more than 100 drops, but for delivery to retail stores the total number of drops would be nearer 10. The problem is to determine the extent to which journey costs should be allocated to each delivery. To solve that problem, it is necessary to examine the work involved in making the journey.

By way of illustration, Figure 19.1 depicts a typical analysis of the nine-hour working day of a local delivery driver. The analysis involves six elements, each of which merits some explanation.

Depot time is the time spent by the driver at the depot at the beginning and the end of the journey. Some duties are the specific

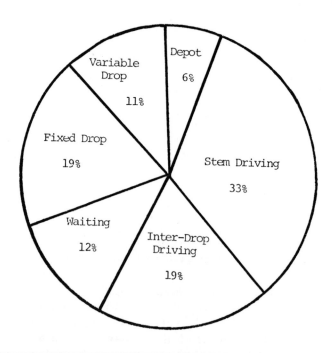

Fig. 19.1   Delivery journey time analysis

responsibility of the driver and must be undertaken before the journey begins. These include the routine daily check of the vehicle and the collection of instructions and documents related to the work on the journey. The duties undertaken at the end of the journey may include such tasks as paying in cash and writing a journey report. Where practicable, it is beneficial for warehouse staff to load and unload the vehicle during the driver's off-duty time, thereby increasing the journey time available to the driver.

Stem driving time is the time devoted by the driver to travelling to and from the delivery area to be serviced. That driving is likely to be on main roads and, therefore, at a higher average speed than inter-drop driving.

Inter-drop driving time is the time devoted to driving between delivery locations. It is possible that this will be mainly urban driving, and average speeds may be fairly low.

Waiting time is the time, in excess of that which is normal and reasonable, that the driver spends waiting his turn to deliver at a delivery point.

Fixed drop time is the time required at the delivery location to perform all the tasks associated with making the delivery – except the time taken to actually unload the vehicle and, if necessary, deliver the goods into the customer's premises. Fixed drop time includes the normal waiting time as well as that required to position the vehicle, open the doors, and hand over the goods and documents, close and secure the vehicle, and depart.

Variable drop time is the time actually spent on unloading the vehicle and moving the goods into the customer's premises. This represents a fairly small proportion of the driver's day; it is, however, the only time during that day when revenue is being generated! Any stops, therefore, which result in an increase in this proportion of the driver's day must be beneficial.

DELIVERY COSTING

Trunk transport is usually costed by journey. For many such journeys, the total consignment is destined for one delivery location; in such cases, the journey cost equates to the delivery cost. However, because local delivery journeys can involve a multiplicity of deliveries, the question arises as to how each such local delivery should be costed.

A common approach is to approximate certain charges on the basis of time standards. Depot and stem driving times are not identifiable with any particular delivery drop and should therefore be allocated equally to each delivery made. Waiting time should be attributed directly to the delivery locations at which it occurs. Using time standards, it is possible to allocate the inter-drop driving time and the fixed and variable drop times to the delivery locations serviced. However, for most purposes, it is sufficiently accurate to average these elements of cost. Hence it is relatively simple to obtain a satisfactory approximation to the cost of each delivery.

For example, the rigid van described in Table 19.1 was used for delivery on 225 days in a year. On one of those days it made a local delivery journey involving a driving distance of 90 stem miles and 22 inter-drop miles; eleven deliveries were made, totalling 390 cases of merchandise. That situation is shown diagrammatically in Figure 19.1 and the analysis of the costs involved is given in Table 19.2.

Table 19.2
Delivery journey cost

	Standing charge (%)	Standing charge (cost) £	Running cost @ 35p per mile £	Total £
Depot	6	4.05		4.05
Stem driving (90 miles)	33	22.29	31.50	53.79
Inter-drop driving (22 miles)	19	12.84	7.70	20.54
Waiting	12	8.11		8.11
Fixed drop	19	12.84		12.84
Variable drop	11	7.43		7.43
	100	67.56	39.20	106.76

The cost per delivery is calculated on the basis that the total journey cost is attributable to the time spent in the delivery area. Accordingly, the cost of waiting time can be calculated as follows: waiting time cost = £106.76 × 12/61 = £21.00. The cost of each delivery is found as follows: delivery cost = (£106.76 − £21.00)/11 =

£7.80. Therefore, the cost of delivery involving waiting time (as defined earlier) is £28.80, while the cost of each normal delivery is £7.80.

From the analysis it can be seen that the cost of the variable drop time is a modest proportion of the total cost and that even for delivery journeys involving no stem driving the cost would, in that case, be only 14 per cent of the total. The general conclusion is that local delivery costs are, for practical purposes, independent of the size of the delivery. The major cost is in putting the vehicle in a position to make the delivery.

Factors affecting cost per delivery

A number of factors have a direct influence on delivery cost. The following merit particular attention:

1 *Waiting time:* As can be seen from the above example, the cost attributable to waiting can be significant. Even more important, the time devoted to waiting reduces the time available to make deliveries. The cost of the normal deliveries on the journey is increased and, worse still, a second journey to the delivery area may be necessary. If the example of the rigid van mentioned earlier is used again, in the absence of waiting time it might have been possible to make twelve deliveries rather than ten. Those extra deliveries might have involved further inter-drop driving of five miles. The journey cost would be calculated as follows: original journey cost = £106.76; additional mileage = $5 \times £0.35 = £1.75$; total journey cost = £108.51. On the other hand, had it been necessary to make a second journey to the delivery area, for customer service reasons perhaps, to make the final two drops, and if the vehicle had been used exclusively for that purpose on the day in question, the total journey cost would have been much greater. The costs of waiting time could be assessed as follows: first journey (ten deliveries) cost = £106.76; second journey (two deliveries) − standing charge = £67.56; running costs = $95 \times £0.35 = £33.25$; journey cost = £100.81. The total journey cost for the twelve deliveries over two days would have been £207.57. Against that, the journey cost for making twelve deliveries on the one day would have been £108.51. The cost of waiting time on the first day can be evaluated, therefore, at £99.06. Accordingly, great care should be exercised in computing waiting time. It is particularly relevant for assessing whether or not the trading terms with customers to whom

delivery usually involves waiting are appropriate and reflect adequately the costs associated with servicing them.

2 *Receiving time restrictions:* The effectiveness of the use of the time spent by a local delivery vehicle in a delivery area is directly influenced by the hours during which consignees are prepared or able to receive deliveries. For example, retail butchers prefer deliveries in the morning, retail store managers prefer deliveries early in the week rather than on Fridays, social club stewards are only available to accept deliveries at certain times of the day, and so on. Other more general causes of restriction include lunch breaks, half-day closing, pedestrianised area vehicular access times, and so on. Increasingly, consignees require transport operators to 'pre-book' delivery times. This practice is acceptable if such timed drops can be integrated into an operable sequence of deliveries. Costly operational problems can occur, however, if preceding delays result in late arrivals and subsequent refusals of deliveries. In such cases a second attempt must be made to effect the delivery.

3 *Vehicle carrying capacity:* The weight capacity of a vehicle is dictated by its official licence; the volume capacity will be determined by the configuration and physical dimensions of the body. In situations where the weight or cubic capacity of the vehicle limits the number of vehicles that can be planned for a journey and results in a greater number of journeys than would otherwise be necessary, consideration should be given to the use of a larger vehicle. It is recognised that there might be a restriction on the size of vehicle which could gain access to a delivery location, but this situation does not arise frequently. In the examples given in Table 19.1, doubling the carrying capacity results in a 24 per cent increase in standing charges and a 26 per cent increase in running costs. By using a large vehicle, comparatively modest additional operating costs are incurred but the result could be that fewer journeys are made. That would reduce total operating costs. An example will make the point more clearly, perhaps. Ten deliveries totalling 12 tons in weight have to be made in a delivery area which is 45 miles away from the depot. The only vehicle available has a 10-ton carrying capacity. Two journeys will, therefore, be necessary. The costs would be estimated as follows: standing charges = £67.56 × 2 = £135. 12; stem driving costs = 90 × 2 × £0.35 = £63.00; inter-drop driving costs = 27 × £0.35 = £9.45; total journey cost = £207.57. Had a 12-ton vehicle been available, only one journey would have been necessary. The standing charges and running costs for that 12-ton

vehicle are estimated to be 10 per cent higher than those for the 10-ton vehicle. On that basis, the journey costs would be as follows: standing charge = £74.32; stem driving costs = 90 × £0.385 = £34.65; inter-drop driving costs = 27 × £0.385 = £10.40; total journey cost = £119.37. Use of the larger vehicle would result in a cost saving of £88.20, a reduction of some 42½ per cent.

Stem distance and delivery cost

As can be seen from Figure 19.1, there are two main elements of the work associated with a local delivery journey. First, there are the tasks undertaken outside the delivery area, the depot duties and stem driving; second, there are the tasks undertaken within the delivery area, the inter-drop driving and the tasks at each delivery location.

Table 19.3
Delivery costs for different stem distances

Stem distances (miles)	10	30	50	70	90
Deliveries possible	17	14	11	8	5
Total inter-drop distances (miles)	43	35	28	20	13
Standing charge (£)	67.56	67.56	67.56	67.56	67.56
Stem driving cost (£) (@ 35p per mile)	7.00	21.00	35.00	49.00	63.00
Inter-drop driving cost (@ 35p per mile) (£)	15.05	12.25	9.80	7.00	4.55
	89.61	100.81	112.36	123.56	135.11
Cost per delivery (£)	5.27	7.20	10.21	15.45	27.02

It follows that the greater the distance from the depot to the delivery area, the greater will be the proportion of the driver's time devoted to stem driving. In turn, this reduces the time in the delivery area and the time available for making deliveries. The greater the stem distance, the greater also will be the running costs for the journey. To examine this problem more clearly, the estimates presented in Table 19.3 can be made. The significance of those calculations becomes clearer when represented graphically, as in

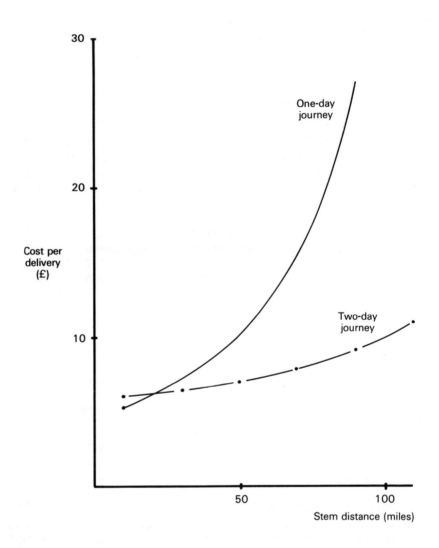

Fig. 19.2 Stem distance and cost per delivery

Figure 19.2. As the stem distance increases, the cost per delivery rises at a disproportionately greater rate. The figure also shows the relationship between the cost per delivery and stem distance for a two-day journey. It has been assumed in drawing those curves that the size of the deliveries and the nature of the merchandise being delivered is such that the carrying capacity of the vehicle is not exceeded. It is not unusual to find, as in this case, that the cost per delivery on a two-day journey is less than for a one-day journey, even for journeys involving a modest stem distance from the depot. Clearly, substantial economies can be achieved if sufficient deliveries can be accumulated to justify one two-day journey rather than two separate one-day journeys. For greater stem distances, journeys of even longer duration may be justifiable.

Second deliveries

As a customer service, many companies adopt the procedure that any items which are not available when a customer's order is being despatched become the subject of a balance order. In that way, the unavailability of one or more specific items does not hold up delivery of the bulk of the order. An objective of such companies will be to so manage finished goods stocks that most goods will be available when ordered.

As has been shown earlier, the delivery of a small order costs virtually the same as the delivery of a large one. Hence, the delivery of a balance order costs almost as much as the delivery of the main order. Thus, a small shortfall in order fulfilment can result in a significant increase in total distribution costs. Commercially, that may be tolerable, but it must be recognised that some of the items in balance orders may cost more than the gross margin on those items. It would be advisable, therefore, for such companies to consider the adoption of a policy which requires that balance orders of less than a specified value will be cancelled, the customer having the option of re-ordering such items with his next regular order.

Balance orders give rise, of course, to other costs in addition to those associated with delivery. For instance, there would be extra clerical and administrative costs, extra order assembly costs, and extra packaging and despatching costs. A balance order for goods with a gross margin of 20 per cent, involving transport costs of £10 and other costs of £7, would need to be worth at least £85 to break even.

Delivery frequency

In the same way that balance order policy has a direct impact on delivery costs, so does order frequency. If each order placed by a customer gives rise to a delivery, then order frequency directly influences the number of deliveries to be made. It follows, therefore, that if, for example, it were commercially acceptable to deliver once a fortnight to a customer rather than once a week, and if the delivery size doubled as a consequence, delivery costs would be halved. Coupling this with all the other costs associated with processing and filling an order, it becomes clear that substantial cost savings can be made from reducing delivery frequency.

In some circumstances, order frequency is directly associated with the frequency of salemen's or representatives' calls. The discriminate selection of customers, whose business is inadequately contributing to corporate profits, for servicing at a reduced frequency could result in a marked improvement in the profits earned.

DEPOT LOCATION

Having discriminated between the two types of transport, trunking and local delivery, the problem remains of deciding where trunking should end and local delivery begin. The easy answer, of course, is at the depot where local delivery vehicles are based. That could be a 'stocked' depot or a 'cross-docking' depot at which goods are transferred directly from trunking vehicles to local delivery vehicles. If demountable bodies are used, the depot may be little more than a concreted area where the bodies can be interchanged between the two vehicle types.

Further questions then arise. These involve deciding how many depots are required, where they should be located, and which delivery areas should be serviced from each depot. The resolution of these problems requires trading-off three costs:

1. the cost of operating trunking vehicles from each of the sources of goods – factory locations or ports of entry;
2. the cost of operating the depots – building and occupancy costs, storage costs, stockholding costs, and so on;
3. the cost of local delivery from the depots to the customers in each delivery area.

Those three costs must be aggregated for each possible combination of depot locations, to determine the combination which gives the lowest total operating cost.

Additionally, operational data are needed for the assessment of each option. Such data include:

1 the number of delivery areas to be serviced;
2 the identification of a focal point (city or main town) in each delivery area;
3 the rate at which goods have to be moved from each source to the customers in each delivery area;
4 the number of deliveries each year that each tonnage quantity represents;
5 the number of potential depot locations;
6 an operating cost profile for depots of varying tonnage throughput rates;
7 a matrix of costs per delivery for each delivery area from each potential delivery depot location;
8 a matrix of costs for operating trunking vehicles from each source to each potential depot location.

The results of these trade-off evaluations can be shown graphically, as depicted in Figure 19.3, which shows the minimum total operating cost for networks of depots from one to ten in number. It does not follow, of course, that the particular depots featured in any one optimal network will necessarily be the same as those featured in the optimal network which is one depot greater in size.

Figure 19.3 reveals that, in the situation on which the graph is based, the minimum total operating cost corresponds to a network of five depots. However, if it were thought that a network of seven depots was desirable (perhaps from customer servicing considerations), such a graph would help to determine the additional cost that would be incurred in providing that level of service. Such a move is revealed by the two horizontal dotted lines on the graph; to move from five depots to seven depots would cost a further £400 000 a year.

USING TRANSPORT CONTRACTORS

The nature of the transport costs incurred by own-account operators and by transport contractors are essentially similar. The differences lie in the interpretation of those costs. That interpretation is heavily

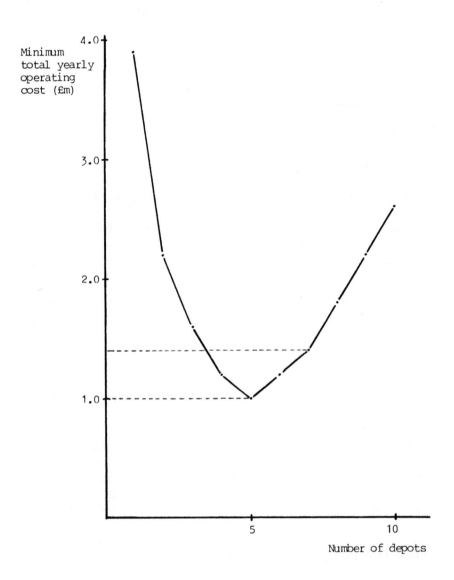

Fig. 19.3 Depot numbers and total operating cost

dependent upon the size and nature of the consignments carried, the opportunities for operational economies, and the level of service required.

If an own-account operator makes a long distance journey to deliver a 20-ton consignment to a customer, it is most unlikely that there would be a return load from that customer. The vehicle will return empty and the operator will incur the whole cost of the round trip. Had the same consignment been transported by an outside contractor, it is possible that he would have been able to arrange a return load from another shipper. So, although the contractor will require a suitable profit margin on the round trip, he has two possible sources of revenue and could probably quote attractive freight rates to both shippers as a result. The contractor may not be able to transport the goods as speedily as the original shipper would like or require, as it may take time to arrange a suitable return load. In those circumstances, a commercial decision is required as to whether the delivery can be delayed to take advantage of the outside contractor's lower transport rate or whether an own-account vehicle should be used to provide quicker, but more costly, service.

In the case of local delivery, a similar kind of commercial decision may be necessary. If the shipper has sufficient orders for delivery in a particular area to permit an efficient (that is, cost effective) journey to be planned, the cost per delivery will be known and the company will retain control over the timely delivery of the goods. A transport contractor might be able to make the deliveries more economically, but it is unlikely that he would match the company's own vehicle plans for speed.

Nonetheless, contractors frequently quote rates on a weight carried basis, reflecting the economies of consolidation. When these rates are compared with own-account delivery costs, it may be found that some deliveries could be made less expensively by using the services of outside contractors. This is particularly likely in the case of deliveries to remote areas and those to which insufficient quantities of goods are consigned. Discriminating use of contractors can, therefore, be most beneficial.

Looked at from the contractor's viewpoint, the key to success is the ability to have access to, and to be able to coordinate, sufficient consignments to make the best use of his vehicles. For trunking, this means ready access to return loads; for local delivery, it means the accumulation of sufficient traffic to each delivery area. Both these requirements call for effective systems and methods of communication to facilitate the required coordination.

Additional advantages accrue from the facility to avoid complex and ever-increasing legal requirements, and from the opportunity to avoid extensive capital investment in vehicles and support facilities – see Dowsett (1981) for a practical analysis of the advantages of using outside carriers for the transport of parcels.

CONCLUSION

The physical distribution manager can achieve worthwhile and substantial savings by taking a structured view of transport costs and alternatives. Directly, the manager can achieve better cost control by planning the more effective use of drivers, by getting the number and mix of vehicles right, and by selecting the most appropriate and effective network pattern for depots and support facilities.

The physical distribution manager will be constrained in his decisions by a number of factors outside his direct control: customer service standards, demand and order patterns, delivery frequencies, and trading terms.

It is essential that such managers understand the cost implications of their activities so that they can contribute effectively to the decision making processes in the organisation. The management accountant, in his turn, is well placed to take an integrated view of the cost of distribution and to encourage senior management to take a corporate view of all the functions involved in the physical distribution of manufactured goods and products.

REFERENCES AND FURTHER READING

Aylott, D. J., and Brindle-Wood-Williams, D., *Physical Distribution in Industrial and Commercial Marketing,* London: Hutchinson, 1970.

Bowersox, D. J., Smykay, E. W., and LaLonde, B. J., *Physical Distribution Management,* New York: Macmillan, 1968.

Christopher, M., Walters, D., and Gattorna, J., *Distribution Planning and Control: a Corporate Approach,* Farnborough: Gower, 1977.

Christopher, M., and Willis, G. (eds), *Marketing Logistics and Distribution Planning,* London: Allen & Unwin, 1972.

Cox, B.,'Transport costs', *Management Accounting,* February 1981.

Dowsett, B., 'Outside carriers for parcels', *Management Accounting*, October 1981.

Frain, J., *Transportation and Distribution for European Markets*, London: Butterworth, 1970.

Gattorna, J. (ed), *Handbook of Physical Distribution Management*, 3rd edn., Aldershot: Gower, 1983.

Glendinning, R.,'Management of physical distribution', *Management Accounting*, February 1981.

Institute of Directors, *The Director's Guide to Storage, Handling, Freight and Distribution*, London: Institute of Directors, 1980.

Longman, D. R., and Schiff, M., *Practical Distribution Cost Analysis*, Homewood, Ill.: Irwin, 1955.

Sawdy, L. W. C., *The Economics of Distribution*, Epping: Gower, 1972.

20

Value Added and the Management Accountant

Bernard Cox

The concept of value added (or added value, in many treatments) has been widely discussed for decades, but only in the past few years has it become familiar to company managements and the readers of corporate reports. Value added is the increase in market value brought about by an alteration in the form, location or availability of a product or service, excluding the cost of bought-in materials or services. The author shows in this chapter that there are other ideas on what constitutes value added and describes and discusses their uses. The expression 'value added' is used to cover a whole range of valuations, mainly for convenience; sometimes the distinction is important, but more often it is not. The author's conclusion is that value added brings a different and useful perspective to the management of a company's affairs and offers significant planning and control advantages in many circumstances. The danger of an over enthusiastic concern with value added is that managements may forget that they are in business to make a profit, argues the author, rather than just to create added value. Value added is a most helpful measure of a firm's output and can be put to good use as one of a range of management tools. There are, however, significant hazards in a naive approach to the interpretation of value added results and users need to be aware of the dangers of relying on such simplified representations of corporate results.

When the discussion document on the future of corporate reports was published by the Accounting Standards Steering Committee (1975), one of the new accounting statements advocated was a 'statement of value added'. The committee said that such a statement was the simplest and most immediate way of putting profit into proper perspective *vis-á-vis* the whole enterprise as a collective effort of capital providers, managers and employees. Value added was the wealth the reporting entity had managed to create by its own, and its employees', efforts.

The rationale behind that thinking is not hard to discern. Anyone with cash or credit can buy products and use his own capital and skills to turn them into items of greater value. The greater his skill, the greater the wealth produced. If the person is not a single individual but a manufacturing and trading organisation, the same considerations apply. In addition, the identification of value added gives interested parties the chance to measure the efficiency of the organisation in various ways.

A simple calculation of value added will serve to illustrate the concept. A market trader sells women's dresses for £20 each, having purchased them direct from the manufacturer for £15. The dress manufacturer bought the cloth to make a dress for £5 from a cloth manufacturer. The cascade of transactions is shown in Table 20.1, and it can be seen that wealth has been created as follows: stage 1 (the cloth manufacturer) – £2; stage 2 (the dress manufacturer) – £8; stage 3 (the market trader) – £3; total value added – £13. At each stage, the total value added is the fund from which the particular enterprise will pay wages, salaries and other employment costs, the costs of obtaining capital, the costs of consuming capital (depreciation), dividends to shareholders, and taxes. In the simple example presented here, all the conditions of the opening definition have been met. Further, the final market value has been realised. In real life, there will usually be work in progress and unsold stocks at the end of the accounting period. How these will be dealt with is discussed later in this chapter. Having set the scene, the company statement of value added can be considered.

COMPANY STATEMENT OF VALUE ADDED

Suggested layouts for value added statements abound, and one such is shown in Table 20.2. That example emphasises the two aspects of value added – the means by which it has been created and the ways in which it has been used. In broad terms, the beneficiaries were employees (71 per cent), capital providers (5 per cent), government (11 per cent), and the company (13 per cent). In a survey

Table 20.1
The value added picture (£)

	Purchases	Value Added	Sales
Stage			
1 Cloth manufacturer			
Sells cloth to the dress manufacturer			5
Incurs costs;			
Raw materials, dyes	2		
Rent, rates, and other bought-in expenses of factory	1		
	3	2	5
Stage			
2 Dress manufacturer			
Sells the dress to the market trader			15
Incurs costs:			
Length of cloth	5		
Rent, rates and other bought-in expenses of factory	2		
	7	8	15
Stage			
3 Market trader			
Sells the dress			20
Incurs costs:			
Price of dress from manufacturer	15		
Rent for the market stall	1		
Running cost of motor van	1		
	17	3	20

of listed companies, Gray and Maunders (1980) found that around a fifth of large companies presented such a statement in their published reports. The larger the company, apparently, the more likely it was to publish a statement of value added.

Companies have experimented with different forms of value added statement and the manner of presentation has varied considerably. Fanning (1978) discussed alternative formats and their constituents, and other writers have conducted similar analyses. A

Table 20.2
Typical value added statement

%			Year to 31 Dec. (£ million)		Previous year (£ million)
	Turnover		103.9		102.3
	Bought-in materials and services		67.6		72.1
	VALUE ADDED		36.3		30.2
	Applied in the following way				
	To pay employees				
71	• wages, pensions, fringe benefits		25.9		17.3
	To pay providers of capital				
	• interest on loans	0.8		0.6	
	• dividends to shareholders	0.9		0.9	
5			1.7		1.5
	To pay government				
11	• corporation tax payable		3.9		3.1
	To provide for maintenance and expansion of assets				
	• depreciation	2.0		1.8	
	• retained profits	2.8		6.5	
13			4.8		8.3
100	VALUE ADDED		36.3		£30.2

number of problems arise in preparing a value added statement for publication:

1 the treatment of investment income;
2 the treatment of work in progress and stocks;
3 the treatment of payroll costs.

Investment income

Where a company has income from associated companies or royalties, should that income be added to turnover in the source section of the value added statement? The alternatives are to add it to turnover (identifying it separately, of course), or to obtain a value added calculation from sales less purchases and then to add the other income. If the non-sales income is not very large, the distinction may not matter too much, but the company should be consistent it its presentation.

Work in progress and stocks

In company financial accounts, work in progress and stocks are valued at the lower of cost or market value; only in the case of long term work in progress will that valuation include an element of profit. However, if true value added is the *increase in value* created by the company, changes in stocks and work in progress should be included at market value. This is, in fact, the case in the National Accounts discussed later. However, for published accounts, generally accepted accounting principles argue against the inclusion of unrealised profit. As long as that distinction is understood, users of such statements can draw their own conclusions.

Payroll costs

The other main difficulty with published statements concerns payroll costs. Should they be the actual costs incurred in the period, or the costs which are related to the sales achieved? Where companies reveal separately the aggregate amount of payments to employees, it seems illogical to include a different amount in the value added statement. At the same time, if there is a substantial change in finished stocks and work in progress, part of the period's actual costs will be included in the valuations carried forward. Most companies simply show the total payroll costs for the period.

Usefulness of statements

Despite many anomalies and possible inaccuracies, Cox (1979) reported that management has found such statements especially useful for explaining company results to employees. The very concept of 'profit' is often an emotive one and employees may well find the concept of 'creating wealth' or 'adding value' more acceptable. Whether value added statements are useful to outsiders is more questionable. The statements contain summarised information and rarely give any data of vital import. It is unlikely that the management accountant would find disaggregated area or sector data in competitors' value added statements. Value added figures are rarely sufficiently detailed for valid conclusions to be drawn. The management accountant's most useful source of information will be government statistics – especially the Census of Production reports used in calculating the National Accounts.

VALUE ADDED AND NATIONAL INCOME

As discussed above, value added at the company level can be considered in two ways – its creation and its distribution. The same standpoints are used in calculating national incomes. Indeed, at the macro level, there are three measures, which should produce the same answer, subject to errors in estimation. National income is calculated as follows: either by adding together the income of all residents (including income from employment, company trading profits, public bodies' trading surpluses, rents, and an imputed charge for the consumption of non-trading capital), or by adding together the expenditure of all residents (including consumers' expenditure, general government final consumption, fixed capital formation, increases in stocks, and net of the value of imported goods and services), or by adding together the wealth created by all activities of all residents.

In general terms, each of those methods produces an approximation to gross domestic product at factor cost. To that value are added the amounts of net property income from abroad, giving gross national product; deducting the value of capital consumed gives national income.

The most useful part of the UK National Accounts for the management accountant in manufacturing is the Census of Production. Each year, all manufacturing companies are required to submit a return of vital statistics. The government publishes the results of the census in the Business Monitor series, as Monitor PA 1000. A serious disadvantage of the report is that its publication is delayed for some considerable time, owing to the exigencies of collection, collation, analysis and publication of the figures. Because of that delay, most companies will not use the report's analysis for short term comparisons but will use it for the study of long run trends in their own industries. As an example of the nature of the information presented in the report, Table 20.3 gives the reported figures for two contrasting industries: the shipbuilding and marine engineering industry, and the pesticide manufacturing industry.

Table 20.3
Census of Production figures (UK)

		Shipbuilding etc. (£ million)	Pesticides (£ million)
1	Sales of goods produced, receipts for work done, and services rendered	1 715.9	174.8
2	Merchanted goods	24.3	161.6
3	Increase during the year in work in progress and goods on hand for sale	85.6	6.5
4	GROSS OUTPUT (1+2+3)	1 825.8	342.9
5	Cost of purchases	807.0	172.3
6	Cost of industrial services, increases during the year of materials, stores, and fuel	142.0	1.7
7	NET OUTPUT (4−(5+6))	876.8	168.9
8	Cost of non-industrial services, rates, motor vehicle licenses	69.0	14.1
9	GROSS VALUE ADDED AT FACTOR COST (7−8)	807.8	154.8
Employment			
11	Operatives (Thousands)	134.3	2.2
12	Others (Thousands)	41.2	1.9
13	Total number of employees	175.5	4.1
Wages and Salaries			
14	Operatives (£ Million)	564.4	8.4
15	Others (£ Million)	207.7	9.2

(The reasons for choosing these two industrial sectors will be discussed later in this chapter.) For the sake of brevity, the table only gives the figures for 1978.

As can be seen from the table, the various constituent items are sub-totalled as gross output (line 4), net output (line 7), and gross value added (line 9), and the distinctions between those values can be seen readily enough. Many companies which claim to use value added in planning or periodic management accounts are, in fact, using net output. That difference may not be important, as long as users and preparers are aware of the distinction, but comparisons must be made in terms of similar quantities or categories.

DERIVING VALUE ADDED FROM MANAGEMENT ACCOUNTS

If a company intends to use value added to compare its performance with that of other companies in the same industry, or simply to compare one part of its business with another, it will need a more accurate calculation than that obtained by the published corporate statement of value added described earlier. The procedure need not be complicated, but some items of expense will call for special treatment. Table 20.4 gives the results of a typical company, analysed in value added terms.

Column A shows the results before analysis, and each line is then examined and transferred to the appropriate category column, divided where appropriate into different heads of expenditure. In the example, £100 000 had been transferred to the fixed asset accounts, being the cost of homemade fixed assets; since it represents value created, however, it has been brought back into the accounts and treated as sales revenue, with the bought-in costs of £30 000 and employee costs of £70 000 being transferred to their appropriate category columns. Column H shows an adjustment to profit of £50 000 being the residual book value of fixed assets scrapped during the year; it is taken back to profit since it is neither wealth created not wealth distributed during the year. Similarly, adjustments are made for such movements as increases in bad debt provisions, depreciation charges, and the like.

This form of analysis provides a simple and systematic approach to the calculation of value added and ensures that less straightforward items are considered properly and adjusted as necessary. It provides a suitable basis for interim employee reports and for the calculation of a range of management ratios for inter-group comparison. This approach can be called the 'cost of sales method' of calculating value added.

If it is intended to compare the results of such an analysis with Census of Production results, certain fundamental differences must be borne in mind. Census results include an element for increases in the value of work in progress and stocks. Census figures for wages and salaries do not include the employers' cost of social security and superannuation. Census wages and salaries are those incurred in the calendar year, whereas management accounts' figures will be those of the income period being reported. Few companies fit happily into one census industrial category; the company's results might have to be disaggregated to render comparisons valid.

Table 20.4
Value added and management accounts

	A	B	C	D	E	F	G	H (£000)
	Management accounts	Sales and income	Bought-in costs	VALUE ADDED	Employee costs	Depreciation	Profit	Adjustment to profit
1 Sales	+12000	+12000						
2 Cost of sales	− 8000		−3900 − 30		−3650 − 70	−400		−50
3 Gross profit	+ 4000							
4 Other income	+ 500	+ 600	− 100			− 50		+50
5 Admin expenses	− 1230		− 300		− 920	− 10		
6 Selling expenses	− 500		− 400			− 25		
7 Financial expenses	− 320		− 300			− 20		−75
8 Profit before tax	+ 2450						+2450	
9							+ 75	−75
10		+12700	−5030	7670	4640	505	2525	

Value added creation

Sales & income	12700
Deduct bought-in	5030
	£ 7670

Value added distribution

Employee costs	4640
Depreciation	505
Profit before tax etc	2525
	£ 7670

Value added ratios

Different authors have suggested a number of value added ratios, with some ratios proving more reliable than others. Table 20.5 shows those suggested value added ratios and their more traditional financial accounting counterparts. The list is not exhaustive, but for the most part it is self-explanatory.

There are three specific difficulties in using value added ratios: the treatment of depreciation; the valuation of work-in-progress and finished goods; the impact of inflation.

Table 20.5
Value added ratios

	TRADITIONAL	VALUE ADDED
Gross Margin	*Gross profit* Sales	*Value added* Sales *Operating profit* Value added
Stock turnover	*Sales* Stocks	*Gross output* Stocks
Fixed assets turnover	*Sales* Operating assets	*Value added* Operating assets
Labour productivity	*Sales* No. of employees *Operating profit* No. of employees *Sales* Employment costs *Operating profit* Employment costs	*Value added* No. of employees *Value added* Direct hours worked *Value added* Employment costs
Capital productivity	*Net profit* Capital employed	*Value added* Capital employed
Rate of investment		*Capital expenditure* No. of employees

Depreciation has been considered, up to this point, as an application of value added. Some authorities, such as Morley (1978), insist that net value added should be used in preference to gross value added. The argument is that depreciation is as much a cost of the period as materials consumed and that it cannot be distributed without damaging the substance of the business.

National accounts report a notional profit in respect of value added to work in progress and finished goods, so should company accounts follow suit? There is no sound reason why a company should not follow that practice in its internal management accounts. Although many accountants will be reluctant to take credit for unrealised profits, the value added results will be markedly distorted in some cases if that element of profit is not included.

The effect of inflation on ratios cannot be ignored. Where the denominator is a non-financial ratio (such as number of employees or hours worked), comparisons between one period and another will be distorted by the impact of inflation on the numerator. The application of some index or of the techniques of current cost accounting will go some way to alleviating these difficulties.

An example or two

Using the information presented in Table 20.3, an elementary form of ratio analysis can be undertaken. The reasons for choosing two such divergent industries are simple: by illustrating extremes, it is easier to draw conclusions and provide pointers for the management accountant dealing with less disparate manufacturing units within a company group. Table 20.6 gives four ratios, extracted from the Census of Production, for the two industrial sectors chosen for study.

Table 20.6
Comparative value added ratios

	Shipbuilding	Pesticides
Gross value added per head	£4 582	£36 872
Ratio of gross output to stocks	1.0	3.5
Net capital expenditure per head	£ 441	£ 2 095
Wages and salaries as a percentage of gross value added	95.6%	11.4%

These ratios can be examined in turn. Each employee in the pesticide industry creates about eight times as much wealth as the employee in the shipbuilding sector. Some underlying explanations might be, for example, that the pesticide manufacturing industry is more capital intensive, with machines doing most of the work, or that each employee in the pesticide industry is more productive. It might be safe to assume that productivity in shipbuilding is lower than in the pesticide industry.

The ratio of gross output to stocks reveals that stocks are turned over once a year by the shipbuilders and more than thrice a year by pesticide industry workers. The higher the turnover rate, the better the results are likely to be in terms of cash flow and financing charges avoided, and the more efficient is the business.

Net capital expenditure per head is five times greater in the pesticides industry than in shipbuilding. Such a conclusion would need much more careful study over a longer period to determine previous levels of capital investment and so on before it could be acted upon in any sensible way.

The proportion of wages and salaries as percentages of gross value added offers the greatest degree of divergence between the two industries. In the shipbuilding industry, employment costs, excluding social security and pension payments, amounted to some 96 per cent of gross value added. Other inescapable costs of employing people, such as social security and pension payments, would easily add 20 per cent or so to those costs. Thus, the total costs of employment exceeded value added, leaving nothing whatsoever for other purposes. That is the picture of a bankrupt industry – borne out by everything else reported about the shipbuilding industry. By contrast, the pesticides industry appeared to be in a particularly healthy position.

VALUE ADDED BONUS SCHEMES

One of the significant uses of the concept of value added is its incorporation in company incentive schemes or bonus schemes. These schemes originated in the United States in the 1930s and have been in use in the United Kingdom since the 1950s, although it was not until the late 1970s that they came into vogue as typical self-financing productivity schemes.

The schemes work by establishing a base ratio of value added to payroll costs, thereby creating a base index. If the index moves positively upwards in later periods, a bonus is payable to scheme members. Research being conducted by the author on some fifty such schemes reveals a number of different aspects worthy of further consideration and the remainder of this chapter describes some of the more important variations.

Calculation of bonuses

There are two principal methods of using the base index to calculate bonuses. Under the first method, the company calculates a productivity ratio by relating value added to payroll costs. For example, a value added total of £720 000 and a payroll cost of £480 000 would give a productivity ratio of 1.5:1. For each subsequent bonus period, the company will pay employees a part of any improvement in value added generated. If the next period resulted in a value added total of £72 000 and actual payroll costs of £40 000, the productivity improvement would be calculated by comparing the value added achieved against the actual payroll cost multiplied by the productivity ratio of 1.5. In this instance, the improvement would be calculated at £12 000 (£72 000 less £60 000). Most commonly, that improvement is shared between the company and the scheme members in pre-agreed proportions. This method uses a productivity ratio calculated on the basis of a standard value added expected for each £1 of payroll cost.

The second method approaches the calculation from a different angle, using a reciprocal of the productivity index and calculating, in effect, an expected or standard payroll cost for each £1 of value added generated. Using the same figures as before, the productivity ratio is calculated at 0.667 (£480 000/£720 000), and the expected payroll cost for the ensuing period would be calculated at £48 000 (£72 000 × 0.667). The actual payroll cost was £40 000, giving a productivity improvement of £8 000.

Two quite different results can be derived from the same set of figures and the same underlying rationale. The two methods can be expressed in algebraic terms, and a number of schemes have failed to ensure that the actual cash implications of those algebraic formulations have been made clear to employees – thereby reducing the significant motivational impact of such incentive schemes. Clear communication of the 'nuts and bolts' of such productivity-encouraging schemes is essential if they are to work well.

Alternatives and problem areas

One of the first points to consider is the definition of value added which will be employed in the scheme – gross value added or net value added. Additionally, payroll costs must be more closely defined and should generally include social security and pension payments costs. Some schemes have made a sound case for excluding certain items of expenditure from their calculations, on the grounds that employees could neither control nor influence certain classes of expenditure such as rent and rates.

There are, in addition, considerations of who should be eligible for participation in such schemes and to what extent absentees should be allowed full participation in bonus payments for periods during which they were away sick or on holiday. The period of the base time for calculating productivity indices and ratios would need to be defined precisely and it would be a subject for negotiation. The practice of using historical data is widespread, but there are instances of firms using current budget figures to compute a base ratio. Whether to include all classes of employee or to restrict membership to specific classes is a further possible source of contention.

The frequency with which the bonus payment is made will have a significant impact on the enhancement of productivity, and managements tend to pay such bonuses monthly – although the absolute amount of the bonus payment is another important consideration.

Results so far

Of the schemes examined by the author, ten have failed to make a bonus payment at all and have either been abandoned or held in abeyance. The others have paid regular bonuses over a number of years. The bonuses actually paid ranged from 60 per cent on gross pay to 0.5 per cent. Generally, sponsoring companies see the schemes as helping to generate employee interest in company affairs and enhancing productivity. The schemes are often regarded as complementing annual pay negotiations and, in some cases, as making up for otherwise unfavourable pay rises.

All the companies that paid bonuses can claim increased productivity and the expressed intention of their managements to continue with the schemes is a clear indication of perceived value.

CONCLUSION

This chapter has considered the use of value added in reporting company results, in the analysis of ratios within companies, and in the operation of incentive schemes. Time and time again, there is welcome evidence of the enthusiasm of practising managers for the wider use of value added concepts in planning and control. It brings a different and useful perspective to compny affairs, and in the words of Wood (1978), it is the key to prosperity:

> Creating added value is a fundamental objective of good management. By creating more added value we can all enjoy a higher standard of living.

REFERENCES AND FURTHER READING

Accounting Standards Steering Committee, *The Corporate Report: A Discussion Document,* London: ASSC, 1975.

Bentley, T., 'Added value and contribution', *Management Accounting,* March, 1981.

Cox, B., *Value Added: An Appreciation for the Accountant Concerned with Industry,* London: Heinemann, 1979.

Fanning, D., 'Banishing confusion from the added value equation', *Financial Times,* 13 December 1978.

Gilchrist, R. R., *Managing for Profit,* London: Allen & Unwin, 1971.

Gray, S. J., and Maunders, K. T., *Value Added Reporting,* London: Association of Certified Accountants, 1980.

Morley, M. F., *The Value Added Statement,* London: Gee, 1978.

Rutherford, B. A., 'Five fallacies about value added', *Management Accounting,* September 1981.

Wood, E. G., *Added Value – the Key to Prosperity,* London: Business Books, 1978.

21

Management Accounting in Not-for-profit Organisations

Duncan Bennett

Most of the other contributions to this handbook have been concerned, at least implicitly, with the planning, management and control of the activities of profit-seeking enterprises. However, a significant part of the economic activities of most countries is accounted for by not-for-profit organisations – central and local government, charities, educational establishments, and the like. For the most part, the processes of planning and control in not-for-profit organisations are the same as in profit oriented concerns. There are, however, a number of important differences. The prime difference, of course, is in the pursuit of an objective other than the profit or wealth-maximising aim of industrial and commercial organisations. Organisations in the not-for-profit category exist to provide a service and their effectiveness is measured by the nature and quality of those services and the costs and benefits to the community in which they operate. Further, there are huge differences in the areas of ownership, power and management. Ownership is generally in public hands – governments, local authorities, hospital or education authorities, trustees, and so on. Management is by professionals, and there is a general lack of adequate management controls, although that situation has been changing for the better over the past few years. Generally, not-for-profit organisations operate in monopoly markets, and the market place assumes a much less important role in the planning and strategic processes of the organisation. Not-for-profit organisations tend to be controlled and directed by politically-oriented persons or to operate subject to the oversight and control of political masters. All in all, the management and control of not-for-profit organisations pose several challenging questions for management accountants anxious to control costs, to perform effectively and efficiently, and to measure performance.

All organisations, whether or not they are attempting to trade, have a common need for funding in order to maintain themselves. They share another feature: each has an objective which it was set up to attain.

Control of any organisation depends upon the information which is available to the controller. The more timely and relevant that information is, the better the controller's ability to design decisions likely to attain the organisation's objective. Thus, there can be no fundamental difference in the role of the management accountant as intelligence officer to management in either type of organisation, profit seeking or otherwise. Management must be provided with accurate, timely and relevant information and must make decisions based on that information, using the skills, experience and judgement available.

Not-for-profit organisations comprise a very wide spectrum, ranging from central government and local government, through charities, friendly societies, and clubs to miscellaneous voluntary organisations. Central government practice is unique and is outside the scope of this chapter.

For broad discussion purposes, then, not-for-profit organisations can be classified in two main groups. The first category requires initial capital outlay and is self-funding thereafter. Such an organisation, having been set up by a capital payment for premises, land, fittings and equipment, makes a charge for its services at a level which sustains it without leading to an unallocated financial gain. An independent college is a good example. Income from fees may well exceed the cost of providing the service given, but any surplus will be used to further the aims of the college rather than to reward an entrepreneur or investors.

The second group is supported by regular contributions or grants, rather than by selling a service. This group includes central and local government, supported by taxes, rates, levies, duties, and so on – largely of a compulsory nature. Additionally, other members of the group, such as charities, churches, private health services, and the like, are supported by voluntary contributions.

Support of central and local government organisations is backed by the concept of equity. The individual contributor has the right to a say in the creation and execution of policies; he or she has a vote which can be used to exert some influence on the policies and practices of national or local government, albeit at arm's length. Other organisations in the not-for-profit sector may, or may not, grant some form of participation to supporters.

A unifying theme in the sector is that its members exist to provide a service – running buses, rescuing mariners, housing pensioners, educating students, researching diseases, building roads. It is here that the management accountant will find the most difficult aspects of his work in this field. Allowing for all the problems of defining and measuring profit, it is still a clear enough item and it is measurable. Services are not susceptible to such clear-cut analysis, and the degree of successful provision is not so easy to measure or report.

Table 21.1
University income and expenditure

	£
Income:	
Tuition fees	2 880 000
Research grants	860 000
Government grants	7 610 000
	11 350 000
Expenditure:	
Teaching costs	6 890 000
Research costs	780 000
Student and staff facilities costs	200 000
Maintenance, equipment and miscellaneous costs	2 670 000
Administration costs and loan charges	1 210 000
	11 750 000
Deficit:	400 000

Equally, there is a distinct lack of available guidance on the application of management accounting and control techniques to not-for-profit organisations. The controller has to depart from the traditional practice of measuring a quantifiable profit and adopt a cost-benefit approach to the organisation's activities. Dobbins and Fanning (1981) described the case of a university of medium size, regularly in a position of operating deficit, because costs always exceed income. Table 21.1 illustrates the income and expenditure statement for such a university. Its activities resulted in a deficit of £400 000. The university can and should be seen, however, in a

Table 21.2
University benefits and costs

	£
Benefits:	
Increased value of students	X XXX XXX
Value of research	X XXX XXX
	XX XXX XXX
Costs:	
Teaching costs	6 890 000
Research costs	780 000
Administration and other costs	4 080 000
	11 750 000
'Social' profit:	X XXX XXX

social context. What benefits does it produce for society, and what are the associated costs to society? The alternative statement presented in Table 21.2 shows one way of approaching the quanti-fication of such a judgement. Some not-for-profit activities are not susceptible to such an analysis, however.

DISTINCTIONS

Gross and Warschauer (1979) identified five principal accounting differences between commercial organisations and not-for-profit undertakings, and a brief discussion of these distinctions will point up the nature of the problems facing a manager and controller of the latter. The first difference is that accounting in not-for-profit organisations is for cash, ignoring accruals and payments in advance, for instance, and most records are of receipts and payments. Secondly, fund accounting is adopted as a usual practice by many not-for-profit organisations, such funds as 'general', 'capital', or 'endowment' being set up to account for the particular resources made available for those purposes. The third accounting difference is in the treatment of fixed assets. Many organisations in the not-for-profit sector write off fixed assets on acquisition. Where assets are donated, they will not be depreciated and may not appear in the organisation's accounts. Fourthly, not-for-profit organisations make transfers between separate funds, or make appropriations to funds for future purposes, thereby departing significantly from commercial accounting practices. The final distinction is in the treatment of outstanding income. For the commercial organisation, debtors are treated in an unequivocal way; owing money is factual and enforceable. In not-for-profit organisations, the enforceability of a pledge may be doubtful; its subsequent collection will be a matter of hope rather than probability.

Distinctions of a more urgent kind have been identified by Anthony and Herzlinger (1980), and those differences are more meaningful for management accountants and controllers than mere book-keeping differences.

The distinctions arise from the nature of a not-for-profit organisation and the essential differences in its objectives and policies. Each of the distinctions presents significant difficulties in a management control context.

Absence of profit measure

There is no profit motive in the not-for-profit organisation; the motive is to provide a service as effectively and efficiently as possible and at a level consonant with the needs and criteria of those for whom the service is intended. In those circumstances, some outputs can be quantified – so many bus routes, so many graduates, so many hospital admissions, and so on. Other outputs, however, cannot be quantified so easily; and even where it is possible to quantify outputs it will be impossible to find a single measure of organisational effectiveness. There is no 'bottom line' figure to use as an indicator. There is no profit measure, and the absence of such a measure renders the management control process exceptionally difficult.

There is no single criterion for evaluating alternative courses of action, since there is no single objective function for a not-for-profit organisation. Decision making becomes a much more complicated and less clear-cut process than in a commercially oriented undertaking. As Anthony and Dearden (1976) commented:

> The management team of a nonprofit organization often will not agree on the relative importance of various goals; members will view a proposal in terms of the importance that they personally attach to the several goals of the organization.

In essence, profit is the difference between the costs of the organisation's inputs and the results of its outputs. As such it offers a tangible measure by which benefits and costs can be compared. While the inputs (that is, costs) of a not-for-profit organisation can be ascertained and measured in precisely the same way as those of a profit-oriented organisation, the outputs are seldom susceptible to measurement in a manner which facilitates comparison between inputs and outputs.

There is, therefore, no single measure of performance in a not-for-profit organisation, and it is virtually impossible to compare organisational units or separate organisations in an effective and realistic way.

Reduced impact of market forces

The activities of a commercial, profit oriented organisation are governed by the demands of the market in which it operates. It must act within the demand and supply constraints created by the market place. Its goods must be wanted, acceptably priced, and competitive. Most not-for-profit organisations have little cause for worry from competition, and most offer the services they think best rather than those the consumers would like.

Again, as Anthony and Dearden (1976) emphasised:

> In a profit oriented organization ... the new client is an opportunity to be vigorously sought after; in many nonprofit organizations, the new client is only a burden, to be accepted with misgivings.

For an airline, the pursuit of more passengers is a profitable objective; more patients for a clinic is a costly outcome. More customers generate fresh resources for a commercial undertaking, whereas more clients consume existing resources in a not-for-profit organisation.

One of the principal influences in the market place is that of competition. In the presence of competition resources must be used effectively and efficiently and managers will be judged, and motivated, by considerations of how effectively and efficiently they use the resources entrusted to them. By contrast, the not-for-profit sector provides no such incentive, and managers are motivated by considerations of a personal and qualitative nature.

Competition does exist, of course, in one important way: there is competition for funds, both between organisations and between departments or units within an organisation. In those circumstances, managers are rewarded (in the sense that they get the resources they want) as a result of their status and political skills rather than for their effectiveness or performance.

Comparative absence of accountability

The archetypal commercial organisation has to account for its actions and their outcomes to its owners and, to some extent, its creditors. Shareholders expect that the company will be run in their best interests and they demand regular reports of the results of that operation. Additionally, they expect sufficient profits to be generated to pay dividends to shareholders, interest to lenders, taxes to government, and so on, and to provide funds for future activities or investment.

Not-for-profit organisations, on the other hand, are characterised by a comparative lack of accountability. There are no owners, except in the general sense that the community owns central and local government or that club members own a social club. Power in not-for-profit organisations is not exercised in the same way as in profit oriented concerns. Additionally, by their nature, most not-for-profit organisations are 'governed' by part-time, often unpaid, elected or nominated amateurs. The need for a strong, effective, experienced and specialist board is much greater in a not-for-profit organisation; paradoxically, the reverse is more often the case in practice. That creates severe problems for management control, and makes effective planning and strategic analysis much more difficult.

Having less rigorous control mechanisms, and being largely traditionalist, the majority of not-for-profit organisations have neglected to adopt comprehensive and sophisticated management accounting and information systems. The advances in theory and practice in the areas of management planning and control have been ignored by their managements, which tend to see their role as a fiduciary one, keeping the system relatively honest, rather than a stewardship one, managing the resources effectively and beneficially.

BUDGETING

The performance of an organisation can be monitored only in the knowledge of what should have been achieved. Some element of

439

budgeting must be present in any organisational planning, especially
in not-for-profit organisations where there are seldom profits to be
maximised but where costs must be minimised. One cannot say
'good' of something without being aware of what 'bad' is; there must
be some form of standard against which performance can be
measured.

The budgeting processes for a not-for-profit organisation follow
the same paths and take the same directions as those for commercial,
profit oriented enterprises (see Chapter 9 for a discussion of
budgeting), and there are few integral differences. The first step is to
estimate the amount of revenue that will be received for operating
purposes during the coming period. Budgeted expenses are calculated to match revenues; expenses measure the extent to which the
organisation is filling its role in society, since, broadly speaking,
society will provide what it regards as sufficient revenues to produce
a desired level of service. To have revenue surpluses is to have spent
too little, to have provided a lower standard of service. The budget
will be formulated in terms of responsibility centres (see Chapter 11
for a description of responsibility centres and responsibility
accounting), and centre managers will generate their own budgets
subject to any guidelines from senior managers and consistent with
the attainment of the objectives of each centre.

Generally, such budget estimates will be based on current levels
of expenditure, but occasionally budgets will be prepared on a
programme basis rather than a centre-by-centre basis. The concepts
of the programmed budgeting process have been discussed elsewhere
in this handbook, as they apply equally to profit-conscious organisations and not-for-profit entities. In a narrower sense, programme
budgets will refer to the budgeted costs of a specific programme of
action over the coming period or periods. Table 21.3 gives a budget
projection for a three-year period for a programme designed to
reduce injuries and deaths caused by motor vehicle accidents in
which driver drunkenness is a contributory factor. The costs and
the components of the programme are fictitious, as is the programme itself. The personnel costs are based on an average number
of employees engaged full time earning an average salary of
£11 000 a year in 1984, increasing by some 9 per cent annually
thereafter. Advertising costs are expected to rise by 10 per cent
annually, publication and administration costs by 12 per cent, and
monitoring costs by 5 per cent. Inflation is expected to run at an
additional average of 10 per cent over the three-year period. The

Table 21.3
Three-year programme budget

	1984	1985	1986
	£	£	£
Personnel costs	242 000	264 000	288 000
Advertising costs	1 250 000	1 375 000	1 512 500
Publication costs	300 000	337 500	379 700
Monitoring costs	100 000	105 000	110 300
Administration costs	250 000	281 300	316 400
	2 142 000	2 362 800	2 606 900
Discounted present value (@ 10%)	1 947 078	1 951 673	1 957 782
Total estimated actual cost over three years			7 111 700
Total estimated discounted present value cost over three years			5 856 533

total estimated actual cost over the three-year period is calculated at £7 111 700; discounted at 10 per cent, the total present value cost is calculated at £5 856 533. The programme would be funded by the government department responsible for transport and would be mounted by the accident prevention units within that department. Funds would be provided from the total departmental budget. Responsibility would be allocated to a senior civil servant who would be seconded from existing duties within the department and who would manage the programme on a full time basis.

As with any budget for an input-using operation, the most difficult part of the process would be to determine the estimated costs for different elements of the programme.

The preparation of the budget would be undertaken hand-in-hand with a cost-benefit analysis of the probable inputs required and the likely outputs derived from the programme. The outputs would be the number of injuries and deaths prevented, quantified in some amenable way. It might be possible to ascertain some quantifiable benefits and to attribute some monetary value to those benefits before attempting the detailed establishment of a budget, on the basis that an injury or death prevented had an intrinsic value which could be compared with the cost involved.

Cost-benefit analysis

Cost-benefit analysis is an ideal tool for the management accountant engaged in not-for-profit activity measurement. Typically, most government agencies have employed cost-benefit analysis techniques to justify proposals for new projects or programmes. The drawback is that such an analysis can only be applied to those outcomes which are susceptible of quantification. Most instances involve important qualitative considerations which cannot be encompassed in a numerical cost-benefit analysis. Equally, rendering considerations into quantitative elements of the analysis will tend to narrow the focus of management's judgement and concentrate decision making in too mechanistic a way on unimportant or misleading considerations.

In addition, there are significant dangers in employing cost-benefit analysis in too trusting a way. While the calculation of benefits and costs for one programme may prove realistic and sensible, there is a danger that other completely different programmes designed to attain different objectives will be judged together on the basis of their benefit-cost relationship. Nonetheless, the systematic analysis of inputs and outputs will tend to improve the decision making process. The application of cost-benefit analysis can be illustrated by reverting to the example used in Table 21.3. The benefits of the programme will be the reduced injuries and deaths attributed to drunken driving. Those benefits can be quantified in a relatively straightforward way.

The first step is to determine the proportion of current injuries and deaths, and projected injuries and deaths, that might be avoided by implementing the programme. Table 21.4 presents estimates of projected road casualty figures for the period 1984–86; it is emphasised that these are hypothetical estimates and are not based on any official or accurate projections. The table also shows the estimated proportion of those casualties that might be averted by the programme's impact.

On that basis, it can be calculated that the programme will result in the reduction of injuries and deaths over the three-year period by a total of 14 300 (375 deaths and 13 925 injuries), at a total present

Table 21.4
Road casualty estimates and programme impacts

	1984	1985	1986
Road users killed	7 500	7 700	7 900
of which due to driver drunkenness	*750*	*770*	*790*
Road users injured	350 000	380 000	410 000
of which due to driver drunkenness	*26 250*	*28 500*	*30 750*
Programme impacts:			
deaths averted	*75*	*125*	*175*
injuries averted	*2 625*	*4 575*	*6 725*
	2 700	*4 700*	*6 900*

value cost of £5 856 533 – an average present value cost of £409.55 per incident averted.

The analysis would proceed by calculating the present value cost in lost earnings and associated expenditure for each injury and each death. The calculation of those costs for injuries would be based on average lengths of off-work time, sickness benefits, employer opportunity costs, and the like; it would include an estimation of the costs of police, fire and ambulance services' involvement at the scene of accidents, legal and court costs of any subsequent proceedings, road repair and maintenance costs, vehicle repair or replacement costs, and so on. The underlying procedure can be illustrated by limiting the analysis at this stage to a consideration of the programme's effect on the occurrence of fatal injuries.

Table 21.5 shows the calculation of the probable 'savings' (that is, reduced costs) from averted deaths as a result of the programme's impact.

The values shown in Table 21.5, under the heading 'Discounted earnings', are derived from a consideration of the likely lifetime earnings of males and females of different ages, adjusted to take account of the likelihood of unemployment or removal from the labour force and for mortality rates due to other factors than road accidents. Those likely earnings were then discounted at 10 per cent. Taking the likely number of users saved from death and multiplying those numbers by the average discounted earnings of persons in the different age ranges, the resultant earnings figures were then

Table 21.5
Savings from averted deaths

Age of user	Numbers Males	Females	Discounted earnings (£000) Males	Females	Total
Under 14	25	15	2 500	1 125	3 625
15–24	40	20	6 000	2 250	8 250
25–34	55	30	9 900	4 200	14 100
35–44	40	20	8 400	3 300	11 700
45–54	35	20	7 175	3 100	10 275
55–64	30	10	5 700	1 200	6 900
Over 64	25	10	4 500	800	5 300
	250	125	44 175	15 975	60 150

discounted back to the base year, 1984, using a rate of 10 per cent, and the estimated discounted present values of the earnings of those whose lives would be saved are those shown in the table.

It can be seen that over the three-year programme, the present value of the lifetime earnings of all those whose lives would be saved is estimated at £60 150 000. The present value of the costs of the programme was estimated at £5 856 533. The present value of the savings from other sources (that is, reduced public service commitments to road accident attendance, vehicle repairs, road repairs, and so on) had been calculated at £6 500 per accident averted, giving a total benefit over the three-year period of some £2 437 500 in respect of fatal accidents averted.

The program cost per death averted was estimated earlier at £409.55; the savings per death averted averaged £166 900, giving a cost-benefit ratio of 407.5:1.

Cost-benefit analysis can be undertaken even where there is uncertainty about the values or savings of outcomes. One of the American departments prominent in the advocacy of cost-benefit analysis displays the motto: 'It is better to be roughly right than precisely wrong'. If the outcomes or outputs cannot be quantified, it is still possible to employ cost-benefit analysis techniques. For example, if a local authority has two alternative social welfare proposals under consideration, each costing £525 000 in a full year, it can proceed by evaluating the likely qualitative benefits flowing from each proposal. If the money is spent on additional social workers, will that create more social benefit than spending the money on increased welfare facilities? Alternatively, which proposal would have the greater benefit to a university engineering department? A further full time lecturer at a salary of £11 000 or a new measurement machine costing £66 000 and having an expected life of six years?

MANAGEMENT MOTIVATION

In the absence of the profit measure and without such managerial performance yardsticks as return on investment or residual income (as discussed in Chapter 17), management must adopt different measures for appraising performance. Management by objectives is a more or less formal procedure that stresses goals and outputs and depends for its success on feedback and performance reports.

In the not-for-profit organisation, the objectives can be stated fairly clearly, and it may well be possible to express them in a quantified form – so many homeless families housed, for instance, or so many passenger/miles operated by local bus services. In that way, managers can be judged by their attainment or surpassing of the objectives set by them or for them.

In most not-for-profit organisations, the principal criterion is the level of service provided or the effects of the programs implemented. Costs are a secondary consideration in that context, although any measurement of managerial effectiveness must include an evaluation of cost control performance and adherence to budgeted levels of expenditure.

CONCLUSION

Not-for-profit organisations have many shared characteristics with their profit oriented counterparts in the industrial and commercial sector, but equally they have many distinctive problems. The absences of the profit motive and a profit measure are formidable obstacles to a proper system of performance appraisal. Nonetheless, the adoption of such techniques as cost minimisation and outcome maximisation will assist the management accountant in his role as management controller for such an organisation.

Cost-benefit analysis and a programmed approach to budgeting offer significant advantages to the controllers of not-for-profit organisations, and the motivation of managers may be achieved by following the 'management by objectives' approach.

Not-for-profit organisations are judged by the extent to which they contribute to the welfare of the community or interests they exist to serve. That measurement may be extremely difficult to make, and there are obvious dangers in adopting either a cost minimisation tactic or an outcome maximisation one, in isolation.

With notable exceptions, the particular problems of the not-for-profit organisation have been overlooked by writers and researchers and, by and large, by the professional bodies and the standard-setting authorities. The idea has been advanced (Charnes et al., 1980) that:

> Managerial accounting... will move away from its present almost exclusive emphasis on private enterprise decision making. That is, the movement will be toward perfecting and developing tools in these disciplines as aids for improved decision making and managerial evaluation in the large and continually growing sector of not-for-profit entity activities.

If so, the discussion in this chapter may go some way towards assisting that process.

REFERENCES AND FURTHER READING

Anthony, R. N., and Dearden, J., *Management Control Systems: Text and Cases,* 3rd edn., Homewood, Ill.: Irwin, 1976.

Anthony, R. N., and Herzlinger, R., *Management Control in Nonprofit Organizations,* Rev edn., Homewood, Ill.: Irwin, 1980.

Canadian Institute of Chartered Accountants, *Financial Reporting for Non-profit Organizations,* Toronto: CICA, 1980.

Charnes, A., Cooper, W. W., and Rhodes, E., 'An efficiency opening for managerial accounting in not-for-profit entities', *in* Holzer, H. P. (ed), *Management Accounting 1980,* Urbana-Champaign: University of Illinois, 1980.

Dobbins, R., and Fanning, D., 'Social accounting', *in* Pocock, M. A., and Taylor, A. H. (eds), *Handbook of Financial Planning and Control,* Farnborough: Gower, 1981.

Gross, M. J., and Jablonsky, S. F., *Principles of Accounting and Financial Reporting for Nonprofit Organizations,* New York: Wiley-Interscience, 1979.

Gross, M. J., and Warschauer, W., *Financial and Accounting Guide for Nonprofit Organizations,* 3rd edn., New York: Ronald Press, 1979.

Hay, L. E., *Accounting for Governmental and Nonprofit Entities,* 6th edn., Homewood, Ill.: Irwin, 1980.

Henke, E. Q., *Accounting for Nonprofit Organizations,* 2nd edn., Belmont, Ca.: Wadsworth, 1979.

Henke, E. O., *Introduction to Nonprofit Organization Accounting,* Belmont, Ca.: Wadsworth, 1979.

Sizer, J., 'Developing quantitative and financial performance indicators in non-profit organizations', *in* Sizer, J., *Perspectives in Management Accounting,* London: Heinemann, 1981.

Sorenson, J. R., and Grove, H. D., 'Cost-outcome and cost-effectiveness analysis: emerging nonprofit performance evaluation techniques', *The Accounting Review,* July 1977.

22

Control Theory and Management Accounting

David Fanning

One of the more persistent themes in the various contributions to this handbook has been the notion of control. The concept of control is central to the theories of managerial accounting and to most theories of management. Control theory covers the broad spectrum of the design, operation and analysis of control systems. As such, it has important insights to offer management accounting and a great deal to contribute to the further development of management accounting theory. In this chapter, the Editor introduces the elements of modern control theory and examines ways in which that theory can be applied to management accounting situations. The management accountant occupies a vital position in any firm, playing a central role in the planning and controlling processes. Modern control theory techniques and principles offer considerable assistance in the effective execution of that role.

Brogan (1974) has defined a control system as any set of systematically related elements:

> which exists for the purpose of regulating or controlling the flow of energy, information, money or other quantities in some desired fashion

and has represented control systems as having either open-loop or closed-loop feedback characteristics. Figure 22.1 shows the elements of each type of feedback control system. Open-loop systems have the quality that the output of the system does not modify either the input or the operation of the system. Control laws are fixed and pro-

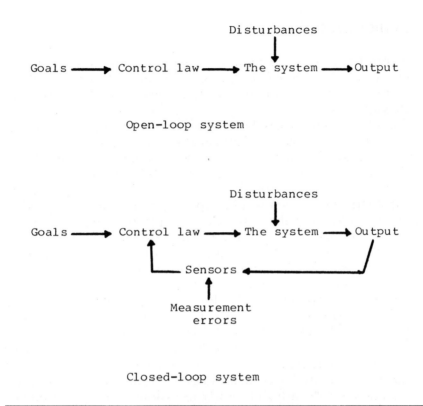

Fig. 22.1   Open-loop and closed-loop systems

grammed in advance and feedback does not exist in the accepted sense; information is retrieved, of course, but at too late a stage to affect the current operations. Feedback in that open-loop system will perhaps be used to modify or formulate future operating plans.

The closed-loop system, a representation of the conventional view of feedback, has the characteristic that the output of a system is monitored regularly and the control laws are applied to the output to determine whether or not the system should be adjusted. In a closed-loop system, for instance, management would modify stock purchasing practices if it was revealed that the sales of products using a particular raw material were declining. The open-loop system would encourage the continued purchase of standard quantities of that raw material – at least until year-end inventory checks precipitated a re-evaluation of stock purchasing practices.

CONTROL SYSTEMS

A control system has a number of simply understood elements: control objective; control strategy; control variables; state variables; disturbance inputs; dynamic relationships between control and state variables.

The control objective is the maximisation of an objective function – for example, the output of finished products from a production line. In that circumstance, the control objective would be to minimise the deviation of actual output from desired output. To achieve that objective, the systems would include one or more control strategies which would depend on the values assigned to certain control variables. In the example mentioned here, the control variables would be the number of machine hours to be worked, the number of finished products to be manufactured in each hour by each machine, and so on. Affecting the control situation would be a number of state variables – the location and number of suitable machines, for instance, or the labour force available to work those machines. The system will be affected from time to time by exogenous variables, the disturbance inputs of control theory, which cannot be predicted with any accuracy or controlled to any extent. Strikes by transport drivers in supplier industries or natural acts such as floods or droughts, for instance, are examples of disturbance inputs; recessions or booms are others. The dynamic relationships between the variables in the system, both state and control variables, would be represented in some form of mathematical model.

Brogan (1974) further described the various configurations of control systems, classified along a number of dimensions; Figure 22.2 reproduces his classification system. The following description of those classes derives from Brogan (1974) and from Buckley and O'Sullivan (1980).

Where the parameters of a system are extended so that values of a parameter are not uniform across the entire continuum, the system is classified as distributed. In a lumped parameter system, the values are either distributed uniformly across the extension or have a finite number of discrete selected occurrences. In a deterministic system, output is predictable – given specified input, operating conditions and control forces. A stochastic system exists in random conditions or where objective and subjective probability judgements must be made. Most management accounting applications of control theory

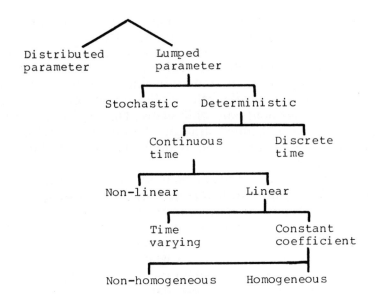

Fig. 22.2   Major classes of control systems

are stochastic. A continuous time system is one in which all variables are continuous functions of time, whereas a discrete time system is one in which some variables assume or are assigned variables at discrete intervals. Relationships between variables in systems may be linear or non-linear. Time-varying systems are ones in which functional relationships, constants and coefficients will change over time. An homogeneous system is one in which no external inputs are received and performance is determined solely by initial conditions at the commencement of the system's operation.

Control theory

Wiener (1948) defined cybernetics (the underlying foundation for control theory) as:

control and communication in man and machine

and argued that control needs goal setting and planning. Control systems must be purposive, as in social, political, and economic systems. The goals or objectives set for the system are outside the field of control theory, although subgoals may be changed as a result of control actions elsewhere in the system.

Comprehensive descriptions and discussions of control theory have been provided by Brogan (1974) and by Bensoussan et al. (1974). The complexities of modern business and the size of most business undertakings call for the application of sophisticated and enhanced management control systems. The increased need for coordination and integrated strategic planning has developed the demand for a wider application of mathematical control theory to management practices.

The essentials of a control system model comprise a control unit (whether it be human or artificial – a computer, for instance) and the grouping of units into subsystems and supersystems, etc. The model details requirements but does not specify the means of their satisfaction or the agents of that satisfaction. Goals will be determined, whether for the system as a whole or for subsystems; data will be required to feed back goal formulating or changing information; the possible or probable disturbances must be identified and provision made for their detection. The channels of information must be open, susceptible to control in terms of thresholds, and adequate for their purposes. The system needs sensors and memories which are mechanically capable, integrated and associative. The system needs to be able to learn and adapt, and its essential processes should be capable of being controlled and monitored by subsystems – for example, by an internal auditing process.

MANAGERIAL ACCOUNTING APPLICATIONS

A number of applications of control theory to management accounting can be identified, and a brief discussion of three of those possible areas of application will serve to illustrate the particular concerns of control theory.

The inventory control model (discussed in Chapter 5) is a typical example of the application of control theory approaches to management problems. Anticipated demand for a stock item is known; the problem is to minimise the costs of carrying and ordering, to avoid having stocks of that item and to determine an optimal ordering schedule. In addition to the actual outlay costs, opportunity costs will be associated with inventory control mistakes or practices.

The control objectives are: ordering costs; carrying costs; stockout costs. The control variables in the system are the order time or interval and the order quantity. The state variables are the level of demand of the item in question, the available supply of that item, and the inventory level.

Ordering costs include those of requisitioning, ordering, acquiring, receiving and processing; associated opportunity costs will be the imputed interest charge on ordering costs. Carrying costs include those of insurance, storage, obsolescence, pilferage, spoilage, and so on, with opportunity costs deriving from imputed interest on inventory cost. The stockout costs are those of making special orders to rectify the situation, but opportunity costs can be more damaging in their impact – the lost contribution and the lost goodwill resulting from being out of stock are two principal examples of such opportunity costs.

Turning to the problem of production control reveals a further application of control theory. In this case, the control objectives are production setup costs, switching costs, and smoothing costs (hiring and firing workers or paying overtime rates, for example). Control variables are the production rate and the production time, while the state variables are demand, supply, inventory level and production rate.

The control of research and development expenditure is a further area in which control theory can be applied. There, the control objective is the expected profitability generated by that activity; control variables are the form and timing of research and development expenditure and the expenditure itself; state variables are goodwill and expected sales.

Those three applications are summarised in Table 22.1, and it can be seen that management accountants have a considerable impact in such areas and, therefore, need a closer appreciation of control theory concepts and applications. Anthony and Dearden (1976) have discussed the whole area of management control and provided one of the more comprehensive treatments of the subject.

FUTURE DEVELOPMENT

Management is in the process of grafting modern scientific thought from the engineering, mathematical and social sciences on to the art or craft of managing (see Hanika (1965) for a review of developments in management thinking at that time, conducted from an enthusiastic

Table 22.1
Applications of control theory

	Control objectives	Control variables	State variables
Inventory control	Ordering costs Carrying costs Stockout costs	Order quantity Order timing	Demand Supply Inventory levels
Production control	Production setup costs Switching costs Smoothing costs Carrying costs Stockout costs	Production rate Production time	Demand Supply Inventory levels Production rate
Research & development control	Expected profitability	Expenditure Form Timing	Expected sales Goodwill

and refreshing viewpoint). That development began when Wiener (1948) advanced the notion of feedback as a principle of communication and control. From being reviewed and assessed descriptively, management activities were treated in a scientific and analytical way.

Considerable advantages can accrue to management accounting from the wider application of control theory precepts to business practices. Control theory can be applied with equal effect to the profit oriented sector and to the not-for-profit sector. The essential requirement is that there should be a goal or goals, the control objective or objectives; there is no specification of what a goal should be or what form it should take. Maximisation of profits or minimisation of costs, sales of a product or provision of a socially beneficial service – each goal is valid under control theory.

It can be argued that the role of the management accountant has less to do with accounting and more with control than has hitherto been recognised. Perhaps the time has come to abandon the term 'management accounting' and use instead 'management control'; perhaps the management accountant should be relabelled a management controller. In the same way that the orientation of the profession moved from cost accounting to management accounting, so it should now move from management accounting to management control. The controller would not be a 'doer'; rather, he would be a coordinator, ensuring that the system was installed and functioning effectively and adequately. He would not collect the feedback data, but would ensure that they were gathered and presented in a relevant form; he would not act as a monitor or regulator, but would ensure that such devices were in position and functioning; he would not set goals or formulate objectives, but would ensure that goals and objectives were delineated, described and communicated efficiently.

Thomas (1980) has argued that the time has come:

> for a significant shift in the theory of managerial accounting. When a theory has been in existence for some time, a dissonance may build up.

He identified such dissonance as typified by the inconsistency developed by the use of standard costing for both product costing and control purposes, and held that management accounting has:

> come to comprise whatever the accountant is interested in doing and/or has a talent for doing.

The very term 'management accounting' is a constraining influence on the development of any new theory of business control. The evidence that management accountants are interested in widening their traditional roles has been adduced in this handbook, and there is every opportunity, now, for the development of a new theory for management accounting, embracing the accounting, behavioural, decisional and organisational aspects discussed in the opening chapter. Several areas have been identified for further study and research, not least the reconciliation of the apparent conflicts between the impersonal emphases of control theory and the behavioural considerations implicit in the theory of the firm and its operation.

What is clear – even from this brief and indicatory overview of the potential for the application of control theory in managerial accounting – is that the modern enterprise is of such a complex and intricate nature, of such social and economic importance, and of such wide ranging and fundamental power that only a proper application of techniques of matching strength and power will assist in the task of managing the enterprise effectively, efficiently and beneficially. Control theory offers those techniques.

In a systems approach to any activity or set of activities, there are four essential elements or components: the goals to be achieved; the decision rules to facilitate the choices to be made in achieving the goals; the prediction models which indicate goals and events; the data bank of facts derived from past experience which facilitates decision making and the choice of decision and prediction models. The systems approach requires goals and is directed towards goal achievement. The goals for management accounting are essential parts of a systems approach; as such, they are normative goals, statements of what management accounting should be. Figure 22.3 presents a systems view of a normative theory for management accounting, incorporating the concepts of control theory. Initially,

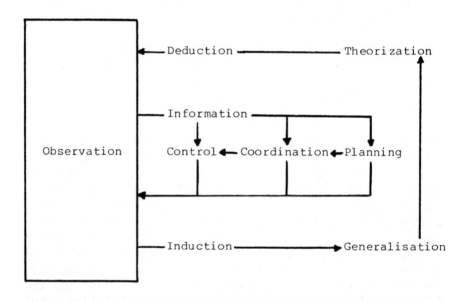

Fig. 22.3   A systems view of a normative theory for management accounting

generalisations about phenomena must be induced and from that inductive reasoning may be deduced a theory for management accounting. From the accounting output, it will be possible to predict real-world phenomena and thereby validate the theory by comparing predicted phenomena with observed phenomena.

The normative theory for management accounting will focus attention on the goals to be achieved, the means of their accomplishment, and the processes of evaluation and adaptation to change. The systems approach will facilitate the production of accounting output which can be used for decision making, for planning, for coordination, and for control.

REFERENCES AND FURTHER READING

Anthony, R. N., *Planning and Control Systems: A Framework for Analysis,* Cambridge, Mass.: Harvard Business School, 1965.

Anthony, R. N., and Dearden, J., *Management Control Systems: Text and cases,* 3rd edn., Homewood, Ill.: Irwin, 1976.

Ashby, R., *Introduction to Cybernetics,* London: Chapman & Hall, 1961.

Bensoussan, A., Hurst, E. G., and Naslund, B., *Management Applications of Modern Control Theory,* Amsterdam: North-Holland, 1974.

Brogan, W. L., *Modern Control Theory,* New York: Quantum, 1974.

Buckley, J. W., and O'Sullivan, P., 'Control theory and management accounting', *in* Holzer, H. P. (ed), *Management Accounting 1980,* Urbana-Champaign, Ill.: University of Illinois, 1980.

Hale, F. J., *Introduction to Control System Analysis and Design,* Englewood Cliffs, N.J.: Prentice-Hall, 1973.

Hanika, F. de P., *New Thinking in Management,* London: Hutchinson, 1965.

Ijiri, Y., and Thompson, G. L., 'Applications of mathematical control theory to accounting and budgeting', *The Accounting Review,* April 1970.

Thomas, W. E., 'Control theory as a basis for management accounting theory', *in* Holzer, H. P. (ed), *Management Accounting 1980,* Urbana-Champaign, Ill.: University of Illinois, 1980.

Wiener, N., *Cybernetics,* New York: Wiley, 1948.

Index